MW00784190

Apocalyptic and the Future of Theology

APOCALYPTIC AND THE FUTURE OF THEOLOGY

With and beyond J. Louis Martyn

Edited by
Joshua B. Davis
and Douglas Harink

CASCADE *Books* · Eugene, Oregon

APOCALYPTIC AND THE FUTURE OF THEOLOGY
With and beyond J. Louis Martyn

An earlier version of chapter 8, Beverly Roberts Gaventa, ""Neither Height nor Depth": Cosmos and Soteriology in Paul's Letter to the Romans," was originally published as "Neither Height nor Depth: Discerning the Cosmology of Romans" in the *Scottish Journal of Theology* 64/3 (2011) 265–78. Reprinted with permission.

Cascade Books
An Imprint of Wipf and Stock Publishers
199 W. 8th Ave., Suite 3
Eugene, OR 97401

www.wipfandstock.com

ISBN 13: 978-1-62032-087-7

Cataloguing-in-Publication data:

Apocalyptic and the future of theology : with and beyond J. Louis Martyn / edited by Joshua B. Davis and Douglas Harink.

xvi + 406 pp. ; 23 cm. Includes bibliographical references and indexes.

ISBN 13: 978-1-62032-087-7

1. Apocalyptic literature. 2. Martyn, J. Louis (James Louis), 1925– . 3. Bible. N.T. Epistles of Paul—Theology. 4. Eschatology. I. Title.

BS646 A591 2012

Manufactured in the U.S.A.

Contents

Contents

Acknowledgments

WHILE THIS VOLUME IS not a *Festschrift* for J. Louis Martyn, it neverthe-less would not be possible without his life, work and witness in the cause of God's liberating Gospel in Jesus Christ and the Spirit. We (the editors) owe a great debt of gratitude to Lou in many things, not least for the generous time he gave us in May 2009 to interview him on matters per-tinent to the theme of this volume. The brief word that Lou contributes here captures an important aspect of what we learned from him in those interviews, that is, his deep indebtedness to the work of Ernst Käsemann. As the reader will soon discover, Käsemann is often in the background of these essays, and sometimes is himself the focus of attention. This vol-ume seeks the future of theology "with and beyond" J. Louis Martyn. Lou reminds us of what came before; more important, he reminds us of the Subject that binds his and Käsemann's and our work in a common purpose.

We are profoundly grateful to each of the authors who, at our re-quest, and at their own cost of time and effort, contributed to this volume. It is due to the superb quality of their work that this volume can make its claim upon our readers' time.

Two student research assistants at The King's University College made essential contributions to our work. Elly Doef tackled the painstak-ing and time-consuming task of transcribing recordings of our interviews with Lou Martyn. Patrick Doerksen did the initial editing and formatting of all of the essays and prepared the bibliography. We are grateful to these dedicated and talented young scholars. Nicole Brandsma prepared the indexes. David Congdon provided valuable help during the final phase of editing.

Thanks are also due to The King's University College for providing research funding for each stage of the production of this volume.

The editorial team at Wipf and Stock is an unusually energetic, helpful, and delightful group to work with, and it is wonderful that they have the vision and capacity to continue to publish volumes such as this.

Acknowledgments

Thanks especially to Chris Spinks who skilfully guided this work from beginning to end.

Each of us is deeply grateful to his spouse and family for the patience, support, and encouragement that sustains our work.

Joshua Davis
Doug Harink

Contributors

J. David Belcher (MA, Vanderbilt) is an independent scholar in Durham, North Carolina, and the author of the forthcoming book *The Depth of Divine Things: The Mystery of Baptism and the Liturgical Life of the Church* (Pickwick). His research interests include liturgical theology, ecclesiology, and the theology of the rites of initiation.

Jodi L. A. Belcher is a doctoral student in theology at Duke Divinity School in Durham, North Carolina. Her research interests include feminist theologies, feminist theory, Pauline anthropology, Christology, and the theology of bodies.

Alexandra R. Brown is the Jessie Ball Dupont Professor of Religion at Washington and Lee University in Lexington, Virginia. She is currently writing a commentary on 1 Corinthians for the New Testament Library series. Her book *The Cross and Human Transformation: Paul's Apocalyptic Word in 1 Corinthians* (1995) is in its second printing (2008).

David W. Congdon is an associate editor of academic books at InterVarsity Press. He is a doctoral candidate in systematic theology at Princeton Theological Seminary, completing a dissertation on Karl Barth and Rudolf Bultmann. He is coeditor with W. Travis McMaken of *Karl Barth in Conversation* (forthcoming, 2013).

Joshua B. Davis (PhD, Vanderbilt) has been Visiting Assistant Professor of Catholic Studies at the University of Illinois Urbana-Champaign and has taught courses for the Loyola University (Chicago) Institute for Pastoral Studies. His research and writing interests include modern Roman Catholic theology, Continental philosophy, and the doctrines of grace, creation, and divine and human agency.

Susan Grove Eastman is Associate Professor of the Practice of Bible and Christian Formation at Duke Divinity School in Durham, North

Carolina. She is the author of *Recovering Paul's Mother Tongue* (2007). Her forthcoming book *Paul's Theology of Participation* (Eerdmans) explores the topics of participation, Christology, and theological anthropology in the letters of Paul.

BEVERLY ROBERTS GAVENTA is the Helen H. P. Manson Professor of New Testament Literature and Exegesis at Princeton Theological Seminary, Princeton, New Jersey. Her publications include *Our Mother Saint Paul* (2007) and *The Acts of the Apostles* (2003). She is currently writing a commentary on Romans for the New Testament Library (Westminster John Knox).

DOUGLAS HARINK is the Dean of the Faculty of Arts and Professor of Theology at The King's University College in Edmonton, Canada. He is the author of *Paul Among the Postliberals* (2003), *1 & 2 Peter* (2009) in the Brazos Theological Commentary on the Bible, and the editor of *Paul, Philosophy, and the Theopolitical Vision* (Cascade, 2010).

STANLEY HAUERWAS is the Gilbert T. Rowe Professor of Theological Ethics at Duke University, Durham, North Carolina. He is the author of numerous books, including the Gifford Lectures, *With the Grain of the Universe* (2001), the commentary on *Matthew* (2006) in the Brazos Theological Commentary on the Bible, and *War and the American Difference* (2011).

CHRISTOPHER R. J. HOLMES is Senior Lecturer in Systematic Theology at the University of Otago, Dunedin, New Zealand, and an Anglican priest. He is the author of *Revisiting the Doctrine of the Divine Attributes: In Dialogue with Karl Barth, Eberhard Juengel, and Wolf Kroetke* (2007) and *Ethics in the Presence of Christ* (2012).

ROBERT W. JENSON is former Senior Scholar for Research at the Center of Theological Inquiry in Princeton, New Jersey. He is the author of numerous books, among them his two-volume *Systematic Theology* (1997, 1999), a commentary on *Ezekiel* (2009) in the Brazos Theological Commentary, and *Canon and Creed* (2010).

NATHAN R. KERR is Associate Professor of Religion at Trevecca Nazarene University, Nashville, Tennessee. He is the author of *Christ, History, and Apocalyptic* (Cascade, 2009), and coauthor of *Kingdom-World-Church: A Theological Manifesto* (Cascade, forthcoming). He researches and writes in the areas of dogmatics, ecclesiology, and the church's mission to the poor. He serves in a ministry to prisoners.

WALTER J. LOWE is Professor Emeritus of Systematic Theology at Emory University. He is the author of *Theology & Difference: The Wound of Reason (1993)*. He is currently working on a seeker's guide to Christianity and the Western tradition.

JOSEPH MANGINA is Professor of Theology at Wycliffe College in Toronto. He is the editor of the journal *Pro Ecclesia* and the author of two books on the theology of Karl Barth. He contributed the commentary on *Revelation* (2010) in the Brazos Theological Commentary. His current research interests include ecclesiology and the sacraments.

J. LOUIS MARTYN is Edward Robinson Professor Emeritus of Biblical Theology at Union Theological Seminary, New York. He is the author of *History and Theology in the Fourth Gospel* (3rd ed., 2003), *Theological Issues in the Letters of Paul* (1997), and the commentary on *Galatians* (1997) in the Anchor Bible.

CHRISTOPHER MORSE is the Dietrich Bonhoeffer Professor of Theology and Ethics at Union Theological Seminary, New York. His publications include *Not Every Spirit: A Dogmatics of Christian Disbelief* (2nd ed., 2009) and *The Difference Heaven Makes: Rehearing the Gospel as News* (2010).

FLEMING RUTLEDGE is an Episcopal priest with 22 years of parish ministry. She is known today as a preacher and teacher of other preachers, and as the author of a number of collections of sermons, most recently *Not Ashamed of the Gospel* (2007), on Romans, and *And God Spoke to Abraham* (2011), on the Old Testament. She is presently completing a major work on the meaning of the crucifixion.

PHILIP ZIEGLER is Senior Lecturer in Systematic Theology at the University of Aberdeen, Scotland. He is the author of *Doing Theology When God Is Forgotten: The Theological Achievement of Wolf Kroetke* (2006) and the editor of several volumes, including *The Providence of God* (2009) and *Explorations in Theology and Ethics* (2009). His research interests include Christology, soteriology, the political and ethical significance of the doctrine of grace, and the theological legacies of Bonhoeffer and Barth.

A Personal Word about Ernst Käsemann

THE AUTHOR OF THE Gospel of Matthew knew that a concern with genealogy can be made to serve the proclamation of the Good News. Something similar can be said about an interest in the ancestry of the sterling pieces that make up this volume. As several of them have as one of their grandparents Ernst Käsemann, a brief personal word about him may be welcome here.

NEW HAVEN: A NON-DIRECTIONAL COUNSELOR
AND THE HAND OF PROVIDENCE

It was September of 1956. Very fortunate to be at Yale, I was sitting in the office of Paul Schubert, my learned and generous-spirited Doctor Father, reporting on the work of the preceding summer and seeking advice about the dissertation, still in its infancy. After listening attentively, Schubert came to what he correctly discerned to be the major point, asking whether I was confident of finishing in May. To my emphatically cautious answer he responded with a thoughtful suggestion: "It may be wise for you to apply for a Fulbright, in order to spend next year in Germany."

In a matter of months, surprised to have received the grant, I was again in Schubert's office:

Myself: Good news! I applied for a Fulbright, and it is now in hand! I will be glad, then, to have your wisdom yet again. You grew up in Germany, and did your first doctorate there. Tell me what you think about the various theological faculties, and specifically about the New Testament professors here and there.

Schubert: What I think is not the question. Which *Neutestamentler* have you read recently, thinking afterwards you would like to spend the remainder of the evening talking with that scholar?

Myself: That is easy. Ernst Käsemann of Göttingen.

Schubert: Now you know where to go and what to do.

GÖTTINGEN AND THE ACQUISITION OF A PERMANENT TEACHER

In a matter of several additional months, Dorothy and I, with our two little boys, were off to Göttingen, where we rather quickly saw that we were being led once again by the hand of Providence. Having thought of German professors—somewhat incorrectly—as exceedingly stern and largely unapproachable, I was delighted with the relatively young scholar who was quickly interested to know in what direction I was already headed, and what theological questions I thought worth exploring.

It was the beginning of a time of grace in which teacher became acquaintance, acquaintance became friend, and friend became comrade, all the while remaining my indelible teacher. Altogether there were four decades for which I am still today profoundly thankful. He was and is my permanent comrade and teacher.

What have I learned from him? Numerous things, all of them related to two aspects of his own life.

Coal Minor's Pastor

First there was his having served as a pastor to a church of coal miners for a decade, precisely in the forefront of tensions and inner-church warfare in the 1930s. He has himself spoken about this time.[1] I will add only that his consistently combative spirit was clearly sharpened as he discerned that, truly perceived, the inner-church warfare against the "German Christians" of the Nazi period was at its root an instance of the cosmic struggle between God and Satan.

---

1. See his "A Theological Review," xii-xxi in Ernst Käsemann, *On Being A Disciple of the Crucified Nazarene* (ed. R. Landau; trans. R. A. Harrisville; Eerdmans, 2010).

Professor as Disciple and Witness

When he returned from the war and his period as ordinary soldier and prisoner of war, he was called to be a university professor. That was not, however, retirement from what he called "the front." He brought into the lecture hall the riveting, militant passion characteristic of his work in the pastorate, developing indeed a lecture style that was unexpected in a thoroughly scientific German professor.

He would arrive with his manuscript, and he would read from it. Then, at a point he judged to call for a sharp and vigorous debate, he would remove his glasses, fix his gaze on the students, and combine the professorial lectern with the pastoral pulpit, as he captured the room with an exegetical concentration that mesmerized all present. It was a rare combination of substance and passion.

I recall especially his proving to be the utterly respectful and thoroughly rebellious student of Rudolf Bultmann.[2] The issue of human existence, he said, does not consist of our making in our own right and as individuals a series of decisions vis-à-vis certain possibilities. Indeed, instead of being a matter of possibility and decision—two of Bultmann's favorite terms, and obvious marks of his debt to Martin Heidegger—the central issue is focused, he insisted, on militant power, having acquired that focus by God's invincible act of invading the world in the sending of his Son to deliver all human beings from the powers of Sin and Death, powers that deceive and slay us all.

God's own love for us is thus shown in his victorious deed of invasion in which he liberates us, and calls into existence against all odds the New Creation, the community in which the Spirit of his Son bears daily fruit in the form of communal love, joy, and peace.

From the pulpit in Gelsenkirchen, then, to the lectern in Göttingen and beyond, this disciple bore his contagious witness in the name of his Lord. Speaking for contributors to this volume, I give hearty thanks for the words we still have from this faithful disciple whose steady concern was that of pointing to his Master.

---

2. For a mature analysis of Käsemann's respectful and radical departure from Bultmann see Martinus C. de Boer, "Paul's Mythologizing Program in Romans 5-8" in *Creation, Conflict, and Cosmos* (ed. Beverly R. Gaventa; Baylor University Press; forthcoming).

INTRODUCTION

The Challenge of Apocalyptic to Modern Theology

Joshua B. Davis

God is not nice

God is not Uncle

God is an earthquake

—GILLIAN ROSE[1]

THE ESSAYS IN THIS volume are responding to the challenge that apocalyptic poses to modern theology. That challenge is ambiguous. At the turn of the previous century, when apocalyptic was discovered to be central to the New Testament's vision of the kingdom of God, the challenge of apocalyptic was seen by many as a threat to the very possibility of Christian faith in the modern world. This was how the historical theologian Franz Overbeck saw the matter. In fact, he went so far as to argue that the apocalyptic character of the primitive Christian faith stood in

---

1. Rose, "Final Notebooks," 9. I have spent a great deal of time wrestling with Gillian Rose in the last year. I have not walked away unscathed. She anticipated many of the questions and answers I had already devised, but the pressure she applied to them transformed them in ways I am sure I have yet to perceive. What I have learned from her, especially from *Hegel contra Sociology*, I have brought to bear on this essay and I hope, in my own way, to apply pressure to the set of questions that drive it. As I have also learned to say from Peter Candler, it is an act of charity to acknowledge one's debts. I gladly do so here with the hope that Rose might be an angel with whom more of us might wrestle, an *angelus* of annunciation and incarnation.

opposition to theology per se. And yet, this same challenge that so many saw as destructive was readily embraced by others as providing an opportunity for renewal. Karl Barth's *Epistle to the Romans*, which without doubt established the template for the theological appropriation of biblical apocalyptic in modern theology, was in large measure an attempt to reconstitute theology by faith alone in the possibilities that follow from the apocalyptic encounter. Apocalyptic's challenge was both a trial and a provocation: a trial by which to judge the authenticity of modern faith, and a provocation to restore its primordial rigor.

All of the contributors to this collection are wrestling with the theological significance of the questions raised by this two-pronged challenge. What role does apocalyptic play in the theology of the New Testament? What does it mean to continue to do theology after the rediscovery of the significance of apocalyptic? How does recognition of apocalyptic transform traditional theological categories? What impact does apocalyptic have on Christian practice and our understanding of the nature of Christian theology? The authors believe that, for the sake of its future, theology cannot avoid the challenge entailed in these questions.

Now is a strange time to talk about returning to apocalyptic, despite the urgency of its challenge to theology, and despite the fact that we have been living in decidedly apocalyptic times since at least 1914. In this century following the inception of the First World War, anxieties about the horrors of modern warfare, and environmental, economic, and political degradation can be all-consuming. In the nineteenth century, novels like Mary Shelly's *The Last Man* (1826) and H. G. Wells's *The War of the Worlds* (1898) began to anticipate the world's destruction under circumstances beyond human control. In the twentieth and twenty-first centuries we have witnessed a steady proliferation of artistic expressions of the apocalyptic imagination those writers championed. Examples now abound in literature, film, television programs, comic books, graphic novels, and video games. Our culture—our Western culture, at least—is permeated by the fantasy of the decimation of our world. We call it entertainment. We also call it "apocalyptic."

Theologians have also been talking about apocalyptic since 1914. Those thinkers responsible for reviving the apocalyptic imagination in theology, the dialectical theologians, had an enormous impact on modern theology, though their time together was short. Young, brilliant, brash, and no doubt highly ambitious, their theologies were exceedingly paradoxical and radically <u>expurgative</u>.[2] Developing the critiques of bourgeois, liberal religion in Nietzsche, Kierkegaard, and Overbeck,[3] they transformed the Protestant rejection of the *theologia gloriae* into a virtual mysticism, profoundly resistant to every positive objectification of God.[4] It is these thinkers who have for the last century set the tone for what is now known as apocalyptic theology and for how it has been received by theology as a discipline.

<u>Ernst Käsemann</u>, the New Testament scholar whose generation succeeded the dialectical theologians, further influenced theology's use of apocalyptic. His famous declaration that "apocalyptic is the mother of all Christian theology" has been a clarion call to many.[5] Though Käsemann shared much of the perspective of the dialectical theologians, his w<u>ork was palpably influenced by Marxism</u>, to a much greater degree than that of his predecessors.[6] Käsemann, due in large part to his strong leftist sensibilities, inspired the two most important apocalyptic theologians of the latter half of the last century, <u>Jürgen Moltmann and Johann Baptiste M</u>etz. Both Moltmann and Metz appealed to apocalyptic to oppose bour- ‖ geois religion, and in doing so drew heavily on Käsemann's emphasis on the eschatological future. Moltmann combined this focus on the future with <u>Ernst Bloch's utopian Marxist vision of ho</u>pe, while Metz married Karl Rahner's theological method to <u>Käsemann's eschatolo</u>gy and Walter Benj<u>amin's disruptive function of memory</u>.[7] The past forty years have seen

---

2. See Robinson, *Dialectical Theology*, vol. 1.

3. See Dorrien, *Barthian Revolt*, 61–71.

4. Barth's theology in *Romans II* is so highly negative that it approaches Protestant apophaticism at times, reveling in a kind of linguistic ecstasy, but one that retains Luther's emphasis on the cross rather than glory as the basis for true theology.

5. Käsemann, "Anfänge christlicher Theologie," 180. The English translation is collected in *New Testament Questions*, 102.

6. Though he is of the same generation as the Frankfurt school of critical theory, I know of no study of the influence of Marxism, or particularly Marxist social theory, on *key* Käsemann. Their influence—or at the very least common sensibilities—are redolent in his work. One passage in Käsemann notes the connection between the gospel and Marx: ". . . in a certain respect the gospel is more Marxist than Marx because it does not believe that we ourselves can break our chains, and thus it invokes the Almighty in our worldly game and makes this hell on earth the place of revelation" (Käsemann, *New Testament Questions*, 237). See also his discussion of Matt 5:6 and the necessary association of the gospel with the poor in ibid., 147.

7. The influence of Ernst Bloch on Moltmann is well known and acknowledged. His *Theologie der Hoffnung* is a homage to Bloch's *Das Prinzip Hoffnung*. On Benjamin's influence on Metz, see Metz, *Faith in History*, 169–72.

Thomas J. J. Altizer make apocalyptic an increasingly central trope for his later work,[8] Catherine Keller develop a critical and hesitant advocacy for a "counter-apocalyptic" that is neither apocalyptic nor anti-apocalyptic,[9] and Cyril O'Regan begin a multivolume study of the different types of theological apocalypticisms and their varying structural relationships to Valentinian Gnosticism.[10]

It is more common these days for theologians to invoke apocalyptic to underwrite their opposition to "the world," or to include it as an aspect of their byzantine meditations on the legacy of "modernity," than it is for them to use apocalyptic to express, as in literature and film, concrete anxieties about our economic and social life. In this regard, apocalyptic has come to serve a purpose quite different for contemporary theology than it did for the ancient world.[11] In fact, since the advent of dialectical theology, the tendency has been for theologians to deploy apocalyptic somewhat ambiguously, more as a matter of style than as a designation of positive content.[12] What is now in many quarters thought of as apocalyptic is deeply indebted to Barth's inspiring dialectical negation of objectivity and the perpetual disruption of fixed theological concepts.[13] And where it has not carried this explicit connotation, as with Moltmann and Metz, the impression is given that theological content could just as well be reduced to political theory[14] or (as Edward Farley said of Moltmann) to science

yes [margin note]

political theory [margin note]

8. See Altizer, *New Apocalypse* and *Genesis and Apocalypse*. He has an expected volume entitled *The Apocalyptic Trinity*.

9. Keller, *Apocalypse Now and Then*.

10. See O'Regan, *Gnostic Turn* and *Gnostic Apocalypse*; his succinct articulation of his typology of apocalyptic is given in *Spaces of Apocalyptic*.

11. It certainly is true that concern about economics, politics, and the environment cannot be separated from "opposition to the world" and concerns about "modernity." Nonetheless, it is true that apart from Moltmann and Metz, the place of apocalyptic in theology is not primarily to address historical, material problems.

• 12. I am using the term "style" in the way similar to Rose's discussion of Adorno in *Melancholy Science*, 11–14.

13. With this claim and the preceding invocation of style, compare Theodor Adorno's deployment of negative dialectics in his "Essay as Form" and *Minima Moralia*. Adorno's *Negative Dialectics* is an "objective" presentation of the stylistic method he deploys in the other works. But I have in mind here his use of disruptive and ironic inversions to explore any objective standard for *wissenschaflich* thought as itself a lie, the impossibility of speaking truth straightforwardly when the criterion for its validity is a falsehood. When I refer to "methodology," "style," or "irony" in this essay, I have his approach in mind.

negative dialectics [margin note]

style [margin note]

14. Carl Schmitt's notion that politics is secularized theology is a good example, and particularly his appeal to the deutero-Pauline notion (2 Thess 2:1–12) of the

4

fiction.[15] We are fairly clear on what it means to do theology *apocalyptically*, but the definition of *apocalyptic theology* remains elusive. •

What, then, does it mean to say that theologians are returning to apocalyptic, thereby taking seriously its challenge for modern theology? If it is true that apocalyptic is at its height as a trope for our culture's anxieties, and has become recognizable as a distinct and particularly unruly theological style, in what sense can the contributors to this volume be retrieving an idea that purports to beckon the future of theology?

The simple and most direct answer to that question is that the contributors resist the notion that apocalyptic is simply a matter of style or method, and are seeking to recuperate the meaning and use of apocalyptic found in Scripture. In fact, most of the contributors to this volume are looking specifically to the New Testament to recover a distinctively apocalyptic theology. Some authors wish to raise serious questions about the goals and even the possibility of such a theology, but all recognize that the place of apocalyptic in the New Testament has important consequences for the tasks and content of Christian theology in general.

That is the simple and straightforward answer. A more complex and thorny response exists, leading through the thicket of the relation of knowledge to belief in modern theology. Understanding that relation is essential for grasping the full significance of the challenge that the rediscovery of apocalyptic poses to modern theology, and exploring that relation's variances is the goal of the remainder of this introduction. Apocalyptic appeared to pose a threat to theology at the end of the nineteenth century because it both adopted and disturbed the accepted relation of knowledge to faith that had developed over that century. When it was theologically appropriated at the beginning of the twentieth century in dialectical theology, it was as an adaptation of the very relation that had been disturbed. The contribution to the future of theology that the editors of this volume see in apocalyptic lies at just the point that the New Testament vision is allowed to transform this heritage.

---

apocalyptic necessity of the *katechon* (the "restrainer") to hold at bay the encroachment of chaos. This notion appears at various points throughout Schmitt's writings.

15. See Farley, *Divine Empathy*, 313.

KNOWLEDGE AND BELIEF: FROM KANT TO OVERBECK

Dualism and Its Opponents: Kant, Schleiermacher, Hegel

Seated at the heart of modern theology, and especially of modern Protestant theology, is the vexing and still unresolved problem of the relation between knowledge (*Wissen*) and belief (*Glaube*).[16] Immanuel Kant's dualistic configuration of that relation is responsible for causing this problem. As I will show in this introduction, the most profound promise that apocalyptic poses for the future of theology lies with the possibilities it offers for thinking beyond the separation Kant imposed. Yet, in order to begin to glimpse those possibilities, it is necessary to have some sense of how the rediscovery of apocalyptic at the end of the nineteenth century disrupted

---

16. Some explanation is in order of my use of the words "knowledge" and "belief" with reference to *Wissen* and *Glaube*, respectively. Kant describes *Wissen* as that which has the highest degree of certainty in cognition (*Erkenntnis*) because it is both objectively and subjectively held to be true (*Critique of Pure Reason* [henceforth *CPR*], A822/B850). And in the preface to the second edition, where Kant distinguishes knowledge from belief, he uses the word *Wissen* (see n. 17 below). When I use the term "knowledge" in this essay, I have in mind this specific meaning. It is because of this Kantian background that I have not focused on *Wissenschaft*, which is generally more common among theologians. I have done so because I want to emphasize not simply how Christian belief is related to science, but how belief comes to be associated with an aspect of life that is categorically distinguished from critical thought and in a way that is integral to the theological appropriation of apocalyptic up to and following Johannes Weiss and Franz Overbeck. However, my use of "knowledge" should be understood to include science (*Wissenschaft*).

I have also chosen to use the English word "belief" in reference to the German *Glaube* in order to emphasize this Kantian background. Though the term also means "faith" in the strictly theological sense, I want to highlight how the meaning of Christian *pistis* during this period of modern history always brings the baggage with which Kant saddled it, namely, as a form of cognition (*Erkenntnis*) for which one has only subjectively sufficient justification. The term also carries with it connotations from Jacobi of an immediate, ungrounded certainty that are distinctively religious. It is this ambiguity that I want to highlight, and which I do not think the use of the English "faith" (to which the religious connotations are much more explicitly attached) would readily imply. It is this ambiguity that I believe is at work in much of the theological appropriation of apocalyptic in the twentieth century. Where I use the word "faith," the meaning is explicitly referring to the New Testament's *pistis*. Note that this is not how Pluhar exposits the difference in his translation of *Critique of Pure Reason*, p. 747.

Finally, it is common to view the nineteenth century through the lens of this tension between knowledge and belief. My genealogy here was inspired by my reading of Hans Frei and John Elbert Wilson, both of whom view nineteenth- and twentieth-century theology through that lens. See Frei, "David Friedrich Strauss"; and Overbeck, *On the Christianity of Theology*. See also n. 105 below.

the fundamental contrast on which modern theology had developed, and yet was nonetheless misrecognized as a radical expression of that same contrast. Thus, a survey of that history is in order.

As Kant clearly stated in his preface to the second edition of *The Critique of Pure Reason*, he understood the work of the critique to have "canceled knowledge in order to make room for belief" (*Ich musste also das Wissen aufheben, um zum Glauben Platz zu bekommen . . .*).[17] In this context, "belief" is concerned with rational inferences pertaining to the coherence of practical reason, inferences that do not rise to the level of scientific knowledge. According to Kant, traditional metaphysical concepts like God, freedom, and immortality had been misused because they were mistakenly and dogmatically equated with "knowledge." That presumption had confounded both the proper use of theoretical reason and the practical, moral significance of God, freedom, and immortality. In noting that these concepts were matters of "belief" rather than "knowledge," Kant did not intend to reject them but to allow their full importance to come into relief. In fact, Kant took the real source of Enlightenment unbelief (*Unglaube*), which was its own form of dogmaticism, to be the refusal of traditional metaphysics to submit its claims to critical evaluation.[18]

That submission to critique was directly related to the universal moral obligation. Morality, which depended on God, human freedom, and immortality, would be impossible if those categories possessed the kind of transcendental necessity required for objective knowledge.[19] The claim to have knowledge of God, freedom, and immortality vitiated their proper moral meaning and propagated the tyranny of the old order. Knowledge (*Wissen*) could only properly refer to propositions that are both objectively and subjectively certain, while belief must be reserved for those propositions that are only subjectively certain.[20] Belief was not at all to be an irrational matter of consent to the traditional forms of religion, but was instead to be entirely an affair of morality. Though this dualism of belief and knowledge became in time the hallmark of modern theology,
• Schleiermacher and Hegel first fundamentally challenged the assumptions on which it was established.

17. German taken from Kant, *Kritik der reinen Vernunft*, 30 (Bxxx). The quote continues, ". . . *und der Dogmatismus der Metaphysik, d.i. das Vorurtheil, in ihr ohne Kritik der reinen Vernunft fortzukommen, ist die wahre Quelle alles der Moralität widerstreitenden Unglaubens, der jederzeit gar sehr dogmatisch ist*."

18. *CPR*, Bxxx.

19. See ibid.

20. Ibid., A822/B850.

While it is true that Schleiermacher accepted Kant's strictures on knowledge of the absolute, and in a qualified sense upheld his distinction of theoretical and practical reason,[21] Schleiermacher did not dissociate belief from knowledge.[22] In *The Christian Faith*, which is his most mature treatment of the matter, Schleiermacher linked belief directly to the certainty (*Gewissheit*) of the immediate feeling of utter dependence (*schlechthinige Abhängigkeitsgefühl*), but noted that this certainty is the effect of God's action, which when cognitively reflected on is the basis for knowledge of God.[23] There can be no doubt that his use of this idea is indebted to Jacobi's invocation of "feeling" (*Gefühl*) and "belief" (*Glaube*) as a critique of Kant.[24] Yet for all that he learned from Jacobi, Schleiermacher made the notions of *Gefühl* and *Glaube* his own.[25] Where Jacobi used "feeling" and "belief" interchangeably to designate the ungrounded, immediate affirmation of the absolute,[26] Schleiermacher understood "feeling" as

21. See Frank, "Metaphysical Foundations," 15. Frank notes that Schleiermacher placed ethics as a system of action alongside metaphysics as a system of description, and understood the transcendent as that to which both were oriented but which neither could reach. They could not reach it because Schleiermacher had eradicated Kant's distinction between transcendental (as the condition of possibility for experience) and transcendent (lying outside possible experience). For Schleiermacher, these two are the same, which means that knowledge of God can no more be confined to one rather than the other since God is equally beyond both. Nonetheless, the transcendent can be indirectly known through both theoretical and practical reason. He aimed, Frank notes, at "a science of knowledge transcending the opposition between knowing and doing, theory and praxis" (16).

22. One must note that the issue of the feeling of absolute dependence, as a preconceptual form of consciousness, is a thorny one in Schleiermacher, and one about which specialists do not seem to be entirely clear—sometimes even being unable to keep it clear in a single essay! Nonetheless, Schleiermacher notes in *Der christliche glaube*, §4.4, that he has no interest in disputing the question of an original, conceptual knowledge of God, but only of treating the matter in relationship to Christian piety. Piety is not separated from knowing and doing (§3.3–5), but is the mediating link between them, as the consciousness of being absolute dependent (§3.4). Piety influences and determines both knowing and doing as that which mediates between (*vermittelt zwischen*) knowing and doing while exciting (*aufzuregen*) them both.

23. Schleiermacher, *Christliche glaube*. The German is taken from this edition. English translations are taken, unless otherwise noted, from *Christian Faith* (henceforth *CF*). This is not knowledge of God in Godself, but knowledge of God through God's effects on us.

24. See Jacobi, *Über der Lehre des Spinoza*. See the discussion in Frank, *Selbstgefühl*, especially 190–98.

25. See Frank, *Philosophical Foundations*, 205. See also 70–78, 165–73.

26. Ibid., 57ff.

the awareness of the unity of subject and object that precedes and affects thought and action[27] and defined "belief" as "nothing but the certainty concerning the feeling of utter dependence, as such, i.e., as conditioned by a Being placed outside of us, and as expressing our relationship to that Being."[28] Such certainty is a conceptual knowledge of God as the "whence" of the feeling of utter dependence, but has its content determined by Jesus Christ, by whose action (*Einwirkung Christi*) the state of being in need of redemption (*der Zustand der Erlösungsbedürftigkeit*) has been abolished (*aufgehoben*).[29] It is the certainty of redemption that arises from one's relation to Jesus that constitutes one's belief in Christ (*diese Gewissheit ist eben der Glaube an Christum*), and which alone yields conceptual content and knowledge of God.[30] One's relation to Christ determines the immediate awareness of God in feeling. That knowledge is not objective and theoretical, but is instead the prior determination of the character of objective knowledge and moral action. In this way, Schleiermacher believed in a different order than objective, critical knowledge and ethical action, an order that preceded, determined, and accompanied (*begleitet*) both as the vehicle through which God, the self, and the world were truly perceived.[31]

Schleiermacher maintained Kant's critical strictures against metaphysics, but did not sever the intimate connection between belief and knowledge. Because feeling refers to the affective unity of the subject and object that is presupposed by thought, there can be no final contradiction of belief and knowledge. However, no definitive reconciliation of the two can occur in critical thought either, since it is that separation that makes discursive thought possible. Only a dialectical correlation of the two can be expected in thought, even if the fundamental unity of the two must be presupposed.[32] It was the misunderstanding of this subtle and peculiar affir-

27. See Frank, "Metaphysical Foundations," 26–31.

28. Schleiermacher, *CF*, §14.1.

29. Ibid.

30. Ibid.

31. Ibid. Robert Merrihew Adams in his "Faith and Religious Knowledge" makes this point that Schleiermacher's account of God does not refer solely to human consciousness. However, I believe that Adams' account is significantly hindered by his account of the relation between discursive thought and the non-conceptual immediacy of feeling (cf. 41–42), which tends to think of the feeling of absolute dependence as absent apart from its conceptualization. I believe this betrays a misunderstanding of the relation of thought to immediate self-consciousness and feeling, which also impacts the understanding of the relationship of belief to knowledge.

32. See the discussion of transcendent ground in Frank, "Metaphysical Foundations." That unity of knowledge and belief is a truth in reality not ideality, which means

mation of a necessary distinction without separation between knowledge and belief—which was consistent with the Romantic understanding of the absolute—that would be misunderstood and critiqued by the idealists of the Tübingen school.[33] Specifically, Baur and Strauss claimed that the christological archetype to which Schleiermacher appealed as the object of belief could not be identified with the historical Jesus as the object of knowledge. They did so through a reading of Hegel's speculative system.

Hegel recognized Kant's distinction of knowledge from belief as a profound problem for Enlightenment Christianity from the time of his earliest theological writings. In *Faith and Knowledge* (*Glauben und Wissen*), he began to develop his critique of "the culture of reflection," which would become a theme in all of his work leading up to the *Logic*.[34] Belief (*Glaube*) was one's subjective trust in the immediate certainty of the unconditioned ground of experience. Such certainty marked the differentiation of self-consciousness from objective immediacy and implied the important recognition of a differentiation between God and consciousness. It was on the basis of this difference, Hegel argued, that belief was distinguished in the Reformation from the dogmatic objectivity of Catholicism and properly recognized as constitutive for the New Testament understanding of *pistis*.[35] Nonetheless, because this early notion of certainty lacked any objective correlate, he understood it to be a state of subjectivity that is outside the province of truth and not properly knowledge.[36]

From the *Phenomenology of Spirit* (1807) forward, however, Hegel transformed this understanding of belief into the initial moment of immediacy in the process of Absolute Knowing.[37] In his *Lectures on the*

---

that it must be dialectically represented in thought. For the reading of the relationship of the general and particular in Schleiermacher, one that has had significant effect on the philosophical significance of Schleiermacher but little on his theological interpretation, see Frank, *Individuelle Allgemeine*.

33. On the difference between the Romantic and Idealist notions of the absolute, see Bowie's "Introduction" in Frank, *Subject and the Text*. The reader will also see a discussion of the significance of negative determination to Spinoza in this section, which is important to both Frank's and Bowie's wider work, and to which my own use of this idea in this essay is indebted.

34. See Hegel, *Faith and Knowledge*, 55–66; and Rose, *Hegel Contra Sociology* (henceforth *HcS*).

35. See Inwood, *Hegel Dictionary*, 46.

36. Ibid.

37. Ibid.

Philosophy of Religion (1827)[38] and the *Encyclopedia Logic* (1830),[39] Hegel applied this understanding of belief in his speculative account of the dual mirroring (*speculum*) of mind in nature and nature in mind, and associated belief, as Hodgson notes, closely with an "intuition" (*Anschauung*).[40] It is the subjective certainty that was known as feeling (*Gefühl*)[41] and mediated by representation (*Vorstellung*). It became true knowledge only when it was elevated to the concept (*Begriff*).[42] Because representations were objective mediations of subjective consciousness, they were historically conditioned presentations of both nature and thought, which referred to both sensible (mythical) and non-sensible (i.e., God and creation) objects.[43] In this way, Hegel made no separation of belief from knowledge, but understood the entire history of knowledge as the conceptual apprehension of their essential unity (reconciliation).

Despite these important oppositions to Kant by the two most influential theological thinkers of the nineteenth century, Kant's separation of belief from knowledge remained dominant. It was propagated in subtle and sometimes unwitting ways by thinkers who returned to Kant from within the paradigms that Schleiermacher and Hegel developed to overcome him. The mistake of those thinkers was to presuppose the separation between belief and knowledge in their attempts to move beyond it. This had not been the case for Schleiermacher or Hegel. Though Schleiermacher agreed that critical philosophy makes traditional metaphysics impossible, he understood knowledge and belief are different aspects of a common reality whose unity is presupposed by thought. Hegel likewise insisted that belief is the immediate certainty of the essential unity of God and humanity. But when Schleiermacher's later followers (viz., Ritschl) mistook his essentially realist position as subjectivist, and attempted to retrieve a supposedly lost objectivity, they transposed Kant's separation of belief from knowledge into an abstract analysis of validity (theory) and value (practice). But it is among Hegel's followers that this return to Kant first began, when Baur and Strauss failed to grasp the significance

38. Hegel, *Philosophy of Religion*, 133–37.

39. Hegel, *Encyclopedia Logic*, §445–68.

40. Hodgson, *Hegel and Christian Theology*, 107–8.

41. Ibid., 108–11. Note that this inverts Schleiermacher's understanding of the relation between belief and feeling. Hegel's account of feeling is entirely subjective, in contrast to Schleiermacher's appeal to the unity of subject and object.

42. Ibid., 111–13.

43. Ibid.

of Hegelian speculation and reconfigured the relation of knowledge and belief as one of reflective, negative determination.

The Logic of Opposition: The Tübingen School

It is F. C. Baur who is most responsible for transforming the place of Hegel's speculative system in modern theology. The common reading of Baur sees his historical theology as a straightforward application of Hegel's speculative method to the history of Christian doctrine. Yet, because Baur did not adopt Hegel's complete account of consciousness, his understanding of speculative method differs from Hegel in some decisive ways. Unlike Hegel for whom speculation involves the mutual reflection (mediation) of belief and knowledge in history, Baur understands dogmatic speculation (theology) to be the conceptual mediation of the opposition between belief and knowledge, which reconciles temporal consciousness with its abstract archetype (essence). What was for Hegel an account of the concrete identity-in-difference of belief and knowledge was for Baur an account of their abstract difference-in-identity. In this way, Baur unwittingly reverted to Kant's dualistic assumptions.

That reversion to Kant was due to Baur's unique synthesis of his influences. As Hodgson has shown, the key moments of Baur's thought were developed from Schleiermacher and Schelling, not Hegel. When he did finally adopt Hegel's system, Schleiermacher and Schelling continued to influence him in ways not entirely consonant with Hegel's goals. From Schleiermacher, Baur learned that the focus of post-Kantian theology should be on consciousness,[44] and this was reflected in his first major work, *Symbolism and Mythology*, which adapted Schelling's idea of myth (from *The System of Transcendental Idealism*) as the poetic and religion expression of the essential unity of God and humanity.[45] This more archetypal understanding of consciousness remained in Baur's use of the concept of the "idea" to describe his dynamic understanding of the reconciliation of God and humanity in history.[46]

Baur's most important difference from Hegel, though, concerns the relation of history to the absolute, which lies at the center of his speculative

---

44. Morgan, "Ferdinand Christian Baur," 272.

45. Hodgson, *Historical Theology*, 92. Hodgson gives a succinct account of Bauer's intellectual development (12–36).

46. Ibid., 15–20.

interpretation of Christian history.[47] In his *Textbook on the History of Christian Dogma* (1837), Baur notes that the scientific articulation of the concept of dogma is the final stage of the unfolding of Spirit in history. It is only in this scientific epoch that there emerges speculative knowledge of history as "the eternally clear mirror in which the Spirit contemplates itself, considers its own picture, in order to be for itself, for its own consciousness, what it is in itself; and to know itself as the moving force behind what has come to pass in history."[48] With this statement, Baur shows he has understood Hegelian speculation in the terms of the philosophy of reflection it was specifically developed to overcome. Baur speaks of history's mirroring (*speculum*) in exactly Fichte's terms of a one-way reflective determination of the ego by the non-ego.[49] History is posited (*setzen*) by consciousness as the mirror within which it knows itself through its contrast (*Gegensatz*).[50] This understanding of speculation attempts to make traditional subject/predicate logic dynamic by transforming each predicate into a subject in its own right.[51] He does not recognize that speculative reasoning is not intended to show the formal identity between the subject and predicate, but to bring to awareness the constitutive misrecognition that is internal to the experience of their separation.[52]

Baur was hamstrung by his fidelity to Spinoza's monistic immanence.[53] Like his belief that consciousness is the proper locus for modern theology, Baur also believed Spinoza's identification of God and the world must be the baseline for our concept of God.[54] He shared this conviction

---

47. Ibid., 162–67.

48. This is Morgan's translation of the passage in "Ferdinand Christian Baur," 265. The German, taken from *Lehrbuch der christlichen Dogmengescheschichte*, 59, reads: "*Was die Geschichte überhaupt ist, als der ewig klare Spiegel, in welchem der Geist sich selbst anschaut, sein eigenes Bild betrachtet, um was er an sich ist, auch für sich, für sein eigenes Bewusstsein zu sein, und sich als die bewegende Macht des geschichtlich Gewordenen zu wissen, das concentrirt sich in dem engern Gebiete der Dogmengeschichte zu einer um so intensivern Bedeutung.*"

49. See Fichte, "First Introduction" in *Science of Knowledge*.

50. Morgan, "Ferdinand Christian Baur," 270–71. As Baur says in *Lehrbuch*, 257: "'The absolute idea is God as the Absolute Spirit who mediates himself with himself through the process of thought." Translation taken from Hodgson, *Historical Theology*, 92.

51. This was how Marx describes Hegel in *Hegel's Philosophy of Right*, 11. See the discussion in Rose, *HcS*, 52.

52. See Rose, *HcS*, 53.

53. See the discussion in Hodgson, *Historical Theology*, 45 and 134–41.

54. Ibid., 45.

with Hegel and it overlapped significantly with Schleiermacher's revision of the doctrine of election.[55] However, Schleiermacher and Hegel both developed accounts of the fullness of being that transcended Spinoza's idea of finite being as the negative determination of infinite substance.[56] This same idea of negative determination lay at the heart of Fichte's philosophy of reflection.[57] Thus, whereas for Hegel speculative thought involved recognition of the false divisions that conceptual thinking introduced into reality, those misrecognitions that could only be overcome in the concretely ethical (*sittlich*),[58] for Baur speculation was the conceptual negation through which the identity of the finite with the infinite had determinate content. That this is a reversion to Kant's separation of belief from knowledge is most apparent in Baur's account of the christological idea.

Hans Frei's counterintuitive claim that David Strauss is the preeminently christocentric thinker is perhaps more appropriately applied to Baur.[59] Strauss's arguments, which led Frei to this judgment, were first developed by Baur against Schleiermacher in his inaugural lecture at Tübingen (1827). In this lecture, Baur argued that Schleiermacher could not sustain his claim that Jesus of Nazareth, the historical person, was the fullness of the christological ideal, the object of Christian belief, because the only notion of the redeemer that could be derived from Christian consciousness would be a generalization of subjectivity. No finite consciousness could so completely represent an infinite consciousness as to be

55. See Schleiermacher, *CF*, §§136–39. See also the illuminating study by Matthias Gockel, *Barth and Schleiermacher on the Doctrine of Election: A Systematic-Theological Comparison* (Oxford: OUP, 2007).

56. On Schleiermacher, see Frank, "Metaphysical Foundations," especially 31–33. This claim is perhaps a bit more controversial with regard to Hegel, for whom there are multiple contrasting readings. I am basing this claim not simply on the priority of essence in his *Logic*, but also on the reading of the speculative relationship of essence and existence, their mutual reflection, which is previously laid out in this essay.

57. See Rose, *HcS*, 197–217. This a dominant theme in the mutually related work of Andrew Bowie, Manfred Frank, and Dieter Henrich. See Henrich, *Between Kant and Hegel*, 184–85; Frank, *Philosophical Foundations*, 92; and Bowie, *Aesthetics and Subjectivity*, 49–52.

58. Rose, *HcS*, 197–217. The reasons for this, according to Rose, are due to the tendency of post-Kantian thought to eradicate "intuition," as the mind's immediate connection to nature, in favor of concepts. This tendency blinds modern thought to its determination by bourgeois property right, and ultimately the Roman legal distinction between "person" and "thing" on which that right is based.

59. See Frei, "David Friedrich Strauss," 225–28; and Hodgson, *Historical Theology*, 100–121.

identical with it.[60] And, what is more, if Jesus was the complete historical realization of God, then he would not have a history—and without a history he would not be human. Thus, in claiming that Jesus was the fullness of the christological idea, Schleiermacher wrongly attributed the archetypal truth of the essence of human consciousness (the divine-human unity) to the historical person of Jesus of Nazareth.

Baur's reasoning on this point is perfectly Spinozan: the infinite has its determination in the finite, which is the negation that makes the content of the finite known. It is likewise perfectly Fichtean: the absolute ego of God has its determination only in its finite non-ego. Unlike Schleiermacher, Baur accepted that Jesus of Nazareth, the object of scientific historical inquiry, could not be the fullness of the christological idea, and argued instead that only the idea was perfectly realized in every single historical individual considered as an aggregate. Jesus of Nazareth could be shown to be the one human being for whom the non-being of the idea was at its lowest possible degree.[61] This meant that the realization of the christological idea was entirely abstract, and that the historical unity of God and humanity was the regulative ideal of the totality of humanity.

Dogma was the historical form of this christological idea, the speculative mediation of knowledge and belief.[62] In bringing thought to bear on belief, dogma articulated the inner unity of the objective contrasts of history, the contrasts within which Spirit knows itself and becomes explicitly known. In creatively reworking contrasts (e.g., Jewish and Gentile) to reflect the more comprehensive unity in which their general correspondence to the christological idea is known, theology reveals the formal identity that is disclosed in those contrasts. That reconciliation is never properly concrete because it is only grasped in and through the conceptual union that synthesizes the differences of finite determination. Baur's method of identification is, as Nietzsche would later say, a creative act, a *factum*.[63] Contrary to Baur's intent, the unity that he perceived is not discovered so much as it is created through the negation of the differences that make something what it is. This is the consequence that David Strauss saw more clearly and developed into his own critique.

60. Hodgson, *Historical Theology*, 47–50.

61. Ibid., 105.

62. Ibid., 237–44.

63. "Adorno is more concerned with the Nietzschean perspective that to say that two things are identical is to make them identical, than with the Hegelian emphasis that to say that two things are identical is to assume incorrectly that they are independent of each other" (Rose, *Melancholy Science*, 22–23).

As Baur's student, Strauss was deeply influenced by his critique of Schleiermacher. That influence is seen in the conclusion to Strauss's *Life of Jesus* (1835), as well as in the arguments of *The Christ of Faith and the Jesus of History.*[64] In the *Life of Jesus*, Strauss also relied heavily on Baur's notion of myth from *Symbolism and Mythology.*[65] But, believing that the way to make Christianity intelligible to the modern mind lay with Hegel's elevation of the religious representation to the philosophical concept, Strauss moved beyond Baur to emphasize the critical negation at the heart of speculation.[66] As a result, though he worked within the structures of Baur's account of speculative thought, Strauss transformed that account into a method for conceptually establishing the objective legitimacy of religious affirmations, which required him to make the characteristically left-wing Hegelian separation of critical method from the system as a whole.[67] That separation was an explicit insistence that Kant's critique be intensified by the sublation of the mythical representation into the philosophical concept. In this way, he obliquely reintroduced the separation of knowledge from belief.

The decisive element in this transformation was the methodology laid out in *Life of Jesus*, and developed in *On the Defense of My Life of Jesus Against the Hegelians* (1837). Where Baur saw the need for a speculative demonstration of the essential identity of religious representation and scientific inquiry, Strauss saw only an ever-widening gap of dissimilarity. The contrast of myth and concept, which is the basis for the contrast of belief and knowledge, became a fundamental opposition for Strauss because he could see no way that the elevation of mythical religious representation to theoretical knowledge was not a false objectification of humanity's essential unity with the divine.[68] Unlike Baur, Strauss understood the philosophical force a choice between belief and knowledge,[69] one that allowed him to universalize the christological idea.[70]

Strauss was not simplistically inverting Baur's approach. Rather, he was making its presuppositions explicit. Strauss recognized the negative,

64. Strauss, *Life of Jesus* (henceforth *LJ*), 757–84. Also see Strauss, *Christ of Faith.*

65. See Keck's Introduction in Strauss, *Christ of Faith*, xxi and l–lv.

66. See the discussion in Hodgson's Introduction in Strauss, *LJ*, xxv–xxxvi.

67. This case is made extensively and defended in Strauss, *Defense*, especially ch. 3. See also Massey's discussion in the Introduction, xiii–xxv and xxvi–xxix.

68. *LJ*, 87–92, 757–58, 777–84. See also Strauss, *In Defense*, 3–20.

69. See Hodgson's Introduction to Strauss, *LJ*, xxv–xxxvi.

70. *LJ*, 757–58.

dialectical relation between representation and essence in Baur's system.[71] In other words, Strauss saw the dialectic at just the point that Baur saw reconciliation.[72] Because of this, Strauss could entirely jettison any need for mythical representation in favor of the direct correspondence of abstract humanity with the christological idea.[73]

Both Baur and Strauss transformed Hegel's speculative reason into a logic for judging the correspondence of historical experience to the christological idea. Yet, only Strauss saw what was being done. Nonetheless, just as Baur failed to see that Kant's critical moment was not abandoned in the speculative elevation to the concept, Strauss missed that this same moment redoubled to expose his own subjectivity as a knower to the empirical critique of the mediating history of mythical representation.[74] For both thinkers, the idea remained abstract. The reconciliation of belief and knowledge that both Baur and Strauss sought was first premised on a more fundamental division of theoretical and empirical reality; which were held together only as mutually determining contrasts. Thus, ironically, the very abstraction that united them was equally and simultaneously the origin of their separation. This was the general logic of reflective determination that was deployed in Spinoza and Fichte, a covert return to Kant that transposed his dualism into the essence of the christological idea, making that division into the engine of an illusory abstract union they called "reconciliation."[75]

It was this subtle and unwitting reversion to Kant in the Tübingen school would be the foundation for theology's reception of apocalyptic in the theology of *krisis*. Though the theologians associated with this movement would come to embrace virtually everything that Strauss opposed, they did so in a manner entirely consistent with his method of negative

71. Ibid., 80. Strauss here writes, consistent with the claim about Baur's Fichtean understanding of speculation: "This is the key to the whole of Christology, that, as subject of the predicate which the church assigns to Christ, we place, instead of an individual, an idea; but an idea which has an existence in reality, not in the mind only, like that of Kant. In an individual, a God-man, the properties and functions which the church ascribes to Christ contradict themselves; in the idea of the race, they perfectly agree."

72. See Massey's Introduction in Strauss, *In Defense*, xxvi.

73. See Frei, "David Friedrich Strauss."

74. See Rose, *HcS*, 149–84.

75. I am aware that the most recent philosophical attempts to overcome this dualism appeal to Spinoza as their inspiration. Yet, the nature of Spinoza's conception of knowledge requires the embrace of the necessity of the opposition rather than their final reconciliation.

dialectic. Before arriving at this point, however, it is helpful to understand how the influence of Kant's dualism continued to spread throughout the remainder of the nineteenth century.

The Crisis of Apocalyptic: Albrecht Ritschl, History of Religions, and Franz Overbeck

. The irony of the Tübingen school was that its reconciliation of knowledge and belief was premised on and achieved within a logic that made that division absolute. Reconciliation within a monist metaphysics can only be abstract and ideal, since every finite determination of a common essence must be posited in opposition to the infinite, and every other finite singular. The Tübingen school's conception of reason was therefore essentially dependence on Kant's dualism. But what was only implicit in Baur and Strauss became explicit in the work of several major philosophers and theologians during the last half of the century, such as Hermann Cohen (1842–1918), and his teacher, Hermann Lotze (1817–1881). It was Lotze who was most influential on the shape of Protestant liberalism[76] through the adoption of his work by Albrecht Ritschl. Lotze's lasting influence lay in his translation of Kant's division of belief from knowledge into an emphasis on value and abstract validity. A brief introduction to Lotze's ideas is thus in order.[77]

76. The work of the Finnish school of Luther interpretation has been instrumental in bringing to light the influence of Lotze's philosophy on Ritschl and his students. A complete study on the matter is Saaranin, *Gottes Wirken auf uns*. The school has questioned the transcendental school of Luther interpretation, which claims that we know nothing of Godself, only God's effects on us. They have also questioned the idea that in Luther our union with God is a union of wills, and is not ontological. However, focusing on ontology and transcendental claims, while perhaps significant for drawing distinctions between nineteenth-century Lutherans and Luther himself, does not get to the heart of the questions about critical reason with which nineteenth-century theologians were wrestling. Closer analysis of the role of the validity/value distinction is in order in relation to the issues they have already raised.

77. It is Gillian Rose who has done the most to uncover the full range of Lotze's influence on European sociology and social theory. She showed that Lotze's work is the conceptual framework presupposed by the two dominant schools of neo-Kantian philosophy and of sociology (Marburg/Durkheim and Heidelberg/Weber). In the present section, I have followed Rose's reading of Lotze and adapted her interpretation of his legacy to illuminate the contours of the knowledge/belief relation as it is developed in theology after Ritschl. See Rose, *HcS*, 2–14.

As Gillian Rose recognized, Lotze was profoundly influential on the whole of German intelligentsia in the latter half of the nineteenth century, shaping the basic assumptions of the dominant schools of neo-Kantianism, sociology, and social theory.[78] Particularly important was his modification of Kant's distinction of theoretical and practical reason into a three-part division of validity, cognition, and value.[79] Where Kant had relied on transcendental analysis of the conditions of experience to determine the *a priori* categories of the mind and the validity of its concepts, Lotze understood validity to be a judgment about the correspondence of abstract propositions to the reality of experience. Validity was distinguished from value specifically in order to supply some basis other than empirical sensation for these judgments.[80] Such judgments were made by applying logical rules that make no appeal to empirical experience.[81] The Tübingen school's use of the christological idea in many ways anticipated this aspect of Lotze's transformation of Kant's transcendental categories into validity.

But, in addition to adding the category of validity, Lotze also uniquely developed the meaning of Kant's practical reason by associating it with value, a category more expansive than ethics. Lotze understood value to be a matter of conviction, belief (*Glaube*), rather than knowledge, and (much like Jacobi's "*Glaube*") its perception was ungrounded, immediate, and certain, requiring no further cognitive or propositional demonstration. However (unlike Jacobi), Lotze linked value to public, cultural, and ethical actions, not subjective feeling. It possessed *sui generis* significance alongside knowledge and validity, and, as the immediate source and aim of all value, it was the proper aspect of life with which to perceive God. As with Schleiermacher's "belief," Lotze's "value" made the object of experience present to the subject through its effects.[82]

---

78. Ibid., 2–14.

79. Ibid., 6–7.

80. Kant had retained an intimate connection between empirical sensation in his transcendental method. The results were circular in that his arguments moved from experience to the conditions of the possibility of experience, and Lotze was concerned to provide an entirely logical basis for judging even whether a certain experience is an accurate representation of reality. See Rose, *HcS*, 2–5.

81. It is significant that this way of talking about the distinction between propositions and experience is one of the ways in which Louis Martyn's "bifocal" vision can be interpreted. See n. 160 below. I think this is the least helpful way to understand the idea, for reasons that will be given below, and that where it is so understood it is self-defeating.

82. See Hefner's Introduction to Ritschl, *Three Essays*, 27.

By translating knowledge and belief into the categories of validity and value, Lotze removed any reference to empirical experience that had otherwise been retained by Kant and Baur. It was on the basis of this separation from empirical experience and the connection of value to the immediate perception of God that Albrecht Ritschl returned to Kant from within Schleiermacher's framework. Ritschl adopted Lotze's notion of value as a way of linking the immediacy of God's presence to ethical action rather than consciousness, which also differentiated it from objective, scientific knowledge. The notion of value underscored the public, cultural, and ethical orientation of the community of believers, to what he understood as "the kingdom of God."[83] In fact, Ritschl identified the "peculiarity" of Christian knowledge of God to consist in its association with "value-judgments."[84] Value judgments are connected directly to the believer's justification and reconciliation. Justification is the immediate certainty of value bestowed by God on the self, while the world and reconciliation of relationship with God and others was the Christian community's public, communal, ethical expression of that value.[85] This greater stress on practical action gave Ritschl a means of combining Schleiermacher's emphasis on the church as the community of believers with a more dynamic conception of God's immediacy than Schleiermacher had.

That dynamism was best captured in the notion of the kingdom of God, which would become, under Ritschl's influence, the dominant theme of liberal theology in Schleiermacher's tradition (Wilhelm Herrmann and Adolf von Harnack).[86] The strongly ethical and political emphasis would later be radicalized and brought sharply into view by Johannes Weiss's account of the apocalyptic content of Jesus' preaching.[87] But for Ritschl and his followers the kingdom of God was decidedly liberal and bourgeois.[88] It was grounded fundamentally in Kant's distinction of freedom from the

83. Ritschl, *Doctrine of Justification and Reconciliation* (henceforth *DJR*), 3:§§1–5, 38–39. Henceforth cited as *DJR*. See also Ritschl, *Three Essays*, 186–87.

84. Ritschl, *DJR*, §28.

85. Ibid., §§13–14 and 62–68.

86. Schleiermacher himself had been the first to envision the kingdom in this way, imagining the eventual cultural triumph of the Christian community over the entire world. But Ritschl notes that Schleiermacher did not understand the full significance of this (*DJR*, §2).

87. In fact, it will be specifically the apocalyptic orientation of Jesus' preaching of the kingdom of God that will be a keenly important notion in this regard.

88. See Ritschl, *DJR*, §§62–68.

objective necessity of knowledge,[89] and led Ritschl to give priority to practical value over theoretical validity. As a result, though theological reflection began with the historical Jesus, Christian belief was only a matter of judgment concerning the value of scientifically determined truths.

It was the history of religions school that took the opposite position and prioritized validity. The goal of this school was to develop a notion of religion as an entirely sociocultural and historical phenomenon. These scholars, many of them theologians, were concerned to show how and on what basis Christian belief was a cultural value arising out of a prior network of social conditions, and in that light to assess the basis on which Christian belief could be a valid modern sociocultural value.[90] To this extent, the history of religions school stood in continuity with the Tübingen school. However, it replaced the role played by the christological idea in the Tübingen school with scientific analysis of the social and historical conditions that gave rise to the religion. In many ways, Strauss's argument that the sociocultural fact of Christian belief was invalid under the conditions of modernity anticipated the approach of the history of religions school. For Strauss, such conditions were the conceptual realization of the universality of the christological idea. For the history of religions school Christianity was the highest and most modern form of religion. Wilhelm Bousset's *What Is Religion?* was perhaps the best example of this stance. Throughout the work, Bousset consistently judged religions and their historical development according to their "value," which he understood as an established social and historical fact of their distinct sociocultural conditions. He argued for recognizing the "eternal"[91] and "supreme"[92] value of the social and historical fact of Christianity[93] on the basis that it embodied the most universal, most cosmopolitan, and therefore most modern of values. Others, such as Rudolph Otto, sought more precisely to identify this standard of validity by correlating these social and historical facts of religious value to a *religious a priori* in humanity that could be socioculturally apprehended.[94]

[Marginal annotations: • Kant; Lessing; modern values; Otto]

89. Ibid., 28.

90. See Rose, *HcS*, 14–23. The reader may find Rose's discussion here of the differences between Weber and Durkheim illuminating for the contrast I am here drawing.

91. Bousset, *What Is Religion?*, 292.

92. Ibid., ix

93. Ibid., 292.

94. Otto, *Idea of the Holy.*

This emphasis on the socio-cultural conditions of religion is most apparent in the development of form criticism, pioneered by Hermann Gunkel.[95] Form criticism isolated the literary patterns and strata of oral tradition that contributed to the present condition of Biblical texts (particularly the Hebrew Scriptures), and linked those patterns and strata to the discrete sociocultural conditions of their production (*Sitz in Leben*). This critical approach had enormously fruitful impact on the study of the biblical material, but often with wildly varying results. Bousset, for example, drew an entirely Hellenizing portrait of the apostle Paul as one who reinterpreted Jewish-Christian belief into the cultural-religious patterns of Hellenistic *kyrios* mystery cults.[96] A similar conclusion was drawn, to opposite ends, by the Roman Catholic liturgical historian Odo Casel,[97] who argued these mystery cults were the setting for the development of the Christian liturgy of the Eucharist and the theology of the paschal mystery. This argument was itself similar to the work of Albert Eichhorn.[98] But on the other hand, the same methods produced the work of William Wrede, who drew a portrait of the apostle Paul that was thoroughly situated within the context of first-century Palestinian Jewish religion and culture. Albert Schweitzer developed this portrait in a way that would become known as "the new perspective on Paul" in the twentieth century.[99] The key figure for the present study, however, is Johannes Weiss.

Weiss

It was Weiss's *Jesus' Proclamation of the Kingdom of God* (1892) that decisively established the status of apocalyptic in the preaching of Jesus.[100] With one small study, Weiss cut off Ritschl's path to the kingdom of God as the ethical value for the Christian community by showing that the content of Jesus' preaching of the kingdom of God, which the Ritschlians had adopted as the critical norm for all Christian value judgments, was the first-century sociocultural Jewish messianic expectation of the imminent divine judgment and end to the world.[101] Such preaching did

95. See Gunkel, *Genesis* and *Legends*, especially 37–122.

96. See Bousset, *Kyrios Christos*.

97. See Casel, *Mystery of Worship*.

98. See Eichhorn, *Lord's Supper*.

99. See Wrede, *Paul*; and Schweizer, *Quest*, 330–403.

100. Weiss, *Predigt Jesu von Reiche Gottes*. The English translation is *Jesus' Proclamation of the Kingdom of God* (henceforth *JPKG*). It must be noted that many of the contemporary representatives of the quest for the historical Jesus, like Marcus Borg, reject that Jesus was in any way an apocalyptic prophet. The general consensus has sided with Weiss.

101. See Weiss, *JPKG*, 84–92. On this point, see Schweizer, *Quest*, 223–69 and 330–403.

not resemble Ritschl's bourgeois, liberal notion of the kingdom of God as fraternal love. Rather, it anticipated the subjection of all human works to God's judgment, as well as the dawn of the new age of the Messiah's reign.[102] Nonetheless, those findings revolutionized how biblical scholars and theologians conceived the kingdom of God. And, in directly correlating the kingdom of God with Jewish apocalyptic, Weiss raised the issue of Christian belief in the modern world to a pitch it had not previously known. Christian belief was now specifically a question for knowledge.[103] Not only was there no sense in talking about the cultural expression of an apocalyptic, world-denying value and the imminent end of the cosmos, but neither could one any longer talk about the distinct but mutual correlation of value (belief) with validity (knowledge). The scientific knowledge of the apocalyptic content of primitive Christian belief meant that modern theology could only be conducted honestly as an inquiry into the validity of this value; that is, whether it was plausible for modern Christians to *right* believe the apocalyptic content of the primitive Christian kerygma.

Two results followed from this. First, because apocalyptic forced the prioritizing of validity over value, the result was the transformation of any transcendental, dialectical, or speculative relation between them into an antinomy. *Antinomy* Scientific knowledge showed that valid Christian belief was essentially apocalyptic, making any form of valid Christian belief antithetical to scientific knowledge. The rediscovery of apocalyptic had forced a choice. Albert Schweitzer saw it clearly when he noted in *The Quest for the Historical Jesus* that, in Weiss's wake, the theologian must *Choice* choose between thoroughgoing (*konsequente*) skepticism and a "thoroughgoing eschatology."[104] A rigorous skepticism takes the knowledge of primitive Christian apocalyptic to be the dissolution of the possibility of any modern Christian belief, and a rigorous eschatology takes fidelity to the apocalyptic order of Christian belief to be the dissolution of modern knowledge. Importantly, it is Kant's dualism of knowledge and belief, framed according to an abstract application of the logical rules of validity, ✓ that is responsible for the antinomy.

The second point has already been briefly noted. Both horns of the dilemma are premised on the priority given to the question of the validity of Christian belief, which is specifically a matter of scientific knowledge.

102. Weiss, *JPKG*, 129–36.

103. The issues had always in some sense tended to pivot around the place of eschatology, going back even to Strauss. See Strauss, *LJ*, xxi.

104. Schweitzer, *Quest*, 328.

Whether the validity of belief is determined according to a thoroughgoing eschatology or a thoroughgoing skepticism, it is knowledge that has precedence in that judgment. The object of that knowledge, paradoxically, is belief. As a result, the rediscovery of apocalyptic renders Christian belief a question specifically for knowledge, which has serious ramifications within the antinomy of knowledge and belief. Like the christological idea of the Tübingen school and the sociocultural conditions of the history of religions school, Schweitzer's dilemma situated apocalyptic as an abstract norm for historical experience, one that set it up as a logical methodology and a perverse form of knowledge.

These consequences were hardly discerned in Schweitzer's time but they were recognized and developed somewhat extensively some twenty years prior to Weiss by Franz Overbeck. It is Overbeck who I maintain is the subaltern influence for the theological appropriation of apocalyptic into the present. It is Overbeck's project that spells out what it means to see apocalyptic in these abstract, normative, and methodological terms.

It is not as widely recognized as it should be that Franz Overbeck was the first to claim that both the form and content of primitive Christian belief was apocalyptic. Unlike Weiss, whose work was focused on Jesus' preaching, Overbeck developed his arguments in relation to the history of the sociocultural conditions of the earliest Christian communities. He argued not simply that these communities believed in the imminent destruction of the world, but that their commitment to this truth had direct bearing on their way of believing. In other words, it was not simply that early Christians believed Jesus would return at any moment to end the world, but that their fidelity to him obliged them to be hostile to any accommodation with worldly culture or knowledge. In this way, Overbeck both recognized and affirmed the apocalyptic antinomy of belief and knowledge, and became the immediate forebear of the otherwise very different theological project of dialectical theology. It is true that Overbeck advanced a relentless critique of the Ritschlian liberalism and apologetic theology of his day, and was thus of use to dialectical theology. However, Overbeck was at root elaborating on the same problem of the mediation of knowledge and belief that had occupied other scholars of his generation— a problem that dialectical theology would seek, if not directly to repudiate, then utterly to confound. Nonetheless, Overbeck saw with the greatest clarity of anyone of his time the intensity of the challenge that apocalyptic posed to modern conceptions of belief and knowledge.

24

Overbeck was not a member of the history of religions school, although he viewed religion in exactly the same sociocultural terms as they. However, abjuring any formal association with a methodological school, Overbeck did acknowledge that he was closest to being a "*Tübinger*,"[105] owing an important debt to Baur's project of historical theology. Like Strauss, Overbeck separated the critical method from the speculative system, yet he maintained Baur's goal of developing a specifically theological reconstruction of early Christianity. Going beyond even Strauss, however, he extended the critical apparatus to theology per se, laying out what he called a "profane church history" (*Profane Kirchengeschichte*),[106] in which the history of theology was seen as an elaborate transgression of the integrity of belief rather than the articulation of its correspondence with the christological idea.[107] As if willingly perverting Baur's notion of theology as bringing thought to bear on belief, Overbeck wrote: "[I]n so far as theology brings faith [*Glaube*] into contact with rational knowledge, it is in itself and by its very nature always irreligious."[108] Or again: "For, if Christianity is considered as a religion, then it is rather the case that, like every religion, it has the most unambiguous antipathy *towards*

---

105. Overbeck, *How Christian Is Our Present-Day Theology?*, 12–16. The title of this book is a Straussian question from *The Old Faith and the New*, if ever there was one, and emphasizes the priority of the question of the validity of belief as a cultural value. The reader is also directed to the excellent study by Henry, *Franz Overbeck*. Other than Henry's study and introduction to his English translation of *Über die Christlichkeit unserer heutigen Theologie* (*How Christian . . .*), John Elbert Wilson has completed his own translation (as *The Christianity of Theology*) with extensive introduction and notes. It was from reading Wilson, who frames the matter in terms of mediation, and whom I interpreted in light of Frei's essay on Strauss (see n. 16 above), that the important role of the *Wissen* and *Glaube* distinction in the intellectual trajectory running from the Tübingen School to Barth occurred to me. Wilson points to Overbeck's acknowledgment of his debt to Baur in this text, and then seeks to develop a close link with Barth in order to defend the argument that Overbeck was in fact the ironic believer that Barth initially thought he was. I have a very different reading of the nature of the connection than Wilson, and remain unconvinced by what I think is his tendentious reading of Overbeck. I prefer Henry's analysis. The reader is directed to consult Henry's assessment of Wilson (Henry, *Franz Overbeck*, 29).

106. Overbeck, *How Christian*, 15–17. See Henry, *Franz Overbeck*, 9.

107. Like the history of religions school, Overbeck saw religion as entirely conditioned by its culture. See Henry, *Franz Overbeck*, 36–41. Henry also notes that Overbeck's view of religion, and the nature of religious belief as distinct from knowledge, is deeply characterized by his commitment to certain aspects of Romanticism. This is a theme of the entire study, but see especially 35–63.

108. Overbeck, *How Christian*, 32.

rational knowledge. I say 'like every religion', because the antagonism between faith [*Glaube*] and knowledge [*Wissen*] is permanent and absolutely irreconcilable."[109]

Clearly, Overbeck agreed with Strauss that Christian belief could not be mediated to knowledge and, therefore, it had persisted in the modern world only as a relic. But his reasons for this claim were very different than Strauss's.[110] He certainly believed with Strauss that Christianity was incompatible with modernity, but he was more interested in showing that modern, liberal Christianity was a violation of the radical, ascetic, and apocalyptic rejection of culture and scientific knowledge of the primitive Christian communities. What fascinated Overbeck was that the apocalyptic form of earliest Christianity realized perfectly the natural antagonism between knowledge and belief.[111] This focus on the apocalyptic dimension of primitive Christianity led Overbeck to elaborate the idea that the very notion of a "Christian theology" was the perversion of belief. As he wrote, primitive Christianity "no more expected to have a theology than it expected to have any kind of history on this earth. Indeed, Christianity entered this world announcing its imminent end."[112] The very idea of a modern, rational theology represented the transformation of Christian belief into knowledge, which is its betrayal.[113]

This was the central assertion of Overbeck's controversial and best known work, *How Christian Is Our Present-Day Theology?* (1873). In it, he levied several critiques of Ritschl, apologetic theology, and David Strauss.[114] Within those critiques, Overbeck's primary goal was to show that the same modern theology that works to keep Christianity intelligible and alive sets it in opposition to its own constitutive apocalyptic essence and horizon and thereby transforms it into its opposite: an expression of culture. What it purchases in the way of theoretical coherence comes, ironically, at the cost of the viability of its status as a belief, rendering it an extension of the objectifying knowledge of its sociocultural conditions.[115] Much like his friend Nietzsche, he sought a transvaluation of all Christian values.[116] The

109. Ibid., 30.
110. Ibid., 28–46.
111. See ibid., 39.
112. Ibid., 34.
113. Ibid., 34–46.
114. Ibid., 74–104.
115. Ibid., 39–46.
116. Ibid., 21–27 and Henry's "Introduction" xvi–xli. Compare also Micheal

point was not to highlight the conflict between belief and knowledge, but to bring to light that the very beginnings of Christian theology created the oxymoron of a Christian culture. Like a parody of Harnack, the perverse kernel of the truth of Christianity was that the whole thing was husk. • ZIZEK

In Barth's wake, the temptation is to read Overbeck as a supreme ironist, one for whom valid Christian belief means the perpetual exposure of theology as unbelief.[117] Overbeck is then associated with Kierkegaard's indirect communication, demolishing the idealist abstractions that are surrogates and foils for the truly concrete demands of the religious life. // This is a gross simplification and dangerous misunderstanding of Overbeck's point, which was quite literally the opposite. Overbeck was much more of an ironist than even Barth detected. He maintained that the perversion of the essence of Christianity was so great in its correlation with culture that the only valid recuperation of its apocalyptic opposition to culture and knowledge could be as an explicit act of knowledge, the direct avowal of disbelief. Within a Christian culture, such an act represents the truest and deepest expression of the apocalyptic heart of Christianity. It identifies an overtly unbelieving knowledge as the distinctively religious *form* that this understanding of belief must take under the sociocultural conditions of modernity. So thoroughly is this the case that even the attempt to revive ancient Christian apocalyptic as opposition to knowledge can only remain a form of knowledge, a parody of what it seeks to revive.   yes

This is, ultimately and unfortunately, what the dialectical theologians did.   • THESIS

THEOLOGY DONE APOCALYPTICALLY

It was Overbeck who saw most clearly and prior to anyone that apocalyptic set belief in opposition to knowledge, which forced, as Schweitzer would later see it, an unacceptable choice between a doctrinaire skepticism and eschatology. The first theological responses to this dilemma adapted Overbeck's ideas about the form of Christian belief into different accounts of the eschatological rupture of all cultural and scientific

Henry's discussion of Nietzsche and Overbeck in *Franz Overbeck*, 65–111, with the discussion of Adorno and Nietzsche in Rose, *Melancholy Science*, 17–26.

117. But this would be to adopt the position of Ritschl to which Overbeck is opposed, claiming that the Christian community is the objectification of its apocalyptic values rather than that its apocalyptic form is authorized by its sociocultural context. Christian belief is, according to Overbeck, deeply paradoxical in that the sociocultural context gave rise to a form of religious belief that set it against those social relations.

Style

analyses. Apocalyptic became a style of doing theology that transformed Strauss's negative dialectic into the primary method for reintroducing an

• eschatological reserve.

This method developed the transvaluation of Christian values that they found in Kierkegaard, Nietzsche, and Overbeck into a critique of the regnant liberal theology. With a Romantic taste for subversive irony, they wanted to fracture the hubris of bourgeois culture and academic theology so as to better communicate the scandal of the gospel. Barth's early way of expressing this was in the dialectical articulation of God's "No" to all human knowledge and culture, which was in fact a deeper and more profound "Yes" to humanity and the whole of the created order. The concern was to continually expose the church and theology to the dialectical negation of theology's irreducible eschatological remainder. The result was the paradoxical claim that the only valid form of Christian belief was the perpetual rupturing of the discourses of validity. In its apocalyptic mode,

theology done apocalyptically

theology was an infinite, practical, and disruptive task. Three distinct but overlapping examples will illustrate this formalistic appropriation of apocalyptic in theology.

Neo-Kantians

Several important studies have shown the significance of Marburg neo-Kantianism on Barth's theology and the work of Lotze's student Hermann Cohen.[118] Bruce McCormack has made the significant argument that neo-Kantian elements remain in Barth's thinking even into the *Church Dogmatics*. He appeals to Lohmann's identification of anti-subjectivism, the *Ursprung*, and opposition to "the given" as the three neo-Kantian elements of Barth's early theology. Of these, anti-subjectivism and opposition to "the given" are retained, while the *Ursprung* is transformed into the doctrine of election in *CD* II/2. The significance of this claim for our present argument is considerable, and works at cross-purpose to the use to which McCormack puts it.[119]

The three points the early Barth drew from Cohen are interwoven. Cohen resisted subjectivism by demonstrating the immediate and underived identity of thought and being in an unknowable origin (*Ursprung*) that precedes any differentiation of the two in discursive thought. Because this identity precedes cognition, the unity of thought and being is not the result of a synthetic operation of the mind to unify empirical experience.

118. On this point, see the close study of the relationship in Fischer, *Revelatory Positivism?* It has also been closely noted by McCormack, *Karl Barth's Critically Realistic*, 31–67 and 216–40.

119. McCormack, "Review of *Karl Barth und der Neukantianismus*," 305–7.

This original unity of thought and being gives the mind immediate access to the ontological principles that make experience possible, which like Lotze's validity are the abstract and logical basis for critical judgments of experience. As a result, when the early Barth used the term *Ursprung* to describe God as "wholly other" in *Romans*, it was in just this originary, abstract, and normative sense. As Hans Frei often pointed out, at this point Barth spoke of God as absolutely unintuitable (*unanschaulich*) because of how immediately intuitable (*anschaulich*) humanity was to itself.[120] This observation lifts out the deeply Fichtean resonances of what Barth learned from Cohen, and underscores the extent to which Barth was insistent that God could be in any sense "given" in empirical experience. God is not even, properly speaking, subjectively apprehended, but is instead the normative principle and criterion for all valid Christian belief. Christian belief is what lies in the wake of the revelation of the true God, the absolute rupture of every attempt to ground knowledge of God in a natural correspondence between God and the world (natural theology).

Paradoxically, though belief is diametrically opposed to knowledge, it remains essentially a form of it. Belief simply is the embrace of the contradiction between knowledge and belief. Barth writes:

> Indeed, only when that which is believed on is hidden, can it provide an opportunity for faith. And moreover, those things are most deeply hidden which most clearly contradict the obvious experience of the senses, . . . The Gospel of salvation can only be believed in; it is a matter for faith only. It demands choice. This is its seriousness. To him that is not sufficiently mature to accept a contradiction and to rest in it, it becomes a scandal—to him that is unable to escape the necessity of contradiction, it becomes a matter for faith. . . . He who *knows* the world to be bound by a truth that contradicts it; he who *knows* himself to be bound by a will that contradicts him; he who, *knowing* too well that he must be satisfied to live with this contradiction and not attempt to escape from it, finds it hard to kick against the pricks (Overbeck); he who finally makes open confession of the contradiction and determines to base his life on it—he it is that believes.[121]

This passage displays the extent to which Barth embraced Schweitzer's dilemma, even noting a dependence on Overbeck in this use of contradiction. True belief is the knowledge of the contradiction and its acceptance.

---

120. See Frei, "Realistic Narrative."
121. Barth, *Romans*, 39. Also, note Barth's comment on Overbeck at p. 3.

Just as with Strauss, the resolution of the conflict between knowledge and faith is the result of the embrace of their mutual, negative determination. This perhaps explains Barth's glib declaration that "[p]roper theology begins just at the point where the difficulties disclosed by Strauss and Feuerbach are seen and laughed at."[122]

Yet, as Barth later wisely realized, if belief is only validated through the application of an abstract logic of negative dialectics, then Strauss and Overbeck were right in their conclusion that theology is impossible.[123] If belief simply is the embrace of the contradiction of knowledge, then any attempt to develop a positive theological content would violate this injunction.[124] By the time Barth wrote *CD* II/2, it is clear that he had resolved this conundrum, not by abandoning his method of abstract logic, but by invoking the purportedly concrete norm of "Jesus Christ" as the logical criterion for that same validity. Because belief in *CD* IV/2 is the subjective, practical appropriation of the benefits of the objective, universally valid truth of reconciliation with God, it is clear that Barth never abandoned this fundamental dualism. Even his appeal to Jesus of Nazareth remains a variation on Baur's and Strauss's abstract christological idea. What Barth retained, as Bruce McCormack has argued, is a form of Marburg neo-Kantianism that transforms a philosophy of reflective, negative determination into a Trinitarian theology of God and divine election.[125] The christological idea of reconciliation thus remains abstract, just as for Baur. This aspect of Barth's legacy continues in various guises in the forms of contemporary theology that retain a sharp distinction between knowledge and belief.[126]

122. Barth, *Protestant Theology*, 554.

123. Bruce McCormack has argued extensively against such a realization. However, it is important to note that if McCormack is right, then Barth's later theology remains ensnared by these abstract principles.

124. Barth does speak of Jesus as the content of the knowledge of the Unknown God in *Romans*. However, this knowledge remains abstract.

125. See McCormack, *Karl Barth's Critically Realistic*, 216–40; and Lohmann, *Karl Barth und der Neukantinimus*, 392–402.

126. This is perhaps most particularly true, in general, of those approaches to theology advocated by so-called postliberalism. It certainly is not a necessity for those positions. It is perhaps especially the case for those claims that Barth's use of philosophy is merely strategic and carried out for his own ends, but that this does not commit him to a more general philosophical method. That is certainly true, as far as it goes, but it doesn't say much at all. What it does not make clear is that Barth can only make such claims because his entire system—which I want to insist is different from his best isolated insights on Christology, the Word of God, and the reading of Scripture—is an abstract formalism, a logic of validity that stands apart from and judges

It is in the terms of this abstract method that Barth sought in both his early and later work to appropriate the apocalyptic form of early Christian belief into contemporary theology as a formal, dialectical eschatology. •

The same must also be said of Rudolf Bultmann, whose work, as different as it was from Barth's, was forged in the same mould of *krisis*. Bultmann's work was also deeply indebted to the legacy of Marburg neo-Kantianism, though much more so to its hermeneutic interpretation than was Barth.[127] As a result, he retained the focus on the general criterion of validity of Christian belief, but developed the very different project of demythologization. Demythologization of the original Christian message, for Bultmann, was an extension of his commitment, in common with Barth, to the radical resistance to any objective bases for Christian belief, any cultural expression of Christian values. In this way, Bultmann remained opposed to Ritschlian liberalism. Yet, he was trained in and retained a basic loyalty to the history of religions school, which determined the validity of Christian belief as a value according to the social and historical preconditions in which that belief is lived. The Word of the *kerygma*, according to Bultmann, is the scandalous contradiction of every empirical experience, a contradiction that constitutes the crisis, the demand for decision evoked by God's revelation. That Word is the proclamation of Jesus' cross and resurrection as God's saving deed. Bultmann knew that the earliest form of the proclamation of the cross was apocalyptic, and within this social and historical setting the mythical representations of apocalyptic made this scandalous reversal of objectivity apprehensible and existentially meaningful. Yet in the social and historical context of modernity, the same mythical representations occlude that message and thus must be demythologized in order that the revelatory contradiction may be encountered. Such a translation is simply preaching the Word of the cross. It was in this way that Bultmann sought to elaborate the contemporary theological appropriation of apocalyptic.

A paradox similar to Barth's attends Bultmann's conception of the validity of belief. For Bultmann, belief is directly correlated with obedience.[128] It is the taking up of one's own cross as a disciple of Jesus in re-

---

these philosophical uses as objectifications in exactly the same way it judges empirical experience. The consequence of this is virtually the direct opposite of what most Barthians want to claim for it. It renders it an almost completely pure system of thought. •

127. David Congdon underscores this point in his essay on Bultmann in this volume.

128. Bultmann, *Theology of the New Testament*, 1:317–19. I am here pointing to Bultmann's discussion of the relationship between obedience, knowledge, and the

sponse to the proclamation that the cross of Christ was the event of God's saving action. Belief is decidedly not knowledge (*Wissen*) of historical events. As he notes, belief is "no teaching about external matters which could simply be regarded as true without any transformation of the hearer's own existence," but it is a turning away from oneself and the acceptance of the Word of the *kerygma* that "all that he is and has, he is and has through that which God has done."[129] Historical reportage is not proclamation of the *kerygma*. When the Word of the cross is preached, it will always evoke a *krisis*, the awareness of a contrast that demands a decision to determine one's existence in relation to that Word. Reception of that Word and the eschatological transformation of the believer into the new being are coterminous with belief. In all of these ways, belief is an entirely subjective rather than objective matter. Nonetheless, Bultmann insisted that in this obedience the believer *knows* herself differently, as having the new existence made possible alone by God's act in Christ. This is the eschatological existence, argued Bultmann, in which the believer exists paradoxically outside of history within it, knowing the infinite and eternal truth of history in contrast to her existence in finite temporality. It is in this sense that Bultmann remained within the logic of abstract validity. As with Barth, the validity of the gospel, in its preaching and its response, is determined not according to knowledge of objective history but according to its evocation of the apocalyptic antinomy, the *krisis*, of knowledge and belief that demands decision.[130] It is this rupture of knowledge that is God's revelation, the proper determination of knowledge of God.

Because this proper apocalyptic form of the gospel frames belief as the contradiction of knowledge, it remained as abstract for Bultmann as for Barth. The gospel's apocalyptic contradiction meant the shocking confrontation with the inadequacy of abstract objectivity, requiring concrete subjective obedience. Yet, this emphasis on acts of obedience remained locked in the formal logic of validity, which imposes the authentic rule of the gospel's apocalyptic disruption of knowledge on the domain of objective experience. As with Barth, belief remains the negative contrast

---

content of belief. The topic of belief as obedience is discussed specifically on pp. 314–17.

129. Ibid., 319.

♦ 130. I am using the term "apocalyptic" in reference to Bultmann to describe his use of the *krisis* as the demand for a choice and the determination of one's life. Bultmann did not believe there was any use for apocalyptic in theology apart from its demythologization into eschatology. This is another aspect of the priority he gives to validity.

of knowledge, the rupture of its self-identity, which ironically gives it its proper determination as knowledge of God.

It is on this point that Käsemann's use of apocalyptic is most sig- Käsemann nificant. Käsemann acknowledged his great debt to the theology of *krisis*, noting that his study of those theologians was responsible in his eyes for helping him see the true meaning of the Reformation doctrine of justification and how easily the historicist and idealist tendencies of the *heilsgeschichlich* schools could be appropriated to the Nazi cause.[131] In fact, it was because of his deep and abiding commitment to what he had learned on these points that he developed his critique of Bultmann.

Käsemann insisted that as important as Bultmann's interpretation of Paul was in its major themes, it was significantly flawed in its orientation toward the individual. Käsemann noted in particular that this was evident in Bultmann's understanding of the body (*soma*), which Bultmann rightly understood in terms of "relation" but wrongly as "self-relation." For Bultmann, subjective self-relation is the key to evading the beguiling influences of objectifications of the gospel, which occlude the demand for decision and obedience. It was on this basis that Bultmann had insisted not only that the quest for the historical Jesus behind the *kerygma* was doomed, but that any other focus than the *kerygma* was a false objectification.[132] But Käsemann insisted that it was just this focus on the individual that was the source of Bultmann's errors. Focused as he was on the self-relation of the individual believer, Käsemann argued that Bultmann could not make the fundamental distinction of Christology from ecclesiology and anthropology, and could not distinguish ecclesiology from anthropology either. As Key

131. Käsemann, "Rechtfertigung und Heilsgeschichte," 114–15. The English translation is "Justification and Salvation." On *Heilgeschichte*, see Cullman, *Christ and Time* and *Salvation in History*. See also Munck, *Salvation of Mankind*. As Martyn notes in his foreword to this present collection, Käsemann's thought was shaped by his time as a churchman, working ten years in the parish with coal miners, and under suspicion by the Nazis. What drives Käsemann is a concern with what is truly real, *who* is the *kurios* of this world. That same Marxian influence is at work in his polemic against *heilsgeschichlich* theology. Sharing with *Heilgeschichte* a concern to combat Bultmann's individualism and subjectivism, Käsemann was entirely opposed to the notion, propounded by Krister Stendahl, that Paul's primary concerns are expressed in Roman 9–11 and are situated in a context of overarching salvation history. For Käsemann, this perspective is at odds with Paul's insistence on the justification of the ungodly, which key shatters any notion that one's righteousness is determined by historical continuity and right behavior. The cross, for Käsemann's reading of Paul, is the critical norm, standing over every historical, human action.

132. Bultmann's emphasis on the *kerygma* as an interpretation of history is where the influence of hermeneutical neo-Kantianism is most apparent.

a result, Käsemann recognized that the abstractness of Bultmann's conception of the eschatological transformation of the believer's consciousness was indistinguishable from the religious ideology of "enthusiasm."[133] This was a stunning critique coming from Käsemann, since it carried the implication that Bultmann was perpetuating the historicist and idealist tendencies that he intended to overcome. In that way Bultmann failed to maintain the proper Reformation teaching on justification.

What Bultmann lacked, Käsemann argued, was an appropriate sense of corporeality as a relation to what lies outside of the self. Bultmann needed to understand the self not in terms of consciousness but as "that piece of world we ourselves are and for which we bear responsibility," a signification of the essential "worldliness" of humanity, which is tied ineluctably to "the ability to communicate."[134] Bultmann could only interpret this relation to what lies outside the self as an objectification that jettisons the scandal of the cross, evades the *krisis*, and reduces both to knowledge. It was for this reason that Bultmann refused any place for historical Jesus research in theology. Yet, Käsemann argued that it was this very external reference to the historical Jesus that primitive Christianity appealed to as the basis for the assertion of the absolute priority of Christ in salvation, leading the believer beyond "self-centeredness."[135] Ironically, noted Käsemann, it could only be by retrieving the historical Jesus as the critical norm of all valid Christian belief, the only proper external relation, that what Bultmann feared in "objectification" could properly be allayed.

Importantly, that retrieval also preserves the worldliness of Käsemann's understanding of justification. Because the normative criterion for belief is not subjective obedience to the *skandalon* of the cross, but is Jesus of Nazareth as the exemplar (*Urbild*) of belief,[136] what is at stake in justification is identification of and devotion to the true sovereign (*kyrios*) of the cosmos. This is a question that asks whether the piece of the world that one is and over which one has responsibility is possessed by the rebellious principalities of the world or is free in its service to God's rightful dominion. Bodies communicate, disclose the world of the reality they serve: demonic revolt or God's righteousness. In this way, as with Bultmann, being a disciple of Jesus of Nazareth is coterminous with belief

133. On the his use of the term "enthusiasm," see Käsemann, "Primitive Christian Apocalyptic."

134. Ibid., 135–36.

135. Käsemann, "Blind Alleys," 63–64.

136. Käsemann, "Philippians 2:5–11," 74.

in him, but it is an embodied witness to the truth that the Nazarene who lived and died is the sovereign (*kyrios*) of the cosmos.[137] Because God's act of making righteous (justification) is always directed toward the radically ungodly, which disrupts any pretention to special status before God on the basis of one's people or good deeds, it is an objective transformation in the material circumstances of the world. The believer's historical existence is the site of this conflict with the powers that resist the sovereignty of the crucified Nazarene.

Käsemann's development of the significance of apocalyptic as concerned with cosmic sovereignty rather than individual consciousness made vital corrections to the abstract logic of validity developed by the dialectical theologians. He carried forward their concerns to undermine historicism and idealism, and showed the abstractness of Bultmann's own proposals. However, Käsemann's concern with objectivity, with the correspondence of the idea with the real, showed that he did not break completely with the logic of validity that informed this trajectory. Barth and Bultmann were preoccupied with imposing the *krisis* of belief and knowledge on theological discourse, a contrast that both Schweitzer and Overbeck had both recognized as the consequence of apocalyptic. By contrast, Käsemann explicitly refused every correspondence of belief with the consciousness of the believer and insisted on its irreducibly material significance in reference to God's cosmic sovereignty. This would appear to preclude the possibility of any abstract conception of belief, and yet a constitutive aspect of Käsemann's opposition to religious ideology and enthusiasm is his insistence that apocalyptic means the perpetual disruption of any objective correspondence between discipleship and redemption.[138] The believer is constantly thrown off of her self-centeredness, dispossessed, and driven beyond herself by the recognition that the whole cosmos is not yet subject to God's sovereignty in Christ, which makes the future the apocalyptic, dialectical horizon of discipleship. In this way, Käsemann remained within Bultmann's strictures against objectification, but transposed them into a temporal disruption of any pretense of correlation between the ideal and the real. Despite his very important movement beyond consciousness, this ensured that Käsemann's thought remained locked in the negative, dialectical, and abstract frame of Kant. It is no less preoccupied with itself than Bultmann just because it is captivated instead

137. See Käsemann, "Primitive Christian Apocalyptic," 135. See also Käsemann, "Corporeality in Paul," 44–45.

138. David Belcher's essay in this volume makes this point.

with its own "mode of intervention."[139] Käsemann remained, in this way, hoisted by his own petard.

From Barth, Bultmann, and Käsemann, the theological appropriation of apocalyptic is an odd inversion of the general principles of the Tübingen school. They accepted that theology is the correlation of science and belief, yet insisted with Strauss and Overbeck that this correlation is not their reconciliation but their breach (*krisis*). As the normative criterion for belief, this form of apocalyptic remains a form of validity. All three thinkers were haunted by the fact that their ferocious dedication to transform theology's crippling separation of belief from history nonetheless perpetuated that problem. In relying on a dialectical eschatology, each made his own discourse an exception to the dialectic. It did not cut the Gordian knot that had become modern theology, but only wove it tighter.

Those theologians who followed these developments and sought to make apocalyptic an explicit and guiding dimension of their theologies, like Moltmann and Metz, were essentially locked within this apocalyptic hardening of the Kantian dualism into an antinomy. They developed it even further in relation to social theory. Moltmann made extensive use of Ernst Bloch's notion of utopian hope, which was premised on a Marxist vision of the liberative dimension of hope as a form of belief. Similarly, Metz drew on the work of Walter Benjamin, for whom perpetual mourning rendered the memory of suffering into the revolutionary potentiality of the future. With the aid of social theory, both thinkers developed major critiques of bourgeois religion and visions of political liberation that are deeply indebted to Käsemann. But for that reason, they also repeated Käsemann's mistake of refocusing on the perpetual displacement of discipleship toward the future, which, while practically confounding any conceptual knowledge of the unity of the real and the ideal, nonetheless remains abstract by presuming that a method focused on the infinite, practical, and politically inflected task of perpetual invasion can be the sole guarantee of validity. This practical orientation of belief to the future is understood to break open the static, reflective self-obsession of the present into the outward-moving hope of the future (Moltmann) or the revolutionary memory of suffering (Metz).[140]

139. See Rose, *HcS*, 35.

140. And most of the secular philosophical interest in Paul and apocalyptic can be understood as repetitions of precisely these same Kantian separations, which suggests that the most recent convergences of philosophy and theology on questions of apocalyptic should be understood as the mutual recognition of a common Kantian lineage rather than as a significant recuperation of biblical themes in philosophical thought.

THE CONTRIBUTION OF J. LOUIS MARTYN

It is in the light of just this heritage of interpreting the theological (or conceptual) significance of apocalyptic in terms of <u>determinate negation</u> • <u>of knowledge</u> that J. Louis Martyn's work is so important. Martyn has reinterpreted the place of apocalyptic in the New Testament in ways that illuminate new and important dimensions of its importance for Paul that open new avenues <u>beyond</u> this <u>inevitable abstractness</u> of an apocalyptic • thought <u>cast in terms of the binary of belief and knowledge</u>. Though his work does not always evade the impasses discussed above, he does make important discoveries that can point the way forward.

Though it is true that Käsemann's influence is palpable, Martyn has developed the centrality of apocalyptic in Paul to an intensity that even Käsemann did not sustain. This is in part because Martyn's work lacks the polemical invective that Käsemann directly associates with apocalyptic.[141] • less polemcd. Not that polemic is absent from Martyn's work. He is certainly concerned to combat the errors of a *heilsgeschichlich* interpretation of Paul. However, where Käsemann tended to adopt Paul's own polemical stance as his own in the presentation of Paul's theology, Martyn focuses on the polemic within the texts, allowing it to serve its own (medicinal or intoxicating) purposes and carry its own connotations. As a result, Martyn's portrait of the apocalyptic Paul is a much more broadly drawn and complex figure.

• The implications for theology of Martyn's apocalyptic Paul reach well beyond Käsemann's contrast to "early catholicism" and "enthusiasm."

One of the central reasons for the uniqueness of Martyn's work with apocalyptic is <u>his reconnection of apocalyptic to New Testament theol</u>ogy, <u>which has done a tremendous amount of work to dis</u>tinguish the place <u>of apocalyptic within theology from its status as a litera</u>ry genre or trope. Käsemann began to do this with his emphasis on the cosmic dimension of justification, but in Martyn what emerges is a total theological vision of | Apocalyptic God, sin, humanity, history, redemption, and triumph that is apocalyptic | theological through and through. This can be seen from four interconnected themes | vision of his work.

The first is his reconfiguration of the meaning of Paul's theology of justification justification. Käsemann's influence is clear. However, where Käsemann placed the dialectical *krisis* at the heart of the Reformation doctrine of justification and understood the Reformation doctrine as truly Pauline,

---

141. This is not to say that there is no polemic in Martyn, only that the focus of that polemic is through the texts, where he identifies his enemies, rather than with Käsemann who, it appears, identifies the texts with his enemies.

Martyn uncovers some subtle but significant differences.[142] Agreeing with Käsemann against Bultmann, Martyn understands justification as an objective change in the world's affairs and not only a subjective change of self-relation, and sees this objective change as a thoroughgoing transformation of conditions of existence under creation's true *kurios*. Yet, he understands this objectivity to be obscured by the traditional translation of Paul's word *dikaioō* as "to justify," which reinforces the traditional Reformation emphasis on subjective change. Instead, he renders *dikaioo* as "rectify," which captures two important dimensions of the word that are often overlooked. On the one hand, it maintains and highlights the Reformation teaching that it is God alone who redeems and strongly emphasizes the priority of God's action in that doctrine. Redemption is specifically and solely God's act, an act of rectification. On the other hand, it stresses that the object of God's action is the afflicted cosmos. In the apocalyptic frame, Sin is a power that has invaded the cosmos and taken it captive, and God's act of rectification is an invasion of these hostile forces to liberate their prisoners and end their insurrection.[143] This is a subtle but important difference in emphasis from Käsemann, who in casting justification in terms of God's sovereignty focused attention in an almost Anselmian fashion on Godself as the object of redemption, the restoration of God's rightful property and honor. Martyn's language of rectification instead focuses on God's gracious act of intervention on behalf of the afflicted to revolutionize their circumstances.

Martyn also recognizes that Paul's doctrine of rectification is set in contrast with another existing Jewish-Christian tradition on God's rectification. The tradition that Paul opposes is promoted by Paul's opponents in Galatians, missionaries from the Jerusalem church whom Martyn dubs "the Teachers." Their tradition, Martyn recognizes, was developed within the Deuteronomistic tradition of the "two ways," the decision that God places before the people of Israel: the way of life and the way of death (Jos 24:15; Jer 21:8; Deut 27:12–13; Sir 2:12; 15:16; Matt 7:13–14; Jas

---

142. Douglas Campbell has since lifted out this difference all the more, relying heavily on Martyn throughout. See Campbell, *Deliverance of God*.

143. Bultmann, *Theology of the New Testament*. Bultmann notes that justification is a "forensic-eschatological" concept in Paul, pertaining to the yearning to have God pronounce one righteous on the Day of Judgment, 274–87. Martyn's apocalyptic interpretation is strictly opposed to this reading, associating it with the theology of the Teachers, and preferring instead a cosmological apocalyptic. In this regard, he follows Käsemann in juxtaposing apocalyptic to Bultmann's perspective.

2:8–13).[144] The focus of their teaching is on human rather than divine ~~human~~
agency. It teaches Gentile Christians that they will stand rectified before ~~agency~~
God when they move out of the cursed status of the Flesh (uncircumcision) into the blessed status under the Law (circumcision). But Paul ~~no choice~~
vehemently resists this idea, insisting that life according to the Flesh is
a bondage that is cosmic in scope and does not allow for this choice of
taking the path of blessing or cursing.[145] It is God alone who acts to rectify ~~direction alone~~
these conditions. As Martyn notes, ". . . Paul's rectification polemic against
the Teachers is nothing other than a <u>reflection of *God's* rectifying polemic</u>
against his enemies."[146] This interpretation shows Martyn's profound debt
to the apocalyptic tradition flowing from the dialectical theology and specifically to Käsemann's critique of Bultmann within that tradition. Martyn
shows here, in a different light, the importance of rectification not being
merely a renewed self-relation, but <u>a relation to what lies outside the self, a</u> ~~!! Key~~
<u>transformation of the very conditions of human agency</u>. Yet, in recogniz-
ing that Paul's apocalyptic rectification is developed in opposition to the
Deuteronomistic "two ways," Martyn also opens important possibilities
beyond the abstract construal of apocalyptic in terms of antinomy, decision, and *krisis*. This point will be developed in more detail below.

2 Second, Martyn's focus on <u>rectification as God's incursion of</u> the
<u>enslaved cosmos</u> is not simply about the cross as the revelation of God's
righteousness as a scandal to reason (Bultmann) or *sub contrario* (Käsemann). Instead, Martyn makes important use of Richard Hays's argument
for <u>the centrality of the subjective rather than objective reading of</u> the

---

144. Martyn's own polemic against advocates of the New Perspective on Paul, such
as E. P. Sanders and N. T. Wright, can be detected here. See Martyn, *Issues*, 300.

145. When I refer to "the flesh" in the following, it carries the specific meaning it
holds in Martyn's work in its association with the "the impulsive desire of the flesh."
See the work of Joel Marcus on which Martyn relies: Marcus, "Epistle of James" and
"Letters of Paul." Marcus shows that the Jewish tradition of the impulsive desire of
the flesh was the background for Paul's argument in Galatians and that it was most
likely a common tradition of Jewish moral theology that he shared with the Teachers.
Martyn's argument presumes a deep connection in the Teachers' theology of rectification between the foreskin and the impulsive desire of the flesh. As Martyn notes in
his hypothetical reconstruction of the Teachers' argument, they may have argued that
the reason there was divisions within the Galatians community was because of their
failure to excise "the flesh" that was the root of the division, discord, and domination.
Paul's counterargument is that Teachers fail to see reality and are living in the old
order, unwittingly perpetuating the idolatry and division that they believe they stand
against. The Epistle of James also draws heavily on the tradition, suggesting that it was
important to the Jerusalem community.

146. Martyn, *Issues*, 155.

genitive in Paul's phrase "*pistis tou Xristou.*" The result is certainly not the rectification of the individual, which Käsemann had already rejected, but the notion that God's agency in overcoming Sin and the Flesh, the very character of God's invasion, simply is the faith of Jesus Christ. That faith is God's confrontation with the powers and principalities of Sin and the Flesh that enslave the world. It looks like the ministry that leads to Jesus' cross, where those powers are finally broken. This is what Martyn calls, infelicitously, God's "weak power," a power that does not triumph according to the divisions and dominations that define the power of Sin and the Flesh, but as the fidelity and unity revealed by Jesus as God's own loving self-bestowal.[147]

3   Third, since this offering in Jesus' faith is the redemption of the enslaved cosmos, it is incorrect to conceive of it as a linear continuation of the historical past. It was the old order of the enslaved creation that was put to death in his cross and an entirely new reality constituted in his resurrection. His cross introduced a fissure into the continuity of reality that marked the beginning of an entirely new creation. Importantly, this means that Paul's objection to the Teacher's "two ways" theology also heralds the obsolescence of "religion" as the ritualized and cultic differentiations of sacred and profane that purportedly constitute happy relations with God. In the light of God's apocalyptic act in the faith of Jesus, the Teachers' adherence to the religious distinctions of the Law is ironically revealed to be the same idolatry they fear in uncircumcised Gentile Christians because it is based in the same constitutive domination and antagonistic separation that are the work of the very "flesh" they demand be excised. On this basis, Paul argues that the Teachers' theology of rectification, founded on a continuity of historical ethnic lineage and religious purity, perpetuates the old order of bondage to Sin and stands opposed to the new reality of unity and love in Christ. Because even the religion of Israel's Law is powerless over Sin, the only solution to the desires of the Flesh is to live by the Spirit in the new creation.

Finally, all of these points are drawn together in Martyn's unique insight into the apocalyptic implications of Paul's invocation of the Christian baptismal formula in Galatians 3:28, which Martyn takes as expressing the essence of Paul's apocalyptic theology. The redemption wrought by Jesus' cross must be understood as both cosmic in its implications[148] and an act

---

147. Cousar, *Theology of the Cross*, 164–70.

148. See Martyn, *Issues*, 136. He refers to Paul's declaration that in Christ's cross he has been crucified to the cosmos and the cosmos to him.

of God's apocalyptic judgment because the declaration that there is no longer "Jew nor Greek, slave nor free, male and female" is to pronounce the dissolution of the constitutive principles of created reality.[149] Though these elements are invoked in Galatians 3:28, it is specifically in 4:3 and 4:9 that Paul mentions the *stoicheia tou kosmou* and states that the human relation to those elements has changed since Christ's advent.[150] Specifically, what has changed is that humanity is no longer enslaved to these elements. But what Martyn goes on to show, pointing to Philo and other ancient authors, is that invocation of the phrase *stoicheia tou kosmou* explicitly meant that these elements were "the pairs of opposites [*t'antantia*] that constitute the oppositions foundation of the cosmos."[151] These opposites in the Pythagorean tradition and others divided the world "into equal parts, referring to the elements themselves as pairs of opposites." The arrangement was generally of four categories, rare vs. dense and light vs. heavy, within which were arranged the various oppositions of earth, air, fire, and water. [152] Martyn underscores the specifically apocalyptic implications of Paul's argument in Galatians:

> In writing Gal 6:14–15, Paul expects the Galatians to understand his testimony: the cross of Christ separated him from a cosmos that consisted of pairs of opposites . . . [t]hus, a Christian baptizand acquainted with a traditional list of oppositional pairs—in whatever form—would have recognized in the baptizer's words a list of the oppositional *elements* that have now found the terminus in Christ, and thus a declaration of the end of the cosmos that was constituted by those elements.[153]

These oppositions, which Martyn refers to elsewhere as "antinomies," no longer enslave humanity because they have been replaced by unity in Christ. As Martyn astutely recognizes in an observation that stands in some tension with his persistent characterization of Paul's theology as "polemical," Paul's argument with the Teachers does not pivot around a polarity of "law observance or non-law observance" but is the negation of the opposition between them, of "both law observance and non-law observance."[154] Because the fullness of the new creation has not yet been revealed, the only opposition Christians recognize in the time after Christ's advent is what

149. Martyn, *Issues*, 125–40
150. Ibid., 125–28.
151. Ibid., 138
152. Ibid., 137
153. Ibid., 138
154. Ibid., 115.

persists in the Flesh's resistance to the work of the Spirit. It is on just this point that Martyn's work on the total vision of Paul's apocalyptic theology is so significant for the future of theology.

Martyn shows us, beyond Weiss, Overbeck, and those that came after them, that the place of apocalyptic in the New Testament is much more significant than a preoccupation with the imminent end of history. For Martyn, apocalyptic is the engine of Paul's entire theological vision. It is not simply a first-century Jewish sociocultural condition for his "thought world" or the highest ascetic expression of religious opposition to culture and knowledge. It is integral to the meaning and content of his arguments. It is the heart of his theology of redemption. As Douglas Campbell's recent work has shown, wrestling with this aspect of Martyn's argument can lead to some striking reinterpretations of Paul's letters.[155]

Martyn's work is then vital for helping us assess the place of apocalyptic in the future of theology. His works carries two insights that can decisively contribute to overcoming the impasses that have been identified in this essay.[156] The first point has already been adumbrated. Martyn's reading of Paul entirely alters our understanding of the role apocalyptic plays in New Testament doctrine. In doing so, Martyn distinguishes between an apocalyptic sensibility, style, or formal method and a genuinely apocalyptic theology that addresses the full form and content of the Christian faith. The place of apocalyptic in the future of theology remains to be seen, but the shape it must now take is to uncover the light apocalyptic sheds on the whole of church doctrine. This is a task that will also require deeper and more sustained dialogue between theologians and biblical scholars, and perhaps even a greater blurring of the lines of specialization, than has been recently customary.

The second and most important point is that the heart of Martyn's reading of Paul's apocalyptic theology is its radical and uncompromising repudiation of dualism. This point alone marks an extraordinary

155. See n. 142 above.

156. It would be inaccurate to claim that Martyn's work evades all the problems identified in this essay with such an approach. For example, in numerous passages Martyn states that he believes Paul's emphasis on the "punctiliar" dimension of God's apocalyptic action and the radical discontinuity of the new creation from the old come into close proximity to dualism. He suggests that Paul might affirm aspects of Marcion, except his rejection of the God of Israel. Sometimes it is disturbingly difficult to determine whether Martyn is arguing that Paul believes the original creation is ontologically depraved or if this is simply an epistemic failure of sinful humanity. Because of the presence of these elements (and others), any theological application of Martyn's work must be critical and nimble.

transformation of the conventional understanding of apocalyptic as essentially dualistic—an implication of his work that appears to elude even Martyn himself. Though theologians will have to continue to work out the metaphysical and/or ontological implications of this claim, Martyn has advanced the formidable argument that Paul's doctrine of rectification eradicates from the cosmos any ontological principle of constitutive opposition. What is more, he has asserted that the advent of Christ is the advent of the new creation of unity in the Spirit under the rule of Jesus Christ as the true cosmic *kurios*. These are ontological, metaphysical claims about the truth of reality. They renounce determination of that truth according to the creative freedom of human agency, the ritualized and cultic differentiations of religion, or the conflicts and dominations of the world's ruling principalities. Instead, they name such oppositions as expressions of idolatry, the fruits of "the impulsive desires of the flesh," hostility to God, and enslavement to Sin. Reality, Paul's apocalyptic theology declares, is only now freedom under Christ's lordship.

Viewed in light of the genealogy developed in this introduction, this repudiation of dualism raises again the specters of Schleiermacher and Hegel, each of whom rejected the premise of Kant's dualism. Walt Lowe has already written on the significance of the Hegelian *aufhebung* in light of Martyn's work, and his contribution to the present volume continues to reflect on the importance of maintaining the unity of subject and object.[157] Other fruitful convergences with readings of Hegelian speculation that do not conform to the presuppositions of the Tübingen school remain to be developed. But the most interesting and unexpected convergences may be found with rereadings of Schleiermacher that highlight the importance of his presupposition of the unity of belief and knowledge, together with his rejection of their final, systematic reconciliation in thought. Though neither Schleiermacher nor Hegel can be assimilated to apocalyptic without considerable alteration, their texts may prove to be astonishingly fertile ground for theological reflection carried out in the light of Pauline apocalyptic and with greater sensitivity to the problems induced by Kantian dualism.

What is clear is that an apocalyptic rejection of dualism entirely transforms the relation of belief and knowledge as it has developed in modern theology. Since Kant, the great theological struggle has been how to reconcile what critical reason separated. It was the theology of *krisis* that audaciously sought to reestablish theology as an explicit affirmation of

157. See Lowe, "Is There a Postmodern Gospel?"

that separation. But as inspiring as this gesture was to many across nearly the whole of the twentieth century, it did not prove to be finally any different from the compulsions that drove Walter Benjamin, Theodor Adorno, Gershom Scholem, Jacob Taubes, Carl Schmitt, or Erik Petersen,[158] each of whom sought to disclose the political significance of apocalyptic thought from within the same post-Kantian frame. Presently, the same impulse drives Continental philosophy's interest in Paul and apocalyptic themes.[159] Yet, Martyn's work clearly shows this long heritage of separating belief from knowledge to be a mystifying variation of the Teachers' "two ways," ensnared by the very principle of opposition it set out to overcome.

On this point, it cannot be overlooked that it is critical thought (*Wissenschaft*) on Scripture and not its pious use that is responsible for the rediscovered importance of apocalyptic. Whether for sectarian or secularist reasons, the isolation of belief from knowledge compromises the integrity of both. In light of Martyn's work, perhaps we can claim that apocalyptic is not at all the mark of the separation of belief from knowledge, or of theory from practice, or of any other aspect of the line moving from Strauss to Käsemann, but is instead a cataclysm of the frame, the overturning of the totality of conditions that render dialectical negation possible. Perhaps apocalyptic makes possible a renewed recognition of *faith*—as opposed to belief—as the proper form of all knowledge throughout the whole of the distinct but mutually interpenetrating sensual, conceptual, and practical dimensions of life.

For this path to be taken, new avenues of thought will not only need to be explored but perhaps even created. These avenues must eschew the abstract logics of reconciliation (Tübingen school) and rupture (dialectical theology) that have conditioned the place of apocalyptic in theology for the last century. However, this does not mean that we must slough off the past. On the contrary, although Bultmann's and Käsemann's thought proved to be abstract, their insistence that faith is coterminous with discipleship is the right place to start, and especially Käsemann's emphasis on the body as the locus of communication and "the disclosure of a world." It is in this context that one's recognition that Christ is the *kurios* matters so significantly. Käsemann recognized but was unable to fully articulate that apocalyptic is explicitly concerned with the historical, material, and

---

158. See the essays collected in Taubes, *Religionstheorie und politische Theologie*, vol. 1.

159. See Badiou, *Saint Paul*, and Agamben, *Time*. Žižek is now explicitly adopting an apocalyptic rhetoric, and this language was not entirely absent from the phenomenological approach of Michel Henry.

political reality of God's kingdom. It is in our bodies that it is real, and it is as embodied that it is actual. The significance of Christ's reign is not at all abstract, but a worldly actuality. Knowledge of the truth that there is no longer Jew or Greek is not a call to *believe* that our experience of these distinctions is not real or to *impose* this ideal on the empirical experience of those distinctions (which can amount to the same).[160] It is a summons to move deeper into the social reality of these divisions, allowing our thought to be shaped by the concrete unions forged from that engagement and the divisions that persist, all the while knowing that this unity is the work of the Spirit, drawing the world into the freedom of the children of God. Žižek

[margin note: abstract logics]

Apocalyptic is, ultimately, about the worldly significance of God's self-communication (*Selbstmitteilung*). It names not only the worldly nature of that communication, but its character as well. That communication is much more than the simple announcement or transmission of information. It reaches much deeper than the mere disruption of human attempts at meaning. It is the offer and reception of Godself. The apocalyptic division disrupts because what is given in God's act is Godself, and yet that act is our redemption because the gift, in excess of all we dared ask or imagine, is all that we have yearned for all along. This is most decidedly not merely a transcendental condition of our experience, but the transformation of the conditions of all experience, the embodied reality of God's purposes, for matter in history.

[margin note: TH (circled)]

If apocalyptic is to be at all significant for modern theology, it will be because, in returning to it now—as we seek to do in this volume—we will be enabled to perceive in new ways the coincidence of our faith and our knowledge in God's act of self-communication, which can be no merely academic, theoretical affair. In times like these of increasing political turmoil, and standing in the midst of what appears to be a monumental crisis of capitalism, this is no insignificant claim to make.

[margin note: TH (circled)]

In the present volume, we have sought to bring together a number of diverse thinkers to address the place of apocalyptic in the future of theology. Each author's contribution, in its own way, intersects with the history and set of questions outlined in this introduction. Some of the essays approach apocalyptic with a deeply critical, even suspicious eye. Others

160. Martyn himself interprets Gal 3:28 not as an affirmation of concrete differences, but as an abstract "seeing as-if" those distinctions were not real. This is a decisive mistake, but one that is entirely consistent with the tradition I have traced in this essay. See Martyn, "Galatians 3:28," specifically p. 41.

wholeheartedly embrace it as the most important category for theology's future. All of them, however, recognize and struggle with the theological issues for which apocalyptic stands as either question, answer, or both.

The volume is broken into three parts. The first part, entitled "Apocalyptic and the Nature of Theology," looks at what role apocalyptic does or should play in theological reflection. Right at the outset, with Walt Lowe's essay, we are situated in the network of questions raised by this introductory essay. Lowe is concerned to reflect on the poverty of metaphysical theism, which has imposed a false subject-object division upon God. Lowe insists, in his characteristically whimsical prose, that apocalyptic is more deeply connected with the mystical traditions than might otherwise be thought, glimpsing a God who is more intimate to me than I am to myself at just the point that we might be most tempted to view God's self-disclosure as somehow "outside" of us.

Douglas Harink's essay focuses on the question of what it means for human beings to be made participants in God's apocalyptic work in Jesus Christ. He isolates three categories within which to consider such participation: scriptural interpretation and commentary, the character of time and history, and the nature of human agency. Harink argues that in each of these three areas Martyn's work makes a critical contribution for contemporary theology to heed. With Alexandra Brown's essay we have a wonderful example of a biblical scholar bringing the art of exegesis to bear on a reading of Paul that attempts to show what biblical scholars themselves have to learn from contemporary philosophical appropriations of Paul. She seeks to show the convergence between the Paul discovered from scientific biblical exegesis and the speculative Paul of philosophical reflection. Christopher Morse's contribution asks the question of "form," which is a philosophical question if ever there was one. But he asks this question in the light of the place of apocalyptic in the biblical tradition. Morse's essay also overlaps with many of the themes of this introduction, noting and wrestling with the question that Schweitzer put to theology in the wake of Weiss's discussion of the centrality of apocalyptic to Jesus' preaching. Finally, Robert Jenson offers a very critical voice to the place of apocalyptic in contemporary theology. Though deeply respectful of Martyn's contribution to biblical scholarship, and noting his admiration for many of those who count themselves Martyn's students, he believes that many of the recent attempts to incorporate apocalyptic into theology fail to ask or wrestle with some vital questions—questions that biblical scholars are methodologically content to simply leave unaddressed. These are questions such as how apocalyptic is to be placed in relationship to those other texts that affirm ideas perhaps antagonistic to apocalyptic commitments. Ultimately, he insists that some form of *Heilgeschichte* (the bane of Martyn's work) is necessary for the theologian who sees her responsibility as fidelity to the whole of the biblical witness, even though this is not the obligation of the biblical scholar.

The second part of this collection focuses on the relationship of apocalyptic to Christian doctrine. Susan Eastman argues that Pauline apocalyptic discloses an incarnational and participatory logic in which God's movement to humanity is carried out through Christ's union with the sinful in his flesh, and to such an extent that his flesh is the site of Sin's overcoming, placing those who now share in his flesh at the forefront of God's triumph over Sin in the cosmos. Beverly Gaventa takes up similar themes, arguing that cosmology and soteriology are inextricably bound up with one another in Paul's thought. The cosmos is, on Gaventa's reading, the site where the battle for salvation is waged, with Sin and Death defeated but not yet vanquished. Apocalyptic is the form for the articulation of that vision. Continuing with the theme of the cosmic scope of redemption envisioned in apocalyptic, Philip Ziegler focuses on Käsemann's apocalyptic soteriology and advocates for the power of the *Christus victor* model of atonement, which he says properly accounts for human bondage to and responsibility for Sin while understanding redemption as liberation. Drawing on Käsemann's claim that the "nerve center" of redemption is Paul's claim that "Christ must reign," Ziegler contends that the apocalyptic viewpoint is concerned with Christ's lordship. Christopher Holmes's reflections focus on the apocalyptic concern with the truth about reality. Holmes situates this concern with reality on the nature of rectification as the result of Christ's action to "realize in us what he is." Jodi Belcher raises some very important and even difficult questions about apocalyptic themes, primarily its predominant imagery of war, invasion, and discontinuity, which, she notes, "clashes with feminist attention to identity formation through complex racial, ethnic, sexual, class, national, colonialist, and able-bodied dynamics." She argues that Martyn's invocation of an apocalyptic "bifocal vision" too closely reiterates the problems of a standpoint epistemology, which neglects the importance of human embodiment, a theme in Paul's account of redemption in 1 Corinthians 11:17–34 and 12:12–27. David Belcher's essay has similar concerns about embodiment, which he has focused on the place of sacramental theology. He argues that the apocalyptic trajectory of theology has been too closely aligned with the Bultmannian emphasis on the centrality of the cross to the diminution of the resurrection, and that this results in a vitiated account of the concrete, material life of the church. He contends that only a full perception of the unity of cross and resurrection can give the kind of material transformation that is needed in contemporary theology.

The final part addresses the vision of the church's practices, mission, and political witness through the lens of apocalyptic. Fleming Rutledge's contribution to the volume is concerned with the practice of preaching in response to Martyn's vision of apocalyptic. Her reflections most appropriately correspond to the emphasis in Martyn's work on the performative, rhetorical dimension of Paul's letters, which would have been originally read aloud to a group of people and made ready use of the ancient conventions of rhetoric to persuade and exhort. Nathan Kerr's essay further elaborates on the project of apocalyptic theology that he began in his important earlier attempts to recuperate apocalyptic in contemporary theology. Subtitling his project "A Response to Christianity's Cultured Defenders," Kerr summons Schleiermacher to mind in offering a critique of those theologians—Robert Jenson specifically—who would view Christian faith as the preservation and perpetuation of a culture rather than as insurrectionary service to "the least of these," the *eschatoi*, as he calls them in connection with this reading of Mark. Joseph Mangina's essay focuses on the important place of baptism in the church's life as the site of the transition from the old world of Sin to the new world of Christ's lordship. Stanley Hauerwas shows how apocalyptic gives a vision of the church as the political people who live beyond the demand for sacrifice, and particularly the sacrifice of war.

What joins the diversity of voices in this volume, many in implicit accord and others in explicit dissonance, is a recognition of the importance of apocalyptic to the New Testament vision of redemption and an insistence that contemporary theology must be more attentive to that vision in its work. Though the consequences of such engagement are judged to be much more far-reaching by some contributors than for others, all agree that theology cannot remain aloof to apocalyptic or remain unaffected by it. It has been our hope to give the reader a greater sense of the theological conversations about apocalyptic, a taste of some of the more significant voices in that conversation, and to inspire others to wrestle more intently with the questions these reflections raise. Such is the work of theology.

PART ONE

Apocalyptic and
the Nature of Theology

1

A God Nearer to Us
Than We Are to Ourselves

Walter J. Lowe

EXHORTATORY PREFACE

• THE POVERTY OF THEISM *is reflected in its imposition of a subject-object framework upon theology. On this straitened view, revelation consists of (i) God providing information or inspiration that (ii) awakens latent (God-given) potentialities, e.g. decision, that (iii) complete the relationship. The apocalyptic news J. Louis Martyn discerns in Paul commands our attention because it is at once far richer than this tradition and more orthodox.* •

The crucial insight is that revelation in Jesus Christ is not a machination God performs at some remove, withholding God's full Godhood as it were. Rather God's invasion is the inbreaking of God's very Being. This Event EVENT *changes everything—it changes our world, our very cosmos. Yet at the same* | *time we are remarkably constrained as to what we know about* how God *has* recreating *wrought this new creation. The world may seem unaffected.*

Thus we know little of the "how" (i.e., the economy, the inner workings) little of the *of the God-world relationship,* pace *atonement theory. Rather, the gospel's* "how" *attention is firmly fixed upon the "That" of God's triumphal invasion, the good news that it has happened. Christianity is the glad announcement of this "That," which (to strain language) is "the That" because it is the break-* • incursion *ing into history of God's very Being—the act of Actuality itself. Actuality*

trumps possibility (Bonhoeffer); it trumps human potentiality. To reveal =
‖ *"to apocalypse": it requires no human completing.*

Hence our present state of glad unknowing, which is glad because it has been freed from enslavement to religion, to self-obsession, to some putative "point of contact" (Anknüpfungspunkt) between God and the human self. Contra the ideology of our times, Christ is not "in us." Rather we—all of humankind (go figure)—are now "living into" (and resisting) the new "how" of God's relation to the world. We are learning willy-nilly that the Being of all beings is now their being-in-Christ.

"A God nearer to us than we are to ourselves." This haunting phrase has been with me for many years; so many, in fact, that I am no longer certain where I first came upon it. My best guess is the work of Karl Rahner. Certainly it is consonant with Rahner's formative conviction that when Christ does come, he comes not as a stranger. No doubt as many attest, the Christ of doctrine may seem alien to the familiar Jesus of Scripture; and no doubt, as the Gospels themselves attest, when Christ came we knew him not. But our not knowing Christ does not alter the fact that Christ comes as one who *knows us* from within. The somewhat disorienting notion of "a God nearer to us than we are to ourselves" helps us imagine how this might be so. A God who could get *that* close to us might be experienced as "invasive," in Martyn's apt term; and yet there would be a fit with the "givens" of the human condition. It is this interaction of invasion and fit—a relation deeper than our self-awareness, deeper than human "immanence" itself—that the present essay wishes to explore.

William Placher has traced the "domestication of transcendence" in late medieval and modern Western history.[1] In the language of this essay, that eclipse occurred at the hands of a "scholasticism," Protestant as well as Catholic, that sought by means of an obtuse monism-*cum*-dualism to "comprehend" (etymologically, to "grasp together") God's revelation. If it is true that "to reveal" is "to apocalypse,"[2] and if apocalyptic betokens God's freedom, then the scholastic project is exposed as an effort to map, to grasp-together, the ungraspable. Otherwise stated, theistic scholasticism is possessed by a false apologetic. It wants to argue that in order to explain or understand the world, you need to include God. It wants to show that other worldviews fail because they lack, they do not include, the crucial theistic ingredient. It is an argument for including (i.e., enclosing)

1. Placher, *Domestication of Transcendence.*
2. See Martyn, *Galatians,* 98–99.

God. But what would this mean, to "include" God? It would mean placing God *within* some larger explanatory context. It would mean *contextualizing* God.

In contrast, the present essay, and perhaps the present volume, contends that, Christianly understood, the crucial task is rather to understand oneself as *being contextualized by* God.

MARTIN BUBER: "THE WORLD IS TWOFOLD"

While the language of "being contextualized" may be novel, the notion it represents is not. In describing the I-Thou relationship, Martin Buber raised to awareness what we already know about being contextualized.

Let us return to the common predilection for placing experience within a subject-object framework. In Buber's judgment this predilection has the effect of extending the realm of the I-It. If the world is but an assemblage of subjects and objects, the richness of human existence is lost. One is reduced to speaking in terms of subjective feelings and objective facts. Resisting such a prospect, Buber's calm, descriptive account of the elusive I-Thou offers something extraordinary, a vision of transcendence firmly rooted in everyday life.

Already with his opening words, Buber places us beyond the exclusive rule of the subject-object framework. Within that framework, subject and object are generally taken to be fundamental entities, each existing in its own right. They may enter into a relationship, the one entity affecting the other in some manner, but the relationship is commonly regarded as a secondary matter. Buber turns this assumption on its head. Recalling Genesis and the Gospel of John, he writes: "In the beginning is the relation."[3] Accordingly, *I and Thou* does not begin with two distinct terms—not even "I" and "Thou" (or "I" and "You")—which he might then seek, through piety and ingenuity, to relate. Rather he begins with the word pairs I-You and I-It, and even before that he begins with the opening sentence, "The world is twofold for [us] in accordance with [our] twofold attitude."[4] The world is twofold for us, and irreducibly, inescapably so. Buber's insight establishes a firm point of reference for our subsequent reflections.

"But surely," one may respond, "the I-It and the I-Thou have at least one thing in common. They are forms of experience. They are both to be understood within the great, inclusive context of human experience."

3. Buber, *I and Thou*, 69.
4. Ibid., 53.

After all, isn't that where subject and object come into contact—in experience? Isn't all of science built on experimentation, which is experience made rigorous? And in the meaningful events that most illumine our lives, do we not speak of "peak experiences"? And for theology throughout the modern period, conservative as well as liberal, is there any court of appeal more determinative than one or another form of "depth experience"?

This suggestion seems innocent enough, but Buber, with uncharacteristic vehemence, rejects it out of hand. One reason is Buber's belief that an all-encompassing appeal leads to monism. A further is his belief that the term "experience" propels the discussion in one direction, namely that of the I-It. What experiences afford us "is only a world that consists of It and It and It, of He and He and She and She and It."[5] One senses from Buber's tone that this is not a minor issue. He continues:

> All this is not changed by adding "inner" experiences to the "external" ones, in line with the non-eternal distinction that is born of mankind's craving to take the edge off the mystery of death. Inner things among external things, things among things! . . .
> And all this is not changed by adding "mysterious" experiences to "manifest" ones, self-confident in the wisdom that recognizes a secret compartment in things reserved for the initiated, and holds the key. O mysteriousness without mystery, O piling up of information! It, it, it![6]

participation

What is at stake here is that "[t]hose who experience do not participate in the world. *For the experience is 'in them' and not between them and the world.*"[7] Buber's concern is that in the very act of invoking mysterious experiences, or religious experiences, even transcendent experiences, one may still be regarding experience as somehow *within oneself*. And why does this matter? Because if the experience is somehow within oneself, then one is not in relationship. If experience is within oneself, one cannot be contextualized by it.

Such experience is a form of possession. In contrast, "Whoever says You does not have something; he has nothing. But he stands in relation."[8]

Having no thing, he has nothing to stand on. And yet the miracle of real relationship is such that he stands nevertheless: "he stands *in* relation." Now it is important not to romanticize, and throughout our discussion we

5. Ibid., 55.
6. Ibid., 56.
7. Ibid. (emphasis added).
8. Ibid., 55.

will strive not to do so. Having nothing to stand on is inherently unsettling, a source of anxiety. There is no thing to grab hold of. And yet one may stand *in* relation. One may find oneself "suspended" within a larger, richer reality, a reality larger than the self, because "You has no borders."[9]

ALBERT SCHWEITZER: THE TWOFOLD BECOMES ANTINOMY

To gain entry to Albert Schweitzer's thought, one might well begin with a childhood memory of overhearing a group of adults as they looked back upon their lives. They recalled

> the idealism and capacity for enthusiasm of their youth as something precious to which they ought to have held fast, and yet at the same time they regarded it as almost a law of nature that no one should be able to do so. This woke in me a dread of having ever, even once, to look back on my own past with such a feeling; I resolved never to let myself become subject to this tragic domination of mere reason, and what I thus vowed in almost boyish defiance I have tried to carry out.[10]

As Schweitzer was later to observe, "The world affirms itself automatically."[11] Mere reason alone is unable to resist the ironically "tragic domination" of such affirmation. What was needed was a countervailing stance of world-negation. Not negation for its own sake, but negation to open up the necessary space for one to find and follow a vocation. Tacitly, Schweitzer acted on Buber's principle: life must be twofold, else it is unlivable. This, I am on the way to proposing, is one of the primary givens of human existence. And it has got to be highly significant for our project of linking the givens to apocalyptic that it should be Schweitzer of all people, a person so at grips with the existential conditions, who saw what others could not see—the apocalyptic Jesus.

To return to the passage just quoted:

> The world affirms itself automatically; the modern spirit cannot but affirm it. But why on that account . . . spare the spirit of the individual [person] its appointed task of fighting its way through the world-negation of Jesus, of contending with him at every step over the value of material and intellectual goods—

9. Ibid.

10. Schweitzer, *Memoirs*, 97–98.

11. Schweitzer, *Quest*, 400.

a conflict in which it may never rest? . . . It is only by means of the tension thus set up that religious energy can be communicated to our time.[12]

"It is only by means of the tension . . ." This is what the boy intuitively grasped. Christianity is not a scholastic monism, but neither is it a form of dualism, apocalyptic or otherwise. Rather, Christianity "carries within itself unresolved, the antinomy between monism and dualism, between logical and ethical religion."[13]

The key here is the word "antinomy." The point is somewhat subtle, but if we pause for a brief clarification, the theological payoff will be substantial. At the University of Strasbourg, Schweitzer studied Kant.[14] In such a context, "antinomy" refers to the conflict between "two opposing conclusions, each beginning from plausible premises, and issuing from valid steps of inference."[15] Kant's *Critique of Pure Reason* achieved something of a revolution by delineating certain basic antinomies that arise from close reflection upon the seemingly simple "givens" of experience. For example, Kant holds that one can argue equally plausibly that the world or universe has a beginning in time and that it has no beginning in time (a topic of no small interest for apocalyptic). But if the world as it presents itself is implicitly inconsistent, then that suggests that the world as it presents itself is not the last word; and that we should be wary of affirming that world just because it affirms itself.

Such logical reflections might already be enough to expose the profound questionability of "this world," but there is more. One must move from mere perception to human existence at large. That is what happens when Kant places his *Critique of Practical Reason*, which treats the grounds of moral existence, alongside the first *Critique*, which treated the grounds of scientific knowledge. And yet even at this level, antinomy persists. The claims of the first *Critique* and of the second, the claims of the Is and the Ought, so to speak, are irreducible; yet neither can be dismissed. *That* is perhaps the ultimate antinomy.

 practical reason

12. Ibid., 400.

13. Schweitzer, *Christianity*, 82.

14. Schweitzer "held doctorates from three Strasbourg faculties: philosophical (with a dissertation on I. Kant's philosophy of religion [1899]), theological (with a dissertation on the problem of the Lord's Supper [1901]), and medical (with a dissertation on the psychiatric study of Jesus [1913])." It is noted that he had "an unbelievable capacity for work" (Grässer, *Dictionary of Biblical Interpretation*, 2:449–50).

15. Reese, *Dictionary of Philosophy and Religion*, 19.

And Schweitzer says as much. In his terminology there is an antinomy of "world-view" and "life-view," where the latter is understood to include the issue of ethics, the issue of how one is to engage an ambiguous world, the issue of how to live humanly. In short, it was the "life-view" that the adults Schweitzer overheard had not engaged with passion. Schweitzer, for his part, addresses the antinomy between maintaining a dispassionate "world-view" and risking one's wellbeing for a demanding ethical "life-view," neither by suppressing the antinomy nor by simply opting for one side against the other—for either of those choices, *nota bene*, would have the effect of denying the twofold character of existence, however that is defined. Rather, Schweitzer chose to give a relative primacy to one side of the antinomy, namely the ethical, while simultaneously retaining full awareness that the primacy was not itself a given but a result of his finite human choosing—in the face of a world of facts, of "its," that remained indifferent to his values. There is a kind of existential heroism here, akin to what Kierkegaard calls "Religiousness A," a religiousness that can proceed without certainty of God, a mysticism of this world, courageous in the nakedness of its humanity. For Schweitzer it is enough to know that

> Our view of life is not dependent on our view of the world in the way that uncritical thought imagines. It does not wither away if it cannot send its roots down into a corresponding world-view, for it does not originate in knowledge. . . . It can safely depend upon itself alone, for it is rooted in our will-to-live.[16]

And what message does the will-to-live deliver once it is accorded the priority that is its due?

> From an inner compulsion to be true to itself and to remain consistent with itself, our will-to-live enters into relations with our own individual being, *and with all manifestations of the will-to-live which surround it,* that are determined by the sentiment of reverence for life.[17]

For Buber the I-Thou is not restricted to relations between persons. One could discover oneself in an I-Thou relationship with a tree. But Buber and Schweitzer are at one in their refusal to romanticize. Buber never claimed a direct I-Thou relationship with God. In this sense Buber and Schweitzer share a kind of *ad hoc* agnosticism. And this too must be part of the human logic of apocalyptic.

16. Schweitzer, *Civilization and Ethics*, xvii.
17. Ibid. (emphasis added).

One very positive effect of such agnosticism is reflected in the following. Schweitzer writes:

> When you preach the Gospel, beware of preaching it as the religion which explains everything. . . . For ten years, before I left for Africa, I prepared boys in the parish of St. Nicholas, in Strassburg, for confirmation. After the War some of them came to see me and thanked me for having taught them so definitely that religion was not a formula for explaining everything. They said it had been that teaching which had kept them from discarding Christianity, whereas so many others in the trenches discarded it, not being prepared to meet the inexplicable.[18]

We, like Schweitzer, teach our students without knowing what forms of the inexplicable they may be destined to confront.

SØREN KIERKEGAARD: THE SCANDAL OF PARTICULARITY

In *For Self-Examination* Kierkegaard invites the reader to look at herself in the mirror of Scripture. Perhaps Christian theology may benefit from regarding itself in the mirror of apocalyptic. Kierkegaard distinguishes between the scholarly task of "translating" Scripture and the task of truly reading it. He compares the Christian reading Scripture to a person who has received from a loved one an enigmatic letter. The text is susceptible to more than one interpretation but it seems to contain

> a wish, something the beloved wished her lover to do. It was, let us assume, much that was required of him, very much; any third party would consider that there was good reason to think better of it, but the lover—he is off at once to fulfill his beloved's wish.[19]

Without overtaxing the parable, one may note that the apocalyptic attributed to Jesus requires much; and that one naturally wishes to invoke its enigmatic character, not least the issue of its authenticity, as justification for keeping it at a speculative distance. But speculative distance may become a defense against a properly theological reading of the apocalyptic attributed to Jesus. Kierkegaard's parable presses the question—what would it mean to ascribe truth to apocalyptic, and to hold open the possibility that the truth might be radical?

18. Schweitzer, *Christianity*, 89.
19. Kierkegaard, "Self-Examination" and "Judge for Yourself," 27–28.

My hypothesis is that if Kierkegaard's parable invites reflection on apocalyptic, it may be because Kierkegaard himself in much of his work may be reflecting, directly or indirectly, on the possible meaning or meanings of Christian apocalyptic. For central to Kierkegaard is the pivotal, revolutionary insistence that "Christianity is not a doctrine but a fact."[20] Christianity is not a scholastic treatise; it is the fact that "God came into existence through a particular human being at a particular point in history."[21] Consider how in saying this Kierkegaard strikes a balance with regard to the ever perilous subject-object framework. Christianity is a fact. That fact is specifically an event. But that does not mean that the event is to be understood or "hermeneutically interpreted" as an event "in our experience." (If this seems hermeneutically impossible, if it seems that to be meaningful any event must be an event in our experience, remember that Buber's insistence that the I-Thou is in effect an event but not an experience.) This fact, this particular particular, viz., that "God came into existence through a particular human being at a particular point in history," is a particular fact unlike other facts. For unlike other facts it cannot be grasped or contextualized within the familiar alienating dichotomy of (merely) objective fact and (merely) subjective experience. Straining language, we can say that (on Christian testimony) this one lowly particular fact happens to be, by God's gracious choosing, the one truly comprehensive Fact within which all else is grasped, comprehended—and borne up with Christ from the dead.

And this is what viewing Christianity apocalyptically proclaims.[22] The common way to contextualize apocalyptic is to locate it on or within a historical timeline of one sort of another. The rationalist treats apocalyptic, or belief in it, as a historical phenomenon. In doing so, the historian assumes *a priori* the very continuity of history that apocalyptic would question—into the dustbin of history goes the notion that history is headed for the dustbin. But a similar distortion occurs when believers inscribe apocalyptic within a cosmic timeline, be it ever so celestial. At least some concerns about the triumphalism of Christian metanarrative might be allayed if Christians took more seriously the gospel admonition that "about

20. Kierkegaard, *Provocations*, 65.

21. Ibid.

• 22. This paragraph and the following are drawn from Lowe, "Postmodern Christian Theology," 23.

the day and hour no one knows, neither the angels of heaven, nor the Son, but only the Father" (Matt 24:36).[23]

Timelines of whatever stripe serve to suppress the scriptural testimony to any apocalyptic without reserve. The suspension of all things human within an unqualified apocalyptic—a suspension that is unqualified *because* it is apocalyptic—is perhaps the possibility glimpsed by the Theology of Crisis of which Barth's *Römerbrief* is paradigmatic.[24] Modernity had sought to bracket traditional apocalyptic between a modern, enlightened Christianity at the one end, and a less threatening Jesus of history at the other. But for a moment at least, at the time of the Great War, all that was made to tremble. For a moment at least it was modernity itself that was relativized and bracketed—with an earlier, apocalyptic Christianity at the one end and at the other end the contemporary apocalypse, the self-dismantlement of modernity by mustard gas and Gatling gun.[25] The Theology of Crisis has long since passed, of course, into the relativizing embrace of history, its apocalyptic circumscribed within the events of a safely distant day. But it was that apocalypticism that generated Christianity's distinctive postmodernism. And it is that apocalypticism that needs to be reclaimed and rethought today.

Key

REFLECTION: GOD'S INDIRECTNESS TRUMPS HUMAN IMMANENCE

The theme of the twofold continues throughout *I and Thou*. One reason for this is that *the I-Thou itself* is irreducibly twofold. It honors the Thou as other, unassimilable to the I. Yet there is no dualism within the I-Thou; there is relation, there is duality. As noted, through most of the book Buber proceeds in a manner that is consistently descriptive (albeit descriptive in a poetic manner.) But for a brief moment in the last, brief paragraph at the end of Buber's Part One all this changes. Suddenly Buber speaks directly to the reader: "And in all the seriousness of truth, listen: without It a human cannot live. But whoever lives only with that is not human."[26]

---

23. A prominent proponent of end-time scenarios reportedly declared that while we may not know the hour or the day, we can know the year and the month.

24. The revised second edition served not to erase Barth's great debt to Kierkegaard, but rather to clarify the nature of the debt, which lay beyond existentialism.

25. See Fussell, *Great War*. For firsthand testimony, do not miss Forché, ed., *Against Forgetting*. More recently, see Hochschild, *To End All Wars*.

26. Buber, *I and Thou*, 85.

In a sense Buber still speaks descriptively. If I live in a particular way, it is the case that I will not be human. But now *the word "human" itself* is no longer just descriptive. It has acquired normative force. Buber's brief address to the reader contains an imperative. It makes explicit an "ought" that was previously implicit. But Buber does not moralize. He brings to awareness an "ontological ought" (cf. more recently, Emmanuel Levinas on the face of the other). Thus we have one further sense in which the world of *I and Thou* is twofold; it attests to the duality of the Is and the Ought.

In Schweitzer that duality becomes antinomy. The contradiction must be confronted, for "[i]t is only by means of the tension thus set up that religious energy can be communicated to our time."[27] It is a tension of not knowing, or of knowing only that there is no religious "explanation" of the world. It is perhaps that not knowing and that knowing that one does not know that could make a person susceptible to one who, in the final words of Schweitzer's *Quest*,

> comes to us as One unknown, without a name, as of old, by the lake-side, He came to those men who knew Him not. He speaks to us the same word: "Follow thou me!" and sets us to the tasks which He has to fulfill for our time. He commands, And to those who obey Him, whether they be wise or simple, He will reveal Himself in the toils, the conflicts, the sufferings which they shall pass through in His fellowship, and, as an ineffable mystery, they shall learn in their own experience Who He Is.[28]

The tension of antinomy is only heightened when we come to Kierkegaard. He is as insistent as Schweitzer that the world is not as it seems. What stands before us in self-evident immediacy is untrustworthy because it covers over the twofold character of human existence. Already in treating the aesthetic stage or sphere, Kierkegaard labors against the entropic drift toward immediacy. The struggle mounts from the aesthetic to the ethical, then from the ethical to Religiousness A.[29]

---

27 Schweitzer, *Quest*, 400.

28. Ibid., 401.

29. It is widely recognized that there are intricate and important issues regarding SK's use of pseudonyms and the extent to which the "stages" actually constitute some sort of succession. Certainly anyone who speaks of stages must mentally juxtapose the less linear language of "spheres." Regarding Religiousness A and Religiousness B, see Westphal, *Becoming a Self*, 175–76, 186–87. For an extraordinary distillation of Kierkegaard's overall argument, see Hannay's *Kierkegaard*, 12–18.

Science

ethics

Now at some interpretive risk, I shall reintroduce the fundamental Kantian antinomy, reflected in the difference between "pure reason" and "practical reason," which can be characterized quite simply as the difference between the Is and the Ought. In Kierkegaard's "aesthetic" stage/ sphere there is little regard for the Ought. It remains possible to regard the Is as a simple given. When Kierkegaard moves to the "ethical," however, the world becomes undeniably twofold; the claim of the Ought is recognized, but still it is possible to believe that the path of right conduct is fairly apparent. With Religiousness A however, the twofold is fully antinomic. It is no longer possible to assume or intuit to some larger explanatory context in which the tension of Is and Ought can be reduced. One finds oneself contextualized by the tensive character of human existence. The fantasy of some single harmonizing reality recedes once confronted with the givens—plural—of our actual condition. It is a given never to be denied that one lives in the world. But it is simultaneously the case that we are called by conscience—called to something that is simultaneously important and unclear. This is to say that the call, like the world, is a given; but its "how" is different. It is not given *in the manner of* this world. With attention, reason can discern certain givens, but sober judgment about oneself and an empathic awareness of others are required if one is to live accordingly. Therein lies the basis for what one might call a rational existentialism.

Break

But for Kierkegaard we have still not arrived at Christianity. For that there is required a further decisive break, a break with "immanence." Let us begin with the notion of immanence itself, and then proceed to the notion of breaking from it. Fortunately we already have a foothold, thanks to Buber's conviction that the I-Thou is not reducible to experience. But one might wonder whether Buber does not exaggerate. "Experience" seems such an innocuous word. What problem could be serious enough to warrant talk about some sort of "break with immanence"?

To show what is at stake, let me offer a reflection of my own on the difficulty of religious witness in contemporary culture.[30] When a person ventures to proclaim Christ today, it is commonly assumed that one is attesting to some "experience" of God (for without the warrant of experience, the testimony is instantly deemed inauthentic)—and thus to some "contact" with God. Claiming some *Anknüpfungspunkt*, some point of contact, is virtually required just to get a hearing. Moreover, the contact is assumed to be a matter of like to like; and since God must be understood

---

30. The remainder of the present paragraph is drawn from Lowe, "Postmodern Theology," 631.

as a spiritual reality, the speaker must be attesting, *ipso facto*, to her own efficacious spirituality. The result is that an effort to point away from oneself to Christ is received as being *self*-referential. To use Paul's negative term, it is heard as boasting—indeed, boasting of one's own salvation. For to have an inner affinity to God, a relation of like to like, and to have that inner potential brought to life by actual contact—is that not in itself to be saved?

Effectively, Buber's point is that while one may have within oneself something associated with a relationship (e.g. the memory of the other person's voice), it is fantastical to think that one has *the relationship itself* within oneself. There are various forms of transcendence that are based on one's own capacities, potentialities that one "has within" oneself, even spiritual capacities. One finds a certain transcendence, for example, in the free exercise of one's imagination. But ironically such forms of transcendence can become an obstacle to relationship, a diversion from the I-Thou. Ultimately one must surrender one's fantasies to attend to the actual living person—the otherness of the other. Thus relationship is not part of my experience. Rather I am part of the relationship—the glory of which is precisely that it takes me out of myself.

With Kierkegaard the distrust of immanence is redoubled. In the [*ŽIŽEK*] *Postscript* Kierkegaard's Johannes Climacus writes, "All paganism consists in this, that God is related to [the human] directly, as the extraordinary is to the astonished observer."[31] If God were to appear in the form of a great green bird with a red beak perched on the village green and whistling in an extraordinary manner, it would get the attention of those who passed by, but the interest would not last. There would be no real relationship.[32] For there to be relationship in truth, the situation must be quite different from the merely aesthetic. There must be in the human subject an intensification of passionate engagement that somehow corresponds "to the divine elusiveness that God has absolutely nothing obvious about [God], that God is so far from being obvious, that [God] is invisible."[33] And as there is nothing obvious about God, so too there is nothing obvious or direct about the God-human relationship. Each movement toward what is in truth an intensification of connection and communication is hidden by what is, in the eyes of the world, a further diminishment of our immediate, experiential access to God.

31. Kierkegaard, *Concluding Unscientific Postscript*, 245.
32. Ibid.
33. Ibid.

With regard to this paradoxical situation, Schweitzer and others like him occupy a pivotal position. On the one hand they have broken with the aesthetic, as with conventional conceptions of the ethical. They exist within antinomy, they live the world's questionability; and yet they live out of a sense of human worth and integrity. If they are religious at all, it is with regard to a god who may not exist—so different is that god vis-à-vis the world that affirms itself. That is roughly what Kierkegaard means by "Religiousness A." It is a position greatly to be honored. Whoever would go "beyond" this position, e.g., by making larger claims with regard to God, must exercise constant vigilance, lest, so far from actually passing "beyond," they actually slip back into something less demanding, something less haunted by the ethical; which is to say, into religious aestheticism.[34]

yes

THOMAS MERTON: "TO FORGET OURSELVES ON PURPOSE"[35]

It has been said that Christianity is a young religion. We are still figuring things out. The person seeking to understand Christianity today is still like the young Thomas Merton, who had seen the ancient churches and not understood them; who in an effort to find himself had done things he came to regret; who, happening upon one voice of the tradition that spoke to him, found his life was transformed;[36] who left the world he knew for a Cistercian monastery in rural Kentucky; whose gravestone can be found there among others.

I do believe that a retrieval of a properly *cosmological* apocalyptic[37] might mark an important step in Christianity's ongoing effort to understand itself. In an essay for *The Cambridge Companion to Postmodern Theology* I have made an argument for the promise of a Christian cosmological apocalyptic, particularly as measured against traditional forms of atonement theory, both "objective" and "subjective."[38] Here I will seek to

34. See the discussion of "Socrates as an analogue of faith" in Westphal, *Becoming a Self*, 121–27. Westphal concludes, "the point of the Socrates analogy is to present in concrete form the generic subjectivity that is the condition of the possibility of the specifically Christian mode of subjectivity" (127).

35. Merton, *New Seeds*, 297/303. Here and in subsequent citations of *New Seeds*, the page numbers for the 2003 Shambala edition follow those for the original 1961 New Directions edition.

36. The book was Gilson's *Medieval Philosophy*. Those who wish to learn about Merton have a valuable resource in Shannon et al., *Thomas Merton Encyclopedia*.

37. Martyn, *Galatians*, 97–98 n. 51.

38. For an exposition of Christian cosmological apocalyptic, particularly as

relate our reflections thus far to the classic Christian tradition by studying Merton's marvelous *New Seeds of Contemplation*. The book, published seven years before his death in 1968, is a kind of harvest from Merton's years of writing and spiritual directing.

Merton begins with a theme familiar to students of spiritual literature. He distinguishes between one's "false self" and one's "true self." The false self recalls the I of Buber's I-It: he has his own interests in mind, he seeks to project a persona that will help bend the world to his purposes. This self "is the man that I want myself to be but who cannot exist, because God does not know anything about him." Yet the false self cannot accept this verdict of nonexistence. "I wind experiences around myself and cover myself with pleasures and glory like bandages in order to make myself perceptible . . ."[39] But the effort is futile.

> My false and private self is the one who wants to exist outside the reach of God's will and God's love—outside of reality and outside of life.

This may sound true enough but fairly familiar. The surprise comes with Merton's recommendation. He does not condemn the false self as superficial and then urge us to a deeper, more truly spiritual level, where the earnest seeker may discover his or her true self. No, in fact Merton sits rather light regarding deeper spirituality. He writes:

> Sometimes contemplatives think that the whole end and essence of their life is to be found in recollection and interior peace and the sense of the presence of God. But recollection is just as much a creature as an automobile. The sense of interior peace is no less created than a bottle of wine. The experimental "awareness" of the presence of God is just as truly a created thing as a glass of beer.[40]

Each of these is an instance of human transcendence. And, if I may interpret, each reflects a human talent or capacity, of which one person may have more and another less just as some people have larger cars and others can't handle their beer.

Merton's statement is, I submit, a remarkable example of realism and humility. I can have an experiential awareness of the presence of God. I

---

measured against traditional forms of atonement theory, both "objective" and "subjective," see Lowe, "Christ and Salvation."

39. Merton, *New Seeds*, 35/37.

40. Ibid., 205/208.

can be that close, so close that I *know* the presence of God. Surely, it would seem, that is the *Anknüpfungspunkt*, our long-sought point of contact. And yet even that is still the exercise of a *human capacity* of which one person will have more and another less.[41] And humankind being as it is, where there is more and less (of power, of repute, of spiritual capacity) there will almost inevitably be competition and resentment.[42] At one point in *New Seeds* Merton asks, "What is the 'world' that Christ would not pray for, and of which he said that his disciples were in it but not of it?" He answers:

> The world is the unquiet city of those who live for themselves and are therefore divided against one another. . . . It is the city of those who are fighting for possession of limited things and for the monopoly of goods and pleasures that cannot be shared by all.[43]

Spiritual excellence itself must be counted as a good "that cannot be shared by all." It still misses the point, which is, in Merton's phrase, "to forget ourselves on purpose."[44] The point is to become "detached even from the desire of peace and recollection"—to become detached, if you will, from our own subjectivity.

But in taking this position, Merton seems to have yanked the rug out from under our entire project. As originally conceived, the project was to counterbalance the seemingly too transcendent notion of an invasive God by finding some point of contact, some point of immanence, so we could find reassurance that this God comes not entirely as a stranger. Admittedly, each of our successive thinkers has put in place a further set of cautions against the common modern fascination with immanence, i.e., experience. But we might still have thought that they would eventually emerge with some point of contact of their own. After all, hasn't all modern theology been a grand dialectical dance of immanence and transcendence? And we might certainly have hoped to find Merton, a spiritual advisor in the classical tradition, affirming some classical, spiritual point of contact.

But he doesn't. Rather, relatively early in the book, in a passage that should be read in full, he sets the terms for what he is up to. He begins, in effect, with creation: "To say that I am made in the image of God is to

41. Ibid., 39/41.

42. On resentment, see ibid., 108–9/110–11.

43. Ibid., 78/80; cf. "The Root of War Is Fear," in ibid., 112–22/114–25. Also see the entire work of René Girard.

44. Merton, *New Seeds*, 297/303.

say that love is the reason for my existence, for God is love."[45] But if love is "my true identity," it follows paradoxically enough that "[s]elflessness is my true self"[46] and even that I must be "holy as [God] is holy, perfect as [God] is perfect."[47] But, Merton asks, "How can I even dare to entertain such a thought? Is it not madness?"[48] Yes, it is madness—unless we begin by confronting how radical our not-knowing is.

> I must begin, then, by realizing that the holiness of God is some-thing that is to me, and to all [persons], utterly mysterious, in-scrutable, beyond the highest notion of any kind of perfection, beyond any relevant human statement whatever.[49]

But even this statement does not go far enough. Merton's exposition goes further, and it does so by shifting into a narrative mode—that of the gospel story. God "emptied" Godself in Christ. Christ

> became a man, and dwelt among sinners. He was considered a sinner. He was put to death as a blasphemer, as one who at least implicitly denied God, as one who revolted against the holiness of God. Indeed the great question in the trial and condemna-tion of Christ was precisely the denial of God and the denial of [God's] holiness. So God [Godself] was put to death on the cross because [God] did not measure up to [humankind's] con-ception of [God's] Holiness.[50]

Everything depends on whether the reader or the hearer of this story finds it to be <u>self-involving</u>. <u>Everything depends on whether one finds oneself "named" by it, whether one knows oneself to be *known*.</u>

CONCLUSION: BEING KNOWN BY GOD

Reflecting on Galatians 4:9, Louis Martyn inserts Comment 43, entitled "To Be Known by God Is to Know That There Are No Holy Times,"[51] which might be restated as "to be known by God is to know that we have not known true holiness"—a fitting exegetical gloss on Merton's spiritual-

---

45. Ibid., 60/63.
46. Ibid.
47. Ibid., 61/63.
48. Ibid.
49. Ibid.
50. Ibid., 61–62/63–64.
51. Martyn, *Galatians*, 412.

theological exhortation. In Galatians 4:8–9 Paul begins with a strong contrast between the previous age and the present life: ". . . formerly, not knowing God, you were enslaved to things that . . . are not gods. But now, knowing God . . ." Martyn notes, however, that Paul immediately corrects himself, writing, ". . . or rather, being known by God . . ." Martyn then proposes that "[t]he resulting sentence encapsulates much of the letter's thrust."[52]

What is there in this brief passage that might encapsulate so much? Let us begin with a sort of structuralist point. Involved in the passage are perhaps four senses or usages of "know." Martyn notes that Paul's initial structure—"formerly" X, "but now" Y—employs "an early Christian formula in which a stark contrast is drawn between life in the Old Age and redeemed life in Christ . . ."[53] The formula's "stark contrast" posits a straightforward either/or between (1) knowing and (2) not-knowing: one is either in the one condition or in the other. But then Paul checks himself and shifts to another use of the term, namely (3) "being known" by another. The result, I would suggest, is to shift the discussion to another level, a level where the premise is no longer one of contrast and exclusion but one of relationship, specifically relationship between "being known" and . . . something else. And what would that something else be? We have the resources for a very suggestive answer. The answer would be, "Something like the I-Thou." The answer would be, "Something like finding oneself 'suspended' without the support of one's customary certainties, and yet finding that one does not fall because one is 'standing in' the relationship." Such relationship does not provide a knowing of the sort that a detached observer might have, yet it is the burden of Buber's book that it does provide (4) another sort of knowing that is deeper and more real.

But Paul speaks specifically of our relationship to God. What is the knowing specific to that encounter? Consider this cardinal passage in which Merton depicts the relationship of faith to reason:

> [f]aith . . . leaves the intellect suspended in obscurity, without a light proper to its own mode of knowing. Yet it does not frustrate the intellect, or deny it, or destroy it. It pacifies it with a conviction which it knows it can accept quite rationally under the guidance of love. For the act of faith is an act in which the intellect is content to know God by *loving* [God] . . .[54]

52. Ibid., 413.

53. Ibid., 412.

54. Merton, *New Seeds*, 127/130–31 (emphasis original).

In faith we know by a light that is not our own. It is not the light of some human potentiality or capacity, however spiritual or "holy." Why not? The answer has already been prepared. It is because even the highest spiritual capacity is still part of our false self; and that false self simply does not exist. It does not exist because God does not know it. Thus the determining truth is not that there are two possible paths, one the way of holiness, the other not, with God, the forensic judge, observing how we choose. Rather, there is but one determining truth, which is our true self—provided we understand that our true self is found not within ourselves, but in God. With this we may arrive at an understanding of how God can be nearer to us than we are to ourselves. It is because our notions of what is nearest, deepest, most holy, and most true about ourselves are dominated by (our attachment to) a false self that, hard as it is to imagine or say, has no reality. It is because we have no self but in God.

If such a state of affairs is seldom soberly affirmed, it is because it is so difficult to imagine or sustain. In closing, I shall argue that one reason for taking cosmological apocalyptic seriously is that it is able to effect just such a contextualization of our ceaseless self-preoccupation. But what is (Christian) cosmological apocalyptic? What is it ultimately getting at? Allow me to suggest that an answer may be found in the Barth of the *Church Dogmatics*, who might seem to have retreated from his early, more patently apocalyptic *Römerbrief*. In their preface to volume 2, part 1, the editors remark:

> Here we have the basis upon which the whole of Barth's teaching rests, for, as he says in this half-volume, the whole of revelation is summed up in the statement that "God is." This is particularly worth noting by those who think that Barth merely resolves all doctrine, and not least the doctrine of God, into Christology.[55] *N yes.*

Early on Barth makes his cardinal distinction between primary and secondary objectivity. "As [God] certainly knows [Godself] first of all, God is first and foremost objective to [Godself]."[56] This primary objectivity is distinguished from God's secondary objectivity, which is "the objectivity which [God] has to us too in [God's] revelation, in which [God] gives [Godself] to be known by us as [God] knows [Godself]."[57] So far so good. It is at this point, however, that we are likely to note that because we are

55. Bromiley and Torrance, in Barth, *Church Dogmatics*, 2/1:vii.

56. Ibid., 2/1:16.

57. Ibid.

finite beings who know God only through the mediation of finite realities, our knowledge of God is only partial. But Barth does not go that route. Rather he says of this secondary objectivity, "It is distinguished from the primary objectivity *not by a lesser degree of truth*, but by its particular *form*, suitable for us, the creature."[58] This seems to me an altogether extraordinary statement. If we join it—"not by a lesser degree of truth"—to the foregoing thesis that "the whole of revelation is summed up in the statement that 'God is,'" we have every reason to affirm that in revelation we have to do with God's very Reality, with God's very Being. Accordingly, we have every reason to believe along with Martyn's Paul that "to reveal" is indeed "to apocalypse." The revelation to which Paul attests is more than a message, more than a "mighty act." It is the invasion or inbreaking of *the very Reality* of God. And that, by its very nature, has its effect.

Yet at the same time we must say that this apocalypsing of the Reality of God occurs, as Barth notes, in a "particular form, suitable for us, the creature." What is this "particular form"? Is it being finite? Is it being visible? Martyn, following Paul, provides an answer:

> This certain hope, grounded in God's invasive action in the advent of Christ, is the apocalyptic good news Paul calls "the gospel." But its being apocalyptic is underlined by the fact that *it is not visible, demonstrable, or provable* in the categories and with the means of perception native to "everyday" existence, native, that is to say, to existence determined solely by the present evil age.[59]

For the present age connotes something that is highly visible, impressive, "awesome": fireworks beyond imagining. But that is what God's apocalypse is *not*. And the fact that it is not is congruent with who God is. For as we were reminded earlier by Kierkegaard's Climacus, "All paganism consists in this, that God is related to [the human] directly, as the extraordinary is to the astonished observer." The result in Martyn's terms is "an epistemological crisis."[60] For Kierkegaard, as we have observed, "There must be in the human subject an intensification of passionate engagement that somehow corresponds 'to the divine elusiveness that God has absolutely nothing obvious about [God], that God is so far from being obvious, that [God] is invisible.'"[61]

58. Ibid. (emphases added).

59. Martyn, *Galatians*, 104 (emphasis added).

60. Ibid.

61. Kierkegaard, *Concluding Unscientific Postscript*, 245.

There is, I believe, a certain convergence between the path traced in this essay and the Christian cosmological apocalyptic proclaimed by Paul. Any effort to think further about the convergence will have to attend constantly to the dialectic, as it were, between what we do not know and what we do know. In closing I will make just a few remarks in this regard.

We have puzzled for a long time about what Paul Ricoeur's notion of a "second naïveté" might mean for Christian theology. It strikes me that Paul's cosmological apocalyptic might provide an answer. Gustaf Aulén's study *Christus Victor* (1931) argues that during its first millennium Christianity was informed by a "classic" understanding of atonement that avoids the subsequent (scholastic) divergence between more objective and more subjective approaches to the subject. Aulén characterizes the classic view as "dramatic."

> Its central theme is the idea of the Atonement as a Divine conflict and victory; Christ—Christus Victor—fights against and triumphs over the evil powers of the world of the world, the "tyrants" under which [humankind] is in bondage and suffering, and in Him God reconciles the world to Himself.[62]

Imagine! We are in prison, off to one side. There is perhaps one small opening through which we see very little. We hear the alarms, the shouting, the sounds of battle. Eventually quiet falls. What has happened? Then voices, a clattering, the door is thrown open—and we stagger into the sunlight, rubbing our eyes as we behold God's new creation.

In Kierkegaard's terms, "Christianity is not a doctrine but a fact." It is this event, God's triumphant act of redemption. Christianity is not a theory of the world. It does not tell us *how* redemption works, but it does proclaim *that* it has happened. For some purposes, a good narrative beats ⚊ a theory any day; and that is because a good narrative "takes us out of ourselves." It tells us that somehow the "point of contact" is not within ourselves but somehow "out there," in relationship. Otherwise put, the point of contact itself is "out there": it has come to us; it has broken through, invading our world, in Jesus Christ. We are in Christ. That is our proper contextualization, accomplished in God's act of redemption.

We live *in* Christ, and therefore, while we live with a "bifocal vision" of this world and of the new creation, our "simultaneous vision is distinctly unbalanced . . ."[63] For "just as God's power is 'much more' than the power

---

62. Aulén, *Christus Victor*, 4.
63. Martyn, *Galatians*, 104.

of Sin" or the fascination of the false self, "so God causes the apocalyptic seer to see the powers of the new creation 'much more' than he sees those of the Old Age (Rom 5:12–21)."[64]

Schweitzer was right, even as he held Christian doctrine at some remove. The world is indeed not as it seems. Our own efforts to articulate the Christian message must never lack the passion this awareness arouses; for in Schweitzer's words quoted earlier, it is "only by means of the tension thus set up that religious energy can be communicated to our time." It seems to me that Paul's cosmological apocalyptic generates the most intense sense of dissonance, announcing the redemption of all things not just as a hope but as an irreversible accomplishment in a world such as ours. On the cross, "God's war of liberation was commenced and decisively settled"; "Paul speaks of a deliverance that has already been accomplished"; "God has already freed us from the malevolent grasp of the present evil age."[65] All that while still respecting our personhood by not relating to us "directly, as the extraordinary is to the astonished observer"!

Is that not how the true God might act if that God firmly desired something like an I-Thou relationship with all humankind, and the whole of creation? The force of Paul's cosmological apocalyptic is to give us ground to stand on, the ground of the new creation, as we witness even against appearances, even in "this world," that it is so.

64. Ibid.
65. Ibid., 101.

2

Partakers of the Divine Apocalypse

Hermeneutics, History, and Human Agency after Martyn[1]

Douglas Harink

WITHOUT J. LOUIS MARTYN, my own theological work as I am doing it today would not be possible. My work on apocalyptic and theology, as the subtitle of the volume says, is "with and beyond J. Louis Martyn"—sometimes beyond, but always with. I am not alone. An increasing number of theologians, some of them writing in this volume, identify Martyn's *Galatians* and *Theological Issues in the Letters of Paul* as of crucial importance for orienting and forming their basic approach to Christian theology. In contemporary parlance, Martyn's work has become for many a theological "game changer."[2]

1. An earlier version of this essay was presented to the Duodecim Theological Society in Princeton, April 2010, at which Lou Martyn was present and generously provided encouragement for the tenor and direction of the paper. The others at that meeting were equally generous in their responses (both affirmative and critical), and I learned much from them. I am especially grateful to Susan Eastman (Duke University) for her careful reading and critique of the essay, which led to some important qualifications and corrections.

2. At the 2009 meeting of the American Academy of Religion (AAR) there were two special panel sessions under the title "Explorations in Theology and Apocalyptic," one of which was given to exploring the theological implications of Martyn's work on John and Paul. There were about 45–50 enthusiastic auditors at that session—and this was AAR, not the Society of Biblical Literature! Walter Lowe, Phillip Ziegler, Benjamin

Partakers of the divine apocalypse: that phrase, a twist on 2 Peter 1:4, rather aptly sums up the gospel as Martyn has helped us to hear it.[3] The gospel is that God has acted uniquely and decisively in the *apokalypsis* of Jesus Christ to invade and liberate the enslaved cosmos, and through the invasive and powerful Holy Spirit, to bring about a new creation, already being formed in a community of free, faithful, and active participants in God's own apocalyptic work. In what follows I will focus on three aspects of this participation in God's apocalypse as Martyn's work sheds light on them. First, what is the character of scriptural interpretation as participation in the divine apocalypse? More precisely, what does scriptural *commentary* look like, understood as such participation? Here I draw attention to certain features of Martyn's commentary on Galatians as an exemplar that yields some answers to that question. Second, what is the character of time and history as a sharing in the divine apocalypse? Martyn's criticism, following Käsemann, of the idea of "salvation history" presents us with important challenges for how to read the past, in particular the history of Israel, in relation to the event of the apocalypse of Jesus Messiah. Third, what is the character of human agency as a sharing in the divine apocalypse? Here I focus in particular on political agency, in the light of what Martyn has to say about "Law" and the "newly created moral agent." Through these three clusters of questions I hope to show how Martyn's work makes a crucial contribution to the task of Christian theology in our time.

HERMENEUTICS: COMMENTARY ON SCRIPTURE AS PARTICIPATION IN THE DIVINE APOCALYPSE

What is theological commentary on Scripture? This question is now receiving growing attention among biblical scholars and theologians. A decade and a half ago I embarked on the writing of a book, *Paul among the Postliberals*, without any clear sense that that work was something like "theological commentary."[4] A few years later, when I was writing a

---

Myers, and David Belcher presented papers. I myself chaired it. Effectively, the panel participants represented three different generations of theologians.

3. I am not unaware of the irony of taking the phrasing of my title from 2 Peter. Ernst Käsemann, who had a profound influence on Martyn, also had a profound dislike for 2 Peter.

4. The several chapters of the book attempted to read together the letters of Paul with various "postliberal" theologians, including Karl Barth, John Howard Yoder, and Stanley Hauerwas, in an effort to show how Paul's letters might speak to important

"theological commentary" on 1 and 2 Peter, I had before me a brief manifesto by R. R. Reno on the nature of theological commentary that set the agenda for the series in which the commentary appears.[5] I think what I did in that commentary more or less meets the criteria of the manifesto; but, given the huge variance in the actual products now available in the series, it is not much clearer to me that we have identified a genre. What complicates matters even more is that, in my estimation, Martyn's *Galatians* is one of the two most important *theological* commentaries of the twentieth century, the other being Barth's *Römerbrief*.[6] But (in contrast to Barth's explicit intention) did Martyn set out to write a "theological commentary"? At first glance it does not appear so; *Galatians* has every appearance of fitting the historical-critical mode, and I think in a certain strong sense it also aims to do just that.[7] What then makes *Galatians* a *theological* commentary?

We might begin by noting that it is not only those who more or less welcome theological commentary who detect that Martyn is up to something different from ordinary historical-critical exegesis. For example, the issue can hardly be more clearly stated than by Troels Engberg-Pedersen, a rigorous historicist, whose book *Paul and the Stoics* received a wide-ranging review and critique from Martyn in the *Journal of New Testament Studies*.[8] Responding to Martyn's review, Engberg-Pedersen detected immediately that "there is a theological and hermeneutical dimension to Martyn's criticism [of *Paul and the Stoics*] that both explains his critical

theological questions of our time through this conversation with the postliberals.

5. Reno's (abbreviated) manifesto is found as the "Series Preface" at the beginning of each volume of the Brazos Theological Commentary. My own contribution to the series is 1 & 2 *Peter*.

6. It was not surprising to me when I read Richard Hays, in his review of *Galatians*, comparing it in stature to Barth's *Römerbrief* (65). For me, *Galatians* had an even stronger theological impact than Barth's commentary. I can think of at least two reasons: 1) even we "Barthian" theologians had long been alerted to the "problems" with Barth's commentary, both as theology and as exegesis, of which we should be wary—a judgment which I have since come seriously to reconsider; 2) Martyn's commentary struck me as a serious theological engagement of Paul *through and beyond* the New Perspective with which I had been enamored since early graduate school days—and "struck me" is the right phrase; I have not been the same since this blow. I have a number of theological friends who attest to a similar experience.

7. Graham Stanton notes that a "major difference" between Martyn's *Galatians* and Käsemann's *Romans* is that "historical questions and historical reconstructions" are more fundamental to Martyn's commentary than they are to Käsemann's (Stanton et al., review of *Galatians*, 66).

8. Engberg-Pedersen, *Paul and the Stoics*; Martyn, "De-apocalypticizing Paul."

verdict of the book as a historical exercise and also skews his reading of it rather strongly."[9] Engberg-Pedersen goes on to specify what he takes to be "the fundamental issue" between himself and Martyn. It is this:

> Should one accept the modern, post-Enlightenment perspective of the "western university" (in Martyn's apt formulation)—basically the perspective of historical criticism—not only as the framework for the historical exegesis of Paul, but also as setting the parameters for the modern theological appropriation of him? Or (in my own formulation of Martyn's position) should one allow certain substantive ideas in Paul's own thought world both to give fundamental shape to the historical analysis of it so as to stress its uniqueness (the "differences," the "Pauline propria") in comparison with other historical phenomena and also, explicitly or implicitly, to carry over into the modern appropriation of Paul in a manner that fundamentally questions the post-Enlightenment worldview? Where I place myself squarely in the former position, I detect a crucial instability in Martyn's position . . . [10]

For Engberg-Pedersen the "crucial instability" is located in Martyn's failure to honor "what . . . is most important in historical criticism: a sense of the distance between then and now."[11]

Engberg-Pedersen gets to the heart of the issue with uncanny clarity. In Martyn's *Galatians* the distance between then and now to a great extent dissipates, as it does in Barth's *Romans*, but differently. While in Barth's commentary the historical distance is to a great extent cancelled, with the then overwhelmingly being taken up and absorbed into the now (in the dialectic of *Aufhebung und Begründung*), in Martyn's historical-critical approach the historical "distance" (not quite the right word) is overcome through a complex interweaving of the then and now, as two aspects of a single apocalyptic time. Martyn himself aims to achieve what he characterizes in the Gospel of John as a "two-level drama."[12] There are two aspects of this character of Martyn's commentary that are worth exploring: first, the *theological* conviction that undergirds the commentary project;

9. Engberg-Pedersen, "Response to Martyn," 103.

10. Ibid., 103–4.

11. Ibid., 104 n. 3.

12. As Richard Hays noted in the form of a question in his review of *Galatians*: "Is Martyn's commentary itself a 'two-level drama' in which, through the medium of expositing Paul's letter, the author simultaneously evokes and interprets events of our own time . . . ?" (Stanton et al., review of *Galatians*, 65).

second, the *literary performance* that brings about the palpable sense of historical co-presence in the commentary.

Unquestionably, as a commentator Martyn *stands with* Paul in the singular apocalyptic reality in which Paul claims to be standing. Should not that in itself explain the fundamentally theological character of the commentary? Still, one can imagine (in fact, one does not have to imagine) any number of modern commentators who would confess strong or even complete *agreement with* Paul's theological vision, who might nevertheless go on to write a "standard" historical-critical commentary in which historical, cultural, textual and linguistic research is employed to explicate the meaning of a Pauline letter as an historical document. Having done so, the same commentator might, *optionally* and as *a second step*, explore some of the "theological implications" or "practical applications" of the letter, "on the basis of" the historical-critical work. This option for so-called theological commentary (shall we call it the "two ways, two-step" approach to scriptural commentary?) is certainly available, even in abundance, on the current scene. But it is not the "option" Martyn takes. Quite the contrary! As any who are familiar with his work know full well, Martyn has little patience for "options" and "two-steps," not least as a commentator. The commentator who stands in a seemingly autonomous relationship of "agreeing" (whether more or less) with Paul's "theology" in any given letter is already standing beyond the reach of the letter; or rather, standing within the reach of the letter, but already in a state of denying its fundamental character, even, and precisely, in "agreeing" with it. The apocalyptic character of Paul's gospel as proclaimed in a Pauline letter does not allow for a supposedly neutral critical distance from which a decision to agree or disagree with it might be launched. For, in being caught up into the apocalyptic event that the letter is, even the modern commentator, like every other human being, is either a slave of the "elemental principles of the [post-Enlightenment historicist] cosmos" or a slave of Christ.[13] That is not to say that the *commentary* is beyond criticism. Its faithfulness as a construal of the apocalyptic gospel, as well as its faithfulness as a reading of the biblical text (which cannot but be aided by critical linguistic

---

13. "Paul not only speaks of the gospel as God's performative Word. He also denies that this performative Word—the gospel of the crucified Christ—is subject to human evaluation, whether that of the Gentiles or that of the Jews (1 Cor 1:22–24). And in this denial Paul obliterates in one stroke the thought that the gospel is subject to criteria of perception that have been developed apart from the gospel" (Martyn, *Theological Issues*, 220).

and historical skills), is always open to judgment about its adequacy.[14] But faithful commentary is in the first place a matter of participation in the apocalyptic event itself, which participation itself is not in the first place under the commentator's control.

For Martyn a Pauline letter such as Galatians is a divine communicative event: "Paul wrote Galatians in the confidence that *God* intended to cause a certain event *to occur* in the Galatian congregations when Paul's messenger read the letter aloud to them. . . . The author we see in the course of reading Galatians is a man who *does* theology by writing in such a way as *to anticipate* a theological *event*."[15] When in Galatians 1:5 Paul utters a doxology and an "Amen," "Paul brings the Galatians climactically into God's presence by inviting them to utter the word 'Amen'" with him.

> It is a signal of his conviction that his own words can and will become the active word of God, because God will be present as the letter is read to the Galatians in their services of worship. One might even say that by using the word "amen," Paul intends to rob the Galatians of the lethal luxury of considering themselves observers. With him, they stand in God's presence. Fundamentally, then, they are dealing with God, not merely with Paul.[16]

As with the Galatians, so also with commentators as readers of the letter; if they grasp its true import, they are "robbed" of "the lethal luxury of considering themselves observers." And if not observers, then what are they but partakers of the same divine communicative event, the *apokalypsis Theou*, of which the letter is an instrument? Martyn's approach to the Pauline letter as a reader and commentator thus exemplifies a fundamental point made by John Webster in an essay on reading Scripture eschatologically: "A dogmatic account of the creaturely activity of *reading* Holy Scripture does not entail the suspension or retirement of . . . language about divine action, but rather its furtherance. . . . Put differently: the ontology of the text—its nature as the creaturely servant of the revelatory presence of the Holy Trinity—is to condition the acts of its readers."[17] Or, as Robert Jenson puts it, "Scripture is not merely a record of divine-human history but a proclaiming of it, not merely an account of God's life with us

---

14. I am grateful to Susan Eastman for clarifying this important matter for me.

15. Martyn, "Events in Galatia," 161 (emphases original).

16. Martyn, *Galatians*, 106.

17. Webster, "Reading Scripture Eschatologically (1)," 245–47.

to date but a voice in that life."[18] By this understanding of what a letter of Paul is and does, the modern historical-critical commentary, as envisaged by Engberg-Pedersen for example, might best be characterized as a work of scholarly historical fiction. Conversely, any commentary adequate to the reality of a Pauline letter is one that *ab initio* understands itself as a participation in the divine communicative event that the letter is by grace and election, both then and now; and only such a commentary is truly theological.[19] Martyn presents us not in the first place with an incremental exegetical "advance" toward an apocalyptic "perspective," but rather with a fundamental shift of hermeneutical stance; that is, exegesis is standing in the midst of the theological earthquake of the gospel, of which Paul's letter is a powerful shockwave, giving an account of what is going on while the quake is still happening.[20] Why has Martyn's *Galatians* laid its hold on so many readers? Because through it we are drawn into the earthquake of God's voice among the Galatians as Paul's letter is read and, by God's grace and election, we are made to share with the Galatians in this divine apocalypse.

There is, no doubt, more than one way to write a theological commentary that reflects the account of Holy Scripture given by Webster and Jenson, and exemplified by Martyn's *Galatians*. In fact, it is hard to imagine how Martyn's performance could be repeated with anything like

18. Jenson, "Scripture's Authority," 34.

19. The point here, again, is not that the commentary is beyond criticism; it is only that participation is the *sine qua non* of a commentary being *theological*. Theological work is always subject to theological judgment in the ongoing task of clarifying what counts as speech true to the gospel.

20. Martyn is inclined to describe the Pauline scholar as one pausing for a moment to issue a report of a journey—i.e., as one mostly on the move, paralleling Paul's own "scholarly" modus operandi (*Theological Issues* 180). We might at this point draw attention to the astonishing recent work by Rowe, *World Upside Down*. Rowe comes to very similar conclusions about reading the Acts of the Apostles: "Precisely because Acts provokes a conflict over the truth of its comprehensive claims, it disallows a response that would seek to sidestep its claim as a whole . . . The book of Acts has a 'kerygmatic intention.' In just this way, the text itself performs the fulfilment of Jesus's programmatic instruction to carry the witness to him to the ends of the earth" (174). "Attending carefully to Acts' irreducibly particular way of knowing . . . requires the development of an interpretive grammar of claim and conflict, which is to say that Acts' mode of discourse will inevitably yield hermeneutical negotiations of its claims in the lives of its readers. To think that our readings of Acts would produce bits and pieces of knowledge that we could, irrespective of our particular convictions or reactions, insert into some wider interpretive scheme is not to practice scholarly (or existential) deferral but is *already* to have offered a counter-reading of the world, one in which the comprehensive vision of Acts is negated in favor of a larger noetic program" (176).

the same effect; other ways may have to be found. But the kind of *literary performance* that Martyn's *Galatians* is, is worthy of some attention. In an important statement about arriving at his own approach to reading Scripture, Martyn invokes "a confluence of the hermeneutical rule of Walter Bauer with the historically dynamic, interpretive framework of Ferdinand Christian Baur."[21] Bauer's rule is that the interpreter should not ask first about the author's intention in writing, but rather about "how the original readers of the author's document understood what he had said in it."[22] From Baur Martyn learned to ask, "Where does the document we are reading belong in the strains and stresses characteristic of early Christian history."[23] Employing Bauer's rule "involves all of the imagination and all of the disciplines necessary for a modern interpreter *to take a seat in an early Christian congregation*, intent on borrowing the ears of the early Christian neighbors, in order to hear the text as they heard it."[24] However, a seat in a congregation of the early church is not often a comfortable pew; rather, seated exactly in that place, the interpreter becomes a participant in the "strains and stresses" of the early church, hearing not only the voice of the theologian who authored the document, but also "the voices of other Christian theologians who prove, more often than not, to be saying rather different things, and in some instances to be saying those different things quite effectively."[25] Working with the interpretive rules of Bauer and Baur, the reader as listener is caught up into an event in which those various voices contend for the minds and hearts of the congregation over matters of great significance. How better to evoke that act of interpretation than in terms of a drama? And so, the opening lines of *Galatians*:

> Reading Paul's letter to his Galatian churches is like coming in on a play as the curtain is rising on the third or fourth act. . . . [T]o read this letter is to be involved in high drama, for one senses between Paul and the Galatians both deep affection and angry tension . . . Paul and the Galatians have a rich history with one another. Important developments antedate the writing and reception of the letter. . . . [W]hat has already occurred has involved a number of persons in addition to Paul and the Galatians. Genuine understanding of the letter involves discerning

21. Martyn, *Theological Issues*, 211.

22. Ibid., 210; Martyn is here quoting Bauer's rule as "a piece of circulating oral tradition."

23. Ibid., 211.

24. Ibid.

25. Ibid., 212.

the roles played by these and other actors, as well as the roles played by Paul and the Galatians.[26]

The first thing Martyn does as an interpreter, then, is to provide "a brief sketch of the players," the *dramatis personae*. As the commentary proceeds, that brief sketch is progressively filled out in a number of ways. Certainly rigorous historical research and reconstruction play a very important part in that task, as we would expect. But given that we are here "coming in on a play," we should not be surprised when we encounter throughout Martyn's commentary numerous shorter and longer "speeches" that the various characters in the play (primarily Paul and the Teachers) might have made, *imaginatively constructed* on the basis of listening carefully for the "strains and stresses" revealed by the letter itself. In other words, the commentary itself (primarily in the 52 "Comments") becomes in essence the writing of the drama that unfolds around the event of the letter to the Galatians.[27] The commentator is the playwriter.[28]

The drama is intense. Conflict is ingredient throughout; and we learn soon enough that it is not primarily a conflict between Paul and the Teachers over the loyalty and affections of the Galatians (as the usual historical-critical interpretive stance would portray it). Rather, it is a conflict in which Christ and the Spirit, via Paul's letter, are engaged in warfare with the enslaving *stoicheia tou kosmou* and *sarx*, via the Teachers, over the actual lives of the Galatians. That warfare, however, reaches beyond the specific occasion in Galatia to which the letter bears its crucial historical witness. Through the letter's witness and the commentator's skilful writing of its drama, we too, the readers of the commentary, also find ourselves taken

---

26. Martyn, *Galatians*, 13.

27. One of the best examples is the discussion of "Christ and the Elements of the Cosmos" in Comment 41 (ibid., 393–406). There we hear the voice of ancient Greek religion as it may have claimed the Galatians' attention prior to Paul's arrival; then (in their own written words) the voices of the Jewish sage who authored *Wisdom*, and of Philo and Josephus. Then we hear the Teachers, as in their "speeches" they voice their criticism of the earlier Greek religion of the Galatians, correct the mistaken message propounded by Paul, announce the way in which the Messiah and the Torah *together* deliver the Galatians from their former ways, and call the Galatians to become observers of the true religion of Moses after the pattern of Abraham. Finally Paul's own voice, via the letter, is heard in the scene announcing God's invasion of the cosmos and deliverance from the "elements" through the singular gospel of the crucified Jesus and the powerful Spirit.

28. By this means, then, a *letter* of Paul begins to work upon us something like a *gospel*.

by the hand and seated in the midst of the early Christian congregation. It is *our* lives that are at stake in this then-and-now moment in which the gospel as Paul's letter is unleashed upon the scene. It is we who are joined with the Galatians in the life-and-death struggle between the Spirit and the Flesh, evoked by the letter, over the loyalty of our hearts and minds. The mode of Martyn's commentary as a kind of drama writing becomes the instrument by which we as readers of the letter are made partakers of the divine apocalypse. The commentary itself aims to participate in and communicate the theological event to which it bears witness. It aims to become an instrument of the Spirit in the gospel's invasion of the world.

An intriguing question remains, however. Does Galatians lend itself uniquely to the kind of drama-writing literary performance that is Martyn's commentary? Probably not, if we consider 1 and 2 Corinthians and Philemon. But what of Philippians and 1 Thessalonians? More dauntingly, what of Romans, written to a congregation that Paul did not found, and that he had never visited? If we cannot for a variety of good exegetical and theological reasons simply repeat what Barth did in *Römerbrief*, how shall a commentary on that letter proceed, such that by it we are taken in hand and ushered into the congregation in Rome, in order to become with the Romans partakers of the divine apocalypse as the letter is read?[29]

HISTORY: PAST AND PRESENT AS PARTICIPATION IN THE DIVINE APOCALYPSE

Implicit in every aspect of Martyn's work of theological commentary, whether in terms of its aims or its methods, is an understanding of time and history as overtaken by and subsumed within the divine apocalypse, that is, of the co-presence of all times within the time of Jesus Christ. That understanding is already given decisive shape in Martyn's work on the Gospel of John in the 1960s, in which the relationship between history and theology in that gospel is explored in detail. It is there that he develops the idea of John's Gospel as a "two-level drama." While John (like Luke) might have told the story of the past and present struggles of the church in his city as a straightforward historical narrative, "instead, we find him presenting a two-level drama in which it is not an apostle but rather Jesus himself who ministers" to John's Jewish-Christian contemporaries.[30] It is the same Jesus who ministered once upon a time among his people in Gal-

29. I pursue this question further in "Time and Politics."

30. Martyn, *History and Theology*, 124.

ilee and Jerusalem who ministers now to the church of the apostle. "John does not in any overt way indicate to his reader a distinction between the two [temporal—past and present] stages. . . . He presents his two-level drama in a way which is obviously intended to say with emphasis: 'This is *the* drama of life.'"[31] Further:

> For John . . . the drama is real precisely because it is played si-
> multaneously on the two levels. . . . These events to which John
> bears witness transpire on both the *einmalig* and the contempo-
> rary levels of the drama, or they do not transpire at all. In John's
> view, their transpiring on both levels of the drama is, to a large
> extent, the good news itself.[32]

As for John, so for Martyn; rather than worrying about displaying a "cru-
cial instability" (Engberg-Pedersen) regarding the relation of history and theology, Martyn fearlessly places John's "two-level drama" understanding of time and history at the very center of his own work, *in order that* his exegetical work might be a participation in *the real*.

For Martyn, the question of history arises most pointedly in both John and Paul around the relation of the gospel to Israel's history, tradition, and Scripture. For John, "[t]he question is whether . . . scripture points to a linear entity that in a linear fashion prepares the way for, and leads up to, the incarnation of the Logos. In this regard, we have simply to note in the Gospel of John the absence of a linear sacred history that flows out of scripture into the gospel story."[33] In fact, in his gospel, John "is waging a battle" precisely against such a view. The Word is without precedent in any history, and cannot be measured by any criterion, including Scripture. Likewise for Paul, "there are no through-trains from the scriptural, patriarchal traditions and their perceptive criteria to the gospel of God's Son."[34] On the contrary, if we are to speak of Scripture, tradition, and history in terms of trains, tracks, and arrows, the trains on the straightforward tracks of Scripture and tradition all arrive at a dead end, and the arrow of history points in the other direction. Paul's own story is the paradigmatic example. Prior to his arrest, conscription, and commissioning by the risen *Kyrios*, Paul embodied in himself in great measure the potentials of Israel's history (*ek genous Israēl, phylēs Beniamin*), Scripture (*Hebraios ex Hebriaōn*), and tradition (*kata nomon Pharisaios*); yet all of this directs Paul in theopo-

---

31. Ibid., 131.

32. Ibid., 142–43.

33. Martyn, *Theological Issues*, 216.

34. Ibid., 224.

litical "zeal" against the people of the Crucified and Risen One (Phil 3:5). Those inherited and acquired potentials, unleashed upon history in Paul's persecuting activity, had to be apocalyptically cancelled (*tauta hēgēmai ton Christon zēmian* [Phil 3:7] or "crucified," as in Gal 6:14); only beyond that cancellation is Paul "found" again, now as witness and apostle. So it is with the history, tradition, and Scripture of Israel; in the apocalyptic arrival of Jesus Messiah they are cancelled as far as their *messianic epistemological "potential"* goes; but found again beyond that—after the messianic apocalypse—as true prophetic witnesses to *this* Messiah, insofar as the Messiah claims, conscripts, and recreates them as such.[35] In the same way, in the Gospel of John, according to Martyn's study of it, there is no "clear trajectory from the scriptural expectations connected with various 'messianic' figures to the figure of the Messiah." The fundamental christological issues cannot be resolved on the basis of further exegesis by the "simple exegetical theologians" in John's milieu because "the fundamental arrow in the link joining scripture and gospel points from the gospel story to scripture and not from scripture to the gospel story. In a word, with Jesus' glorification, belief in scripture *comes into being* by acquiring an indelible link to belief in Jesus' words and deeds."[36]

Imitating John and Paul, Martyn's work is deeply occupied with coming to grips with the way that our concepts of history, tradition, and Scripture must be fundamentally qualified by and reconstituted under the impact of the gospel. There are several aspects of that occupation. First, as

---

35. Here I cite Benjamin's "Theological-Political Fragment," 305: "Only the Messiah himself completes all history, in the sense that he alone redeems, completes, creates its relation to the messianic. For this reason, nothing that is historical can relate itself, from its own ground, to anything messianic. Therefore, the Kingdom of God is not the telos of the historical dynamic; it cannot be established as a goal. From the standpoint of history, it is not the goal but the terminus [*Ende*]." It is not likely that the Jewish philosopher has the "Christian" Messiah in mind, although the possible Pauline source of Benjamin's messianism is convincingly argued by Agamben in *The Time that Remains*, 138–45. For myself, Benjamin's "Theological-Political Fragment" and "Theses on the Concept of History" have penetrated deeply into my understanding of the gospel, precisely because they resonate so profoundly with the apocalyptic character of the gospel that I have learned from Martyn.

A statement made by Origen in his commentary on John also resonates strikingly with both Martyn and Benjamin: "Before the sojourn of Christ, the law and the prophets did not contain the proclamation that belongs to the definition of the gospel, since he who explained the mysteries in them had not yet come. But since the Savior has come and has caused the gospel to be embodied, he has by the gospel made all things as gospel" (*Commentary on John* 1.33, quoted in Behr, *Mystery of Christ*, 91).

36. Martyn, *Theological Issues*, 214, 216.

we have already seen, the kind of theological-historical commentary on Scripture that Martyn practices itself presupposes the relation of gospel and Scripture, apocalypse and history, that he learns from John and Paul. The commentator reads the New Testament documents as a participation in the same singular history—the history of the gospel's apocalypse—of which those documents are themselves witnesses. That singular time—the time of Jesus Christ—is the criterion not only of how Israel's history, tradition, and Scripture "count" as witnesses, but also of how the *church's* history, tradition, and Scripture do so, and so also the commentator's work. "Counting as a witness" depends not upon potentials inherent in the witness, but upon God acting apocalyptically by the Spirit of Christ to conscript the witness to this purpose.

Second, and closely related, we note Martyn's lifelong vigorous op- position to the salvation-historical interpretation of Paul (and John). In good measure the whole of *Galatians* is written against that interpretation, arguing in fact that it is the Teachers, the opponents of Paul (and in John, the "simple exegetical theologians"), who establish their position on the basis of a salvation-historical exegetical paradigm. It is not possible, at least if we are following John and Paul, to speak, as N. T. Wright representatively does, with great authority (and against Martyn, among others), of "God . . . quietly and steadily working his purposes out as year succeeded to year"; of "the age-old promises" being "fulfilled through the long unwinding of Israel's and the world's story"; of a divine plan that "had been steadily unfolding in the mind of God and on the ground in the Middle East" in which the death and resurrection of Jesus comes about as "a new chapter [that] has opened within the story."[37] History for Paul, not only in Galatians but also in Romans, is not "going somewhere" according to a divinely directed, forward moving, continually progressing "plan" of God, culminating in the arrival of the Messiah. In Romans, history—the history of the nations (chs. 1–2), of the Jews (chs. 2–3), of Abraham (ch. 4), of Adam (ch. 5), of a person under the Law (ch. 7), of the creation (ch. 8), even of God's chosen people (chs. 9–11)—is revealed, in light of the messianic apocalypse, as standing under a single sign: bondage. Bondage to the powers of Sin, Disobedience, Injustice, and Death. Every character in this history has been "handed over" to these powers *by God* (only here may we perhaps speak of God's "plan"), kept in prison under them, until the singular event of God's own invasive and liberating act in the

37. Wright, *Paul*, 50–51, 134, 9.

crucifixion and resurrection of Jesus and the coming of the Holy Spirit.[38] History before this event, according to Paul in Romans, is *wreckage*. We are reminded at this point of that stunning image of the angel of history in Walter Benjamin's theses on the concept of history:

> There is a picture by Klee called *Angelus Novus*. It shows an an-gel who seems about to move away from something he stares at. His eyes are wide, his mouth is open, his wings are spread. This is how the angel of history must look. His face is turned toward the past. Where a chain of events appears before *us, he* sees one single catastrophe, which keeps piling wreckage upon wreckage and hurls it at his feet. The angel would like to stay, awaken the dead, and make whole what has been smashed. But a storm is blowing from Paradise and has got caught in his wings; it is so strong that the angel can no longer close them. This storm drives him irresistibly into the future, to which his back is turned, while the pile of debris before him grows toward the sky. What we call progress is *this* storm.[39]

Paul might have written that paragraph. He finds no saving trajectory, no saving *divine* storm of progress, running through and amidst the ungodly storm piling up wreckage; indeed, God himself is the one who has handed all history over to the wreckage it has and continues to become. There is for Paul a singular hope, which only *now, today*, in this *hour* is apocalypsed upon the scene with saving divine power: the Messiah. In his crucifixion even the Messiah is "handed over" to history's wreckage and becomes part of it; but in his resurrection from the dead "by the Spirit of holiness" he is apocalypsed as the one who is able to "awaken the dead, and make whole what has been smashed," that is, to *redeem* history—something that it is impossible for the angel of history to do in the hurricane of "progress," which is the cause of history's destruction rather than its redemption.

It is of fundamental importance, then, that just as we must not try to trace a divine salvation-historical plan in the history "leading up to" the coming of the Messiah, we also must not try to trace such a plan in

38. See especially Martyn's discussion of what might be called the *providential* enslavement under the powers in *Galatians*, 372–73. See also Gaventa, "God Handed Them Over."

39. Benjamin, "Concept of History," 392. Benjamin's philosophy of history stands within a stream of Jewish (apocalyptic) messianic thought that arose after WWI, which includes Rosenzweig, Scholem, and (after WWII) Taubes, who was influenced by Benjamin. Moltmann notes the significance of these Jewish messianic thinkers for Christian theology in *The Coming of God*, 29–46. See also, at greater length, the il-luminating study by Mosès, *The Angel of History*.

the history leading out from the Messiah's arrival—in the history of the church perhaps (or "Christian civilization," or the "struggle for human rights," or "the spread of democracy")—which will now progress in its own power throughout the generations to its culmination in the kingdom of God. Just as "the covenantal promise [to Abraham] did not create its own epoch, calling into existence a corporate *sperma Abraam* that would extend generation after generation—in a linear fashion—through the centuries,"[40] so too the coming of Jesus Christ is "not the beginning of a new, a second, epoch."[41] No more than the history of Israel does the history of the church represent a progressive history of salvation. The church no less than Israel requires at every moment, again and again, to be halted, caught up, and commissioned by the Messiah, that is, to be redeemed in the Messiah from even its own wreckage-making powers, to trust (like Abraham and Sarah and Israel) that it will be "awakened from the dead" and made whole by the God who gives life to the dead and calls into being the things that are not.

If that description captures something of Paul's understanding of history as we learn it from Martyn (assisted by Benjamin), there are a number of important implications. I will explore only two, one of which will be developed in the next section of this essay. For now, I draw brief attention to the closely related questions of Marcionism, anti-Judaism, and supersessionism, which to a significant extent always hover around the edges of Martyn's work (and of which he is always conscious), and which from time to time he addresses directly. Why, he asks, have Christian theologians, from the early church onward, often "attributed a motif [e.g., salvation history] to John or Paul, when in actuality that motif is characteristic of theologians against whom these authors were waging a significant battle"? Martyn answers his own question: "In part, I think, because we have been unconsciously afraid that, if Paul and John should prove to be anti-redemptive-historical theologians, they would also prove to have applied to scripture an anti-Judaic hermeneutic."[42] While Martyn suggests that some arguments might be mounted even from within Scripture itself (Isa 43:18–19) against that fear, nevertheless the concern that "Paul and John unwittingly prepare[d] the way for Marcion" presses upon us. Is it possible, Martyn asks, that in seeking to avoid Marcion's heresy the early church in fact adopted the very redemptive-historical heresy against which Paul and

40. Martyn, *Galatians*, 348.

41. Barth, *Romans*, 77.

42. Martyn, *Theological Issues*, 224–25.

John waged their battle and in terms of which they interpreted these two theologians? But then, having (perhaps rightly and necessarily) expelled the Marcionite heresy, where does that leave us with John and Paul with respect to their supposed anti-Judaism and supersessionism, if Martyn's interpretation is right?

That is a very large question, and I cannot begin to answer it with respect to John's Gospel. I have elsewhere, however, argued with respect to Paul that it is precisely the redemptive-historical approach that tends

• to supersessionism, and perhaps also to anti-Judaism, by way of a chauvinism of historical progress.[43] But, as I have also argued elsewhere, from resources in Martyn and Barth's *Römerbrief*, in Paul there is no such historical chauvinism; rather, there is the priority of the *nun kairos*, the time of the *apokalypsis Theou*, which has the power to redeem and fulfill all times.[44] Nothing and no one in all creation has the capacity to bring about its own fulfillment—unless sheer nothingness, death itself, is embraced nihilistically as a kind of completion, but that is hardly the hope of Israel and the church. It is only as the Messiah—the Lord of all times, and therefore of Israel, the church, the nations, and all creation—enters the realm where Death reigns (history) and reaches out to everyone (indeed, everything) in bondage to death and decay with the strong hand of rescue, that anything at all is brought to its end; or rather, the Messiah himself *comes as the telos*

• of all things, taking all things to himself as their resurrection from the dead. The whole wreckage of history, which Paul in Romans sees in the light of the messianic apocalypse, is in that very same apocalypse addressed by the excessive power of God's grace and resurrection life: Abraham and Sarah's aged bodies are raised from childless death (ch. 4); the Second Adam superabundantly exceeds by his obedience the destruction and slavery brought by the first Adam's disobedience (ch. 5); the person subjected to the slavery of Sin and its captive servant, Law, is rescued for thanks and praise (ch. 7); creation eagerly awaits its resurrection into freedom (ch. 8); Israel awaits the glorious arrival of the Deliverer from Zion (ch. 11); Israel

---

43. Harink, *Paul*, 151–207. In fact, I would now also argue that a purely secular historicism cannot be supersessionist since there is no non-arbitrary criterion by which one historical fact ("Christianity") might be assessed as higher or better than another ("Judaism"), particularly when both have persisted throughout history to this day as "living" facts, i.e., the one has not superseded the other by "living" while the other has "died."

44. Harink, "Paul and Israel," "Barth's Apocalyptic Exegesis," "Jewish Priority." In this latest essay I argue that nothing is prior to the gospel, and election and Jewish priority find their true basis in that.

and the nations, messianically reconciled, rejoice together in the one God of their salvation (ch. 15). The Messiah supersedes all things and comes as the fullness of all things. There is no historical supersession of anything (except by election, in the gospel, of "the Jew first, and also the Greek"); certainly the church does not in any sense replace Israel. If Israel is lost, so are the nations. Nothing perdures in history from its own inherent capacity. But nothing is lost in the singular history that is the messianic apocalypse, the *nun kairos*, stretched out between its inauguration and its fullness because of God's patience, so that his mercy might become known to all. If the nations are saved by the mercy of the Messiah, so also is Israel, and never the one without the other. The *apocalyptic* gospel, we discover, provides us with the only possibility of a truly non-supersessionist theology. If that is not clear from Romans, nothing is.

A question nevertheless remains in Martyn's work about the identity of Israel in history. Noting that in Galatians "election is God's enactment of his promise in Christ, Abraham's only seed," Martyn turns to Romans for another word on the matter of the election of Israel: there "things are dramatically different. . . . Indeed, the whole of the argument in Romans 9–11 presupposes God's election of ancient Israel."[45] Nevertheless, a careful look at 9:6–8 suggests to Martyn that things are not wholly different. He concludes:

> God's election, being free of all presuppositions, cannot be traced through the generations of Israel on any basis other than the act of God himself, the one who issues the promise *newly* in each generation and solely on the basis of his own faithful perdurance; so that his purpose might *remain* without exception a matter of his election (Rom 9:11). An hypothesis follows: Perhaps both in Galatians and in Romans—although in different ways—Paul means emphatically to deny that God's elective grace was enacted in an ethnic, anthropological sense, either in the Abrahamic promise or in the giving of the Law.[46]

Surely the central thrust of Martyn's point here corresponds strongly to Paul's emphasis. But we must still ask: Does God elect *Israel*? That is, does God not elect the *bodies* of Abraham and Sarah (although precisely because of their incapacity and lack of potential; Gen 11:30) and, *through their bodies*, their descendants? In Romans 9:6–13 it is, to be sure, not Ishmael who is elected; but it *is* Isaac, the son of Abraham and Sarah and

---

45. Martyn, *Galatians*, 350.

46. Ibid., 350–51 (emphasis original).

not of another pair, who is created by God's election. And it is not Esau who is chosen; but it *is* Jacob, the "ethnic" son of Rebecca, who is chosen while still in the womb. The point here is not that any of these descendents had anything to contribute of themselves to an ongoing "history of redemption." Each one of these characters is "wreckage" of history in their own right: both Sarah and Rebecca are barren before God resurrects their wombs; Isaac and Jacob can hardly be counted as adding something of moral value to the history of the world, and in any case neither would even exist apart from God's election. With nothing to offer, God nevertheless elects, creates, conscripts, and commissions *their Abrahamic bodies* and not others, through which to work the miracle of his promise. Is there not here at least a minimalist "ethnic" generational presupposition? Is not Israel this chosen fleshly body in the world, and not simply one nation among others, to which God has bound himself in promise? Would Paul have found himself under any compulsion to write Romans 9–11 if that were not so? And if so, what is the theological implication of that?[47]

THE HUMAN AGENT: POLITICAL AGENCY AS PARTICIPATION IN THE DIVINE APOCALYPSE

A matter of focal concern in Martyn's later writings has been that of divine and human agency. Those familiar with his work will now know the phrase, "the three-actor moral drama," by which Martyn refers to 1) the divine agent, 2) the anti-God powers as agent(s), and 3) the human agent; each of these must be taken into account in an adequate description of human agency in Paul.[48] The human agent apart from the gospel is for Paul morally incompetent: the agent does not stand neutrally, as it were, before moral options, freely and competently deliberating between them, then choosing the right or better option and carrying out the action. Such a human agent does not in fact exist, or rather, no longer exists. Martyn traces the Pauline "history of the human agent" in four stages. First there is the "Adamic agent who was created/fashioned by God with moral competence (Rom 1:19–20)." Second, God elects and creates in Israel "a corporate and corporately addressable agent (Rom 9: 4–5)" who

47. I address some of these issues in the essays mentioned in the previous footnote. One must now also consult Eastman, "Israel and the Mercy of God." Eastman generally presupposes Martyn's work in her own, but challenges Martyn, and many others who read *Israēl tou Theou* in Gal 6:16 as a reference to the church.

48. See especially Martyn, "Epilogue" and "Gospel Invades Philosophy."

nevertheless is "repeatedly disobedient. Indeed, there is universal Adamic disobedience (Rom 3:9–18; 11:32)." Third, the disobedient Adamic agent "becomes without exception [morally] incompetent; and, handed over by God to anti-God powers, this agent finds his incompetence deepened (Rom 1:21–28)." In fact, the anti-God powers are themselves "subjects of verbs, actors who do things"; they deceive and enslave disobedient Adamic agents. Fourth, then, the human agent must be delivered not only from disobedience, but also from enslavement. This happens in the apocalyptic power of the gospel:

> In the gospel of Christ (for Paul an event) *God steps on the scene.* Far from allowing the human agent to stand alone at the road fork, this invasive God powerfully meets both the incompetent, enslaved agent and the powers that enslave him in their own orb. . . . And in that meeting the divine agent does something unheard of. Destroying old-age images of the human agent, God *changes* human agency itself. . . . God creates *the corporate, newly competent and newly addressable agent*, forming this new human agent in the image of the crucified Son, *Christos estauromenos*, by sending the Spirit of the Son into its heart (Gal 4:6; Rom 8:29).[49]

This remarkable account of divine and human agency in Paul is worthy of a great deal more attention than I can give to it in a short space. Of particular importance, and often ignored in Christian ethics, is the third stage in this history of human agency: the role of the deceptive and enslaving anti-God powers. Then too, because that stage is ignored, most accounts of Christian ethics also ignore the fact of apocalyptic invasion, deliverance, and the new creation of the human agent. It is these aspects that I want to explore briefly in relation to the question of political agency.

Martyn has not given much direct attention to the (geo)political aspects of Paul's apocalyptic gospel—an emphasis that has, by contrast, occupied a good number among the more recent generation of Paul scholars. In Martyn's case, perhaps it is the nearly exclusive attention to the letter to the Galatians that has in the nature of the case limited his focus on political matters. There is, of course, plenty that is "political" in that letter: the separation of new Galatian converts from the gods of the cities in which they live, which would never have been simply a "religious" matter; the relationship of the churches in Galatia to their founding apostle; the relationship of the churches to the invading Teachers, with their supposed

---

49. Martyn, "Epilogue," 179–80 (emphases original).

political authority from the church in Jerusalem; the factions that would likely have formed from loyalties divided between the Teachers and Paul. All of this is addressed in good measure in Martyn's *Galatians*, and he clearly shows how the politics of the Crucified One is proclaimed by the apostle in the midst of all of that, for its judgment and healing. The gospel of Christ crucified and the powerful Spirit has already called the Galatian churches into being, each congregation being created as a "corporate, newly competent and newly addressable agent."

Indeed, exactly as the churches in Galatia are *corporate* agents created by the gospel, we should not underestimate how they are political entities and agents. The political character of their witness and agency gets somewhat lost, I believe, when Martyn speaks of the temptation of the Galatian churches to become Law observant as primarily a temptation to become (or remain) "religious." Martyn is, of course, emphatic that the gospel is not a "religious" alternative to the Law:

> In the sense in which I employ the word, religion is a human enterprise. Thus in Paul's view, religion is the polar opposite of God's apocalyptic act in Christ. . . . Gal 3:28 shows . . . that in the life of the church, worship of God is the corporate act in which
> - the religious distinction of sacred from profane is confessed to have been abolished. . . . The distinction between church and
> - world is in nature apocalyptic rather than religious.[50]

What is missing here is an explication of how "law"—not simply the Sinaitic Law, but also the "law of the land,"[51] city laws, Roman law—is itself what in good measure defines and maintains any political community as such, preserving it from remaining or disintegrating into a sheer contest of competing powers. To be sure, in Galatians the center of Paul's attention is the Sinaitic Law, and to be sure the Teachers are proposing that that Law must be *done* by human agents under a "two-actor" scheme. But it is important also to see that in this way the Teachers are not only exhorting the Galatians to become "religious," but also (or, precisely as religious) to become members of the theological-juridical-political community of Jews.[52] This would likely even be proposed as a genuine political benefit

50. Martyn, *Galatains*, 37.

51. I read somewhere, recently, that in ancient Greek one inflection of *nomos*, as *nómos*, means "law," whereas differently inflected, as *nomós*, it means the "land" in which a certain *nómos* is in force. If that is the case, there may be a legal-political coincidence in the single word.

52. At least not merely "religious" in the modern sense of religion as a sphere of belief and practice separate from the public, social, and political spheres of life.

to the Galatians, insofar as in becoming loyal to the God of the Crucified One they had separated themselves from the theological-juridical-
political communities (the towns and cities) of which they were previously
members. Left in what must have seemed a legal-political limbo by the
coming of the gospel, the Galatians would have been attracted by the offer
of a new juridical-political status, one that may even have promised some
legal protection.

The point of difference between Paul and the Teachers in this respect
is the same as the point of difference between Paul and the pagan authorities in the Galatian cities: that is, not the difference between religion and
not-religion, but the difference between the political community created
by the gospel, on the one hand, and the political communities created
either by pagan public observance or by observance of the Sinaitic Law,
on the other. Nevertheless, Martyn has clearly identified the fundamental
point of difference between the gospel-created political community and
any other political community: the distinction between church as political
community and world as political communities is apocalyptic. God him- •
self in the invasive gospel is immediately the creator and sustainer of this
political community. Judged from the point of view of worldly political
communities, defined and maintained as such "under law," the church can
only appear to be a-legal and an-archic, since nowhere is it exhorted by
the gospel to "obey the law(s)."[53] From the point of view of the gospel,
however, the apocalyptically created community is political in the most
concrete and direct way not because it obeys laws, which, both in their
being established and in their being obeyed, mediate the political reality
of the community. Rather, the gospel-created community is immediately
obedient to its *Kyrios*, who himself, with the Holy Spirit, is the *nomos* in

53. It is of crucial importance to see that Paul nowhere exhorts Gentiles to obey *Christian*
the laws of their cities or lands. "Not-Law" is as important here as it is with respect to *Anarchy*
Judaism. Failure to recognize this has been in part responsible for Gentile believers
thinking that the only relevant "not-Law" is "not-Sinaitic-Law," which has allowed all
kinds of opportunity for Gentile Christians to engage in various forms of opposition to
Jewish law observance—indeed, sometimes turning that opposition itself into another
law—while being perfectly "lawful" citizens of their lands. The apocalyptic community
is not defined by *any* law as such. Insofar as any nation's law or even a "law of the land"
comes to assume a primary place in the formation of Christians' and churches' identity
or agency and have their allegiance (their *pistis*), that law has assumed the enslaving power of the *stoicheia tou kosmou*. An unusually important, if oddly written (and
therefore somewhat neglected), work in this regard is Eller, *Christian Anarchy*. Eller •
works out a comprehensive vision of "Christian anarchy" by drawing extensively on
Paul, but also on the works of Johann and Christoph Blumhardt, Dietrich Bonhoeffer,
Jacques Ellul, and Karl Barth.

person—*nomos tou Christou, nomos tou pneumatou*; and the political form of life that "fulfills the law" in this community is summed up not in another "law" but in a "word" (*logos*): "love your neighbour as yourself." As Martyn writes, "It follows, then, that mutually loving behavior in the church is not a matter of *Law and order*, the former being the parent of the latter. It is a matter of *order and Law*, in the sense that the order of Christ's love proves to be the foundation for—indeed, proves to be—the Law of Christ ([Gal] 6:2)."[54]

If, in the sense we have just described, the church is most truly and immediately *the* political agent as it is redeemed through the crucified Messiah and moved by the powerful Spirit, we are left with a further question: How does this newly created, newly competent corporate agent enact its political witness among the nations? This question also hovers around the edges of Martyn's work, as he indicates in a recent footnote: "An important project for another setting: How is Paul's understanding of the human agent's history related to his view of the church's life in the civic, Adamic society?"[55] In fact, because this essay is already long, this must also be for me a question for another setting. I will simply conclude with a couple of suggestive comments.

First, as participating politically even now in the divine apocalypse, the messianic community is already being redeemed from the wreckage of worldly political history. And it is being thus delivered because the form of its political agency and witness is the law of Christ, which is love. The "civic, Adamic society," particularly as represented by the "ruling authorities," enacts its laws and "history-making" agency still in the grip of the anti-God powers; the form of that world is passing away. As such, those ruling authorities cannot be viewed by the messianic community as doing much other than adding to the wreckage of history. They serve no *redemptive* purpose. Rather, their work of administering law and punishment, which in Romans 13 Paul says is appointed to them by God, assumes only a negative, indeed, an imprisoning and often deadly "providential" role in history. The "ruling authorities" mete out "wrath." That can never be the calling and task of the messianic community created by the gospel, as Paul makes clear in 12:17–31. In terms of the gospel, the legal-political role of the ruling authorities stands in a contradictory relationship to the true end of history, which has arrived in the messianic apocalypse. While we

54. Martyn, *Galatians*, 513; the discussion of these issues in Comment 48 (502–14) is of crucial importance.

55. Martyn, "Epilogue," 182 n. 29.

"submit" (*hypotassō*) to the authorities, we neither owe them loyalty and trust (*pistis*) nor are we called to "obey" (*hypakoē*) either them or their laws. Simultaneously living beyond the Law and submitting to the authorities that exist, the messianic political community enacts its own political life and witness according to the "word" "love your neighbour as yourself," and so fulfills the law of Christ. In this, it is redeemed from the wreckage of history because it does not seek to bring about just ends through its own power, but has become a participant in the justice of God that has come upon it—the divine apocalypse in Christ and the Spirit.

Second, Jesus Messiah, as himself the end of all things which *comes* in the Spirit, gives power and shape to the messianic community's witness to justice. As Spirit-moved, this community is active and not passive. As Martyn writes, "Led by the Spirit, this communally competent agent is neither alone nor passive, being literally inspired and collectively called by God to vigorous, world-wide activity; for, forming Christ in their communities, God places this communal agent in the front trenches of his war of cosmic liberation *for all*."[56] That said, as cruciform, this communally competent agent is not caught up in locating those points of worldly-political leverage from which it might launch the next "conservative" effort to keep things as they are, or the next "progressive" movement in order to "advance toward" or "bring about" the kingdom of God or at least a "higher" stage of history.[57] Freed from that kind of compulsiveness of purpose through sharing in the crucifixion of its Lord, the "vigorous world-wide activity" of this communal agent is always being *given over* as "weak messianic power" (Benjamin), to the end that *comes* as its fulfillment, that is, to the one who is himself the Love that "never ends."

B. Seems inconsistent with A.

56. Ibid., 182.
57. See Griffiths, "Cross."

95

3

Paul's Apocalyptic Cross and Philosophy

*Reading 1 Corinthians
with Giorgio Agamben[1] and Alain Badiou[2]*

Alexandra R. Brown

STUDIES THAT FIND THE Apostle Paul's apocalyptic orientation to be central to his understanding of the Christ event and the good news he proclaims about that event have proliferated in the last several decades, thanks in large part to the groundbreaking efforts of J. Louis Martyn. That the apocalyptic Paul has taken a place in a growing body of theological work beyond the biblical studies guild is a testimony to the coherence of this portrait and its resilience over time and countervailing trends in Pauline theology. In this essay I hope to contribute in two ways to the growing apocalyptically informed cross-disciplinary conversation: first, I will set an exegetical example for an apocalyptically informed reading of Paul. Second, from the vantage point of this example, I will explore certain characteristics of the contemporary secular philosophical appropriation of Paul with an ear toward the remarkable resonances these studies sound with the apocalyptic Paul.

---

1. Agamben, *Time.*
2. Badiou, *Saint Paul.*

AN EXAMPLE FROM 1 CORINTHIANS

The opening chapters of Paul's first letter to Corinth serve as a sort of apocalyptic map for reading the rest of the letter. The "Word of the cross" discourse in chapters 1–2 functions performatively to dislodge the readers/hearers from intellectual and social structures—Gentile wisdom, Jewish signs—according to which the cross is folly, leaving them open to an epistemology of the cross by which they know Christ no longer in a merely human way, but as knowers of and in a "new creation" (2 Cor 5:16).[3] Applying the insights of the analytic philosopher J. L. Austin, I have proposed elsewhere that Paul's "Word of the cross" functioned as a performative utterance related, in part, to the capacity of language to break down old structures of thought and to create a space for a new world to emerge.[4] This operation in Paul's preaching I characterize as "apocalyptic," using the term Paul himself uses to characterize both the event of God's entry into the world and the cosmic effects of that event (e.g., Gal 1:16–18). The Word of that event (*logos tou staurou*), we might say its "proclamation," has power, Paul suggests, to communicate to hearers in such a way as to bring the new creation to bear on communal life, thus liberating people from enslaving powers that thwart human beings and the whole creation.

Insofar as Paul's letters press for new readings of time and history (*chronos* and *kairos*), cosmos and new creation (*kosmos* and *kainē ktisis*), law and its fulfillment (*nomos* and *teleios*), they envision, to be sure, a new world order already in progress and awaiting a consummation, as Paul says, on the "day of the Lord" (e.g., 1 Thess 5:2). First Corinthians in particular demands our attention to the political implications of that new order by juxtaposing theological and ethical modes of discourse in verbal contexts persistently punctuated by *aporia* and disjuncture. This wedding of content (new creation) and style (disjuncture, *aporia*) in the letter provides a starting point for reading Paul as a thinker deeply engaged in a kind of radical "political" discourse.

In very different ways, two contemporary philosophers, Giorgio Agamben and Alain Badiou, both post-Marxist, secular Europeans, resonate with Paul's apocalyptic announcement in 1 Corinthians 1–2 of the *end* of worldly philosophy (*sophia tou kosmou*). Each sees Paul as the critic

---

3. Here and throughout this paper I reflect the influence of J. Louis Martyn, whose reading of Pauline apocalyptic is central to the questions I pose to the philosophers. His essay on "Epistemology" and 2 Cor 5:16 is particularly relevant to questions relating Paul's thought to philosophy.

4. Brown, *Cross*; Austin, *How*.

of current political and economic systems in which, for example, legal rule becomes the agent of violence (Agamben), or in which capitalist monetary practices at once reduce all to the "count" and encourage increasing fragmentation of competing groups into closed identities (Badiou). In what follows I hope to show certain overlapping areas of discourse between Paul and these philosophers and to highlight aspects of the philosophical readings that are particularly relevant to current debates about the apocalyptic Paul in biblical studies and theology.

PAULINE THEMES AND PHILOSOPHICAL OPERATIONS

To advance the inquiry proposed here, I will set out a few broad categories relevant to Paul's thought (across the letters) that are shared widely by biblical scholars and, in part, by our philosophers. Each set of terms is, by virtue of its centrality in Paul's thought, also pertinent to a comprehensive *apocalyptic* reading of Paul's letters. Indeed the persuasiveness of the apocalyptic reading of Paul rests on its cogency *across* the categories.

History and Revelation

Paul's term "revelation" (*apokalypsis*) describes a divine inbreaking into human time which reconfigures temporality.[5] The implications of this reconfiguring are vigorously debated in analyses of Paul's letters. Whether or not Paul supports a salvation history approach to the divine act in time, such that the apocalypse of Christ *fits within prior events* of salvation history, is a matter of much discussion. An alternative view, characteristic of recent apocalyptic readings of Paul, is that the apocalypse of God's Christ disrupts the salvation history schema, neither restoring the original creation nor completing it, but establishing a wholly new creation radically independent of the old temporal frame (e.g., the schema of this world that is passing away, 1 Cor 1:31). This latter reading reflects the emphasis Paul places on the Christ event as an apocalypse (*apokalypsis/apokalyptō*) in, for example, 1 Corinthians 1–2 and 1 Corinthians 15 and his declaration

---

5. See, for example, arresting temporal language such as that in 1 Cor 7:29— *ho kairos synestalmenos* ("the appointed time is drawn up . . .")—and Rom 11:5— *en tō nyn kairō leimma kat' eklogē charitos gegonen* ("in the now time there is a remnant chosen by grace . . .").

in Galatians 6:14 of the *kainē ktsis* (new creation), which, by implication, replaces the old universe and its standard binary structures.[6]

Paul's ample use of *kairos* (time) terminology reflects this temporal element in his apocalyptic outlook. The "now time" in Romans 11:5 reveals the remnant chosen by grace; *kairos* in Romans 13:5 marks the accomplished transition from night to day; the "drawn-up kairos" in 1 Corinthians 7:29 signals the time in which the *schēma* of the present world is already passing away. Terms like "new creation" (*kainē ktisis*), "end things" (*eschata*), and "ends of the ages" (*ta tēlē tōn aiōnōn*) signal pervasive temporal effects of the *apokalypsis* Paul announces. Also within Pauline temporal discourse—and yet breaking away from standard temporal markers—we find his characteristic iterations of the death of Jesus by crucifixion (*thanatos, stauros*), his resurrection (*anastasis*), and the expectation of his Parousia in glory, all themes that take their bearings in the apocalyptic action of God in Christ.

Election and Peoplehood

Paul's understanding of God's election (*eklogē*) of Israel and the election and calling (*eklegomai, eklektos, kaleō, klēsis*) of the church (*ekklēsia*) are at the heart of much traditional Pauline interpretation, and are also central to the interpretations offered by our contemporary philosophers. Questions concerning the continuity of Jewish law (*nomos*), covenant (*diathēkē*), promise (*epangelia*), and the problem of Jewish-Gentile relations within the churches, including the discussion of the remnant (*leimma*), dominate certain letters (Galatians and Romans) and simmer on the backburner in others. Closely connected are the relation of "all" (*pas, panta*) to "part" (*meros*) and "fullness" (*plērōma*), and questions concerning the body (*soma*), whether the *soma* is the place of circumcision as in Galatians, the locus of sexual relations (1 Cor 7), or the corporate "body of Christ" constituting the church (1 Cor 12).

Soteriological Themes and Themes of Deliverance

A final category takes up those terms and concepts in Paul focused on the *telos* of apocalypse as salvation (*sōteria*) or deliverance (*ryomia/ryomenos*). Soteriological terms in Paul include: justification/rectification (*dikaioō/*

---

6. Martyn, "Apocalyptic Antinomies."

dikaiosynē); faith (*pistis*); salvation (*sōteria*); redemption (*apolytrōsis*); deliver/deliverer (*ryomai/ryomenos*); spirit (*pneuma*); sin (*hamartia*); flesh (*sarx*); slave/slavery (*doulos/douleia*); power (*dynamis*); love (*agapē*); grace (*charis*). These terms are significantly concentrated in apocalyptic contexts in Paul (i.e., contexts in which vocabulary and conceptuality evoking divine in-breaking is prominent) and are strongly represented in the philosophers' accounts. Another term of central importance for Paul's eschatological and soteriological thought is *katargeō*, often translated "nullify," "destroy," or "bring to an end"—as in the fate of Death itself at the end time (1 Cor 15:26)—but by Agamben as "to make inoperative" (Rom 7:5-6). Also in Agamben, the terms "separated" (*aphorismenos*), "use/to make use" (*chresis/chresai*), and "summed up/recapitulated" (*anakephalaioomai*) contribute to what in traditional exegesis and theology might be classified as soteriology.

Each category above contributes to Paul's "political theology," if by "political" we mean, broadly, the implications of his thought for shared life in human community.[7] The situation of the gospel in time and history, its implications for understanding "peoplehood," and the ways in which salvation, redemption, or deliverance of the creation are envisioned all constitute, in this sense, political interests. Each set of Pauline terms likewise finds a place within our philosophers' concerns about the human subject in political community. In what follows I will summarize moments in each thinker's treatment of Paul which link most closely to the key categories of Paul's thought outlined above and which reflect sometimes familiar, sometimes strikingly new, hermeneutical insights. First, to Agamben.

GIORGIO AGAMBEN

The Italian political philosopher Giorgio Agamben (b. 1942) engages Pauline categories most directly in the areas of law and peoplehood. His interest in how law constitutes the political subject draws him particularly to Paul's treatment of the law (*nomos*) and the remnant (*leimma*). For Agamben, Paul's message is messianic in that in announcing the "time of the end" it opens a way to redemption in the present, yet only through a division of law against itself and a people against itself that renders both

---

7. I do not mean to engage directly the sorts of proposals that come from reading Paul as an interlocutor with or critic of the Roman Empire per se, though his cosmology does set him against all cosmic "powers and principalities" that thwart creation and contribute to the longing and groaning of the whole universe.

"inoperative" with respect to possession but "useful" with respect to vocation as we shall see below.

History and Revelation

Paul's messianism and his idea of the distinct messianic time inaugurated by Jesus Messiah[8] constitutes for Agamben a *kairos* that dwells *within* chronological time, neither supplementing it nor completing it, but nevertheless "grasping and fulfilling it." This time is *"the time of the end,"* not *"the end of time,"* and its power is to create the conditions for "grasping redemption 'as though not' grasping it."

> [T]he messianic time is not another day, homogenous to the others. It is rather, *in* time, the disconnection through which we can—by a hair—*grasp* the time, and accomplish it.[9]

Or again,

> The Messiah has already arrived, the messianic event has already happened, but its presence contains within itself another time, which stretches its *parousia*, not in order to defer it, but, on the contrary to make it *graspable*. For this reason, each instant may be, to use [Walter] Benjamin's words, "the small door through which the Messiah enters."[10]

The messianic signs of this "graspable" time become evident to Agamben in the various ways Paul renders the key notions of law (*nomos*), the remnant (*leimma*), and calling (*klēsis*) in his letters.

Law and Its Status in Messianic Time

Paul's critique of law (*nomos*), in Agamben's view, is consonant with a reading of law as capable of producing its own "state of exception," the legal exemption sometimes deemed appropriate by the sovereign authority of the state for stepping outside the rule of law in the public interest. The defense of totalitarianism is grounded in such an exception. An individual or group excepted from the rule of law is *homo sacer*, "sacred

---

8. For Agamben, *Christos* is, in this sense, a political designation.

9. Agamben, *Time*, 72.

10. Ibid., 71.

man," outside the law, and indeed outside the lawful community.[11] For Agamben, imprisonment without due process at Guantanamo Bay is a current instance of this legal violence in action, and the Nuremburg laws (1935) a historical instance.

But lest we misunderstand Agamben's intent to be the *dissolution* of law in order to eliminate its subversive power,[12] it is important to see how Agamben attends to the nuances of *nomos* in Paul. Reading across selected passages in Romans, 3:11–12, 27 and 31 and 7:12, he finds that

> Paul goes to great lengths to specify the way in which *nomos* is set against *epangelia* (promise) and *pistis* (faith). At stake is the law in its prescriptive and normative aspect. . . . Rather than being an antinomy that involves two unrelated and completely heterogenous principles, here the opposition lies in the *nomos* itself, between its normative and promissive elements. . . . The messianic law is the law of faith and not just the negation of the law."[13]

To understand the "non-normative" aspect of law in messianic time, Agamben lands upon the Pauline word *katargeō*, which he translates "I make inoperative, I deactivate, I suspend the efficacy of . . ." Paul, he notes, makes frequent use of this word, which is used very rarely in Greek literature before him.[14] Shunning the translation "I destroy"—"even the most elementary knowledge of Greek," he notes, "would have shown that the positive equivalent of *katargeō* is not *poieō* but *energeō*"—he cites Romans 7:5–6 as a sample case:

11. "The first thing to note about this 'sacred man' is that he was not sacred in any reverential sense—in fact he was closer to the opposite. *Homo sacer* is a juridical term from archaic Roman law designating an individual who, in response to a grave trespass, is cast out of the city. . . . This 'sacred man' is thereby removed from the continuum of social activity and communal legislation; the only law that still applies to him is the one that irrevocably casts him out" (Durantaye, *Agamben*, 206).

12. An insightful argument that contradictions arise across Agamben's oeuvre regarding the nature of state sovereignty and the ways he envisions beyond it is offered by Passavant, "Contradictory State."

13. Agamben, *Time*, 95. At least hints of the nuance offered by Paul Meyer ("Worm at the Core") concerning the law's vulnerability to be taken into the hands of Sin seem to echo here. See also the related argument in Martyn, "Nomos."

14. So, in Euripides, in the context of "hands left idle," and in Polybus, with the meaning "to be inactive." 26 of the verb's 27 uses in the NT, Agamben notes, belong to "Pauline" letters. Two of those uses, however, occur in 2 Timothy and Hebrews. Thus, my count renders 25 uses in undisputed Pauline texts of 28 uses in the NT. Agamben, *Time*, 96

For when we were in the flesh, the passions of sin were enacted [*enērgeitō*] through the law in our members to bring forth fruit unto death. But now we are deactivated [*katergēthēmen*, "made inoperative"] from the law.

Later in this context, Agamben develops the "inoperative" as a taking out of the *energeia* that corresponds to *dynamis en astheneia teleitai*, "power realizing itself in weakness" (2 Cor 12:9). The fulfillment of the law in Romans 10:4 can only be understood in light of its "deactivation." And if we ask, what of Romans 3:31?—"Do we then deactivate [*katargoumen*] the law by faith? By no means! We uphold (*histanomen*) the law"—Agamben answers, "that which is deactivated, taken out of *energeia* is not annulled, but conserved and held onto for its fulfillment."[15] The dialectic rehearsed in Agamben's treatment of *katargeō*[16] echoes Luther's, then Hegel's, then Barth's rendering of *katargeō* by way of the German verb *aufheben*. Luther, aware of the double meaning "to abolish" and "to conserve," sets the stage for Hegel's dialectic, which Agamben characterizes as "nothing more than a secularization of Christian theology."[17]

The weight of its influence over time warrants a look at Paul's fuller use of the term *katargeō*. In what would seem the least ambiguous use of the term in 1 Corinthians 15:26 we read, "The last enemy to be *katargeitai* is death." Is Death here "made inoperative" or is it "destroyed?" Or again, in 1 Corinthians 15:24, is every rule and authority "made inoperative" or "destroyed" (*katargēsē*)? In these heightened eschatological instances, translations more often render "destroy."[18] In 1 Corinthians 13:10–12, however, as the imperfect "passes away" (*katargēthēsetai*), the analogy is to the passing from childhood to adulthood, a model of development, not destruction. Elsewhere, Paul's language about law and its status suggests a meaning closer to "deactivate:" "Do we deactivate/destroy [*katargoumen*] law through faith? Certainly not! But law is upheld [*histanomen*]!" (Rom 3:31). The related and notoriously difficult text in 2 Corinthians 3:13—"not like Moses, who would put a veil over his face so that the Israelites might not gaze at the outcome of what was being brought to an end/fading away/

15. Ibid., 98.

16. *Kata* (down) + *argos* (inactive, idle, delayed).

17. Agamben sees in *aufheben/Aufhebung* that "Hegel used a weapon against theology furnished by theology itself and that this weapon is genuinely messianic" (*Time*, 99).

18. RSV, ESV, and NIV all render "destroy" in both vv. 24 and 26. KJV renders "put down" in v. 24 and "destroy" in v. 26. The ASV renders "abolish" in both verses.

being nullified [*katargoumenou*]"—demonstrates perhaps most clearly the openness of Paul's expression to Agamben's dialectical rendering.

Certainly this is second-order language, rich in semantic possibilities. Elsewhere Paul can pose even the Word of the cross as something that might be "emptied" by preaching in "words of [worldly] wisdom" (1 Cor 1:17). Something of the sort may be in play where, for Paul, law and even death are, in a sense, emptied of effectiveness, that is to say, made inoperative by the world's standards. Finally, Agamben suggests a law of faith set against the law of works, the Abrahamic promissory law against the Mosaic Law, but nevertheless a law within which the messianic subject lives.[19] The continuing vitality of law thus conceived and its constitutive character for the messianic community is evident too in Agamben's understanding of the remnant in Paul.

The Remnant

Through his notion of the "remnant" (*leimma*), argues Agamben, Paul points to a linguistic and conceptual apparatus that addresses both the insidious legal division of exception and its messianic *Aufhebung*. In Paul's "remnant" (Rom 11:5) Agamben finds

> a transcendental . . . operation that divides the divisions of the law themselves and renders them *inoperative*, without ever reaching any final ground. No universal man, no Christian can be found in the depths of the Jew and Greek, neither as a principle nor as an end; all that is left is a remnant and the impossibility of the Jew or the Greek to coincide with himself . . .
>
> At a decisive instant, the elected people, every people, will necessarily situate itself as a remnant, a not-all.[20]

Agamben's remnant discourse is dense in part because he seems to go against the plain reading of the text to argue that Paul's remnant is neither a numerical portion of Israel nor a way of designating Israel as a whole.[21] What remnant (*leimma*) signifies, rather, is a particular relation of part to whole, *meros* to *pas*, a relation proper to messianic time, "the now time" (*en tō nyn kairō*; Rom 11:5) when a remnant is produced, "chosen by grace." For Agamben, the characteristic Pauline and messianic response to

19. See Passavant, "Contradictory State," 165–66.

20. Agamben, *Time*, 52–53, 55.

21. Ibid., 54–55.

the division of the law is to cut that division with a new division, namely, that of *sarx/pneuma*.[22]

> In this sense, the messianic aphorism (from *aphorizō*, to sepa-rate) can be seen as a cut of Apelles that does not have an object in itself, but divides the divisions traced out by the law. The subset "Jews" is thus divided into "apparent Jews" or Jews ac-cording to the flesh (*Ioudaios . . . en tō phanerō en sarki*), and hidden Jews, Jews "according to the breath (*en tō kryptō . . . en pneumati*; Rom. 2:28–29). The same thing happens to non-Jews (even if Paul does not explicitly say so). . . . This means that messianic division introduces a remnant into the law's overall division of the people, and Jews and non-Jews are constitutively "not all."[23]

The remnant now is more an apparatus than a particular subject, which operates to define experience in the messianic "now" as still *partial*. It is the *instrument* of salvation more than its object. Destined in Paul's eschatological vision for the All (*plērōma*), in "real time" there is nothing other than the remnant. For Agamben, the recognition of this messianic apparatus brings into focus in a new way debates about the particular and the universal, for, as he says, "the messianic cut of Apelles never adds up to a universal."

> For Paul it is never a matter of "tolerating" or getting past dif-ferences in order to pinpoint a sameness or a universal lurking behind. The universal is not a transcendent principle through which differences may be perceived—such a perspective of tran-scendence is not available to Paul. Rather, this "transcendental" involves an operation that divides the divisions of the law them-selves and renders them inoperative *without ever reaching any final ground*.[24]

Agamben insists, then, on the difference between overturning or abolishing a law on the one hand and making it "inoperative" on the other, to show the necessity of a *suspension* within *the law* that resists the collapsing of the law as norm and the law as exception. Of particular in-terest to theological readers of Paul may be Agamben's locution "without ever reaching any final ground." Whether or not Agamben accounts for divine eschatological reservation, he insists on an apparatus of *reservation*

22. Ibid., 49.
23. Ibid., 50.
24. Ibid., 52, emphasis added.

characteristic of Pauline messianic time. More clarity on this point emerges as he turns his attention to the term *klēsis* (calling).

Calling (*Klēsis*) and Salvation (*Sōtēria*)

Together, the coincidence in Agamben's Paul of delay and presence in messianic time and the division of the division of the law so that only a *remnant* remains sets the conditions for messianic "use" but not "possession" of *klēsis* (calling, vocation). The one called, then, is not a new entity with new limits, boundaries, and rights, nor one who is possessed of a *truer* vocation, nor one who withdraws from the world into eschatological indifference. The messianic *klēsis*, participating now in the familiar dialectic,

> calls the vocation itself, as though it were an urgency that works it from within and hollows it out, nullifying it in the very gesture of maintaining it and dwelling within it.[25]

This, for Agamben, is the key to understanding Paul's temporally conditioned *hos me* ("as though not") in 1 Corinthians 7:25–31, where Paul does not set one vocation against another, but <u>every vocation against</u> *itself*—married as though not married, mourning as though not mourning, buying and selling as though not buying and selling. <u>Each vocation is</u> <u>emptied of its possessive quality to be appropriated for a particular mes-</u>sianic *use*. Hence, "[t]o remain in the calling 'as not' means to not ever make the calling an object of ownership, only *use*."[26]

Agamben is doing philosophy, not theology. He is speaking to his colleagues in the saeculum about political life; he is not proclaiming the Word of God. <u>With his starting point in human consciousness and agency,</u>

• he finds a (politically) <u>redeeming apparatus in Paul's language of the rem-</u><u>nant that guards against totalizing schemes of the universal Christian.</u> For him, messianic time relies on what he calls the "recapitulation" (he cites Eph 1:10) of past time in one present moment of *kairos*. The summoning of the past into the present produces, he wants to say, a redemptive moment in time, a faith in "what is lost." Even the linearity of time itself is lost; in its place is something he sees in Paul's vision of the "ends of the ages" having come (1 Cor 10:11). Again, a sort of division of something against itself "redeems," in Agamben's interpretation of Paul. The coincidence of

Key

25 Ibid., 24.

26. Ibid., 22.

past and present in one moment, the "now time" (Rom 13:11) wherein the present recognizes itself in what is passing away (1 Cor 7:31), is key. But if Agamben finds redemption in a certain retrieval of the past that prevents totalitarianism in any given moment, what is "redemptive" for Badiou is something totally new.

ALAIN BADIOU

A Moroccan-born French philosopher long committed to various forms of Marxist and Maoist political activism, Alain Badiou (b. 1937) sees in Paul the "militant apostle of universalism" who was "conscripted by" the truth event of Christ's resurrection.[27] His reading of Paul is very different from Agamben's, and yet the two have been compared as similarly "preoccupied with the complexity of number and counting, with two terms that may be mistaken for one," and similar too in "registering this dialectic as a relation between two rather than a pure one."[28]

Paul as Militant Figure

It is Paul's faithfulness to the truth event of resurrection that makes possible his radical critique and transformation of society. In Badiou's conception,

> a poet-thinker of the Event, as well as one who practices and states the invariant traits of what could be called the militant figure. He brings forth the entirely human connection . . . between a general idea of a rupture, an overturning, and that of a thought practice that is this rupture's subjective materiality.[29]

Resurrection as Truth Event

Badiou employs mathematical set theory to distinguish between "being" and "event," or the set of "there is" and the set of "it happens." *Being* is accessible to knowledge and characterized by multiplicity (it is the locus of individuals and particularisms). *Event* produces the truth of that

---

27. L. L. Welborn notes and admires "Badiou's ability to articulate the relevance of Paul's gospel in a secular idiom . . . for purposes of theologico-political reflection" (Welborn, "Mortal Site," 294).

28. Kaufman, "Saturday of Messianic Time," 40.

29. Badiou, *Saint Paul*, 2.

ontological situation and emerges from it in a "contingent, unpredictable and undemonstrable way."[30] The resurrection of Christ is, though a "fable," the truth event that seizes Paul and renders him a subject. It comes to him as a "caesura, a thunderbolt," totally incalculable in terms of his prior constitution within the knowledge systems of Judaism, Hellenism, and the Roman Empire. In the wake of this eruption of truth, Paul becomes its militant activist "armed" with the singular and universal truth of the gospel. Badiou elaborates the Damascus Road experience:

> Is the term "conversion" appropriate to what happened on the road to Damascus? It was a thunderbolt, a caesura, and not a dialectical reversal. It was a conscription constituting a new subject: "By the grace of God I am what I am (*eimi ho eimi*, 1 Cor 15:10). What his absolutely aleatory intervention on the road to Damascus summons is the "I am" as such. . . . Paul's faith is that from which he begins as a subject, and nothing leads up to it. The event—"it happened," purely and simply in the anonymity of the road—is the subjective sign of the event proper that is the Resurrection of Christ. Within Paul it is the (ré)surgence [(ré)-surrection] of the subject.[31]

For Badiou, the discourse on the cross in 1 Corinthians 1:18–31 (Christ crucified, a stumbling block to Jews and a scandal to Greeks) succinctly states the revolutionary eruption of a truth event that resists classification by any pre-existing master narrative. It reduces to nothing things that are and brings into being things that are not (1 Cor 1:28). While for Badiou the event is not the crucifixion, but the "fable" of resurrection, what the event creates is a radical subject who stands against the status quo, a revolutionary.

Key

---

30. Christopher Morse comments lucidly on Badiou's set theory: "The invention of set theory—by which multiples are presented as belonging together not by prefigured series, or, ontologically stated, in categories of like substance, but by setting of infinitely varied inconsistencies in which what is out of order provides the condition for new orderings—make possible for the first time, so one interpreter as observed, a rational concept of infinity and its functions that does not require reference to a *Deus ex machina*" ("Resurrection as Myth," 261). See also Morse's clarifying attention to Badiou in *Difference*, 66–69.

31. Badiou, *Saint Paul*, 17.

The Subtraction of Difference: "In Christ, no male and female, slave and free, Jew and Greek"

The singularity of the event has as its political corollary the end of identity politics and of law in the hands of a "national model," driven by "identitarian verification."[32] Here Badiou's mathematical set theory demands a "subtraction":

> Paul's unprecedented gesture consists in subtracting truth from the communitarian grasp, be it that of a people, a city, an empire, a territory, or a social class. What is true . . . cannot be reduced to any objective aggregate, either by its cause or by its destination.[33]

In this conviction, Badiou wishes to presage—via Paul as his militant example—"an end to identity politics and solely communitarian ethics." Modern French law is a target of Badiou's critique:

> Abandoning all universal principle, identitarian verification—which is never anything but police monitoring—comes to take precedence over the definition or application of the law. This means that, just as under Pétain, when ministers saw nothing wrong with defining the Jew as prototype of the non-French, all legislation would be accompanied by the required identity protocols, and subsets of the population would be defined each time by their *special status*.[34]

While this last citation comes near to Agamben's treatment of the law and the state of exception, Agamben will eschew any solution that posits a "universal" principle. This marks a major difference in their respective proposals for a more just political life.

The Foundation of Universalism: The One for All without Exception

Paul's genuinely revolutionary conviction, says Badiou, is that the sign of the One is the "for all" or the "without exception."

32. Badiou, *Saint Paul*, 9.
33. Ibid., 5.
34. Ibid., 9.

> That there is but a single God must be understood not as a philosophical speculation concerning substance or the Supreme Being, but on the basis of a structure of address. The One is that which inscribes no difference in that to which it addresses itself. The One is only insofar as it is for *all*...[35]

At the same time, Badiou sees in Paul's truth event an "indifference that tolerates difference." What matters, he says, is that differences show, "through the ordeal of their division," that they are capable of welcoming the universal that "happens to them like grace." Difference matters, but only insofar as it is (and remains) the substratum that allows recognition of the unicity of faith.[36] Hence the convolutions of the argument about head coverings in 1 Corinthians 11, where Paul at once confirms and denies the importance of the difference male/female.[37]

Law and Grace

Whereas Agamben approaches the law and its double division as the *key* to messianic vocation through a certain rendering of the "remnant," Badiou sees law increasingly as the sign of the particular and partial that cannot be inscribed in the One. He finds the same notion in Paul, for whom "law always designates a particularity, hence a difference. It is not possible for it (law) to be an operation of the One because it addresses its fallacious 'One' only to those who acknowledge and practice the injunctions it specifies."[38] Grace, on the other hand, says Badiou, is what comes "without being due."

> The polemic against the "what is due," against the logic of right and duty, lies at the heart of Paul's refusal of works and law. . . . Only what is absolutely gratuitous can be addressed to all. Only gratuitousness and grace measure up to a universal problem.[39]

Here we may understand the "universal problem" as the organization of human life around the void that is death.[40]

35. Ibid., 76.

36. Boyarin's *A Radical Jew* is the clearest articulation of a critique of Paul as a Platonist whose One obliterates the distinction, the particularity, and ultimately the existence of the people of Israel.

37. Badiou, *Saint Paul*, 106.

38. Ibid., 76

39. Ibid., 77

40. Welborn draws out the meaning of Badiou's assertion that "the fundamental

SEARCHING EXEGETICALLY FOR PAUL'S RESPONSE TO HIS PRESENT PHILOSOPHICAL INTERPRETERS

Agamben and Badiou have accomplished remarkably rich and provocative readings of Paul, challenging Paul's usual interpreters to awareness of large ideas astir in the text that have a different sort of application than those imagined in more traditional historical and theological accounts. Insofar as each philosopher focuses on the identity of the singular "subject" and the consequences for collective identity, it is no surprise that Paul's own *topoi* of sovereignty, law, difference (Jew/Gentile), and conversion or transformation (the resurrection as truth event), or messianic recognition of "the time of the end" (eschatology), are prominent in their arguments. Where Badiou and Agamben seem to intersect is in what might be termed the "soteriology of the community." For Badiou, the community will be saved by trust in a universal truth as event; for Agamben, it is through the division of the law and of calling generated in messianic time (read the relation of each instant to the Messiah[41]) and forever leaving the remnant.

But how do these ideas behave when we call them to stand once again in the context—historical, cultural, and theological—of Paul's letters? By taking up specific texts within one letter, 1 Corinthians, with the observations of our philosophers in the foreground, I hope to allow a sort of bifocal vision to stretch my own exegetical practices beyond accustomed boundaries, but also to test the philosophers' use of Paul within his own linguistic, epistolary context. In the end, I am not interested in finding the philosophers right or wrong with respect to their readings of Paul, but rather in hearing with greater acuity the conversation between the "way the words run" in Paul's first-century context and their new constellations in contemporary philosophical discourse.

BACK TO 1 CORINTHIANS

First Corinthians, written ca. 54–55 CE, brings together Paul's longest reflection on the cross (1:17 ff) with his most extensive treatment of the resurrection of the dead (15:12–57), an event that accompanies the destruction (or deactivation; *katargeō*) of all powers inimical to God, after which "God may be all in all [*hina ē ho theos ta panta en pasin*]" (1 Cor

---

ontological characteristic of an event is to inscribe, to name the situated void of that for which it is the event" ("Mortal Site," 298, citing Badiou, *Ethics*, 69).

41. Agamben, *Time*, 76.

15:28). Between chapter 2 and chapter 15 is an extended discourse on the body (*soma*), remarkable for its interweaving of personal, corporate, and political dimensions of somatic life, all of which rely significantly, for Paul, on manifestations of that other entity, the Spirit. Across the letter, there is a persistent pattern of association of part (*meros*) to whole (*pas/panta*), some of it connected directly to *soma* language.[42]

Paul's primary address to the problem of factionalism (*erides*) in the Corinthian church (1:10–11) comes in an extended discourse on the cross of Christ in 1:18–31. In this rhetorically rich and poetic unit, whose aim seems to be to open up a new way of being, we note that for Paul, contra Badiou, the event that provokes *caesura* and rupture is not, in the first place, resurrection, but crucifixion. Even if it is hyperbole, it is surely central to Paul's message that he says in this context, "I decided to know nothing among you except Christ and him crucified" (2:2). Note what happens to the conventions of language as Paul announces the *logos tou staurou*:

> For the word of the cross is to those who are perishing [*apollyme-nois*] folly [*moria*], but to us who are being saved [*sōzomenois*] power [*dynamis tou Theou*].

Already the cosmos as defined by conventional paired opposites (e.g., opposites employed by the Stoics and the Wisdom tradition to confirm the divine order) is crumbling. We expect folly to be paired with its opposite, wisdom, but find power there instead.[43] And from the perspective of the conventionally ordered world, things only get worse. For God makes foolish the wisdom of the world (1:20) and has resolved to save the world through folly (1:21b). Later, the jolting reminder comes again: "the wisdom of this world is folly with God" (3:19). Here the Word (*logos*) works in a particular linguistic context to dislodge readers from their accustomed world. This is an aspect of its dynamic apocalyptic nature, its performative power; by this power to dislocate, the Word begins to create the conditions under which the readers/hearers may be transformed and transferred into a new world.[44] It is the cross (the crucifixion of God's own

---

42. See 1 Cor 12:27: "Now you are the body of Christ and, *part by part* [*merous*], its members [*melē*]. See also the highly significant uses in 13:8–10, 12. 13:9 stands as a useful warning for our efforts here: "For we know in partial ways [*merous*] and we prophecy only in parts [fragments?]."

43. See, for example, Sir 21:16: "Like a house that has vanished, so has wisdom to a fool." In the strange pairing here is what Paul Ricoeur called (in reference to Aristotle's *Poetics*) the "semantic shock" of a good metaphor (Kearney, *Paul Ricoeur*, 40).

44. Brown, *Cross*, 76.

Son) that is power. This event in some sense fulfills or confirms the divine judgment on merely human or worldly wisdom, but also sets in motion the salvation (*soteria*) of God, which culminates in resurrection, when God is all in all. ⌐ key

Paul's use of Scripture in this context is especially revealing. Verses 1:19–21 cite Isa 29:14 LXX directly, with the exception of the last word, where Paul substitutes "I will nullify" (*atheteso*) for Isaiah's "I will hide" (*krypso*). Thus, we read at verse 19:

> I will destroy the wisdom of the wise and the cleverness of the
> clever I will nullify.

Paul's use of this citation seems to echo its larger context in Isaiah, for Isaiah goes on to outline the false, self-exalting perceptions of Israel:

> You turn things upside down!
>   Shall the potter be regarded as the clay?
> that the thing made should say of its maker,
>   "He did not make me";
> or the thing formed of him who formed it,
>   "He has no understanding." (Isa 29:16)

But a new day comes in 29:18:

> In that day the deaf shall hear
>   the words of a book,
> And out of their gloom and darkness,
>   the eyes of the blind shall see.

The word the prophet brings here is in ways like the *logos tou staurou*; it brings judgment against false wisdom and it brings new sight. But *unlike* Isaiah's message, the Word of the cross does not *first* meet failure which is *then* followed by God's reversal. Rather, the Word of the cross, like a parable of Jesus, creates obduracy and comprehension *simultaneously*, so that the single subject lives at the juncture of the old and the new, "the ends of the ages."[45]

The sequence of Paul's ideas in 1 Corinthians 1:21–24 reveals the incongruity of the Word of the cross with any prior epistemology:

---

45. Here recall Mark 4 and the Parable of the Sower, where, unlike its Jewish parallel in 4 Ezra, the parable announces the *simultaneous* growth of good and bad seed, and this, indeed, at the hand of the sower. See Marcus's treatment of the parable in his commentary, *Mark 1–8*. For Agamben on 4 Ezra and 1 Cor 7:29–31, see *Time*, 25.

21   God was pleased to save through folly

22   Jews ask for signs; Greeks seek wisdom

23   We preach Christ crucified, scandal to Jews, folly to Greeks

24   But to the called [*klētois*] Christ, the power of God and the wisdom of God.

Here, Agamben's logic of *klēsis* echoes as each category of humanity (each *part* in the *all*) is divided against its own vocation (seeking signs, finding scandal; seeking wisdom, finding folly). Would it be too far afield to see the ones called as the newly created people of God that comes into being as a new thing out of the categories of Jew and Gentile? Certainly there is a sense in which the *kaleō/klēsis* language in Paul can be understood in Agamben's terms as the key to the messianic transformation of the human community.

One more section of the text closely tied to issues of communal identity in Agamben and Badiou has special resonance here. In 1 Corinthians 1:26–30 Paul engages his audience in a review of the circumstances in which they were called: "not many of you were wise according to worldly standards, not many were powerful, not many were of noble birth." In fact, God chose the foolish, the weak, the lowly, the nothings and nobodies, "lest any human being boast in the presence of God" (vv. 27–29). Throughout this section, and explicitly at verse 29, Paul engages Jeremiah 9:23–24 in a midrash that echoes what Walter Brueggemann calls in Jeremiah an "epistemological crisis."[46] At times of crisis in Israel's history, Brueggemann suggests, the epistemological consensus achieved by the "royal definers of reality" broke down. In such times, the voices of prophets and apocalyptic visionaries were raised. For these "outsiders," traditional wisdom does not hold; God breaks through the façade of wisdom, disrupting the status quo, delivering the dispossessed, the outsider, the unnamed, and all whose inexplicable tragedies find no place in the cosmic order.

Thus far, the apocalyptic Paul is in agreement with his precursor, Jeremiah. But in verse 27 he goes beyond Jeremiah's critique of the wealthy and wise to add his own triad of election terms:

---

46. In part this is to say that the Jeremiah text is not merely a prooftext for Paul but a piece of Israel's Scripture that speaks a new word, powered by ancient memory, in the light of the cross.

27a   God chose [*exelexato*] the foolish things to shame the wise.

27b   God chose [*exelexato*] the weak things to shame the strong.

28a   God chose [*exelexato*] what is low and despised in the
       world, even the things that have no being [*ta mē onta*] in
       order to bring to nothing [*katargēsei*; nullify/make inopera-
       tive?] things that have being [*ta onta*].

Here Paul moves radically beyond the prophetic witness of Jeremiah to
show God to be not only the judge and rectifier of the old cosmos, but the
creator *ex nihilo* of a new world. This apocalyptic God appears in Paul as
the one who breaks in to liberate the groaning cosmos (Romans 8) and
creates anew in electing things that have no being.[47] The series of aporias,
reversals, and paradoxes generated by the divine apocalypse in crucifixion, then, sets the stage for all that comes in the rest of the letter. Every
address to moral and communal (hence political) life in the letter must
now be read in light of the parody of wisdom (the cross) that became true
wisdom for Paul, thereby founding nothing less than a new creation.

RECEIVING PAUL TODAY: SUMMARIZING POINTS OF CONTACT

Perhaps the nearest point of contact between the apocalyptic apostle who
emerges from our exegesis and the philosophers is Badiou's assessment of
1 Corinthians 1:27–28 as "the most radical statement in the text we are
commenting on."

> It is through the invention of a language wherein folly, scandal,
> and weakness supplant knowing reason, order and power and
> wherein non-being is the only legitimizable affirmation of be-
> ing, that Christian discourse is articulated. In Paul's eyes this
> articulation is incompatible with any prospect (and there has
> been no shortage of them, almost from the time of his death ‖ KEY
> onward) of "Christian philosophy."[48]

In Paul's discourse *on the cross* we witness, to be sure, a radical departure from what we normally call "philosophy." Nor is Agamben an

47. Brueggemann, "Epistemological Crisis," 86. For argument that Paul uses the
language of call and election to refer to God's *creative* power and that, therefore, *new
creation* is what the liberating God does in electing, see two essays on Romans 9–11:
Gaventa, "Calling-into-Being"; and Barclay, "Mercy."

48. Badiou, *Saint Paul*, 47.

upholder of philosophical conventions. His deeply dialectical reading of the human subject in messianic time as at once unique, individual, and yet perpetually dispossessed sets him against a great deal of both modern and postmodern philosophy.

If for Paul the human being is "no longer I," but is "in Christ" a new being (Gal 3:20), so also for our philosophers a radically changed subject emerges—from the slight messianic shift in Agamben or from the evental truth in Badiou—to exist in a new and redemptive relationship to the world. While for Agamben the messianic division of the subject, like the division of time accomplished in the small opening made by the Sabbath, leaves a remnant dispossessed but ready for messianic "use" in the open community, for Badiou the new community is drawn out of ("extracted from") the deadening division of law and difference by the conscripting power of the resurrection event. The operations seem quite opposite—one insisting on dialectical division, the other shunning the dialectic and extracting unity out of difference—but both systems point toward a radically new community freed of the potential of bare difference to produce violence. Indeed, Paul's clearest statement of his own conscription into the gospel of God is narrated as a seizure by apocalypse out of a life of violence (Gal 1:13–16a).

The (Absent) Cross

There is no discourse on the cross per se in either Agamben or Badiou. And yet, could it be that Agamben's "complete loss of man" that corresponds to his redemption[49] is pointing to what Paul sees in the cross, where Christ "emptied himself, taking the form of a slave and becoming obedient unto death" (Phil 2:5–11)? Even for Badiou, who cites Romans 6:9 to the effect that "death as such counts for nothing in the operation of salvation,"[50] Christ's death is utterly necessary.[50] For Christ is himself pulled *ek nekron* ("out from the dead") and in this act creates the mortal site, the subjective situation of all to whom the evental truth is addressed. Whereas death is an operation in the situation, resurrection "blasts open the continuum constructed around death."[51] This is, for Badiou, the power of the cross.

49. Agamben, *Time*, 31.

50. Badiou, *Saint Paul*, 70.

51. Welborn, "Mortal Site," 208.

The (Absent) God

The larger, lurking cause of our theological unease with the philosophers is, of course, the absent God. By what agency, we might ask, does the evental truth make its entrance, or what provokes Agamben's subject to realize messianic consciousness? Does there emerge an ersatz deity, say, the flow of time itself, the ideals of the universal or the particular, or, with Badiou, "mathematics as ontology"?[52] Can Paul's theology of the apocalyptic Deity of the cross be transfigured into a philosophical operation on the subject? Certainly these are central questions in the dialogue that may yet open new paths of understanding. Or again, can it be that in the debate between Agamben and Badiou about the liberating operation of the *universal* (Badiou) against the *essential particular* whose remnant is the opening to redemption (Agamben) we might find helpful guides to our perplexities about Paul and the ambivalence of difference? Might we come to know in new ways both the mercy of the always-creating, remnant-preserving God of Romans (chs. 9–11) *and* the God of the "all in parts" of 1 Corinthians?

Here, finally, are two thinkers, themselves "other" to our theological discourse, who see in Paul's ideas, or at least in the *structure* of his ideas, a way forward to a more just and viable human community here and now. The urgency of their own vocations toward imagining and arguing a world in which systemic violence, ethnic strife, and the deadening impoverishment of human and non-human life are overcome—by the seizure of a truth event or the transforming perception of the messianic moment—calls us, at least, to reread through their lenses the texts that have captured their attention. But, to be sure, the *telos* of the secular political philosopher is other, radically other, than the *telos* of the theologian Paul. For Paul, surely, the truth event that creates anew is not the "fable" of resurrection, but the deliverance enacted by the crucified and resurrected Christ, whose entry into death robs death of its victory so that God may be all in all (1 Cor 15:54–55). Made (a) subject with the whole creation in hope, Paul looks resolutely toward the glorious liberty of all (i.e., the creation itself) as children of God (Rom 8:22). The distance of this eschatological hope from secular politics is obvious. The question remains: can any political philosophy drawn from Paul's apocalyptic vision and vocabulary finally ignore a hope that is not merely secular?

---

52. Morse ("Resurrection as Myth," 261) finds this telling phrase in Badiou's book *Infinite Thought*.

4

Eschatologizing Apocalyptic

An Assessment of the Present Conversation on Pauline Apocalyptic[1]

David W. Congdon

THE AIM OF THIS paper is to answer the question, "What does it mean to speak of apocalyptic?" Recent developments in apocalyptic theology make it increasingly difficult to give a clear and definite answer to this question. This paper seeks to clarify the enduring problem posed by this question and to put forward a way of answering it. My own research is in the relation between Karl Barth and Rudolf Bultmann, and if Barth is, for some at least, the grandfather of contemporary apocalyptic theology, then Bultmann is "public enemy number one." It is not an exaggeration to say that apocalyptic theology is an explicitly anti-Bultmannian enterprise. It was my uneasiness about this state of affairs that led me on the path of this essay.

I argue that apocalyptic theology is at a crossroads. There are so many different claims as to what counts as apocalyptic that it is becoming nearly impossible to gain clarity about what the word "apocalyptic" actually

---

1. A revised version of a paper given at the 2011 Annual Meeting of the American Academy of Religion in San Francisco under the title, "Eschatologizing Apocalyptic: Bultmann, Taubes, and the Copernican Turn." The paper was given at one of the sessions of the Theology and Apocalyptic Working Group. The session's theme for that year was Jacob Taubes. I am grateful to Ry Siggelkow and Nathaniel Maddox for their comments on an earlier draft of this paper.

means. I will not claim to put forward a general definition to encompass all the varieties—in fact, just the opposite. We need instead to be honest about our differences and not use ambiguous terminology to disguise our disagreements. I will proceed as follows: first, I will look again at the debate between Bultmann and Käsemann with an eye toward assessing what we mean today by "Pauline apocalyptic"; second, I will turn to the work of Jacob Taubes, whose materialist and messianic conception of apocalyptic warrants critical attention; and third, I will make some general remarks on the current state of apocalyptic theology and what questions need answers before we can make further progress.

I

Those of us who consider ourselves allies in the project of apocalyptic theology recognize our deep indebtedness to the work of Ernst Käsemann. Those who preceded him, such as Johannes Weiss and Albert Schweitzer, pioneered the historical scholarship on apocalyptic, but they were quick to put these ideas behind them. If we have Käsemann to thank, it is because he willingly stood in the dross-clearing light of early Christian apocalypticism. In a footnote to his 1962 essay "On the Subject of Primitive Christian Apocalyptic,"[2] he writes poignantly of the work of the historian: "How many of our students today," he asks, "grasp the truth . . . that he who does not himself mature in the historian's trade will shake nothing but unripe fruit from the tree of knowledge? The principal virtue of the historian . . . is the cultivation of the listening faculty [*Einübung des Hörens*], which is prepared to take seriously what is historically alien and does not think that violence [*Vergewaltigung*, lit. "rape"] is the basic form of engagement."[3]

Käsemann makes this statement in view of two critical articles by Gerhard Ebeling and Ernst Fuchs regarding his 1960 essay on "The Beginnings of Christian Theology."[4] This piece attempts to provide a "reconstruction" of the theological concerns of the primitive Christian community. Whereas Ebeling writes about the "basis" (*Grund*) of Christian theology, and Fuchs on the "task" (*Aufgabe*) of theology, Käsemann focuses on "the beginnings." He does this, he says, because "some have to dedicate

2. Käsemann, "Primitive Christian Apocalyptic" (German ed.: "Zum Thema der urchristlichen Apokalyptik"). Citations to translated works will include the page numbers for the original German publication in parentheses.
3. Ibid., 110 n. 2 (107 n. 2).
4. Käsemann, "Beginnings."

themselves to administering the literary estate [*Nachlass-Verwaltung*] of the historians with the object of preventing the interpreters from settling down too comfortably."[5] It is therefore as a historian that Käsemann is interested in the question of apocalyptic, in opposition to those whom he calls "the interpreters"—by which he means hermeneutical theologians like Ebeling, Fuchs, and of course Bultmann. The famous line from this essay on "the beginnings" regarding apocalyptic being the mother of theology is often treated as a normative claim about theology *as such*, and while Käsemann certainly points in that direction, he first and foremost understands it as a historical claim. We should not forget that a few pages later he says that the apocalyptic hope in an imminent end "proved to be a delusion" and resulted in the collapse of the "whole theological framework of apocalyptic, with its expectation of the parousia."[6] He insists on recognizing the "mythical character" of the early Christian understanding of history.[7] He warns against the notion of a "perennial theology" (*theologia perennis*), a system of thought universally valid for all times and places. And yet he asks "whether Christian theology can ever survive in any legitimate form without this [apocalyptic] theme."[8]

How then does Käsemann define "apocalyptic"? He fully admits that the word, like any other theological term, is "ambiguous" (*mehrdeutig*).[9] In 1960 he writes, "The heart of primitive Christian apocalyptic, according to the Revelation [of John] and the Synoptists alike,"—notice his starting point—"is the accession to the throne of heaven by God and by his Christ as the eschatological Son of Man—an event which can also be characterized as proof of the righteousness of God."[10] He goes on to say that Paul and the Fourth Gospel present basically the same view, though expressed in different forms from a *religionsgeschichtlich* perspective. The apocalyptic hope of the early Christian community is marked by *Naherwartung*, the expectation of something imminent within history.[11] History has a "definite beginning and a definite end" in this perspective.[12] His argument,

5. Käsemann, "Primitive Christian Apocalyptic," 109 (105). More literally, "with the object of disturbing [*beunruhigen*] the interpreters."

6. Käsemann, "Beginnings," 106 (104); translation revised.

7. Ibid., 96 (95).

8. Ibid., 107 (104).

9. Käsemann, "Primitive Christian Apocalyptic," 109 n. 1 (106 n. 1).

10. Käsemann, "Beginnings," 105 (102).

11. Cf. ibid., 99, 106 (97, 103). He appeals to passages like Matt 10:23 as evidence of this apocalyptic expectation.

12. Ibid., 96 (95).

in a nutshell, is that Christian apocalypticism functions as a thoroughgoing critique (and appropriation) of what he calls "enthusiasm," viz., the emphasis on a present possession of the Spirit as the telos of history. The presence of spiritual gifts is identified instead as a pledge of the "impending irruption [*baldig Hereinbrechen*] of the parousia."[13] In his follow-up essay of 1962, he further explicates the apocalyptic expectations of an imminent Parousia with respect to Paul's epistles and addresses the anthropological questions posed by Bultmann. He defines the central hope of the post-Easter community as "the return of Jesus in the role of the heavenly Son of Man."[14] The community's hope is not Jesus himself but rather him only as "the bearer of the Last Judgment . . . to which the correlate on the human side is the general resurrection."[15] It is helpful, I think, to be clear about how Käsemann defines apocalyptic, because it is not a view that many, if any, of the current apocalyptic theologians subscribe to, at least not literally.[16] But that's getting ahead of ourselves.

It is in this context that we should understand the debate between Käsemann and Bultmann on this topic.[17] In 1964, Bultmann writes an essay entitled, "Is Apocalyptic the Mother of Christian Theology?" He begins with an illuminating clarification of the problem:

> In two significant essays Ernst Käsemann has championed the thesis that apocalyptic is the true origin of early Christian theology, indeed, the "mother of Christian theology." I could

13. Ibid., 92 (91); my translation.

14. Käsemann, "Primitive Christian Apocalyptic," 114 (110). The later emphasis in Christian teaching on a chronologically distant hope is the result of the failure of the Parousia to occur as expected. As Käsemann puts it in a footnote, "I speak of primitive Christian apocalyptic to denote the expectation of an imminent parousia [*die Naherwartung der Parusie*]. Where this is changed in apocalyptic literature to the expectation of something far distant in time [*Fernerwartung*], the change occurs because of disappointed hopes and consequent caution in prophecy, without being able to conceal the original phenomenon. We can understand well enough why apocalyptic seldom enjoyed the good will of the dominant church or theology. For this reason it is all the more important to define the limits of the problem which is presented by the fact that the beginnings both of church and theology were conditioned by 'imminent' expectation" (ibid., 109, n. 1 [106 n. 1]).

15. Ibid., 115 (111).

16. I am thinking here of the work of Christopher Morse and Nathan Kerr, in particular. Other Pauline apocalyptic thinkers could be mentioned as well, such as Philip Ziegler and Douglas Harink.

17. For a recent and comprehensive assessment of this debate, see Lindemann, "Anthropologie und Kosmologie."

accept this if instead of "apocalyptic" we speak of "eschatology." Eschatology is the notion [*Vorstellung*] of the end of the world; it is a notion which as such does not intend to include a concrete picture [*Bild*] of the end-occurrence [*Endgeschehen*], which does not even think of the end as chronologically fixed. As Paul and John demonstrate, there is not only "future" but also "present" eschatology. By contrast, apocalyptic is a specific concretization of the eschatological notion. It draws up pictures of the end-occurrence, and it fixes the end chronologically. So because Käsemann chooses the concept [*Begriff*] of apocalyptic, he understands the early Christian eschatological expectation as the expectation of an *imminent* end [*Naherwartung*].[18]

Notice what Bultmann is objecting to in this opening paragraph. His primary problem with apocalyptic is that it (a) fixes the telos of history at a particular point in chronological time and (b) claims to describe the specific form that this chronological telos will take. In support, he points to the fact that this apocalyptic emphasis on an imminent end of history is not the only eschatology present within the New Testament, and he appeals to Paul and John—a different starting point than Käsemann, it's worth noting. Whereas Käsemann states that present eschatology is strictly included *within* a future, apocalyptic eschatology, Bultmann makes a crucial dialectical addition: "As true as it is to say—that is, against the enthusiastic pneumatics—that present eschatology is 'anchored and qualified' [*verankert und eingeschränkt*] by apocalyptic, it is, in my opinion, also true to say, conversely, that apocalyptic eschatology is anchored and qualified by the present."[19]

It would be a mistake, however, to view the Bultmann-Käsemann dispute simply in terms of two different positions on the origins of Christian theology, even though that is how it tends to be received. Bultmann is not nearly as interested as Käsemann in the attempt to reconstruct the theological climate of primitive Christianity, and he has strong reservations about the very possibility of such a project. Bultmann is best read here as a theologian, as one who is seeking to articulate the conditions for the responsible proclamation of Christ's significance for faith today, though certainly he does so on the basis of the biblical text.

Bultmann's real concerns become clear later in his essay, where he turns to Käsemann's specific conception of apocalyptic as referring

18. Bultmann, "Ist die Apokalyptik?," 476. For Lindemann's explication of Bultmann's essay, see Lindemann, "Anthropologie und Kosmologie," 167–70.

19. Bultmann, "Ist die Apokalyptik?," 133 (127).

to Christ's reign and the subjection of the cosmic powers. Bultmann's problem is that, taken literally, this view conceives of apocalyptic as a supernatural battle taking place "over our heads," so to speak. Bultmann says that Käsemann's view is right only "if Christ's reign is understood as his lordship over me." The subjection of the cosmic powers "must be understood as my active participation in this subjection through my obedience."[20] He agrees with Käsemann that Christ's lordship is rooted in the defeat of death in the resurrection, but it is precisely on this basis that Bultmann insists on the existential and anthropological nature of Christian apocalypticism. As Bultmann puts it, with reference to 1 Corinthians 15.57, "Paul thanks God, who gives *us* the victory."[21] Without this intrinsic relation to the particularity of life in the world, apocalypticism becomes little more than mythological or metaphysical abstraction. On Bultmann's reading, however, Paul relocates "belief in the presence of salvation out of the realm of speculation . . . into the realm of concrete human existence."[22]

Bultmann's opposition to apocalypticism is thus bound up with his opposition to all forms of speculation. It is in this sense that he rejects the notion of a saving event that is "objectively" real and effective in the abstract apart from our concrete participation or acknowledgement of it. Bultmann does not mean that salvation is a mental fabrication or a work that we accomplish ourselves. Even though the event of Christ, he says, is "always a new beginning" for us in the sense that it "always demands our decision," the event "is in actuality [*faktisch*] always a beginning for us, whether we want it to be or not."[23] But we cannot assume a neutral posture that would allow us to state in advance what Christ is for each person. One is either obedient or disobedient in relation to Jesus Christ, and this obedience is a contingent response that is new in each particular moment. To speak of Christ is to speak of a concrete active relation between God and a human being, and this relation cannot be universalized as a general

20. Ibid., 480–81.

21. Ibid., 481.

22. Ibid., 480.

23. Bultmann, *Verkündigte Wort*, 237–38. This is from a sermon, "Der Sinn des Weihnachtsfestes," which he preached on December 17, 1926, in Marburg. Bultmann goes on to say: "'The Word became *flesh*,' God became a *human being*. It's not about the miraculous transformation of some cosmic substance, but rather the fact that through the birth of a human being history has been decisively determined. It's also not about the fact that we have sensed God's grace in special contents [*Gehalte*] and special experiences [*Erlebnisse*] as something extra, but rather the fact that in the person of Jesus Christ God's grace and reality have appeared and marked our history" (238).

relation without turning the event into a substance and revelation into something revealed. Bultmann's concern is finally identical with that of the Pauline apocalyptic theologians. He seeks to protect the contingency, otherness, and newness of God's eschatological inbreaking. Is the defeat of death and the subjection of the powers and principalities an event like other occurrences in history and thus capable of articulation by any neutral observer, or is it rather an event that is known and encountered only by the one who actively participates in it by faith and is thus an event that, to use the terminology of Christopher Morse, is never "in hand" but only ever "at hand"?[24]

Why this rehash of the debate between Käsemann and Bultmann? In short, because contemporary apocalyptic theology has (perhaps unknowingly) followed Bultmann, and not Käsemann. Where the decisive points of conflict between "apocalyptic" and "eschatology" are concerned, theologians today have largely—and, in my estimation, correctly—taken the path of a demythologized eschatology over against a literal apocalypse, though most still use the linguistic framework of biblical apocalypticism as a way of fleshing out what is, in fact, a post-Enlightenment interpretation of eschatological hope. The point of drawing out this genealogical connection to Bultmann is *not* at all to suggest that contemporary apocalyptic theology is, in fact, non-apocalyptic. Much to the contrary, the point is to argue that if these recent developments are rightly identified as apocalyptic—and I believe that they are—then there is no reason not to acknowledge Bultmann as a truly apocalyptic theologian.

The work of J. Louis Martyn marks the turning point in this Bultmannian direction, all appearances to the contrary notwithstanding. A full defense of this claim is not possible here, but let me note the following points. One quickly notices that Martyn's work places no emphasis on a chronologically imminent occurrence within world history as the basis for a Pauline apocalyptic, nor is there any attempt to describe some future catastrophic end of the cosmos.[25] The accent throughout is rather on the

24. Cf. Morse, *Difference*, 5–7, 21–25.

25. I credit Martyn as the turning point because it is his Pauline scholarship that forms the theological framework for contemporary apocalyptic theology. He is the one figure consistently cited as exegetical evidence for the apocalyptic position. That is not to say Martyn was a lone innovator. In terms of differentiating Pauline apocalyptic from the version that prognosticates about the imminent future, his work builds upon that of Christopher Rowland. As Martinus C. de Boer points out, Rowland's 1982 study of Jewish and early Christian apocalyptic is responsible for differentiating the concept of apocalyptic from a strictly futurist orientation. Rowland writes, "Apocalyptic is as

transcendent *otherness* of God's redemptive agency in Christ. The promi-nence of language regarding the *cosmic-historical scope* of this apocalyptic invasion does *not* mean for him that the Christ-event is *empirically cosmo-logical* or *chronologically historical*. While Martyn rightly insists that the apocalyptic invasion is never the imaginative creation of an individual, he does not define its "reality" within the category of what human beings generally refer to as the "real world," because this invasion alone deter-mines what is truly real. God's disruptive action in the advent of Christ "is not visible, demonstrable, or provable in the categories and with the means of perception native to 'everyday' existence. . . . The inbreak of the new creation is itself revelation, apocalypse." The invasion of divine grace causes an "epistemological crisis," he says, for those whom it encounters, since the world they inhabit now appears in an entirely new light. The one confronted by the apocalypse therefore "sees bifocally"; that person sees "both the evil age and the new creation simultaneously."[26] Martyn's concept of bifocal vision is, in fact, equivalent to Bultmann's concept of "paradoxical identity." The point for both is that the apocalypse is not an event alongside other events in history, nor does it create a new historical age that appears to all people apart from faith. On the contrary, it is an epistemological crisis in the sense that it alters our very relation to the world. The Christ-event transfigures history for the one who faithfully participates in it.

Where the apocalyptic theologians differ today from Bultmann is not at all where Bultmann and Käsemann differ. Instead, as Morse's book on heaven makes clear, the real point of departure from Bultmann is over the sociopolitical implications of apocalyptic thinking. The assumption is that Dorothee Sölle and others are correct in judging Bultmann's theology to be individualistic and apolitical, and for *this* reason primarily (though not exclusively) he is identified as non-apocalyptic.[27] Whether this judgment

---

much involved in the attempt to understand things as they are now as to predict future events" (*Open Heaven*, 2). Cf. de Boer, "Paul."

26. Martyn, *Galatians*, 104.

27. To be sure, Morse renders a number of other criticisms against Bultmann be-sides the political problem. While he affirms demythologizing in the limited sense of deliteralizing, he also states that Bultmann imposes an "alien framework" and "ex-istential ontology" upon scripture (Morse, *Difference*, 40), as many have done ever since Barth rendered the same verdict. These are, however, passing remarks in Morse's book. He does not spend any time examining the merit of these claims; he mostly takes them for granted as established judgments in theology. His much more important claim is that demythologizing interprets heaven "too exclusively in terms of the self in disregard of a wider social and political world" (39). The significance of this statement

is accurate is a question I cannot take up in any detail here, but notice that this was not the concern in the debate between Bultmann and Käsemann. When Morse criticizes Bultmann for lacking "the sense of any cosmic and political eventfulness associated with heaven," he has already made a de-mythologizing move to associate the cosmic language of apocalyptic with sociopolitical action in the world.[28] As a historian examining the views of the early Christian community, Käsemann understands the cosmic lan-guage to refer quite literally to the future of the cosmos.[29]

is made clear by the fact that Morse devotes an entire chapter to developing precisely the sociopolitical implications of Christian talk about heaven (75–98), not to mention the numerous other places where these ideas appear in the other chapters. This justi-fies my argument that it is the judgment regarding Bultmann's ostensibly apolitical conception of faith that is the real, or at least primary, basis for his rejection among the contemporary apocalyptic theologians. The reasons that someone like Käsemann gave are rarely, if ever, mentioned.

28. Morse, *Difference*, 39.

29. Käsemann as a mature theologian is another matter entirely. In his posthu-mously published writings from 1975 to 1996 (he died in 1998), collected in *On Being a Disciple of the Crucified Nazarene*, Käsemann affirms and extends Bultmann's program of demythologizing in a way that reveals the surprising continuity between Bultmann and apocalyptic theology. See the following passage: "Bultmann was entirely correct to throw out this catchword that so horrified and enraged his opponents. There must be demythologizing. It was only that Bultmann was much too soft when he applied it principally to our worldview and called us from ancient Christian ideas to modern thought. Without question God does not intend that we run about as living mummies of the ancient world, everywhere assuming and making use of the technology of our time, but spiritually and religiously setting ourselves back 1,900 years. Faith must be lived today, and this means it must give thought today and give an account of itself. . . . Nevertheless, demythologizing may not only denote speaking in new tongues and with modern speech" (100–101). In other pieces he explains how demythologizing needs to be extended and furthered today. In an essay on the heritage of the Reforma-tion, he writes: "[Demythologizing] is no doubt necessary and the task of all preachers and teachers, but it must be radicalized. For no one can hear the gospel without being summoned to the reality of earth from illusions about oneself, the world and especially God. Demythologizing must proceed to 'de-demonizing'" (177). By "de-demonizing," Käsemann means that the apocalyptic invasion of God destroys the illusory power structures that enslave the oppressed peoples of the earth. This is made even clearer by another lecture from 1987: "This is why I acknowledge the demand for demythologiz-ing. The ancient worldview, which lived on in the Middle Ages and in our time openly or subliminally still haunts us, has no claim on us. Contrariwise, a demythologizing carried on and given legitimation theologically should not toll for a burial already conducted 200 years ago by rationalists inside and outside the church. Nor should it be used as springboard for a Christian existentialism that no longer needs theological heralds to remain up to date. Today, demythologizing must be more radical than in the days of the Enlightenment, more critical toward its faith in progress and science and toward the postulate of human maturity in the modern era. Not merely texts are to be

My point is that the literature on apocalyptic has tended to obscure the way in which this word has been associated with a variety of different theological commitments, some of them incompatible with each other. The most recent work in Pauline apocalyptic theology is highly actualistic, dialectical, and existential in nature—aspects that come out very clearly in the work of Morse and Kerr, among others. Even the eschatology is largely present tense rather than future tense.[30] In short, apocalyptic theology today is highly Bultmannian in nature, with the one crucial qualification being its explicitly theopolitical orientation. And it is with that in mind that I turn now to Taubes.

---

demythologized respecting their ideological wrappings. In the evangelical sense demythologizing occurs as a battle and resistance against superstition. And superstition, at least according to Luther's explanation of the first commandment, is everything that does not allow us most deeply and without compromise to fear, love, and trust God 'above all things.' Thus demythologizing, evangelically conceived and rooted, denotes ridding humanity and the earth of the demonic" (199–200). Käsemann then goes on to say that the demonic manifests itself today in "the cries of a humanity for centuries exploited by the white race, herded into the misery of slums and starved there, plagued by epidemic, and for the most part treated worse than cattle" (201). In this sense, "the gospel rids of demons" and "deserves to be called mother of the Enlightenment" (203). These passages, pregnant with numerous theological possibilities, reveal how misguided it is to limit demythologizing to deliteralizing or to reject Bultmann's project because it does not seem adequately political in nature. Such critiques do not perceive the radical implications of Bultmann's hermeneutical program. Despite his debates with Bultmann in his younger years, Käsemann later proved himself to be one of Bultmann's most faithful students. Käsemann rightly perceived that New Testament apocalyptic, the program of demythologizing, and liberation theology all belong together. See Käsemann, *Disciple*.

30. Despite the fact Morse concludes his book with a chapter on "the hope of heaven," there is virtually nothing said about the so-called afterlife or a traditional conception of creation's consummation. The chapter is instead a thorough demythologizing of Christian expectations; the eschatological "last day" is indeed the day "at hand," that is, every today. Morse acknowledges that this is a very different kind of hopeful expectation: "What then is the hope of heaven, if any, expressed in these parameters? At the least this much we can acknowledge, to sum up from the foregoing observations: The 'real world' is proclaimed to be one in which there is life currently arriving on the scene, in whatever situation we are facing, that is stronger than any undeniable loss threatening us, including death" (Morse, *Difference*, 117). I am in full agreement with Morse's conclusions, but it is important not to cover up or ignore the way these represent a *fulfillment* of Bultmann's hermeneutical insights and not their rejection.

II

The work of Jacob Taubes stands in stark opposition to Pauline apocalyptic theology, and it does so for primarily political reasons. To understand why this is the case, we have to keep in mind two related strands of thought: the first is Taubes's Hegelian-Marxist philosophy of history, and the second is his analysis of analogical and dialectical theology. Put another way, Taubes is concerned with (1) a revolutionary politics and (2) the revolution of Copernicus. Both of these are affirmed by contemporary Pauline apocalyptic theology, but in a very different way.

Taubes is drawn to the apocalyptic and gnostic traditions, because he shares with them a critique of the status quo, a rejection of the present order of the world. Apocalypticism, he argues, is born out of a prophetic rebellion against the structure of society. This rebellion is a nihilistic overturning of the entire world system, hence the points of similarity with later gnostic thought. "Apocalypticism," he says, "negates this world in its fullness."[31] In its expectation of an imminent end, Jewish apocalyptic is a theology of revolution. God stands beyond and against the oppressive history of humanity, and thus "God's voice resounds as a call to action, to make ready the wilderness of this world for the Kingdom."[32] In a crucial passage, Taubes states that "the paramount question posed in the Apocalypse is *when*? The question arises from the pressing expectation of redemption, and the obvious answer is *soon*. Imminence is an essential feature of apocalyptic belief. The global statement *salvation is at hand* does not satisfy those who want to know the day and the hour."[33] Notice that this view is even more extreme in its emphasis on the chronology of the apocalypse than Käsemann's, and thus quite distant from the position of the Pauline apocalyptic school.[34]

---

31. Taubes, *Occidental Eschatology*, 9.

32. Ibid., 16.

33. Ibid., 32.

34. In addition to accenting the category of imminence, Taubes's discussion of apocalyptic is similar to that of Käsemann on another key point as well. According to Käsemann, the primitive Christian community's apocalyptic understanding of history—in which "the world has a definite beginning and a definite end" and "takes a definite direction"—is what "first made historical thinking possible within Christendom" (Käsemann, "Beginnings," 96 [95]). Taubes makes a similar claim, arguing that the development of an apocalyptic eschatological perspective within Israel is effectively the birth of history. He frames his entire study in *Occidental Eschatology* in terms of the question, "How is history possible in the first place?" He goes on to distinguish between myth, which sees time "as a cycle" and "under the dominance of space," and

Taubes is entirely unfazed by the historical observation that such apocalyptic expectations were unsatisfied. The problem of the Parousia's delay, which consumed the energies of his contemporaries in biblical studies, is *not* a serious concern for Taubes. He understands apocalypticism to be a response to a sociopolitical crisis whose purpose is then fulfilled through revolutionary action. Hence, Marx becomes the model of a truly apocalyptic thinker. For Taubes, there is no loss in the movement from a *theological* apocalyptic to a *philosophical* apocalyptic. This transition is simply the natural consequence of a scientific revolution that has made belief in a transcendent God impossible. The only way to be an intellectually responsible apocalyptic thinker today is to become a left-Hegelian Marxist revolutionary—something we need not reject outright, even if we dispense with Taubes's philosophical and theological framework.

To explain this move from theology to philosophy, we need to look at the key to Taubes, viz., his understanding of the Copernican turn. Taubes divides world history into two eras: the world under Ptolemy and the world under Copernicus. The former is the age of analogy, which posits a correspondence between heaven above and earth below; the latter is the age of dialectic, which posits "either contradiction or identity between man and God" in the form of a "dialectic of antithesis" or a "dialectic of synthesis"—represented philosophically by Kierkegaard and Hegel, and theologically by the early Karl Barth and Paul Tillich, respectively.[35] Ac-

---

the spirit of revelation and redemption that understands time as "irreversibly straining toward something new while inquiring into its purpose." According to Taubes, the eschatological orientation of apocalypticism inaugurated the idea of history in the sense of progress toward a particular telos. "Israel breaks through the cycle of this endless repetition, opening up the world as history for the first time." See Taubes, *Occidental Eschatology*, 3–16.

35. Taubes, "Dialectic and Analogy," 174. Cf. Taubes, "Theological Method," 213. Barth is a common theme throughout Taubes's career. Though he tends to locate Barth in connection with Kierkegaard (in contrast to Tillich and Hegel), he also notes the way in which Hegel is suffused throughout Barth's writings. Barth is a kind of synthesis in himself between Kierkegaardian antithesis and Hegelian mediation. In a third essay from the same issue of *Journal of Religion*, Taubes writes a full piece on Barth's theological trajectory from the first edition of *Der Römerbrief* to *Die kirchliche Dogmatik*. He tracks the development in three stages: (1) a Hegelian "dynamic eschatology" in the first edition of *Romans*, (2) a Kierkegaardian "theology of crisis" in the second edition, and (3) a Hegelian "theology of reconciliation" in *KD*. Taubes is clear that the second stage is where he thinks Barth was best, and when he refers to Barth in other writings, it is usually to the Kierkegaardian Barth of radical crisis and dialectical negation. See Taubes, "Theodicy and Theology." For a related piece on Barth that shares some content with the "Theodicy and Theology" essay, see Taubes, "Philosophic Critique of Religion."

cording to Taubes, the Copernican revolution means that all language distinguishing between heaven and earth "become mere 'metaphors,'" having lost their grounding in the cosmic order. "The vertical axis crumbles," he says, "and above and below can no longer be genuinely distinguished." The result is that "theistic religion and philosophy are forced to retreat."[36] This retreat began with the Protestant Reformation and reached a climax in Barth's rejection of the *analogia entis*. The result of the Copernican revolution is that we live in "an earth without a heaven."[37] In the midst of a discussion of Kant in *Occidental Eschatology*, Taubes makes the following key remark: "Because the space between heaven and earth has become meaning-less, Copernican man seeks to revolutionize the world according to an ideal that can become reality in the course of time. The ideal is no longer the Platonic idea which dwells on high, but is to be found in the future."[38] What future is this? It is the one that *we* make, on the basis of an ideal that *we* devise. He affirms the notion of apocalypse as "a vision of future events,"[39] precisely because it is a vision that we must realize.[40]

We can now reconstruct the line of argument. Taubes works backwards from a kind of messianic Marxism that takes for granted a world without heaven that we must revolutionize according to an immanent historical ideal. Dialectical philosophy provides the intellectual matrix for this revolutionary action. He traces the genealogy of his position back through Thomas Müntzer and Joachim de Fiore, Marcion and Paul, to the apocalyptic prophets of Second Temple Judaism. The logic only becomes clear by the end: the conception of apocalyptic that he develops is one that can survive the Copernican revolution because it is entirely grounded in and oriented toward the immanent political situation. God only serves as a call to action, so that once God drops away with the loss of heaven, the apocalyptic action still survives intact. Insofar as God-talk remains, it has been collapsed into the rallying cries of the revolutionaries. The kingdom of God simply *is* the Marxist utopia. Whether one travels the path of Hegel or Kierkegaard, the move from analogy to dialectic results, according to Taubes, in the *direct identification* of God and humanity. To use Morse's

36. Taubes, "Dialectic and Analogy," 170.

37. Taubes, *Occidental Eschatology*, 108.

38. Ibid., 137.

39. Taubes, "Dialectic and Analogy," 166.

40. Augustine, with his conception of the two cities, represents the Ptolemaic world of analogy, and precisely for this reason is also the key anti-apocalyptic thinker. His theological framework undermines an immanent-futurist orientation, and thus it impedes the development of an apocalyptic politics of revolution.

language, this is a God who is very much "in hand"—literally "in hand," in fact, insofar as God is the sign we raise in protest or the Molotov cocktail we toss across the barricades in order to fashion a new world. The question theology must pose to Taubes is whether there is anything to differentiate his apocalypticism from ideological propaganda.

I agree with Taubes that something has decisively changed in the move from Ptolemy to Copernicus. I further agree with him that any re-pristination of a metaphysical analogy of being is hopelessly misguided. And I agree also that apocalyptic has to be articulated from within the theopolitical situation of the suffering masses. Crucially, however, I side with both Bultmann and contemporary Pauline apocalyptic theology precisely because they articulate a third way beyond metaphysical analogy and immanent dialectics, that is, an alternative to a God who is *above* us and a God who is directly identified *with* us. For Martyn, this alternative appears in the notion of "bifocal vision." For Bultmann, it is his concept of "paradoxical identity." For Morse, it is found in the idea of God's "at-handedness" and the corresponding notion of "incommensurable juxtapositions" that he borrows from Paul Lehmann.[41] What all of these conceptions have in common is the insight that God remains a critical *other* who stands radically beyond the creaturely situation, but in a way that is wholly nonmetaphysical. Heaven is not defined here as a supra-mundane location, nor is God defined as an abstract ontological entity associated with general philosophical concepts like simplicity, impassibility, and causality. But neither is God a "mere metaphor" whose content we define on the basis of our own idealistic projections, such that heaven is what we create for ourselves. God is instead a kerygmatic event whose transcendent-eschatological word addresses us in the gospel of God's present advent and mobilizes a community of revolutionary action within a particular historical moment. Just because one agrees with Taubes that we must dispense with the supernatural does not mean that we must dispense with the transcendent. The two are not coextensive, and abandoning the former actually makes possible the proper articulation of the latter.

III

Apocalyptic theology is at a crossroads. Proponents of such a theology will need to make a decision regarding which path to take. By now it should be clear from my paper that there are two distinct kinds of apocalyptic

41. Morse, *Difference*, 108–11.

theology. The first (what I will call "Apocalyptic A") is the view that the apocalyptic event is something literal, immanent, and directly observable. This can take a number of different forms. It is the tradition of apocalyptic on which Taubes draws, and which New Testament historians like Käsemann and Christiaan Beker emphasize. This is a Jewish apocalypticism rooted in a prophetic critique of imperial oppression and oriented toward the imminent arrival of a cosmic kingdom. Whether one understands the new age in supernatural or political terms, there is a *sequential ordering* of two objective world ages. The second kind of apocalyptic ("Apocalyptic B") is found in the theology developed by the likes of Martyn, Morse, Kerr, and others. This position views the apocalyptic event as something nonliteral, transcendent, and indirectly or paradoxically present. Here the new age is understood in neither supernatural nor political terms, and there is a *simultaneity* of the two ages. It is in this camp that I include Bultmann, alongside Barth and Bonhoeffer, despite some ostensible disagreements. As controversial as it may be for those who wish to posit a continuity between ancient Judeo-Christian apocalypticism and the present form of apocalyptic theology, I argue that we must differentiate very clearly between these two schools of thought. Certainly both share a common language regarding two ages, the old and the new, and both also share a common prophetic critique of the powers and principalities. And yet each approaches the issue in a radically different and mutually exclusive way. The two forms of apocalyptic cannot be harmonized within a more general account.

Apocalyptic A understands the apocalypticism of the biblical texts to be *mythical* in nature. This mythological quality is either (a) emptied of content and viewed as symbolic of political concerns (Taubes); (b) confined in its literal form to the primitive origins of the church but still given some normative significance for Christian theology (Käsemann); or (c) retained entirely as myth (modern fundamentalism and dispensationalism). Apocalyptic B, what I elsewhere refer to as "Pauline apocalyptic," is a *demythologizing* of Scripture, and as Bultmann himself makes clear, demythologizing does not eliminate myth but rather *interprets* it for today.[42] In other words, Apocalyptic B is rooted in an interpretation of the biblical texts from within a decidedly modern—that is, Copernican—framework. It has no interest in historical reconstruction, as if apocalyptic

---

42. Bultmann, "New Testament and Mythology," 12. In his 1952 clarification, Bultmann says that "[demythologizing's] criticism of the biblical writings lies not in eliminating mythological statements but in interpreting them; it is not a process of subtraction but a hermeneutical method" ("Problem of Demythologizing," 99).

has a univocal meaning that must be maintained today. It equally has no interest in speculation: either metaphysical speculation about the being of God, or eschatological speculation about a coming end of history. Instead of positing an earth without heaven, it proposes to rethink heaven itself. While dialectical, its emphasis on paradoxicality means that the relation between history and eschatology is one that must be conceived and posited ever anew. The apocalyptic event of Christ is neither removed to an obscure future, nor reduced to a past datum, nor conflated with a present construction. This event in all its living potency remains paradoxically present within each contingent situation *without ever identifying itself* with any single political mobilization or sociocultural mode of existence. Contrary to Joachim, and so Taubes, the Spirit does not "supersede Christ," but rather the Spirit *is* Christ.[43]

There are, as I see it, *two* primary ways in which Apocalyptic A manifests itself today. The first of these two ways is to identify what is apocalyptic with a particular mode of sociopolitical and intellectual resistance to the world. This can take an atheistic-Marxist form, as it does in Taubes, or it can take the form of Anglo-American postliberalism, within which I include both Hauerwas and Milbank. Common to these views is the notion that heaven or the "ideal" is to be defined by a particular worldview, that is to say, by the political ideology or cultural-linguistic rules of a particular community, whether the proletariat or the church. Because it is all-encompassing, this worldview can only confront "outsiders" by means of violence, whether physical, social, rhetorical, or some combination thereof. All of these in some sense objectify the divine and conflate God with a particular cultural form, historical entity, or intellectual system.

The second way in which Apocalyptic A manifests itself is by identifying what is apocalyptic with a particular mode of metaphysical theology. Instead of conflating the inbreaking of Christ with an empirical community, this conflates the inbreaking with a culturally specific intellectual framework or philosophical *Denkweise*. As with the empirical community, this mode of theological thinking is a contingent and contextual form of the gospel's manifestation in the world, yet it is explicitly or implicitly given a normative status for the articulation of Christian faith. It is explicit when theology baptizes a philosophical system (e.g., Hellenistic substance ontology) as authoritative; it is implicit when theology uncritically or naively imports philosophical notions into its articulation of the gospel. Either way, this second form of Apocalyptic A ends up directly

43. Taubes, "Dialectic and Analogy," 168.

identifying the gospel with a certain philosophical conceptuality. This is most clearly present in the repristination of the *analogia entis*, but it is also evident in those attempts to associate the cosmic-historical nature of the Christ-event with a "soteriological objectivism" that presupposes certain ontological relations as given. It is on this ground, in particular, that one often finds praise bestowed upon Barth or Bonhoeffer for their ontologizing of salvation, whether in Barth's account of Christ's history as the universal history of humanity or in Bonhoeffer's account of Christ's incarnate reality as the bodily assumption of all humanity.

The problem here is not the appropriation of philosophical conceptions in theological reflection. Instead, the problem is that such appropriations often appear to have timeless and universal validity; they are not continually and contextually interrogated in order to assess whether new conceptualities might more faithfully correspond to the event of Christ's inbreaking here and now. I am not suggesting that apocalyptic theology ought to avoid every form of theological ontology—that would be impossible—only that ontological concepts need to be (a) strictly distinguished from the gospel itself (thus emphasizing their contingency and replaceability) and (b) strictly ordered according to the logic of the gospel (thus dispensing with abstract universals in favor of concrete particularities and multiplicities). Apocalyptic A fails to uphold these points, often in spite of the right theological judgments. For instance, the attempt to articulate the basis for a "cosmic" and "historical" apocalypse in light of Barth and Bonhoeffer often ends up taking the form of an account of Christ's universal mediation. While some way of accounting for this is necessary, it is problematic insofar as theology becomes tied up with a specific philosophical conceptuality—especially an outdated one. And lest we encounter the objection that Bultmann is tied to a Heideggerian ontology, we should note that this is one of the abiding myths of our time, one that should have long since passed from serious academic conversation.[44]

44. The seminal work of Roger Johnson has demonstrated that the sources for Bultmann's theology are to be found in Marburg neo-Kantianism and the theology of Wilhelm Herrmann. Heidegger at best fills a very limited role in Bultmann's thought. Moreover, there is the historical question as to whether the relation of dependence was really only unidirectional. In light of the fact that Bultmann and Heidegger had joint teaching assignments and participated in each other's seminars, Johnson draws the important conclusion: "It may well be that we should have to correct our older picture of Bultmann's dependence upon Heidegger. . . . The relationship may well entail a far greater degree of reciprocity than has characteristically been assumed to be the case: Bultmann's own understanding of existence from the perspective of a religiously conceived individuality providing the stimulus to Heidegger's formulation of

Each of these two forms of apocalyptic thinking belong to the first type, Apocalyptic A. What unites them is the way in which what is truly apocalyptic is identified with something given in the world—whether a community of people or a philosophical framework. They are borne out of the Jewish apocalyptic desire to specify exactly *when* the apocalypse will take place, or *what* it will look like. The *what* need not be a description of a future Armageddon; it can also be a certain ontology or a certain religious community within the world. The second type of apocalyptic, Apocalyptic B, which I advocate in this paper, has no interest in the questions of when and what. It speaks rather of a *who*, namely, the crucified Christ, who is the wholly other in our midst, the transcendent one who continually breaks anew into our immanent situation. The "when" is always *now*, and the "what" is always *new*. One cannot describe what the apocalyptic incursion of God will entail in advance of its happening in the particular moment. The invasive event of God in Christ is a contextual and contemporary occurrence. The event is always "new every morning," always demanding a new interpretation within the present historical horizon. To speak of this incursion as *cosmic* is to acknowledge that there are no restrictions to where the risen Christ may manifest himself. To speak of this incursion as *imminent* is to acknowledge that God's forthcoming is never "in hand" but must always happen again and again. As Bultmann puts it, "God is 'the guest who always moves on' (Rilke), who cannot be apprehended in any now as one who remains. Rather . . . God ever stands before me as one who is coming [*der Kommende*], and this constant futurity of God is God's transcendence [*Jenseitigkeit*]."[45]

---

the existentialist interpretation of *Dasein* as the point of departure for a radical new ontology" (Johnson, *Origins of Demythologizing*, 175 n. 1). Beyond the question of just how dependent Bultmann ever really was on Heidegger (the historical question), there is the more important question regarding what Bultmann actually borrows from existentialist philosophy (the material question). On this point, Johnson also correctly reminds the reader that "Bultmann consistently appropriated for his own thought only that which was consistent with his own fundamental philosophical-theological conceptuality. This is true for his theological relationship with Barth as well as his philosophical relationship with Heidegger" (123). In other words, when Bultmann appropriates concepts like authenticity, decision, objectifying, and being-on-hand—not to mention research from the *religionsgeschichtliche Schule*—they are always subordinate to his more basic theological concerns as an existential-dialectical Lutheran theologian.

45. Bultmann, "Science and Existence [1955]," 144. Cf. Bultmann, *Primitive Christianity*, 195: "The grace of God is not visible like worldly entities. His treasures are hidden in earthly vessels (2 Cor. 4.7). The resurrection life is manifested in the world in the guise of death (2 Cor. 12.9). . . . The grace of God is never an assured possession.

The title for this paper is "Eschatologizing Apocalyptic." This is, of course, a way of combining, via juxtaposition, the views of Käsemann and Bultmann. By stating the need to *eschatologize* apocalyptic, I mean that we need to include the concerns of the first type of apocalyptic within the second. The political concerns of Taubes are entirely valid and must find a positive place within theology, *yet* without collapsing the divine into any single form of revolution. Bultmann's objections to apocalypticism are ones that contemporary theologians seem to share, and rightly so in my view. We can no longer sustain the original association of apocalyptic with a chronological and cosmological occurrence. Apocalyptic theology must not be a way of retreating to a premodern conception of history or an uncritical philosophical ontology. The apocalyptic invasion of Christ is properly understood as a concretely existential and eschatological event.

In conclusion, I pose the following questions. First, is apocalyptic functioning to justify the identification of God with a particular form of anti-worldly resistance (however we define "world")? Second, is apocalyptic functioning as a way of keeping the door open for traditional supernaturalism and classical metaphysics without having to sound like a supernaturalist or a metaphysician? If apocalyptic is to have a future, it must, I believe, be unequivocal in saying no to both. Contemporary Pauline theology has the resources to do so. We must simply declare our allegiances.

It is always ahead of man, always a future possibility. As grace, the transcendence of God is always his futurity, his constant being ahead of us, his always being where we would like to be." See also Bultmann's very important essay, especially for the topic of apocalyptic, on "Die christliche Hoffnung [1954]." At the end of the essay he writes: "The God of the present moment is always the God who is coming [*der kommende Gott*]; and only because of that is God the God of the present whose grace frees the human being from bondage to the past and opens that person for the future—for God's future" (90).

5

"If Johannes Weiss Is Right . . ."

A Brief Retrospective on Apocalyptic Theology

Christopher Morse

I remember that Julius Kaftan, my teacher in dogmatics in Berlin, said: "If Johannes Weiss is right and the conception of the Kingdom of God is an eschatological one, then it is impossible to make use of this conception in dogmatics."

—RUDOLF BULTMANN[1]

THE QUOTATION ABOVE FROM Rudolf Bultmann serves to introduce the issue considered in this paper, and a trajectory of thought that informs it, but is not cited to foreclose its assessment. That issue, now more than a century after Johannes Weiss's publication of the first edition of *Jesus' Proclamation of the Kingdom of God* in 1892, and half a century after Bultmann wrote the words above in 1958, is the significance of apocalyptic testimony for dogmatic theology, and, more specifically, the unsettled questions it raises for theology today. How "dogmatics" and "apocalyptic" are each defined will obviously affect what this significance and its questions are determined to be. To keep within the designated limits of these

1. Bultmann, *Jesus Christ and Mythology*, 13.

pages, I will focus selectively upon two critical contexts of New Testament interpretation, considering the first retrospectively with regard to the second.

The first context is that associated with Weiss's late-nineteenth-century monograph declaring Jesus' preaching of the kingdom to be eschatological and apocalyptic in a manner that is contrary to modern theology's talk of the kingdom. This monograph Albert Schweitzer famously credited shortly after its publication as being "one of the most important works in historical theology." "It closes one epoch and begins another."[2] In the preface Weiss states that his aim is "to make clear the completely apocalyptic and eschatological character of Jesus' idea of the Kingdom."[3] He refers to "eschatological-apocalyptical views" without differentiating the terms further.[4] It is these views, he acknowledges, that present the most difficulty for systematic and dogmatic theology (labels he also here uses interchangeably without differentiation). Kaftan's reported quote gives voice to this difficulty from the standpoint of a dogmatician who was a contemporary of Weiss.

The second context, closer to recent times, is the emergence of a reinvigorated inquiry into New Testament apocalyptic influenced by Ernst Käsemann's celebrated thesis first published in 1960 that "apocalyptic was the mother of all Christian theology." And yet, Käsemann writes, "It cannot be disputed that the theology of the Church has to a large extent seen its task as consisting in the vanquishing of apocalyptic."[5] In this second context, as in the first, a perceived conflict is thus acknowledged between the apocalyptic significance of the Gospel message and the theology of church teaching, or dogmatics, that professes faithfulness to the gospel. In this connection the exegetical work of J. Louis Martyn on Pauline apocalyptic published in 1997 offers fresh perspectives and a renewed impetus at the present time for recognizing what the unsettled questions and points of conflict are.[6]

---

2. Schweitzer, *Quest*, 239.

3. Weiss, *Jesus' Proclamation*, 56.

4 Ibid., 131. In a series of subsequent works Weiss addresses the subject of apocalyptic in more detail. See, as one example among others, from the year of his death in 1914, his comprehensive *Earliest Christianity*.

5. Käsemann, *Questions of Today*, 102, 115.

6. Martyn, *Theological Issues* and *Galatians*.

UNSETTLED QUESTIONS FROM WEISS

Johannes Weiss's influential monograph on Jesus' preaching of the kingdom of God provides an apt focal point for two reasons. While it is primarily noted for its pivotal importance in exposing the difference between an eschatological account of the kingdom of God in Jesus' preaching and the modern dogmatic interpretations of the kingdom prominent in Weiss's day—the point to which Julius Kaftan was responding—it also is explicit in affirming Weiss's view as a New Testament exegete and historian of early Christianity that there is a legitimate place for what he calls "dogmatic" as well as "historical" accounts of biblical concepts, so long as one is clear about their distinction. It is inevitable, he writes, that future generations will find significance in ancient testimonies that cannot on historical grounds be said to have been part of their origin. What is necessary for critical theological scholarship is that this later significance for faith, which dogmatics addresses, not be confused with claims for the original historical meaning. In Weiss's view, dogmatic meaning is thus subject to changing circumstances in a way that historical meaning is not.[7]

> Theology must insist on one thing if it wants to remain clear concerning itself and conscious of its procedures, namely, that one should acknowledge whether and how far we today are removed from the original meaning of the concepts, and that one should declare, for the sake of clarity, that [one] wishes to issue the old coinage (*Münzen*) at a new rate of exchange (*Curs*).[8]

Taking Weiss at his own words, in retrospect we may well ask to what extent his own purportedly historical account of the kingdom's apocalyptic significance in the New Testament message must itself be said to be more dogmatic than historical, according to his own definition—issuing "the old coinage at a new rate of exchange." But that question is less important than the more interesting one of whether Christian *dogmatic theology* as a discipline of church teaching can ever be creditably characterized exegetically as *apocalyptic*. Or is it the case, as Julius Kaftan reportedly supposed, that "dogmatic" and "apocalyptic," like the oxymoron of a square circle, are

---

7. The reverse contrast between "dogmatic" and "historical" is drawn by Ernst Troeltsch six years later in "Historical and Dogmatic Method."

8. Weiss, *Jesus' Proclamation*, 59–60. The German original text here translated as "that man wishes to issue the old coinage at a new rate of exchange" is "*dass man die alten Münzen in einem neuen Curs ausgeben will*" (*Predigt Jesu vom Reiche Gottes*, 7). Today the *Curs* in Weiss's German is spelled *Kurs*, and I will subsequently refer to it in this spelling.

contradictory concepts premised upon opposing worldviews—whether it be the view that Harnack, for example, called "the Greek spirit" of Hellenization reflected in the dogma of the ancient church, or what Weiss highlights as the post-Kantian reversal of apocalyptic significance dominant since the Enlightenment in the modern Protestant worldview of his day?

Systematic/dogmatic theology, as Weiss comments, "generally regards its task to be that of *framing* a unified Christian view of the world and life, which is supposed to be *authoritative* both for the individual and for all people for a long time to come."[9] This is a traditional description. Insofar as these two requirements—a unified framing of the world (generally associated with systematic theology's requirement of coherence) and a creditable authoritativeness (associated specifically with dogmatic theology as dealing with communally authorized, or church, teaching)—both entail a world that will further endure, they are premised upon a presupposition of durability that conflicts with what Weiss, as historian and exegete, describes as "the eschatological attitude" of "primitive Christianity." That attitude Weiss designates by citing Paul's testimony in 1 Corinthians 7:31 that "the form [*schēma*] of this world is passing away." This is the distinguishing text in Weiss's explanation of "eschatological-apocalyptical" significance. It has to do with what is taken to be the real world.

> The real difference between our modern Protestant world-view and that of primitive Christianity is, therefore, that we do not share the eschatological attitude, namely, that το σχημα του κόσμου τουτου παράγει. We no longer pray, "May grace come and the world pass away," but we pass our lives in the joyful confidence that *this* world will evermore become the showplace of the people of God.... The world will further endure, but we, as individuals will soon leave it.... We do not await a Kingdom of God which is to come down from heaven to earth and abolish this world, but we do hope to be gathered with the church of Jesus Christ into the heavenly βασιλεία.

"This is not to say," Weiss concludes, "that one ought no longer to use the concept 'Kingdom of God' in the current manner. On the contrary, it seems to me, as a matter of fact, that it should be the proper watchword of modern theology. Only the admission must be demanded that we use it in a different sense from Jesus."[10] In short, according to Weiss, the early Christians were wrong in what they took to be the real world of

9. Weiss, *Jesus' Proclamation*, 131 (emphasis added).

10. Ibid., 135.

the coming kingdom, but modern Christian theologians are also wrong in assuming that what they take to be the real world of the coming kingdom is in keeping with the gospel testimony. They fail to recognize that in referring to the kingdom of God they are issuing the "old coinage" (*Münzen*) of Jesus' preaching at a "new rate of exchange" (*Kurs*)—though it is a rate of exchange that is more consonant with faith in the modern world.

Two questions immediately arise. What is meant by "the form of this world that is passing away," which Weiss holds it is no longer possible for Christian faith to accept? And second, if the "kingdom of God" requires "a different sense" in modern theology from that found in the gospel proclamation of Jesus, by what rule of faith or canon of judgment is this difference to be determined? Church theology as dogmatics by definition is canonical in that it confesses to follow and be subject to a canon or rule of faith, a *regula fidei*. Put into Weiss's terms, what sets the "new rate of exchange" for the "old coinage"?

As to the first question of the meaning of "form" or *schēma* in Paul's testimony, the history of commentary generally shows a distinction drawn between some configuration of the world (*figura* being the Latin translation of the Greek *schēma*) and its material substance. Origen, in the early third century, writes, ". . . if the 'form of this world passes away,' it is not by any means an annihilation or destruction of the material substance that is indicated, but the occurrence of a certain change of quality and an alteration of the outward form." For an example Origen cites Psalm 102:26, where the passing away of heaven and earth is compared with a change in clothing.[11]

John Calvin likewise interprets Paul as distinguishing the *figura* of this world from its *substantia* and registers his objection to Erasmus' preference for the term *habitus* or "condition" because of its implication, in Calvin's view, that this makes the world nothing but a "*monstre et vaine apparence*," a "monstrous show and vain appearance."[12] The statement to which Calvin objected was Erasmus's paraphrase of Paul's testimony in 1 Corinthians 7:31 that "this world holds only the shadows of goods and evils, in which there is nothing substantial, and nothing lasting; to cling to these shadows wholeheartedly is not for those who strive after immortality."[13] For his part, Calvin interprets Paul's meaning to be that

11. Origen, *De Principiis*, 57.

12. John Calvin, as quoted in Pringle, *Epistles of Paul*, 258. One is reminded of the expression, "all hat and no cattle"!

13. Erasmus, *Paraphrases*, 104.

"the form of this world that is passing away" is comparable to the play on the stage of a theater, but not to the theater itself. The instant that the stage curtains fall upon the scene of the play, he writes, "what held the gaze of the audience is immediately swept from their sight."[14] This is consistent with Calvin's repeated references to the created world of heaven and earth as the "theater of God's glory."[15]

In his detailed exegetical notes on Paul's reference to the "the *schēma* of this world that is passing away" some eighteen years later in his critical commentary on 1 Corinthians, Weiss writes, "whether it is correct here to think of the inner structure (*Gefüge*) or the *habitus*, status externus, rather than the stage of a theater is not certain to me," but notes 1 John 2:17, 2 Peter 3:10, and other passages as instances where the world itself is said to be "passing away."[16] In his 1892 monograph, however, he expresses no uncertainty that "the modern Protestant worldview" cannot share such an "eschatological attitude" as is indicated in 1 Corinthians 7:31, but by contrast it "lives in the joyful confidence that *this* world will evermore become the showplace of the people of God" and does not await a kingdom or grace coming down from heaven to earth in contravention of this world.

More recent commentators have used such renderings for Paul's intended meaning of "the *schēma* of this world" as: "all social, personal, and commercial expressions" causing the "anxiety" (*amerimnous*) from which he wants the Corinthians to be free (7:32);[17] "the configuration of this world as we know it [in] its present structural arrangement";[18] "the life situation of the Christian community [that] is transitory since it exists in the final season of the last age [that] is nearly over";[19] and "the outward appearance of the present mode of earthly life [that] is going out of existence, because it is to be transformed as a result of the Christ-event."[20]

As to the second question Weiss's work raises regarding the kingdom of God, his monograph of 1892 proved especially unsettling by arguing (1) that "the modern dogmatic idea" of the kingdom of God prominent in the theology of the late nineteenth century since Kant could not factually be considered a historically accurate idea of the kingdom as it is found in

14. Calvin, *First Epistle*, 160.

15. Calvin, *Institutes*, 1.5.8 (p. 61) and elsewhere.

16. Weiss, *Erste Korintherbrief*, 201.

17. Fee, *First Epistle*, 335–36.

18. Collins, *First Corinthians*, 295

19. Orr and Walter, *First Corinthians*, 221.

20. Fitzmyer, *First Corinthians*, 318.

the gospel preaching of Jesus, but also (2) that, in spite of this inaccuracy, the modern dogmatic idea was nevertheless the one consonant with faith at the present time because the difference in historical situations meant it was no longer possible to share the apocalyptic worldview of the gospel witness.[21]

The classic account of the broader context of Weiss's contribution found in Albert Schweitzer's *The Quest of the Historical Jesus* characterizes the historical investigation of the life of Jesus, of which Weiss's work was part, as a "struggle against the tyranny of dogma," here meaning originally the so-called two natures dogma of fifth-century Chalcedonian Christology. In Weiss's case the "modern dogmatic idea" to which he is responding is that of Immanuel Kant's influential turn to moral autonomy in conceiving of the kingdom of God as an "ethical commonwealth" to be realized, not by the agency of an eschatological inbreaking, but as an immanent religious development, as expressed by such followers at the time as Weiss's own father-in-law, Albrecht Ritschl, and Julius Kaftan, with his conception of the kingdom as "a supreme ethical ideal" requiring human initiative for its actualization. It is this modern idealistic idea of a kingdom to be reached through human initiative that Weiss labels "thoroughly unbiblical."[22] To the contrary, he writes, in the world according to the gospel proclamation of Jesus, "The actualization of the Kingdom of God is *not* a matter for human initiative, but entirely a matter for God's initiative."[23] Notwithstanding, Weiss concludes, such an apocalyptic concept of the coming kingdom with its view of the world proves impossible for the modern Christian believer.

The epoch-making importance that Schweitzer attributes to Weiss in the opening up of eschatological awareness in New Testament interpretation and the problems it poses for theology was by no means limited to Weiss's influence alone. His was only one factor in a larger movement at the time that had its counterpart in such figures as Johann Christoph Blumhardt, the younger Christoph Blumhardt, and Franz Overbeck. The Blumhardts inspired young pastors such as Karl Barth with their practical ministry of prophetic witness and social involvement based upon the eschatological hope of the coming kingdom of God. Barth credited the influence of the Blumhardts with introducing him to the "strange new world

---

21. I have discussed this legacy with respect to the theological treatment of biblical references to "heaven" in *The Difference Heaven Makes*. See the responses by Ziegler, Sonderegger, Eppehimer, Wood, and Duff in *Theology Today* 68/1 (2011).

22. Kant, *Religion*, 91.

23. Weiss, *Jesus' Proclamation*, 132.

within the Bible," a world that was not reducible to religious, moral, or historical frames of reference.[24] The controversial Overbeck, a friend and faculty colleague of Nietzsche at Basel, in a statement Barth later quoted in his essay of 1920, *Unsettled Questions for Theology Today*, scandalized many with his claim that "the contradiction between the original Christian eschatology and the contemporary hope for the future is fundamental."[25] Overbeck, who until 1897, like Weiss, held the title of Professor of New Testament and Early Church History, was unique among his peers in contending that all theology, by definition—and not just modern theology—is antithetical to Christianity. In this respect Overbeck declared modern theology to be "nothing new" and asserted one of his basic theses to be "that theology has always been modern and for this reason it has always been the natural betrayer of Christianity (*Christlichkeit*). Hence the situation in modern theology is only the manifestation of an ancient relationship."[26]

UNSETTLED QUESTIONS FROM MARTYN

In retrospect, major differences between this first context and the second are quite apparent. One speaks with far less confidence today about the so-called historical Jesus and his consciousness as an extract from the gospel testimony itself. Since Weiss's time a breadth of research and analysis has been devoted to defining the word "apocalyptic," both as a literary genre and as a theological concept, and any brief label risks the trivialization of oversimplification.[27] Ernst Käsemann, when pressed for a precise definition, replied, "I speak of primitive Christian apocalyptic to denote the expectation of an imminent Parousia," thus locating the defining sense of apocalyptic as "imminent expectation" in the post-Easter testimony that "the Lord is at hand" (Phil 4:5), with its attendant hope of the vindication of the Son of Man in all things—"on his way to his enthronement," as Käsemann expresses it—rather than, as in the case of Weiss, in the Synoptic testimony of Jesus' preaching that "the Kingdom is at hand."[28] Yet in each case, it should be noted, it is this *at-handness*, signaled by the little Greek adverb (ἐγγύς), that is recognized as basic to the gospel's apocalyptic testimony. For dogmatic theology that seeks to be attentive to this testimony

24. Barth, *Word of God*, 28–50.
25. Barth, *Theology and Church*, 63.
26. Overbeck, *Christianity of Theology*, 151.
27. See Sturm, "Word 'Apocalyptic.'"
28. Käsemann, *Questions of Today*, 107–9.

today, this *at-handness* becomes a crucial point whose significance must be addressed.

In turning to Martyn, the apocalyptic situation as portrayed is more complex as additional factors from Paul's testimony, mainly Paul's letter to the Galatians, are taken into account. We may select as a key defining text for Martyn Paul's testimony in Galatians 6:14–16, which Martyn translates as follows:

> 14 As for me, God forbid that I should boast in anything except the cross of our Lord Jesus Christ, by which the cosmos has been crucified to me and I to the cosmos. 15 For neither is circumcision anything nor is uncircumcision anything. What is something is the new creation. 16 And to all those who will follow this standard in their lives, let peace and mercy be upon them, that is to say upon the Israel of God.[29]

With respect to the statements in this text—which Martyn acknowledges are "of the kind to make the head swim" and even to cause one to "wonder whether they do not constitute a flight from reality"!—Martyn discusses a number of points that would take us well beyond the limits of our inquiry, but highlights three which have particular bearing upon our topic. First, and most fundamentally, is the fact that Paul's testimony makes cosmic reference to the world, or more exactly, in Martyn's words, "two different worlds." Second is the question of the makeup of the world according to Paul, which Martyn characterizes as involving "apocalyptic antinomies." And third is the question of the sense in which the so-called new creation of which Paul speaks is something that may be said to have an embodiment.[30] In each instance Martyn writes of Paul's apocalyptic testimony about the cosmos as being about "the real world," leaving the reader to ask if this is not simply the first-century world of Paul's time, but also "the real world" of our time today.[31]

That for Paul "the cross of the Lord Jesus Christ" is depicted as a cosmic event of such magnitude that it is said to involve the cosmos's own crucifixion, as well as Paul's himself, alerts us in the first instance, Martyn argues, that we are being introduced here to a frame of reference that is not reducible to religious categories or, as we may add, recalling Weiss's words,

29. Martyn, *Galatians*, 10.

30. See Martyn, "Apocalyptic Antinomies," "Elements of the Cosmos," and also Comment 51, "Apocalyptic Antinomies and the New Creation," in *Galatians*, 570–74.

31 See, as examples, Martyn's references to "the real world" in *Galatians*, 502, and in *Theological Issues*, 121, 233.

to a *religious* "framing" of "a unified Christian view of the world and life." Martyn defines what he means by "religion" as "the various communal, cultic means—always involving the distinction of sacred from profane— by which human beings seek to know and to be happily related to the gods or God"; adding, "Religion is thus a human enterprise that Paul sharply distinguishes from God's apocalyptic act in Christ."[32]

From such a claim it follows that a "cultural synthesis" of developing historical phenomena conceived as homogenous data—the sort of cultural harmonization Ernst Troeltsch attributed specifically to the function of religion in society and the task of "constructive theology"—represents a very different framing of "the world," one that from the testimony of the Apostle would have to be considered, again recalling Weiss's words, as "thoroughly unbiblical."[33]

The apocalyptic act of the cross, as Martyn interprets Paul, involves nothing less than an actual "turn of the ages" in that a newly constituted state of affairs is envisioned as taking place in contravention of "anti-God powers" previously holding sway. What is apocalypsed is thus, in Martyn's account, an "invasion" of the course of this world and not its continued development. Or, stated more exactly, it is a rectification, or setting right, in the orb of "the present evil age" (Gal 1:4), whose origin is "outside" that orb in God's sending of the Son and of the Spirit of the Son (Gal 4:4–6).[34] This rectification reveals a world in the thrall of powers inimical to its own good, and finds in the "cross of our Lord Jesus Christ" the crucifixion of that world and the constituting of nothing less than, in Paul's words, "a new creation."

Such rectification involves, in Martyn's description of Paul's testimony, a "three-actor moral drama" that Martyn finds to be in contrast to "theological texts [in which] the orthodox moral drama has two actors, the divine agent and the human agent." A reading of Galatians 5, however, shows Paul referring not only to divine agency, as indicated by the Spirit of Christ, and to the human agency exercised by the Galatians themselves, but to a "third actor" of usurping agency. This "third actor" Martyn describes as "*anti*-God powers (represented here by the Impulsive Desire of the flesh [the *epithymia sarkos*, or in Hebrew *yēser bāśār*], the power which Paul elsewhere calls Sin in the singular)." In contrasting this framing of moral agency with what he attributes to the more "orthodox" two-actor

32. Martyn, *Galatians*, 588.

33. Troeltsch, *Religion in History*, 11–32.

34. Martyn, *Theological Issues*, 82.

view found in "theological texts," it is worth noting by way of definition that Martyn explains, "In the present essay I use the term 'apocalyptic' to refer to the *three-actor* drama."[35]

In interpreting the cosmic dimensions of this threefold understanding of agency that Martyn sees as characterizing Paul's apocalyptic testimony in Galatians, the references to *ta stoicheia tou kosmou* in Galations 4:3 and 4:9 call for special attention. In ancient usage, as Martyn documents, these *stoicheia*, or "elements of the cosmos," were understood to be made up of pairs of opposites. It is these opposites that Martyn calls "antinomies," noting that "for Paul, as for the Pythagoreans, an antinomy is more than an antithesis, for an antinomy lies at the foundation of the cosmos" and is not merely "a form of rhetoric, a product of human thought."[36] By declaring that "the cross of the Lord Jesus Christ" has freed him from the enslavement of the cosmos as constituted, for example, by the antinomy of "circumcision" and "uncircumcision"—has indeed "crucified" that cosmos—Paul testifies to nothing less than "a new creation" from which the cosmos as constituted prior to that crucifixion is no more.

Such an ancient way of thinking about the elements of the cosmos (the *stoicheia*) in terms of opposites would be familiar to those in receipt of Paul's letter. Yet Martyn also acknowledges that *stoicheia* also included in ancient usage the four physical elements thought to comprise the composition of the natural world: "earth, water, air, fire." In the cross, as the "turn of the ages," a reconstituted sense of the *stoicheia's* antinomies results in "a new creation." But the question of the *stoicheia's* four cosmic elements of earth, water, air, and fire is not hereby addressed by Paul.[37] (In a note Martyn points out, "among Christian texts, 2 Peter 3:10 and 12, where the author refers to the dissolution of the world's elements in a final cosmic conflagration," adding, "a Stoic motif."[38])

Significantly, perhaps anticipating dogmatic objections, Martyn remarks that just as the antinomies ingredient in the elements of the cosmos would not in ancient usage be understood simply as "rhetorical antitheses," or conventions of speech, neither can they be equated with Marcion's "ontological antitheses." For Paul, despite Marcion's heretical attempt to marshal his writings in support of contrasting the God of creation with the God of Jesus Christ, the reconstituted antinomies of the turn of the ages that originate in the apocalypse of Christ and his Spirit, distinguishing

35. Martyn, "Gospel Invades Philosophy," 27.
36. Martyn, *Theological Issues*, 115.
37. Ibid., 127.
38. Ibid. See Harink, *1 & 2 Peter*, 175–86.

that new world from the old, are explicitly affirmed as *creation*, God's *new creation*.[39]

Finally, in asking whether this new creation can be pointed to as having an "embodiment," Martyn's exegesis of Galatians finds Paul giving three answers: "The new creation is embodied in Christ, in the church, and thus in the Israel of God."[40] But, according to the foregoing points, it is not the Christ, or church, or Israel of God as defined religiously according to the old sacred and profane antinomies as identified prior to the apocalypse of Christ's advent unto the cross. The real world in Paul's vision is a battleground, but the battle lines are not those drawn apart from Christ's appearing. As "the dawn of the new creation" the embodiments of this dawning conform to no conceptual terrain or territorial establishment of the old crucified cosmos with its antinomies.[41] Rather, Martyn writes, in the new creation of which alone Paul confesses to boast, "The territory in which human beings now live is a newly invaded space, and that means that its structures cannot remain unchanged."[42]

Are we left with an abstract dialectic of a putative cosmic rectification in which an eternal vindication of grace over its opposition never, as it were, touches down to earth or is concretely grounded anywhere? Here Martyn's reading of the Pauline testimony as calling for and calling forth "bi-focal vision" firmly rejects any such view. "To see *bi-focally* in Paul's terms is to see *both* the enslaving Old Age and God's invading and liberating new creation," and to see them "simultaneously." Yet this liberating invasion is "not demonstrable in the categories of the Old Age or with the means of perception native to the Old Age."[43] For concrete examples of such a bifocal envisioning of the world's current inbreaking, Martyn points to the American civil rights struggles of the 1960s and to

39. Martyn, *Theological Issues*, 115. See also the references to Marcion in the index of *Galatians*.

40. Martyn, *Theological Issues*, 122–23.

41. For a critical questioning of what this means, not only with respect to epistemology and ethics but also current "elements of the cosmos" as known in today's cosmological sciences, see Wilkinson, *Christian Eschatology*. Wilkinson acknowledges the influential writings of John Polkinghorne in this connection and provides an extensive bibliography.

42. Martyn, *Theological Issues*, 121.

43. Martyn, "Paul to Flannery O'Connor," 284. See especially Martyn's "Epistemology." In an earlier work on the Fourth Gospel Martyn writes of a "two-level drama" in which the past and present are seen together in earthly events, qualifying the apocalyptic distinctions, but discussing why "stereoptic vision" is necessary. See *History & Theology*, 135–43.

the individual in the World Trade Center on 9/11 who chose to remain at the side of his disabled colleague. In this connection James Cone's recent book, *The Cross and the Lynching Tree*, is most noteworthy.

CONCLUDING OBSERVATIONS

Having looked briefly at these two critical contexts of New Testament apocalyptic interpretation, we may now extend and rephrase Julius Kaftan's reported statement about Johannes Weiss to ask, "If the conception of the real world according to Paul is an apocalyptic one, as Martyn describes, then is it possible to make use of this conception in dogmatics?" No doubt most contributors to this volume, as well as its readers, will in their various and independently critical ways have answered yes, and accounted for themselves accordingly. In doing so they will have encountered a host of still outstanding issues, but also remarkable insights, that Martyn's apocalyptic interpretation presents for today's dogmatic accounting. There are the immediate and rightful questions arising from ecological concerns over environmental responsibility and over the social and political impact of fundamentalist apocalyptic construals. But also there is the great host of issues implicit in Christology regarding, for example, divine and human agency, whether advent does indeed precede epiphany, about good and evil, sin and salvation—all subjects much debated in a history of doctrine where Manicheanism and Marcion are rejected and Luther's "theology of the cross" does battle with Aristotelian teleologies of nature and grace over who is calling things by their right name. By facilitating a renewed awareness of the gospel's apocalyptic testimony, Martyn contributes not only to a deepened understanding of the theological subjects he explicitly addresses, but also, and thereby implicitly, to a rethinking of what a dogmatic accounting involves. This is best shown by considering how Johannes Weiss's claims regarding the task of dogmatics may be said to look when viewed today in retrospect from the context of Martyn's work.

The key issue highlighted here in both contexts of apocalyptic interpretation is what one takes "the real world" to be. With respect to whether the gospel testimony regarding a new state of affairs coming to pass in contravention of an opposing *schēma* of this world that is said to be passing away affords too one-sided or unstable a frame of reference to be dogmatically creditable for "framing a unified Christian view of the world and life," or whether it may be said to be warranted as expressing communally today a faith authored by the gospel, the difficulty has not to do, as it is often mistakenly alleged, with the acceptance of modern science, but rather with the governing rules of univocity that arise with modern attempts to credit dogmatics as a scholarly discipline.

Much was made at the turn of the twentieth century of the alleged scholarly superiority of historical method to dogmatic method in modern theological inquiry. A leading instance in this regard was Ernst Troeltsch's 1898 essay on "Historical and Dogmatic Method in Theology," which served to define the terms "historical" and "dogmatic" for the emerging modern theology.[44] Objecting to dogmatic method as the uncritical abstraction of church teaching from its historical context, Troeltsch argued that all knowing of "the real world," including our knowing of biblical testimony and church dogma, arises out of an environment of interrelated factors such as time, place, and the cultural conditions that constitute the historical context. If by "dogmatic" one means, as Troeltsch does in this essay, authoritarian assertion without critical regard for questions of context—either the originating context of a text or the context of its current hearers and recipients—the objection is well founded. But equally, if by "historical" one means that the only context that counts for real is one limited to the space and time dimensions of earth, when these are viewed, to quote Troeltsch, as a single nexus of "unitary forces" and "analogous occurrences," or what he calls "the univocity and the total interconnection of historical events," most of the gospel's cosmic claims of a "new creation" are disqualified for our hearing from the start.[45] In this case, nothing can be credited as actual that does not qualify as being historically factual.

But if what is coming to pass as "new creation" and the form of this world that is said to be passing away are not heard of in this testimony as unitary forces or analogous occurrences, in Troeltsch's terms, or as the same or "univocal" kinds of events, to judge their reality status accordingly would be to violate the native context of their hearing. Today, however, neither of these so-defined modern meanings of "dogmatic" and "historical" from a century ago finds a scholarly consensus in theology. Historicism as well as dogmatism has come to have its philosophical and theological critics. Attesting the gospel news of the cosmic imminence proclaimed to be at hand thus requires that our inquiry learn from, but not be prejudiced by, these earlier characterizations of modernity and their stipulations regarding "historical" and "dogmatic" accountability. Simply substituting *kairos* for *chronos* short-circuits the problem. Much twentieth-century

---

44. Troeltsch, *Religion in History*, 11–32.

45. Ibid., 13, 17, and 27.

theological consideration of what Weiss called the gospel's "completely apocalyptic and eschatological character" was subsequently spent arguing alternatives to a univocal literalization of apocalyptic testimony through proposals most prominently of myth, saga, and promise. Today it cannot be said that agreement among competing proposals for a deliteralization of apocalyptic testimony has been reached.

What can be said in retrospect, I think, is that Weiss posed the critical insight regarding the difference apocalyptic significance makes for dogmatics, but he did so by exactly misstating it. An at-handness that is proximate but not approximated by prior conditions requires precisely the reversal of the terms by which he allows for the task of dogmatics. It is not "a new rate of exchange" (*Kurs*) for "an old coinage" (*Münzen*) that dogmatics seeks, as if modern theology can only reissue a devalued gospel currency for what the current going rate of interest may allow (the "heaven is whatever we want it to be" school of thought), but "a new coinage" bearing the ever-current imprint of a once-for-all but not all-at-once turn of events in the sending of the Son and the Spirit, as "the old rate of exchange" that a dogmatic theology attentive to a hearing of the gospel as news of a new cosmos now taking place (*apocalypsed*) bears witness.

If we follow the dogmatic implications of this reversal of Weiss's terms, we are challenged to think of the *Kurs*, or "rate of exchange," not as the current trading value of the gospel news of heaven as determined by what the market will allow (which is where Weiss's own appraisal and those of some later cultural synthesizers falters), but as what has traditionally been called the *regula fidei*, or better, to cite the words of the Second Helvetic Confession of 1566, that which is *cum regula fidei et caritatis congruit*.[46] Only now—and this is the decisive point—the faith and love that are congruent with this "rule" are recognized in the first instance as happenings said to be apocalypsed, as taking place (Rom 1:17), and not, as it were, deposits of binding or folded grave clothes forever entombed in place (John 20:5–7), not of the order of what Martyn calls a "nomistic rule."

This apocalyptic sense of *regula* is in keeping with the single instance in the gospel testimonies, Galatians 6:15–16, where the Greek word for "rule," *kanon*, is used for the standard of faithfulness: "For neither circumcision nor uncircumcision is anything," Paul writes, "but a new creation is everything! As for those who will follow this rule [κανόνι]—peace be upon

---

46. For further comment on the dogmatic criteria of doctrine see Morse, *Not Every Spirit*, 45–70.

them, and mercy, and upon the Israel of God" (NRSV). The term "new creation" for the canon or rule of faith, to cite Martyn, "is an expression at home in apocalyptic writings, in which the accent lies on the motif of radical, uncompromising newness. . . . The standard, then, is not a nomistic rule, however novel. On the contrary, the standard is the *real world* that has now been made what it is by the *event* of God's gracious invasion via his Son and the Spirit of the Son."[47]

In following such a canon it is always to a current state of affairs that dogmatics as a theological discipline is called to give faithful account of what Martyn portrays as the reconstituted apocalyptic antinomy of differentiation in the real world between a cosmos "coming to pass" and an old cosmos in defeated opposition shown by this coming to be "passing away," distinguishing what is *at hand* and what is *in hand*, proximate but not approximated. This means that a primary criterion for dogmatics becomes *cruciality* in discerning "the present time" (Luke 12:54–56). Yet this criterion of *cruciality* has as its essential complement the test of *congruence*—that which is *cum regula fidei et caritatis congruit* in keeping with the "canon" Paul exhalts as "new creation" in the words, "And to all those who will follow this standard [χανόνι] in their lives, let peace and mercy be upon them, that is to say upon the Israel of God" (Gal 6:16).

Contrary to the pejorative connotations of unaccountable assertion or unself-critical authoritarianism, dogmatics as a critical appraisal of trustworthiness is an undertaking that Johannes Weiss, as historian and exegete, to his credit affirmed. The ambivalence of his own appraisal of the modern-day significance of Jesus' preaching of the kingdom sparked a century of further interpretations that have become our legacy. In the Synoptic accounts the news of such a new and inbreaking state of affairs at hand is said to be conveyed by way of parables in pointing listeners to a significance in familiar situations of their day not publicly observable according to prevailing preconceptions. Weiss thought that such talk of a coming kingdom could only be taken "*in a different sense*" in the modern world, and that this was a task for dogmatics. In retrospect it is perhaps no small irony to recall from one of the foremost of those twentieth-century dogmatic interpreters these words of Karl Barth:

> We can and must be prepared to encounter "parables of the kingdom" *in the full biblical sense*, not merely in the witness of the Bible and the various arrangements, works and words of the Christian Church, but also in the secular sphere, i.e., in the

47. Martyn, *Galatians*, 565–67.

strange interruption of the secularism of life in the world [*der Profanität des Weltlebens*]. . . . We have ears to hear the voice of the Good Shepherd even there too, distinguishing it from other clamant voices . . ."[48]

48. Barth, *Church Dogmatics*, IV/3.1:117 (emphasis added).

6

On Dogmatic/Systematic Appropriation
of Paul-According-to-Martyn

Robert W. Jenson

IT MUST BE SAID up front: relations between guild exegetes and the church's theologians have long been testy and mostly continue to be. An article with a title like the one above is still an oddity. Indeed, from time to time systematic/dogmatic theologians have become so exasperated with guild exegetes' naive theology[1] and its malign control of their results that they have taken to doing their own exegesis, handicapped in some skills though they may be. There is a current wave of this, to which I belong: I have in the latter years written two commentaries on Old Testament books. In them, I treat the creed as a hermeneutical principle; I attend to the patristic exegetical tradition, and to the Targums and Rashi; and on the way I deploy such historical-critical and linguistic skills as from occasion to occasion seem useful and I can muster.

That said, it must also appear up front: I am not competent to bandy interpretations of Paul, or of any other part of the New Testament, with J. Louis Martyn—though of course I do have an opinion or two. Nor do I

1. No reading of Scripture as Scripture in fact proceeds without theological presumptions. Since many guild exegetes pay no attention to this point, the theology that goes into their exegetical mill is subliminal and almost always childish; and so what comes out is the same. And of course, those scholars who have ceased to read Scripture *as* Scripture are then simply engaged in a possibly interesting antiquarian enterprise, rather like excavating nineteenth-century pots in Manhattan.

include him among the *naïfs* of the previous paragraph—as will appear, if I have a complaint it is of contrary character. When I am with him or read something by him, I am for the most part happy simply to profit from his knowledge and wisdom. What I can do is ask: Supposing that Paul taught the way Lou Martyn says he did, how can or should this Paul's theology determine our present theological labors?

Here I must intrude an excursus on the general role of New Testament theology in the church's continuing theological task. It is certain limitations of that role that I will note in this context. I have three in mind.

The first: There is such a thing as a consensual New Testament theology; but it is not always helpful when help with the continuing theological task is most needed. Since one of the criteria by which the canon was formed was conformity to the *regula fidei* and the baptismal questions, the *theological* consensus among the tradents and authors of the New Testament covers much the same ground as faithful theologians[2] will occupy to begin with. When, on the other hand, we have a theological *problem*, we may find the same problem unresolved in the New Testament, or a selection of divergent positions. The latter is a familiar theme of critical exegesis: e.g., there is the Christology of Paul, and then there is the Christology of Matthew, and they are not easily made to agree, etc. Some slogans of—particularly self-designated—critical exegetes may safely be ignored by the rest of us, but this one demands attention.

I suggest: the New Testament indeed does not furnish us with a *template* for our continuing theological work; what it provides is something more vital, *examples* of faithful theology. It often does not provide answers to our puzzlements, but it does display the kind of reflection needed to deal with them. What the New Testament's canonicity guarantees[3] is that the collected witnesses are engaged in the right theological enterprise, not that they always achieve replicable results.

The second: We should resist harboring a "canon within the canon." Even Paul is just one of the apostles—he could be cavalier about the status of other primary authorities, but we should not be. This is of course a council

---

2. The New Testament's consensual theology will of course be a vital authority when argument breaks out about whether a theological position is in fact faithful. Here I am assuming work on actual problems, new or perennial.

3. Assuming—like the present writer—that canonicity does guarantee something. The history of the church is in any case a mere chaos unless we trust that the Spirit shapes such events as the canon.

of perfection: we will scarcely avoid having our preferences among the biblical witnesses. But we should try not to let our predilections rule—e.g., despite Martin Luther's notorious dictum,[4] also Lutherans must attend to what James has to say.

The third: One should be cautious in exploiting all but the most obvious or unavoidable historical reconstructions. For an example at the highest level of skill and judgment, Martyrn's reconstruction of a Jewish-Christian theology shared for a certain distance by Paul and his opponents is ingenious, intricately argued, and confirms my prejudices, but of course it may nevertheless be mistaken.

Theology should not put too many of the faith's eggs in a possibly fragile scholarly basket. It will indeed sometimes be a promising move to recruit a historical reconstruction to fund or adjudicate a theological decision or development. But we will just thereby take the risk of seeing it, and us with it, debunked by later scholarship—for one that embarrassed me that way, the posit of a divine enthronement liturgy in Jerusalem's temple, by the very exegetes who first made the Old Testament come alive for me.

To turn now to the matter of this essay, what examples does Paul-according-to-Martyn then set us? I perceive three;[5] doubtless there are more.

First: Martyn's Paul is a ruthlessly single-minded thinker. There may be limits past which we ought not follow this example, but in itself and in the context of the present state of the church, it is much needed. In the discourse of Martyn's Paul, all proposals of churchly practice or teaching are judged by a single standard: How does this jibe with the *apokalypsis Christou*, the revelatory fact and message of the Messiah's crucifixion and resurrection? For Martyn's Paul, nothing can be true that if true might suggest that God needs a prior or further revelation or, what is in this theology the same thing, that Christ died in vain. This is surely a good example.

We should note the expansiveness of this principle: perhaps somewhat surprisingly, a theology that obeyed it would be a universal *scientia*. For example, a physical theory that made time reversible could not be true. For example, an ideology that perceived revelation—however peripheral—in a political movement or some group's special critical insight could not be true. And so on.

---

4. All Scripture is the gold of the divine Word in a bed of human straw, but James is "right strawy."

5. Again!

Second: This Paul cannot let go of the question about his people "according to the flesh." What is the Jews' relation to the *apokalypsis Christou*? I cannot see that he comes to an internally consistent answer—here is one of those earlier mentioned opinions—but the attack of his powerful intellect and the fact that he cannot refrain from returning to the problem is surely a mandatory example, again precisely at this point in churchly history.

For both theological development and global forces are now driving synagogue and church together. We will soon stand together or fall together—speaking, that is, "in human fashion." But if we are to stand together, we need to know why that is possible, and a general preference for getting along with one another will not suffice—to say nothing of the jejune solution that all religions are the same anyway. Whatever this may demand from the side of Judaism, the church for her part must now seek a Christian theological interpretation of the continuing existence of Judaism. Is rabbinic Judaism *nothing but* the community of those Jews who reject Jesus as the Christ? Does circumcision now count for *nothing at all* in the eyes of God?

Alternatives to such ancient negations are possible.[6] Perhaps, e.g., old Israel and continuing Judaism are *included* in the revelation of/in Christ. In patristic exegesis of the Old Testament, the figures of the "Angel" or "Glory" or Word" of the Lord, which intervene so decisively in Israel's life—taken together, they are what the rabbis have called the *Shekinah*—are the incarnate Son himself. Thus for the fathers, revelation in Israel belongs directly to the revelation of/in Christ.

But is such a position Pauline in Martyn's sense? The fathers quote Paul—e.g., "the rock was Christ"—in support of their teaching. But it is not clear to me that Martyn's Paul could support all their drastic and ontically intended assertions. Thus Gregory the Great in his homilies on Ezekiel writes that the enthroned and onrushing figure "like a man"[7] who calls Ezekiel to prophecy, looks like a man because he *is* one: Jesus the Christ, appearing in the Glory of God just as—we may add—on the Mount of Transfiguration. Can an *apokalypsis Christou* that comes "straight down from above" allow for such a historically extended and plotted reality of the revelation of/in Christ? More of that later.

---

6. For my attempt, see "Theology of Israel."

7. Ezek 2:26–28, my translation.

Third: Martyn's Paul directly and naturally inhabits Israel's Scripture. Despite his teaching of freedom from Mosaic Law,[8] and some interpretations that are implausible even by rabbinic standards, it does not occur to him that he might belong to a different "community of interpretation" than that of Israel's lawgivers and prophets or of the rabbis of his own time, that he might have to build and traverse a hermeneutical bridge to join them.

This example summons us *ad fontes*. For the nascent church never "adopted" or "accepted" Israel's Scriptures.[9] It went the other way around; the Scriptures funded the church. They were authoritative for the witnesses of the resurrection antecedently to the event. It was not only that the resurrection opened their eyes to the true message of Scripture—as on the road to Emmaus—it was their antecedent life in the Scriptures that enabled them to perceive the resurrection in the first place. It was not long, however, before history reversed the relation, and an active role in the church for Israel's Scripture was thought to require argumentative defense. And it was not long after this that the *regula fidei* and then the baptismal creeds developed, with a narrative of God's saving works that skips over Israel entirely, jumping straight from creation to Mary's conception.

Trying to retrieve an ancient mistake and restore a putatively more authentic original configuration is not always a good idea and is in any case never easy, but in this instance we are, in my judgment, summoned to the effort. Paul's practices—if not all his theologoumena—show us what in fact is the case: we belong to one community of interpretation with the tradents and writers and past and present readers of Israel's Scripture. When "the hermeneutical problem" is conceived as the problem of *establishing* our community with them, it is—at least within the church—a pseudoproblem.

Finally, lest a wrong impression be given, I must note that there are of course particular Pauline theologoumena that may commend themselves quite directly to the continuing theological work—some of which I for my part have simply taken over. Some of these may be little affected by the truth or error of Martyn's general interpretation. I may mention Paul's theology of the body of Christ, particularly from 1 Corinthians 10–11; his doctrine of baptism as incorporation into this body, from Romans 6; or his identification of a general reversal of created relations as the consequence of idolatrous reversal of Creator and creature, from Romans 2. Other lists could doubtless be made.

8. Whatever that may in fact be!

9. Further to this paragraph, Jenson, *Canon and Creed*.

But now, how is systematic theology to deal with the specific features of Martyn's Paul? I confess I do have problems with that—had I none, I suppose I would not be writing an article on this theme.

And at this point let me insert a necessary distinction: between strictly systematic appropriation of a conceptual structure and broader influence. The following touches only on the former. There are many who regard themselves as students of Lou Martyn and whose dependence on his work is very real who are not implicated in the following queries.

To get right to my first and overriding question: Can we say that with the *apokalypsis Christou* God "invades" the world?[10] Is this in fact true, by the whole witness of Scripture? Can we legitimately structure a systematic doctrine of revelation by the claim? We will, I fear, answer these questions affirmatively only if Paul-according-to-Martyn is a very peremptory canon indeed within the canon.

To begin, the doctrine of creation is in the way. According to it, God has no call to invade the world, since he already rules in it. For the doctrine of creation does not say only that God once upon a time initiated the world, it says that he now sustains it by his affirmative will and specific action within it.

To be sure, this doctrine is challenged by the evil infesting creation. In my judgment, no conclusive theodicy is possible; as Luther put it to Erasmus, if we consider how things go, and judge by any standard available to us, we shall have to conclude "either that God is wicked or that he does not exist."[11] Affirmation of God as the present good Creator of a good creation is therefore always a defiant "Nevertheless . . .", but this is a defiance believers are allowed and so required to make, on Jesus' account.

Further, surely the apocalypticism that Martyn finds in Paul must have something to do with the "apocalyptic" mode of prophecy extant in Judaism. And when Paul credits his gospel not to prior authorities but to an "apocalypse of Christ Jesus" surely this qualifies his experience on the way to Damascus as like that of the seers. Martyn has not—we may hope—reinvented the language *de novo*.

Two features characterize the passages of Scripture usually labelled "apocalyptic": an unveiling of God's underlying plot for history, paradigmatically by a glimpse into heaven; and dramatic display of God's conflict with and victory over opposing powers. So far so congenial to Martyn's Paul.

---

10. This question has been raised by others as well.

11. WA 7:784.

But in actual apocalyptic prophecy we do not see God invading earth from heaven. We see instead an extended conflict carried out at once on earth and in heaven, with the heavenly version dramatizing the divine plot of the earthly events. Martyn may be right about Paul—again, I am in no position to argue the point—but if he is, Paul is an eccentric also in that part of the biblical witness to which he is said most to relate. Indeed, he may be seen as out of fellowship with most of the church represented in the canon. And that is a problem for theological appropriation, since Paul is not the only apostolic theologian.

I have a second, related, problem: Do the coordinates "vertical/horizontal" make a good scheme on which to plot God's action? Is revelation/salvation perpendicular to temporal history?

We have to ask where this discourse comes from—just as we ask where "substance" or "being" or "hypostasis" came from. For those of a certain generation, the answer is not far to seek; the linguistic atmosphere is familiar. I too was entranced by Barth's second *Romans* and Bultmann's system—he did have one—and I once read a lot of Ebeling and Käsemann. Perhaps most biographically significant, I awakened theologically in a midwestern Lutheranism in which intellectual sophistication and knowledge of Søren Kierkegaard's thought were more or less equated—it was some time before I knew more about Hegel than that "S.K." disapproved of him. And indeed, much of all that is still in me.

But the critique of "Greek metaphysics" to which it led me finally doubled back on itself. It dawned on me that the late modern discourse of tangents and perpendiculars and incommensurabilities in general was just Platonism stripped to its geometry. What, e.g., does Bultmann mean by "myth"? He means any story of related sequential events that pretends to be about God, which is exactly what Plato meant. The difference is that Plato thought that in this life he could not escape myth whereas Bultmann thought he could see through it.[12] Which is also why Bultmann could recognize his own concerns in Barth's *Romans*, with its talk of a revelation that touches time without extension in it.

The point is not that the Greeks went in for metaphysics and the gospel should do without them,[13] or that there are "Hebrew" and "Greek" ways of thinking and that Hebrew is better. What the Greeks happened to call "philosophy," "love of wisdom," culminated in wisdom about God,

---

12. Plato preserved the *Vorstellung* in the *Begriff*; Bultmann was on Hegel's left wing.

13. A la the most properly so-called liberal theology, in the train of Ritschl.

that is, in what the Christians would come to call "theology." The pagan Greeks developed the theology of one putative God, revealed to Homer and Parmenides, and the witnesses of the gospel developed the theology of another, revealed to the prophets and apostles. The two theologies are contrary; the debate between them has been greatly fruitful, but it *is* a debate. The one is wisdom about a God whose eternity is perpendicular to time and other is wisdom about a God whose eternity both embraces and is involved in time. Much as it goes against the polemical consensus, the notion of a *Heilsgeschichte* maps what Scripture as a whole presents better than can any geometry.

The problem with the old history-of-salvation theology was that it treated the saving history as a plotted sequence of events located *within* the secular construct we now ordinarily call history. The movement was undone by the difficulty of drawing the boundary—if Cyrus belongs to the history of salvation, why not the whole movement of peoples that enabled him? And if that movement . . . ?

But what if the old history-of-salvation theology merely had it the wrong way around? What if the narrative told by Scripture, from Genesis 1 to the end of the Revelation, were itself the embracing historical reality, within which secular constructs, like the Darwinian tale or the standard narrative of the Enlightenment or what the experts tell us about Cyrus, have to find their places and to which they must accommodate themselves if they are to claim a grip on truth? What if Truth itself obligated the church's thinking to take this at once countercultural and hegemonic position? In this essay, I merely throw out the possibility.

PART TWO

Apocalyptic and Christian Doctrines

7

Apocalypse and Incarnation

The Participatory Logic of Paul's Gospel

Susan Grove Eastman

LIKE VERY MANY OTHERS, I owe an incalculable debt to J. Louis Martyn. Martyn himself would no doubt scoff at such a statement, because, as he repeatedly reminds us, there is no *quid pro quo* in the arena of God's grace in Christ; everything is gift, and therein lies the power of the gospel. Nonetheless, there may yet be a happy overflow of gratitude returned to God for the gifts bestowed through God's servants.[1] Let this essay be a testament of such gratitude, above all for Martyn's insistent proclamation of Paul's gospel, in which "the uncontingent, prevenient, invading nature of God's grace shows God to be the powerful and victorious Advocate who is intent on the liberation of the entire race of human beings."[2] This "invading grace" is "the power that Paul saw in the cross, the event in which the name Immanuel was enacted: 'God with us.'"[3] Martyn's own work invites us to think theologically about Paul's letters, and to do so in the sovereign presence of this crucified God. I trust that this volume of essays will serve also as such an invitation, always in conversation with Martyn's own provocative and unsettling reflections.

1. For an illuminating discussion of the overflow of grace and gift, see Barclay, "Manna and Grace."
2. Martyn, *Issues*, 289.
3. Ibid.

In this essay I hope to think through some theological implications of Martyn's pithy claim that the cross is the enactment of "God with us."[4] Martyn consistently identifies the cross as *the* singular, punctiliar apocalypse in which God invaded the enslaved cosmos with liberating power. For example, he writes, "[I]n the thoroughly real event of Christ's crucifixion, God's war of liberation was commenced and decisively settled, making the cross the foundation of Paul's apocalyptic theology."[5] Here even the *commencement* of God's redemptive "war" is located at the cross. Yet, as hinted by the reference to "Immanuel," implicit in that apocalyptic act is the incarnate identity of the Crucified One. This presumption shows in Martyn's own language of "divine invasion," and even more tellingly in his emphasis on the "direction of the line of movement" that always extends first from God to humanity, and only reciprocally as a divinely instigated and enacted movement from humanity to God.[6]

Following these cues, in this essay I will argue that Martyn's portrayal of apocalypse as divine invasion illuminates the incarnational logic implicit in Paul's message of the cross. That logic in turn discloses the Pauline theme of "participation in Christ" as the good news of God's full, paradoxical, and transforming solidarity with Adamic humanity, with important implications for Christology, soteriology, and ecclesiology. With regard to the first, the motif of "divine invasion" needs to be pressed further in its Christological implications, to recover the centrality in Paul's thought of Christ's humanity as well as his divinity. This recovery, in turn, unites Paul's language of "righteousness" (*dikaioō, dikaiosyne*) and participation within the action of God in Christ: Christ's death on the cross is effectively "for" the human race, on our behalf, because it is essentially "with" and even "in" humanity, in the matrices that constrain and construct our present reality. Finally, through union with Christ who participates fully with and for the entire human race, even as it labors under the bondage of Sin, the church discovers its mission as the vanguard of Christ's apocalyptic redemption of the cosmos.

---

4. In keeping with the focus of this volume, I will limit my essay to theological engagement with Martyn's proposals and with the text of Paul's letters. Pauline scholars will recognize the exegetical and translation choices I have made along the way.

5. Martyn, *Galatians*, 101.

6. See, e.g., Martyn, "Events in Galatia," 168: "For Paul, the dominant line is the one along which God *has* moved *into the cosmos* in the invasive sending of Christ and in Christ's faithful death for all. . . .[T]he difference between human movement into the covenant and God's movement into the cosmos is, in the terms of Galatians, the watershed distinction between religion and ἀποκάλυψις."

PARTICIPATORY CHRISTOLOGY

Martyn's construal of Paul's gospel is drawn from Galatians, a text that he reads as decisive testimony to the apostle's distinctive apocalyptic outlook. Galatians discloses this outlook through the temporal markers that thread through the letter, from "the present evil age" (1:4) to "the fullness of time" (4:4) to "new creation" (6:15). Paul provides further evidence of his apocalyptic thinking by framing the situation inaugurated in Christ as one of cosmic conflict between the Spirit of God, given through Christ, and "the flesh," which is associated with both the present evil age in general, and specifically with circumcision (5:16–26; 6:7–8, 13).

In particular Martyn notes Paul's use of the verb *apokalyptō* in 1:16 and 3:23, and its cognate noun, *apocalypsis*, in 1:12 and 2:2. These are key texts for his interpretation of Pauline apocalypse in terms of God's liberating invasion of the old age in which humanity is held captive. In 1:12 Paul insists on the divine initiative that broke into his life with the gospel, apart from human teaching. Indeed, the content of this gospel is not simply a set of teachings *about* Christ, because it is the apocalypse of God's own Son *in* his own life (*en emoi*; 1:16). This divine break-in changed not only the course of Paul's life, but Paul himself, as is testified by his former victims: "He who once persecuted us is now preaching the faith he once tried to destroy!" (1:23). Hereafter Paul's actions will be guided by "apocalypse," and implicitly, therefore, not by human guidance, including direction from the church in Jerusalem. Thus when he does go to Jerusalem to visit the church leaders there, it is not because they summoned him, but because God sent him "according to apocalypse" (2:2). Finally, in 3:23 Paul depicts the time before Christ as a time of confinement under the Law awaiting "the coming faith to be *apocalypsed*." The two parallel sentences that immediately follow explicate this coming of faith as the coming of Christ (3:24, 25). Shortly thereafter, Paul repeats and amplifies this announcement of Christ's arrival on the human scene in terms of God's "sending" of his Son: "When the fullness of time had come, God sent forth his Son, born of woman, born under the law, to redeem those who were under the law, so that we might receive adoption as sons" (4:4–5). As Martyn argues, in these passages there is a tight relationship between *apokalyptō*, the verb *erchomai* ("to come on the scene"), and the verb *exapostellō* ("to send"): "From 2:16, 3:22–25, and 4:4–6, we see that Paul is referring interchangeably to the coming of Christ, to the coming of Christ's Spirit, and to the coming both of Christ's faith and of the faith kindled by Christ's faith."[7]

---

7. Martyn, *Galatians*, 362. See also Tannehill, "Participation in Christ," 232: "Gal

Taken together, these instances of apocalyptic language in Galatians set forth a picture of God's initiative and dynamic presence through the advent of Christ, who dramatically "comes on the scene" with liberating power. In light of Martyn's emphasis on the cross as the singular apocalyptic event, however, it is significant that none of these verses is explicitly about the *crucifixion* of Christ as the punctiliar apocalyptic event. This is not to say that the crucifixion of God's Son is not central to Paul's proclamation of the gospel—*mē genoito*! Yet, particularly in 4:4–6, Paul's focus is on Christ's human characteristics: Christ is the one whom God sent to be "born of a woman, born under the law." This suggests that the redemptive power of that crucifixion is bound up in the human as well as the divine identity of the Crucified One.

Other verses where Paul speaks of God "sending" Christ display a similar emphasis on Christ's incarnation as well as his crucifixion. In Romans 8:3, Paul proclaims: "For God has done what the law, weakened by the flesh, could not do: sending his own Son in the likeness of sinful flesh and for sin, he condemned sin in the flesh." The condemnation of Sin in the flesh implies the crucifixion, but "in the likeness of sinful flesh" implies incarnation; as Morna Hooker notes, "however we interpret these words, they are surely a reference to the incarnation, and an attempt to affirm that Christ shared fully in human experience."[8] Robert Tannehill further expands on the idea of incarnation in Romans 8:3, which

> reveals an important presupposition of Paul's gospel about Jesus' saving death. God has sent God's Son to participate in the human plight. The Son is sent 'in likeness of flesh of sin,' which makes possible effective action against sin and a new kind of life for believers. In other words, atonement for sin presupposes the prior divine action of sending God's Son to participate in the human situation, an act in which the Son identifies with humanity in its need.[9]

Philipians 2:5–11 also discloses this Pauline "presupposition" through its extensive depiction of Christ's humanity "in the form of a slave" and "in the likeness of human beings." Operative here is the participatory logic in Paul's thinking: God in Christ enters into the human condition at its most desperate point, under the dominion of Sin as a cosmic power, and subject

---

3:22–25, in its most natural reading, equates the coming of Christ with the coming of faith."

8. Hooker, "Interchange in Christ," 18.

9. Tannehill, "Participation in Christ," 227.

to condemnation and death. This divine movement in turn instigates and enacts a reciprocal human entrance into fellowship with Christ. Christ came among us in full partnership, suffering the depredations of sin and the judgment of death, so that in and with Christ we might be united with God in a life-giving fellowship.

Paul goes to rhetorical extremes to get this point across: "For our sake God made him who knew no sin to be sin, so that in him we might become the righteousness of God" (2 Cor 5:21); "Christ redeemed us from the curse of the law, having become a curse for us—for it is written, "Cursed be everyone who hangs on a tree"—that in Christ Jesus the blessing of Abraham might come upon the Gentiles, that we might receive the promise of the Spirit through faith" (Gal 3:13–14). As in Galatians 4:4–5 and Romans 8:3, these statements begin with a clause depicting Christ's immersion in the human condition, followed by a purpose clause in which the attributes or benefits of Christ are transferred to human beings. Calvin called this the "wondrous exchange"; Hooker calls it "interchange in Christ"; Tannehill speaks of an "exchange of attributes" and a reciprocal "identification" between Christ and humanity.[10] The picture is not simply one of trading places, because Christ remains divine as well as human, and human beings do not take Christ's place in the Godhead. So, for example, in 1 Corinthians 1:30 Paul names Christ as our righteousness and sanctification and redemption; in 2 Corinthians 5:21 we "become the righteousness of God" *in Christ* even as, paradoxically, this transformation takes place because Christ was "made to be sin." Hence the interaction between Christ and humanity is one of full, mutual participation in which neither party becomes completely absorbed in the other. At the same time, the liberating effects of Christ's actions do presume a relationship of exchange or even substitution: because Christ becomes a curse, we are delivered from

10. Calvin writes, "[W]e cannot be condemned for our sins, from whose guilt he has absolved us, since he willed to take them to himself as if they were his own. This is the wonderful exchange which, out of his measureless benevolence, he has made with us; that, becoming Son of man with us, he has made us sons of God with him; that, by his descent to earth, he has prepared an ascent to heaven for us; that, by taking on our mortality, he has conferred his immortality upon us; that, accepting our weakness, he has strengthened us by his power; that, receiving our poverty unto himself, he has transferred his wealth to us; that, taking the weight of our iniquity upon himself (which oppressed us), he has clothed us with his righteousness" (*Institutes* 4.17.2, 1362). I am grateful to George Hunsinger for directing my attention to this passage, and for alerting me to participatory elements in Calvin's understanding of salvation. For Hooker, see "Interchange in Christ," *passim*; for Tannehill, see "Participation in Christ," *passim*.

the curse; because Christ is made to be sin, although being without sin, we are delivered from Sin; because God condemned Sin in the flesh of Christ, we are liberated from its power so as to fulfill the just requirement of the Law (Rom 8:3–4). Christ both joins himself to us and stands in our place.

PARTICIPATORY REDEMPTION

In all these passages we see a participatory Christology that entails Christ's full immersion into human, bodily existence such that human beings in turn find life "in Christ." Yet another aspect of Paul's participatory thinking is implicit in this Christology. He presumes that human identity is already and always constructed and constrained through being joined with and subjected to external powers. In Ernst Käsemann's formulation, "We are always what we are in the mode of belongingness and participation, whether as friend or foe, whether in thinking, acting, or suffering."[11] Such belongingness entails vulnerability and the unavoidable qualification of one's actions through the network of human and cosmic forces that permeates the cosmos. Belonging to the body of Christ connects one with the power of God, mediated through a "moving and expanding network of saving relationship."[12] But apart from the redemption accomplished through Christ, humanity belongs to what Paul calls "the present evil age" (Gal 1:4) and "the body of death" (Rom 7:24).

This anthropology is thoroughly participatory and apocalyptic, assuming a situation of universal imprisonment under the power of Sin. Thus entangled, human beings live under Sin's tyranny and are also complicit in its rule, thereby standing under condemnation and Death. The result for subjective experience is a vicious circle of culpability and compulsion, from which humanity cannot free itself. The human predicament therefore requires more than forgiveness pronounced from on high; it requires a rescue operation on the ground. Indeed, the rescue operation itself discloses the depth of the problem: "God would not have to carry out an invasion in order merely to forgive erring human beings. The root trouble lies deeper than human guilt, and it is more sinister. The whole of humanity—indeed, the whole of creation (3:22)—is, in fact, trapped, enslaved under the power of the present evil age."[13]

---

11. Käsemann, "On Paul's Anthropology," 21.

12. Williams, "Renewal of Community," 235–36.

13. Martyn, *Galatians*, 105.

Paul's gospel is thus the radically good news that in Christ, God has invaded this world held captive by Sin and Death, in order to set creation and humanity free. To get the full impact of this news, however, I suggest that we need to move beyond the language of "invasion" to that of "incarnation." True, "invasion" does convey the motifs of conflict that are frequent and important for Paul. But it also brings to mind images of masked, invincible commandos who infiltrate the bunker where the prisoners are held, or storm the beaches of occupied territory, overwhelm the enemy, and set the captives free. The problem is that this imagery does not go quite far enough in depicting the depth of Christ's identification with Adam's race as his *modus operandi*. Christ's death with and for us is an "inside job," which frees us in an utterly counterintuitive way. He takes the form of a slave; he becomes one of the captives; he joins them in the prison cell; he assumes the position of powerless trust in the God who alone can save. He dies as one of us. He waits for resurrection, which is always God's deed (1 Cor 15:4; Phil 2:9).

Here divine power condescends to operate in and through human weakness, thereby redescribing the character of power as effective through solidarity. Again in Käsemann's words, "Adam's counterpart makes his appearance and joins himself to the godless, without godlessness but in reverence before the creator."[14] The second Adam, whose obedience, death, and resurrection mark the turning of the ages, is no superhero action figure; he is a human being who "humbled himself, becoming obedient unto death, the death of the cross" (Phil 2:8). As such, he is very much like Abraham, who trusted in "the God who gives life to the dead, and calls into existence the things that do not exist" (Rom 4:17). His life and death are completely within the parameters of human limitations.[15]

How, then, might attention to this participatory Christology help us think through the logic of Paul's soteriology in an apocalyptic context? To probe possible answers to that question, I will follow Martyn's lead in his account of "rectification" in Galatians, and then put that account into conversation with Romans, in particular 8:1–4.

In his commentary on Galatians, Martyn presents a concise interpretation of Paul's deployment of the difficult terms *dikaiosyne* and *dikaioō*. The noun, *dikaiosyne*, has traditionally been translated as "righteousness,"

14. Käsemann, "Saving Significance," 42.

15. See, e.g., Bonhoeffer, *Christ the Center*, 103: "Jesus Christ had his own human individual *hypostasis* and human mode of existence. The man that I am, Jesus also was. Of him alone is it really true that nothing human remained alien to him. Of this man we say, 'This is God for us.'"

and the verb *dikaioō* as "to justify." Such versions obscure the link between the noun and the verb. To be sure, the noun also may be rendered as "justification," thereby making its link with the verb obvious. But because "justification" situates Paul's language in the realm of legal and moral discourse, Martyn explicitly rejects it. Instead, he translates *dikaiosyne* and *dikaioō* as "rectification" and "to rectify," with the sense of "putting right what is wrong."[16] This translation opens a way to speak about "what is wrong" in terms of a universal bondage to hostile powers, including the Law as an enslaving and cursing entity (Gal 3:10, 13), Sin as the prison warden over the whole of creation (3:22), and the enslaving elements of the cosmos (4:3). God's way of rectifying this situation of bondage is through declaring war on it in the apocalypse of God's Son, whose faithful death on behalf of enslaved creation is "*the* apocalyptic event" in which liberation is accomplished: "It is God's declaration of war in Christ against all of the forces enslaving the human race that formed the foundation of Paul's militant doctrine of rectification."[17] So, for example, when Paul says that "Christ became a curse for us" (Gal 3:13), this is because "God has had to make things right by entering into combat *against* the Law, insofar as it enacts its curse (3:10). And Christ's death on the Law-cursed cross is the point at which God has done that (3:13)."[18]

Martyn here gives a very distinctive account of rectification, participation in relationship to rectification, and the disclosure of the human plight: rectification is liberation from the powers that enslave humanity, whether the cursing Law, as in Galatians, or Sin itself as *the* enslaving power that even co-opts the Law of God (Rom 7:8–12); participation is Christ's death on the cross as the apocalyptic event in God's war against Sin; and the human plight disclosed by this divine warfare is one of bondage to Sin and its minions, to the extent that we ourselves become Sin's slaves.

The progression of the argument is quite clear; what is not clear is exactly *how* or *why* Christ's death on the "Law-cursed cross" wins God's victory over the enslaving powers. This question only becomes more urgent when we attend to the depiction of Christ's humanity and death in other "interchange" passages. In Philipians 2:5–11 Christ takes the form of a slave, in the likeness of human beings, and humbles himself, becoming

16. Martyn, *Galatians*, 249–50.

17. Ibid., 275.

18. Ibid. For the image of the cross as Christ's death on the battlefield in God's apocalyptic war against cosmic oppression, see also Martyn, *Issues*, 285–89. Note that Martyn does *not* say that God wars against the Law per se, but rather the Law in its role of pronouncing a curse.

obedient to the point of undergoing a criminal's death. Here the slavery motif is dominant, and linked to Christ's death by the form of execution apportioned to slaves. In 2 Corinthians 5:21 Christ is simply and shockingly "made to be sin, although knowing no sin." In Romans 8:3 the fact that God sends him "in the likeness of sinful flesh and for sin" is somehow central to God's condemnation of Sin itself.

These passages raise further questions about the role of Christ's humanity in God's "war of liberation." Why, for example, is it necessary for the liberator to die the death of a criminal? Why does he take the form of a slave? Why does Paul emphasize Christ's fleshly existence (Gal 4:4–6; Rom 8:3)? Why, indeed, is Christ not only fleshly, but sent "in the likeness of sinful flesh and for sin" (Rom 8:3) and even made to "be sin, on our behalf" (2 Cor 5:21)? Is such a complete identification, not only with oppressed humanity, but with Sin itself, necessary to ensure victory in a war against the tyranny of Sin? And where does Paul's language about condemnation (Rom 5:16, 18; 8:1–4, 33–34) fit into this picture of liberation? How does Christ's participation in human dereliction relate to the situation of condemnation in which humanity finds itself?

To address these questions, we turn to Romans 8:1–4, where motifs of both judgment and participation come together in a ringing declaration of liberation "from the law of sin and death":

> There is therefore now no condemnation [*katakrima*] for those who are in Christ Jesus. For the law of the Spirit of life in Christ Jesus has set me free from the law of sin and death. For God has done what the law, weakened by the flesh, could not do; sending his own Son in the likeness of sinful flesh and for sin, he condemned [*katekrinen*] sin in the flesh, in order that the just requirement [*dikaiōma*] of the law might be fulfilled in us, who walk not according to the flesh but according to the Spirit. (My translation)

This triumphant victory cry is the climax of Romans 1:18—7:25, wherein Paul's account of the human plight progresses from a depiction of humanity's liability to judgment and condemnation under the wrath of God (1:18—5:11), to a cosmic picture of human bondage under the domination of Sin (5:12—7:24).[19] The first account emphasizes human culpability and divine judgment; the second emphasizes human bondage

---

19. Martin de Boer offers a careful and influential analysis of this structural pattern in Romans in "Apocalyptic Eschatology." See also Tannehill, *Dying and Rising, passim*; Eastman, "'Empire of Illusion.'"

and divine liberation. The two strands overlap in both 5:12–21 and 8:1–4.
Thus on the one hand, the motif of judgment is evident in the way in which
8:1–4 echoes 5:16: "And the free gift is not like the effect of the one person's
sin. For the judgment [*krima*] following the one leads to condemnation
[*katakrima*], but the free gift following many trespasses leads to the [ful-
fillment of] the just requirement [*dikaiōma*]." In 5:18 Paul amplifies the
theme of judgment along the same lines: "Then as the trespass of the one
led to condemnation for all, so the act of righteousness of the one leads to
acquittal and life for all." In 8:1, then, the promise of "no condemnation"
announces good news to humanity insofar as it stands under condemnation. Paul drives home this good news in 8:32–33: "He who did not spare
his own Son but gave him up for us all, will he not also give us all things
with him? Who shall bring any charge against God's elect? It is God who
justifies; who is to condemn?" Here is relief from the devastating effect
of human culpability for evil, the condemnation that itself is a form of
bondage.

At the same time, however, the logic of both 5:12–21 and 8:1–4 is
entirely participatory. In 5:16–18 a participatory logic underlies the relationship between Adam and Christ: all humanity suffers the consequences
of Adam's trespass, and all humanity is caught up in the new reality inaugurated by Christ. In 6:6 Paul further develops the theme of redemption in
corporate categories by speaking of crucifixion with Christ. As Tannehill
argues, "In 6.6 the 'old man' is crucified with Christ, which implies that
Christ is related to this 'old man.' Indeed, the fact that the 'old man' and
the 'body of sin' are destroyed in Christ's crucifixion seems to imply that
Christ is the bearer of this inclusive reality of the old aeon."[20] Elsewhere
when Paul talks about Adam and Christ, he uses the same corporate mode
of thought: "For as by a man came death, by a man has come also the resurrection of the dead. For as in Adam all die, so also in Christ shall all be
made alive" (1 Cor 15:21–22). This is Paul's gloss on the creedal formula he
received and passed on to the Corinthians: "Christ died for our sins in accordance with the scriptures" (1 Cor 15:3). The union between Christ and
humanity undergirds and renders effective Christ's death on our behalf.

Moreover, not only is Paul's logic participatory; it is also apocalyptic. That is, Christ's immersion in the bondage of "this body of death"
(Rom 7:24) not only addresses the problem of human culpability for sin,
it also discloses and rectifies the problem of Sin's dominion. Paul sets
forth this liberation in Romans 8:2–3. While 8:1 proclaims freedom from

20. Tannehill, *Dying and Rising*, 27.

condemnation, the two clauses of 8:2–3 proclaim both the christological basis of that deliverance and the paradoxical way in which God has liberated humanity from Sin itself. The key phrase is "condemned sin in the flesh," and the key exegetical questions are, "What sin? Whose flesh?"

A brief reflection on the context of the letter will make the answers to these questions clear. Romans 5:12—7:25 tells us that "sin" clearly cannot be framed only, or even primarily, in terms of human wickedness. It will not do simply to return to 1:18—5:11 to understand what is going on in 8:3. Rather, by this point in the letter it has become clear that Sin "reigns in death" (5:21) and exercises dominion through the Law (6:14). It uses the Law as a military base of operations (7:8, 11) and a weapon of deception (7:11). Sin deals out the wages of death (6:23). Sin, dwelling in human beings (7:17, 20, 23), accomplishes evil through its human subjects, *contrary* to what they want (7:13, 17, 20). Sin is that which terrorizes humanity "in the shadow of Adam," humanity bound up in "this body of death" (7:24), the realm of human futility under Sin's power.[21] When shortly thereafter we read that "God condemned sin in the flesh," surely we are to recognize that this raging tyrant, not mere human wickedness, is the direct object of God's condemnation. Now Sin itself, the horrifying oppressor that holds humanity captive, receives the death sentence.

The location of both *this* Sin and its condemnation is "in the flesh." Again, the context tells us whose flesh is in view. This oppressive occupying power, Sin, is located in the flesh of Christ himself, who through his fleshly existence became united with the "body of death." In other words, Christ in the likeness of sinful flesh is united with the "I" in whom Sin dwells (7:17, 20, and 23), and who cries out for deliverance (7:24). Because Sin operates in and through the network of human relationships mediated by bodily existence, the flesh is Sin's sphere of operation and the arena in which the battle with Sin is waged. In *this* place and *this* way, therefore, Christ becomes the body where condemnation is pronounced and executed on Sin itself, so that its power to tyrannize humanity is eviscerated and its dominion destroyed. Remarkably, after 8:4 "sin" appears only twice in the remainder of the letter (11:27; 14:23), and never again as an enslaving power. This destruction of Sin's rule is the apocalyptic victory of Christ's "death on the battlefield": Christ's death both *with* and *for* us has brought about a regime change through the sentence of death imposed on Sin itself, in the locus of Christ's own body. This is how Christ's participation in

---

21. The phrase "in the shadow of Adam" comes from Hofius, "Der Mensch im Schatten Adams."

the realm of Sin and Death wins the victory in God's war against the forces that oppress and enslave the human race.

Thus Christ's full identification with humanity's subjugated condition under Sin provides the leverage for liberation from "the law of sin and death," on two levels that correspond with Paul's overlapping yet tensive accounts of the human predicament in Romans 1–7. In the first place, Christ's union with sinful flesh allows him to absorb the judgment that brought condemnation on all humanity in the shadow of Adam (5:16, 18). But even more, his union with Sin in the flesh allows him to be the locus of the condemnation passed on Sin itself, which like a cancer that has metastasized throughout the body politic of the human race, has taken on a lethal power of its own. In both ways, Christ's movement into the human sphere and full participation in the realities of Sin and Death dynamically enacts God's salvation-making power, a power that eludes classification.

We might call this a "participatory rectification," enacted not by an individual believer's movement into Christ through faith, but by Christ's movement into human dereliction, culminating in his death on a cross, the premier instrument of execution for slaves and criminals. I suggest that *this* is the participatory category in which "the real bite of [Paul's] theology" lies.[22] If Christ were not "one of us," joined with the ungodly and, even more shockingly, with Sin itself, his crucifixion would have no rectifying effect. It would be an isolated event. But if Christ simply joined himself to us in solidarity with our weakness and bondage and died an ordinary death rather than being executed as a criminal, there would be neither deliverance from the condemnation pronounced on Adam's race nor liberation from Sin's dominion. There would be participation without rectification. But participation and rectification come together in *Christ's* incarnation and crucifixion, which together enact the righteousness of God's powerful, complete, and redemptive involvement in humanity's plight. Together, that is, they comprise the gospel through which "the righteousness of God is being apocalypsed from faith to faith" (Rom 1:17).

22. Sanders, *Palestinian Judaism*, 502: "[Paul] is not primarily concerned with the juristic categories, although he works with them. The real bite of his theology lies in the participatory categories, *even though he himself did not distinguish them in this way*" (emphasis original). By "participatory categories," Sanders has in mind the notion of human transference "into Christ" through faith in Christ; I am proposing a different model.

INTO THE WORLD: PARTICIPATORY ECCLESIOLOGY

Rudolf Bultmann locates his discussion of "participation in Christ" in the category of ecclesiology: "'In Christ,' far from being a formula for mystic union, is primarily an *ecclesiological* formula. It means the state of having been articulated into the 'body of Christ.'"[23] Käsemann disagrees:

> Christ is always drawing us afresh out of our inner-ecclesiastical traditional associations and . . . his sphere of power is the justification of the ungodly. We do not simply enter into this. We must be called to it afresh every day. 'In Christ' is really not primarily an ecclesiological formula at all. To see it as such is to endanger and obscure the primacy of Christology over ecclesiology. 'In Christ' is the state of those who through the gospel are called out of the old world and who only belong to the new creation in so far as they continue to be confronted with the Lord who justifies the ungodly. His sphere of power has, however, for the sake of the gospel, a universal breadth, and also, as the promise to Abraham shows, the depths of salvation history. For both in the primeval period and in the endtime the point at issue is more than individual salvation or disaster; what is at stake is the destiny of the world.[24]

The difference between these two understandings of ecclesiology and participation is monumental, and it concerns what Martyn calls "the direction of the line of movement."[25] In the first, individual believers move *into* Christ and the church; in the second, Christ moves into the world of the ungodly, which is where believers discover what it means to belong to Christ.

In light of these differences, it is instructive to compare Bultmann's memoirs with those of Käsemann. In 1956 Bultmann wrote brief "Autobiographical Reflections," in which he touched on the experience of the Third Reich:

> Then came the time of the Hitler regime, with its coercion and its pernicious methods. Life in the university and in the community at large was poisoned by mistrust and denunciations. One could enjoy mutual openness and growth through common participation in the world of the spirit only within a small

---

23. Bultmann, *Theology of the New Testament*, 311.

24. Käsemann, *Perspectives on Paul*, 101.

25. Martyn, "Events in Galatia," 168.

circle of like-minded acquaintances; and many Jewish friends
were forced to emigrate.[26]

One senses here a retreat to the refuge of the circle of Christian faith, a
like-minded community "of the spirit" that is separated from the world
and makes no claims on it. This is not a vision of the church that compels
one to act in the world. And while it is true that Bultmann was a member
of the Confessing Church, it is also true that he begged Karl Barth to sign
an oath of allegiance to Hitler, as he himself had done.[27] Bultmann expressed concern that Barth's refusal to do so would jeopardize any possible
future "discussion between state and church on the legitimate or illegiti-
mate significance of the state's totalitarian claim."[28] He further indicated
his agreement with their mutual colleague Hans von Soden, who urged
Barth to sign the oath on the basis of the state's "earthly" sovereignty,
which requires that one "render to the state what, according to my conviction, and that of many theologians, are the things of the state."[29]

The image of the church that emerges from Bultmann's reminiscences, as well as his position on the oath of allegiance, is of a place apart,
a separate community "in the world of the spirit" that leaves intact the
rest of human affairs. Thus, although Bultmann certainly speaks of the
lordship of Christ, that lordship holds sway within this separate territory
where the body of Christ is located. To participate in Christ is to move into
this sacred territory, this spiritual fellowship, a place of refuge set apart
from the world.

At first glance, Käsemann may appear to be saying something similar
when he claims, "'In Christ' is the state of those who through the gospel
are called out of the old world." But Käsemann immediately qualifies this
call. It is not a call to a separate spiritual realm, but to discipleship in service of Christ who has joined himself with the ungodly. We can only be in
service to this Lord in the recognition that we also are the ungodly, and
that Christ is to be found in the midst of all humanity, without remainder.
Furthermore, because Christ's "sphere of power has, however, for the sake
of the gospel, a universal breadth," the church cannot find its life apart
from the world, but only in the service of Christ who is the liberator of all

26. Bultmann, "Autobiographical Reflections," 285.

27. Barth, *Karl Barth–Rudolf Bultmann Letters*, 78–79. Barth was willing to sign
the oath, with the proviso that it include a clause saying "so far as I can do so respon-
sibly as an Evangelical Christian," but this proviso was denied.

28. Ibid., 79.

29. Ibid., 135.

human beings. Yes, our loyalty and obedience are due to Christ alone, but Christ's lordship is universal.

This understanding of the relationship between Christ, the church, and the world is played out in Käsemann's experiences during the Third Reich. In brief reminiscences near the end of his life, he describes his work as the pastor of a working-class congregation: "As early as the fall of 1933 I declared that the Reichsbishop was a traitor to the evangelical church. From then on I was hated by the Nazis, later was denounced in the marketplace as a national traitor by the Gauleiter (district leader) in Gelsenkirchen, and was recommended to the higher authorities for assignment to a concentration camp."[30] Käsemann, in fact, was not sent to a concentration camp, although in 1937 he was arrested and imprisoned after a sermon on Isaiah 26:13: "O Lord our God, other lords besides you have ruled over us, but we acknowledge your name alone." At the conclusion of his memoir he writes, "As a last word and as my bequest, let me call to you in Huguenot style: 'Résistez!' Discipleship of the Crucified leads necessarily to resistance to idolatry on every front. This resistance is and must be the most important mark of Christian freedom."[31] The line of movement evident in Käsemann's "fighting words" is into the world, not out of it, and it leads to confrontation with the idols that hold humanity hostage.

It is not for nothing that Martyn's commentary on Galatians is dedicated to Ernst Käsemann. In the writings of both, the dominant motif of Christ's liberating movement *into* the territory of human bondage is front and center, and in both this results in a picture of the church that is stunning in its radicality. Just as the source and direction of "participation in Christ" is Christ's redemptive participation in all things human, so the source and direction of life in the body of Christ is a gracious involvement in the humanity Christ came to liberate. The direction of this line of movement goes all the way down. What else could it mean to be joined with the Christ who took on the form of a slave? Viewed in this light, the church becomes a place of joining with Christ's participation in the lives of all human beings, without distinctions and without remainder.

We may discern this union with all humanity in two aspects of Martyn's interpretation of Paul: his insistence that the crucifixion of the old cosmos dissolves the distinction between sacred and profane, and his vision of the church as "God's cosmic vanguard"[32] in the forefront of God's

30. Käsemann, *On Being a Disciple*, xviii.

31. Ibid., xxi.

32. Martyn, *Issues*, 266.

war to deliver "the whole of humanity—indeed the whole of the cosmos (Gal 3:22; Rom 8:21)—from the grip of the powers of the present evil age."[33] The dissolution of the distinction between sacred and profane is evident in Paul's polemic against the divisive effects of Law observance in his Galatian congregations. By dividing those who observe Torah from those who do not, other missionaries who want to impose Torah observance on congregations of Gentile Christians are upholding a cosmos constructed by a separation between "Law and Not-Law." It is this division, not the Law itself, which is destructive and belongs to the powers of "the present evil age" (Gal 1:4). But Christ's death has brought that divided cosmos to an end: "Specifically, the cosmos that was crucified on the cross is the cosmos that was founded on the distinction between Jew and Gentile, between sacred and profane, between the Law and the Not-Law."[34]

Again, we may ask, how is it that Christ's death has such an effect? Paul's text points us back to the participatory power of Christ's identification with all humanity, not just those who observe the Torah: "Christ redeemed us from the curse of the law, having become a curse for us—for it is written, 'Cursed be every one who hangs on a tree'—that in Christ Jesus the blessing of Abraham might come upon the Gentiles" (Gal 3:13–14). Christ became a criminal. He entered the territory of cursed existence, the territory of all who do not keep the Law, thereby overcoming the gulf between Jew and Gentile that divided all the known world of Paul's day.[35] The church that follows this Lord must therefore be located at the boundaries that divide humanity into categories of insiders and outsiders in our known world.

The second way in which Christ's movement into the human sphere shapes the church is by making it a sign of God's advocacy of every human being. Members of the church are "newly enrolled soldiers called into the obedience of faith and sent into the warfare in which God is regrasping the world for himself."[36] Here is the fruit of "following the invading God":

33. Ibid., 265.

34. Ibid., 140. See also Martyn, *Galatians*, 393–406.

35. The author of Ephesians amplifies this theme: "But now in Christ Jesus you who once were far off have been brought near in the blood of Christ. For he is our peace, who has made us both one, and has broken down the dividing wall of hostility, by abolishing in his flesh the law of commandments and ordinances, that he might create in himself one new human being [*anthrōpos*] in place of the two, so making peace, and might reconcile us both to God in one body through the cross, thereby bringing the hostility to an end" (Eph 2:13–16).

36. Martyn, *Issues*, 65.

a church that enacts God's "genuine love and powerful grace" in the midst of Adam's desperate children.[37] Martyn's military imagery, drawn (let it be noted) directly from Paul, may make us nervous that it will lead to a triumphalist ecclesiology. But Martyn is always clear that the contours of God's battle against the powers that oppress humanity are cosmic, and that the "enemy" is never other human beings.[38] Nor is the arsenal of this warfare discernable in terms of human weapons. It is, rather, the counter-intuitive power of God's gracious union with "every one of us," discerned and enacted in the crucifixion of God's Son.[39] Earlier I suggested that the language of incarnation, even more than the language of invasion, communicates the countercultural nature of this power. God's *modus operandi* is a relentless commitment to be *with* us, in spite of everything. Paul's *modus operandi* is the same. Describing the way in which this gospel upends our ideas of power, Martyn writes:

> We say to Paul, "Look! From Harlem to the ancient valleys of the Tigris and Euphrates, the oppressed are crying out for change, for liberation, for transformation, and we must find the power by which genuine change, liberation, and transformation can be brought about!" Paul responds: "The people are indeed crying out. I myself cry out. Who is weak, and I am not weak? Who is made to fall, and I am not indignant?"[40]

Notice how it is Paul's fellowship in suffering that gives proof of God's commitment to liberation and transformation. Martyn continues by pointing to the cross as God's strange power "that looks like weakness."[41] It is the power of solidarity with the depressed and the oppressed, in the prison cell, at the execution block, enacted in the flesh, expressed in Paul's own anguished cry.

CONCLUSION

The burden of this essay has been to argue that Martyn's depiction of Paul's apocalyptic gospel as divine invasion discloses the participatory logic at the center of that gospel. That logic is one of a movement from God to

37. Ibid., 287.
38. Ibid., 286.
39. Ibid., 297.
40. Ibid., 287.
41. Ibid.

humanity, enacted through Christ's union with Adam's condemned and enslaved heirs. Christ participates so fully in humanity's situation of bondage that his flesh becomes the place where Sin is condemned and stripped of its power. Henceforth, then, the church is to be the vanguard of this liberating action of God, already accomplished by Christ, and carried forward by those who belong to him. The church is the place of participation in Christ who already and always joins himself with the godless—that is, all of us. Or as Martyn puts it:

> [T]he gospel is God's advent! . . . As event, the gospel is inseparable from God because God himself comes on the scene in that proclamation in the fullness of his power (*dynamis theou*).[42]

This is the incarnational heart of Paul's good news.

42. Ibid., 219.

8

"Neither Height nor Depth"

Cosmos and Soteriology in Paul's Letter to the Romans[1]

Beverly Roberts Gaventa

THE SMALL GREEK NOUN κόσμος appears in only two verses of Paul's letter to the Galatians (4:3; 6:14), but it plays a large role in J. Louis Martyn's magisterial interpretation of that letter. The term first appears early in the Introduction to the commentary, where Martyn observes that Paul "takes his bearings from the good news that in Christ—and thus in the act of *new* creation—God has invaded the cosmos."[2] This startling claim, that an invasion of cosmic proportions is the gospel, Martyn unpacks and defends throughout the commentary.

Four texts form the backbone for this argument: 1:4b; 3:22; 4:3; and 6:4. The first appears in the opening lines of the letter, where Paul identifies Jesus Christ as the one "who gave up his very life for our sins so that

1. An earlier version of this paper was read in the Pauline Soteriology Group at 2010 Annual Meeting of the Society of Biblical Literature, at the kind invitation of Professors Susan Eastman and Ross Wagner. I am grateful to them for their invitation, as well as to Edward Adams for his response; to Shane Berg, Nancy Duff, J. Louis Martyn, Paul W. Meyer, Carey Newman, and Patrick J. Willson for commenting on earlier drafts; and to Brittany E. Wilson for research assistance. The paper was subsequently published in the *Scottish Journal of Theology* 64 (2011) 265–78, and is published here in revised form by permission.

2. Martyn, *Galatians*, 22.

he [Christ] might snatch us out of the grasp of the present evil age" (1:4; Martyn's translation). Martyn affirms the exegetical consensus that the first assertion, that Christ died "for our sins," is a pre-Pauline formulation, but he contends that the remainder of the statement reinterprets that traditional affirmation in an apocalyptic direction. This reinterpretation, which is "one of the topic sentences for the whole of the letter," casts the self-giving death of Jesus as the liberation of a humanity "held under the thumb of powers foreign to themselves."[3]

Martyn draws a direct line from 1:4b to the second text, 3:22: "the scripture imprisoned everything under the power of Sin" (Martyn's translation). *Ta panta* ("everything") refers to "creation as a whole," which is "in a state of imprisonment under the power of the 'present evil age,'" which Martyn identifies with the cosmos.[4] The first explicit use of κόσμος appears in 4:3: "When we were children, we were held in a state of slavery under the power of the elements of the cosmos." Here we come to "the theological center of the letter," which Martyn summarizes as follows:

> Like all other human beings, we were held in a state of *slavery* by the very *building blocks of the cosmos* [i.e., the *stoicheia tou cosmou*], the cosmos having fallen to a significant degree out of God's control. But God did not leave us in that state of slavery. At a time selected by him, God *invaded* the partially foreign territory of the cosmos, *sending* his own Son into it, born, as all human beings are born, and *subject to the enslaving power of the Law*, as all human beings are subject to that power. The mission God gave to his Son was to *redeem from slavery* those who were thus caught under the Law's power, so that we who are incorporated into the Son might *receive adoption* at the hands of God himself.[5]

So, when Paul writes in the letter's conclusion, "the cosmos has been crucified to me and I to the cosmos" (6:14), he refers not only to the whole of creation in its captivity but especially to the values, dispositions, and judgments associated with the cosmos, most notably its division of the world into Jew and Gentile, slave and free, male and female, Law and Not-Law.[6]

---

3. Ibid., 90. This cosmological reading of Gal 1:4b stands out sharply against a more narrowly forensic reading, in which the "present evil age" is identified with human sinfulness or separation from God; see the illuminating discussion of the history of interpretation of this text in Riches, *Galatians Through the Centuries*, 77–82.

4. Martyn, *Galatians*, 102 n. 65, 360.

5. Ibid., 388 (emphasis original).

6. Space does not permit discussion of the work done by the category of "antinomy"

THE COSMOS IN ROMANS

As we turn from Galatians to Paul's later letter to Rome, we find that the Greek term κόσμος is used with a different, more neutral, nuance. Instead of the enslaving "building blocks of the cosmos" (*the stoicheia*) and the cosmos that has been crucified,[7] Paul writes that the faith of the Romans is known "in the whole cosmos" (1:8). This shift in usage might underscore interpretations of Romans as a modification of Galatians. I shall argue, however, that Romans does not modify Galatians but rather extends it. Despite the slight change in the use of the term *cosmos*, in Romans as in Galatians questions about the world are overwhelmingly questions about its salvation rather than about the order or the nature of the created world. Just as in Martyn's reading of Galatians, in Romans as well, the most important thing to say about the world is that it is God's, that it is at present under siege by Sin and Death and other anti-God powers, and that God is redeeming it through the death and resurrection of Jesus Christ. In addition, this understanding of the character of God's salvation, which is rightly called cosmic, offers a significant challenge to some contemporary understandings of both anthropology and soteriology.

That there is both range and variation in Paul's usage of cosmos language has been argued convincingly by Edward Adams in his important study *Constructing the World*.[8] Adams reviews the scholarly discussion of cosmos language in Paul, particularly the influential treatments of κόσμος in Bultmann's *Theology of the New Testament*[9] and in Hermann Sasse's article in the *Theological Dictionary of the New Testament*.[10] Both Bultmann and Sasse understand κόσμος as carrying negative theological connotations. For Bultmann, the individual is "in the grip of the world" and is thereby under judgment.[11] For Sasse, the world is "estranged, fallen, and condemned."[12] Both examine the use of cosmos language across Paul's letters, without attending to differences among them.

---

in Martyn's commentary; see ibid., 570–72; and especially "Apocalyptic Antinomies" in *TDNT*. The epistemological concerns in Martyn's discussion of apocalyptic antinomies are closely connected with his classic treatment of 2 Cor 5:16, "Epistemology at the Turn of the Ages" [1967, 1997].

7. In Rom 12:1, however, Paul urges his auditors not to be conformed to "this age," perhaps an echo of the "present evil age" of Gal 1:4b.

8. Adams, *Constructing*. See also his article "Cosmology."

9. Bultmann, *New Testament*, 1:254–59.

10. Sasse, "κόσμος."

11. Bultmann, "Understanding of Man," 78; quoted in Adams, *Constructing*, 17.

12. The phrase is Adams' summary (*Constructing*, 18).

By contrast, among the important contributions Adams makes is his insistence on reading each letter on its own, in its own context. He demonstrates convincingly a difference between the use of the term in 1 Corinthians and in Romans, the two letters where the word κόσμος appears most often. In 1 Corinthians, where κόσμος appears twenty-one times, it does have negative implications. The world has a bankrupt form of wisdom, mere foolishness in God's eyes (e.g., 1:20–21; 3:19). It is the place where God's apostles are a spectacle (4:9, 13), where immorality is the norm (5:10). It is soon to be passing away, so that it is preferable for believers not to be caught up in the concerns of "this" κόσμος (7:31).[13] Adams rightly locates this usage in the framework of the social dualism of 1 Corinthians, where Paul perceives the need to confirm and maintain the boundary between the believing community and outsiders.[14]

In Romans, however, where κόσμος appears nine times, the term is more nearly neutral in its connotations, according to Adams. Here it refers most often to humanity as a whole, as when Paul declares at the outset that the faith of the Romans is known "to the entire cosmos" (1:8), or when he recalls the promise that Abraham's offspring would inherit the "cosmos"[15] (4:13; similarly 3:19; 5:12–13; 11:12, 15). Some of these texts are slightly ambiguous and might mean the earth (i.e., the globe), but even so the reference would be to earth as the location in which humanity is to be found. It is not that God judges the planet earth, when God is said to judge the world. The one instance in which κόσμος clearly refers to something more than humanity is in 1:20, which has to do with God's creation of the cosmos. In Romans, unlike 1 Corinthians, κόσμος does not distinguish those on the "inside" of the community and those on the "outside." Adams rightly concludes from his study that Romans lacks the social dualism

13. In Romans, this critique of the "world's" value system does appear, but it is cast in the language of living "according to the flesh" (8:6–14) and being "conformed to this age" (12:1–2).

14. Ibid., 149. Adams devotes relatively little attention to Galatians, for the understandable reason that κόσμος appears only twice in the letter. He concludes that κόσμος and καινὴ κτίσις "express the spacio-temporal dualism of 'this world' and the 'the new creation'" [sic], and that the usage in several respects resembles that of 1 Cor (221–32; quotation in ibid., 231).

15 Here I diverge from Adams, who argues on the basis of usage in Paul's Jewish contemporaries that κόσμος in 4:13 refers to the future eschatological world that is to be inherited by the faithful (adducing Sir 44:21; *Jub* 17:3; 22:14; 1 *En.* 5:7; Philo, *Somn.* 1.175; Philo, *Mos.* 1.155). See Adams, *Constructing*, 168.

found in 1 Corinthians; in particular, Romans 12:14—13:10 promotes a kind of "solidarity" with the wider society.[16]

A few additional brief observations about the use of the term κόσμος in Romans are in order. First, the use of κόσμος, when considered alongside the use of πᾶς, may reinforce the universal horizon of this letter. As is well known, Paul again and again speaks of God's actions for all, starting as early as 1:5 (the "obedience that stems from faith" is for "all the Gentiles"). The saving power of God's action is for "everyone who believes" (1:16); "all have sinned" (3:23); Adam's one act of disobedience and Christ's one act of obedience likewise affect "all" (5:18); "God confined all in disobedience that God might have mercy on all" (11:32). These two terms mutually reinforce one another. So perhaps Paul's motives are not entirely social.

Second, the use of κόσμος in Romans reflects the letter's emphasis on creation and specifically on God as creator. It is in connection with the claim about creation that Paul contends, in 1:19–20, that humanity knew God from the "creation of the cosmos" and should have acknowledged God. Abraham and his offspring, who are promised that they will inherit the κόσμος (4:13), are the recipients of the action of God "who calls into being things that do not exist" (4:17). All of creation longs for God's redemption (κτίσις, 8:19–22).

Third, the use of κόσμος language in Romans is connected to the notion that humanity exists for the praise of God.[17] Paul early on identifies the refusal of doxology as *the* root of humanity's enslavement to Sin. In 1:19–20, Paul contends that although God is made known "from the creation of the κόσμος," and "they" knew God, they did not "glorify God or give God thanks." He reinforces this claim in 1:25 and 28 with statements that "they" "worshiped and served the creation rather than the one who created," and "they decided not to acknowledge God." The second half of Romans 1 may have only Gentiles in view, but by the time Paul reaches the catena of 3:10–18, he has effectively included Jews in the same charge. "There is no one who seeks God," and "there is no fear of God before their eyes." Speech is emphasized within the catena:

> Their throat is an opened grave.
> With their tongues they deceive.
> The venom of asps is under their lips.
> Their mouth is full of curses and bitterness.

16. Adams, *Constructing*, 220.

17. On doxology in Romans, see Gaventa, "From Toxic Speech" and "'Glory of God.'" This line of investigation was suggested to me by an earlier essay of Minear, "Gratitude and Mission."

The result of this refusal to give God thanks and praise comes in 3:19:

> What the law says to those who are in the law it says so that every mouth might be shut and the entire κόσμος made liable to God.[18]

The entire created κόσμος (again here in the sense of the human population of the world) is deprived of speech because of its refusal to acknowledge its created state. It should not be surprising, then, that Paul later depicts the unity of the diverse Roman congregations as speech in unison: "That you might together with one mouth glorify the God and father of our Lord Jesus Christ" (15:6). This point is reinforced by the numerous doxologies and blessings within the letter (as in 1:25; 7:25a; 9:5; 11:36; 16:20; [16:25–27]), which seem to call for the Romans to assent to Paul's argument with ascriptions of praise and thanksgiving.[19]

Fourth, it is at least worth noticing that, in most cases, the word οἰκουμένη might have been used instead of κόσμος, but οἰκουμένη appears only once in the Pauline corpus and that instance occurs in the citation of Psalm 18:5 in Romans 10:18.[20] It is especially intriguing to note 1:8, which might well read, "your faith is made known through the οἰκουμένη, the entire inhabited world." 3:6 also serves to illustrate this point, as Paul might easily have asked, "How will God judge the οἰκουμένη, the entire inhabited world?" Luke uses the term in just that way when he reports that Caesar's directive for a census went out to the entire οἰκουμένη (Luke 2:1; see also 4:5; 21:26; Acts 11:28; etc.). Similarly, Josephus writes that Cyrus identified himself as having been appointed by God as the great king of the οἰκουμένη (Ant. 11.3); Josephus also refers to the Romans as the "lords of the οἰκουμένη" (C. Apion 2.41; see also Ant. 19.193; J.W. 4.656). It is of course hazardous to speculate about what does not appear in a text, but it may be that οἰκουμένη, which by this time is used in reference to the world as governed, even controlled by, human beings, is less appropriate for Paul, and κόσμος reinforces his notion of the human population precisely as that cosmos is created and sustained by God.

---

18. For this translation, see Gaventa, "From Toxic Speech," 402; and Elliott, *Rhetoric of Romans*, 144–45.

19. Gaventa, "Glory of God," 64; Martyn, *Galatians*, 91–92, 569–70.

20. On which see Wagner, *Heralds*, 184–86.

ANTI-GOD POWERS AT WORK IN THE COSMOS

To this point I have argued that when Paul employs the Greek term κόσμος in Romans, he does so in a way that is neutral. The cosmos is not inherently bad; it is God's creation and in need of God's salvation. This would seem to carry us a long distance from Martyn's reading of Galatians, where humanity needs to be delivered *from* the present evil age (the cosmos) and where the cosmos is crucified (6:14). However, that conclusion proves to be seriously misleading, since in Romans the cosmos (i.e., the human population and indeed the entirety of creation, κτίσις) has been taken captive by anti-God powers. And one important—perhaps the most important—aspect of Paul's cosmology in Romans is that humanity (i.e., the human cosmos) is at present the object of a conflict between God and anti-God powers. That is, the universe is inhabited by powers other than the power of God and the frail power of human beings.[21] Romans then represents not a modification but an extension of the argument of Galatians.

Captivity to Sin and Death

The captivity of the human cosmos to anti-God powers is anticipated as early as Romans 1:18–32, with the repetition of the statement that "God handed them over" in 1:24, 26, 28, where impurity, the passions, and the base mind serve as metonyms for the power of Sin.[22] 3:9 states explicitly that all (πᾶς again) are "under the power of Sin."[23] It is with 5:12–21, however, that the enslaving power of Sin and Death becomes explicit. Through the action of Adam, Sin enters the cosmos and opens the door for Death. The lines that follow depict Sin and Death as establishing control over "all people." Sin and Death rule as kings (5:14, 17); Sin increases in its power (5:20); Sin rules through Death (5:21). In 6:9–11, Paul comments

21. This is consistent with Martyn's discussion of the three-actor moral drama in his "Epilogue." Most of the texts to be discussed in this section do not use the word κόσμος, but it would be short-sighted to restrict discussion of Paul's cosmology narrowly to his use of the term κόσμος. Just as Paul refers to the death of Jesus in Romans without ever using the term σταυρός and has things to say about the Christian community without using the term ἐκκλησία prior to ch.16, there may also be cosmology without the word κόσμος.

22. For argumentation in support of this claim about 1:24, 26, 28, see Gaventa, *Our Mother*, 113–23, 194–97.

23. Martyn, *Galatians*, 370–73.

that even Christ was at one time ruled by Death, and in 6:12–23 he speaks of Sin as an enslaving power.

Additional Use of Conflict Language

These references to the powers of Sin and Death are widely recognized, even if there are significant disagreements about what exactly Paul means by them or what role they should play in understanding the letter.[24] But the full impact of Paul's language comes into view when we take into account the extent to which Romans, especially chapters 5–8, teems with language of conflict:

1. The most explicit and startling example of such conflict terminology is that of weapons. In one of those rare, early imperatives in 6:13, Paul exhorts the Romans, "Do not present your members to Sin as ὅπλα [weapons] of wrong, but present yourselves to God as alive from the dead and your members to God as ὅπλα [weapons] of rectification." In a similar vein, 13:12 admonishes that "we should put away the works of darkness and clothe ourselves in the ὅπλα of light."

2. Consistent with the language of "weapons," at several points Paul employs the term "enemies." 5:10 speaks of "us" as having formerly been God's "enemies," and 8:7 characterizes the mindset of the "flesh" as at enmity with God. 11:28 depicts the part of Israel, which does not yet see Jesus as the Messiah [οἱ λοιποί], as being "enemies" with respect to the gospel.[25]

3. Less explicit but also derived from the arena of conflict is the language of "peace" and "reconciliation," which occurs in 5:1 and in the *inclusio* at 5:11. Now, Paul writes, "we have" peace with God, a declaration that is repeated at 5:11 with "now we have received reconciliation." As Cilliers

24. In addition to the commentaries, recent contributions by Dodson and Southall are instructive. In *"Powers" of Personification*, 120–21, Dodson instructively notes that "personification" is little in evidence in Paul's letters outside of Romans, where it is concentrated in chs. 5–8. His own conclusion is that Paul uses "personification" in order to distance God from evil and to identify the Law as Sin's victim rather than as a villain in itself (139). Dodson provides a helpful discussion of personification as a rhetorical device, but he does not ask whether Sin and Death are something more than or other than personifications, a question addressed by Southall in *Rediscovering Righteousness*, esp. regarding Sin, 96–112. Southall in turn draws on Gunton's instructive discussion in *Atonement*, esp. 53–82.

25. The word occurs also at 12:20 in the biblical citation from Prov 25:21, "If your enemy is hungry, give him something to eat."

Breytenbach has demonstrated, the language of reconciliation has its home in the arena of reconciling warring parties and is not in the first instance religious terminology.[26]

4. The numerous references to "slavery" and to "ruling" or "reigning" are also closely associated with the arena of conflict. Not only did many slaves in the Roman world become slaves as a result of war, but slavery necessarily reflects the suppression of conflict, the defeat of the enslaved, and the overwhelming power of the owner.[27] Orlando Patterson's now classic study of slavery argues that slavery is to be understood, in the first instance, as having to do with power and domination more than with laws concerning property. Slavery, in Patterson's language, is "social death."[28]

5. At 7:11, Paul writes that Sin took the commandment as an ἀφορμή, an "opportunity," using a term that is found elsewhere in military contexts as a pretext for making war.[29] Since Paul goes on to say that Sin "killed" me, the violence of the image is undeniable.

6. At the very end of the letter, Paul solemnly declares that "the God of peace will soon crush Satan under your feet" (16:17).[30]

7. Last but not least in significance, when Paul says that God "handed them over" in 1:24, 26, 28, as when he says that Christ "was handed over" (4:25; 8:32) and that God did not "spare" (8:32) his own Son, he is again using language found in conflict situations. Both in biblical and non-biblical Greek, the verb παραδίδωμι is used to refer to the handing over of someone or something to a third party, often in military contexts.[31] Similarly

26. Breytenbach, *Versöhnung*, 40–83.

27. Bradley, *Slaves and Masters*, esp. 14–15, 113–43.

28. Hence the title of his book, *Slavery and Social Death*. Patterson defines slavery as "the permanent, violent domination of natally alienated and generally dishonored persons" (13).

29. Polybius 3.69; Philo, *Flacc.* 47; Dionysius of Halicarnassus 5.5.3; 6.25.3; and elsewhere. See also Gal 5:13 and Martyn, *Galatians*, 485.

30. Some commentators have argued that 16:17–20 is an interpolation; see, for example, Keck, *Romans*, 377–79, and Jewett, who provides an extensive review of the literature in *Romans*, 986–88. There is no manuscript evidence that supports this theory, however, and I concur with those who hold 16:17–20 belongs with the letter; see Fitzmyer, *Romans*, 745; Moo, *Romans*, 928; and most recently Hultgren, *Paul's Letter*, 591–92.

31. E.g., Herodotus, *Hist.* 1.45.1; 3.13.3; Xenophon, *Cyr.* 5.1.28; 5.4.51; Deut 2:24, 31; 20:13; Josh 2:14, 24; Jer 21:20; Ezek 7:21.

φείδομαι, used in 8:32, often occurs in contexts having to do with the sparing of human life in military conflict.[32]

This extensive use of imagery associated with conflict, even violent conflict, culminates at the end of Romans 8.

Romans 8:31–39

It is possible to grant much of my argument to this point and still insist that by the time we get to Romans 8 this conflict over the lordship of the human cosmos lies in the past. The first half of Romans 8 contends that believers belong to the Spirit and not to the realm ruled by the flesh; therefore, they are God's children, they are Christ's fellow heirs, and so forth. They may be subject to suffering, but they have already been rectified and even glorified (8:29–30). It is common to refer to chapter 8, even to chapters 5–8, as Paul's discussion of the Christian life, a life that may be marred by suffering but is not any longer the landscape of conflict. J. A. Fitzmyer, for example, describes 8:14–39 with the heading, "Christian life, lived in freedom bestowed by the indwelling spirit, has its destiny in glory."[33] Leander Keck's heading for 8:1–30 is "Liberation by the resident Spirit," and for 8:31–39 is "God's love celebrated."[34]

Headings necessarily oversimplify, of course, but the picture of Romans 8 is actually distorted by such headings, especially when we arrive at 8:31–39. This passage demonstrates that Paul regards the human cosmos (even if he never uses the word) as a place that remains disputed territory. God is in conflict with other powers for rule over the human cosmos.

First, the controlling question of 8:31–39 is clearly stated at the outset: If God is "for us" (ὑπὲρ ἡμῶν), who is "against us" (καθ᾽ ἡμῶν)? Cranfield rightly observes that the words "God is ὑπὲρ ἡμῶν" stand as a "concise summary of the gospel,"[35] but it is also true that the question that follows encapsulates the gospel as well. In view of the fact that God is ὑπὲρ ἡμῶν, who can be καθ᾽ ἡμῶν? Elsewhere Paul uses κατά with the

32. Homer, *Il.* 15.215; 21.101; *Od.* 9.277; 22.54; Josephus, *J.W.* 1.352; 4.82; Deut 7:16; 1 Sam 15:3. For argumentation in support of this paragraph, see Gaventa, *Our Mother*, 113–23, 194–97, and "Interpreting Apocalyptically."

33. Fitzmyer, *Romans*, 497.

34. Keck, *Romans*, 8.

35. Cranfield, *Romans*, 435. Similarly, N. T. Wright comments that "the statement that 'God is for us' is about as basic a way as can be conceived of summing up the revelation of God's saving justice in the gospel" (*Romans*, 612).

genitive in similarly forceful contexts, as when Elijah is said to plead with God "against Israel" (Rom 11:2) or when 2 Corintians 10:5 speaks of "high places raised up against the knowledge of God" (see also Gal 5:17). The full implications of this "against" will emerge only in the lines that follow, but the question assumes both that resisting God is finally impossible and also that some agent (τίς) may well attempt to do just that.

Second, the language of both power and powers pervades this passage. Romans 8:32 recalls God's action regarding "his own son," whom God is said not to have "spared" but to have "handed over." As noted above, both these verbs are frequently found in contexts that involve conflict. Verse 34 contains Paul's only reference to Christ as "at the right" of God, in what is widely agreed to be an allusion to Psalm 110. Not only does Christ's presence in the heavenly court indicate his own power, but of course in 1 Corinthians 15:25 Paul cites the next line of this psalm in clear reference to God's final triumph over God's own enemies: "He must reign until 'he has put all his enemies under his feet.'" In addition, when Paul lists in Romans 8:35 the circumstances that may be thought to "separate us" from Christ's love, several of them are directly or indirectly associated with conflicting powers, most notably "the sword," but also hardship and persecution, which regularly come about because of conflict. And Psalm 43:23, which is cited by way of interpreting these circumstances, similarly contains the violent image not only of "dying all day long" but of being put to slaughter.

This brings us to Romans 8:38, which provides the names of the agents that produce the circumstances. The list is a varied one, but at least some of these agents are to be understood as actual powers (especially angels and rulers and "powers").[36] Whatever their ontology, these powers have the intent of "separating" human beings from the realm of God, the love of Christ. That point can be made more forcefully still: what Paul writes here makes no sense if there is not, in his judgment, some intent to separate humans from their rightful Lord. In the face of this intent,

36. On the extensive debate about the list in 8:38–39, see Carr, *Angels and Principalities*, 112–14; Wink, *Naming the Powers*, 47–50; Jewett, *Romans*, 350–55. To say that these powers are suprahuman is not at all to say that they are removed from human life, as is clear in the list of 8:35; it is precisely when Paul *looks at* the reality of human life that he sees the work of these powers. But that is not to say, as has become fashionable in recent years, that Paul is addressing himself to the Roman Empire as such. Resistance to God surely exists within the empire, but it is by no means confined to the empire; and the rescue operation that is God's action in Jesus Christ extends to the whole of creation. On the specific question of Paul and the Roman Empire, see the formidable argument of Barclay, "Roman Empire."

the final item in the list of powers is revealing. Paul says that "no other creature" will be able to separate "us" from the love of God; that is, whatever the power manifested by them, they are in fact no more nor less than another of God's creatures.[37]

Third, and perhaps most important, the passage needs to be understood as a unity that moves in the direction of the final statement in 8:38–39. There seems to be no question among students of the letter that this is true. With "What shall we say about these things?" 8:31 introduces a series of questions, each of which opens with the interrogative τίς. The series concludes in 8:38–39 with the emphatic denial that there is any such thing. Literally, 8:39 says that there is no τις κτίσις.

It is important to underscore the unity of the section because commentators often implicitly undermine that unity by treating 8:31–34 as forensic and then characterizing 8:35–39 as a personal faith statement or emotional outburst. Fitzmyer, for example, describes the passage as situated in the law court but treats 8:38–39 as a statement of Paul's "personal conviction."[38] Barrett regards 8:31–34 as anticipating the last judgment, with Satan as the prosecutor, but then identifies 8:35–39 as referring to believers' fears of astrological powers.[39] It is true that the first and second of these questions may be taken as forensic.[40] It must be acknowledged, however, that the passage drives as a unity toward the last question about separation. And the last question does not pertain to people being judged but to people being pursued by agents that wish them separated from their rightful Lord. In other words, it is about a conflict of powers. Paul's final assertion is that there is no power that has the power to bring about this separation. The conclusion is clear, even if it remains unstated: the powers that attempt this separation will be defeated.

The question that arises rather quickly concerns the ontological status of these powers. What sort of beings are understood by the list in 8:38–39? Similarly, when Paul couples the words ἁμαρτία and θάνατος as subjects with active verbs, does he mean something more than that everyone does things that are wrong? Everyone dies? Paul does not address the ontological question, probably because he assumes the reality of these

---

37. We might recall Ps 104:25, which shrinks Leviathan down to the size of God's plaything or, as my colleague Dennis Olson puts it, God's "rubber ducky."

38. Fitzmyer, *Romans*, 529, 534.

39. Barrett, *Romans*, 173–74.

40. Note, however, that Robert Jewett has recently called into question the forensic interpretation of 8:33 (*Romans*, 539–40).

powers and is more interested in describing the captivity than he is in describing the captors. There is, however, ample evidence in Paul's religious environment for the belief that human beings are subject to evil powers in the form of demons.[41] And it is worth pressing again the question of what sense 8:31–39 makes if there is not, in Paul's thought, the intention of some powers to remove believers from God's love in Jesus Christ. Without some sense of opposition, some actual resistance, to "us" in this passage, the passage becomes nothing more than an emotional outburst, a rhetorical climax that is devoid of actual content.[42]

κόσμος and κτίσις

This examination of cosmology in Romans looks very little like what one would customarily expect from a discussion of cosmology. Little or nothing has been said about the cosmos in the non-human sense of that term (the globe, its other inhabitants, to say nothing of the larger universe).[43] Further complicating matters, I have emphasized 8:31–39, which addresses not the entire human population but "us," presumably Christians, raising the question whether 8:31–39 has anything to do with the salvation of the whole of the cosmos. It is at this point that we return to 8:18–25, where Paul makes a connection between the "us," i.e., those who at present know what God has done, and the whole of the created order (κτίσις).

Although there is at present a near consensus that κτίσις refers to non-human creation, I regard κτίσις as an all-encompassing term, one that refers to everything God has created, including humanity.[44] First, the subjection of creation οὐκ ἑκοῦσα ("not of its own will") has been over-interpreted as a reference to Adam's fall and its consequences. Elsewhere in Greek, the phrase οὐκ ἑκοῦσα is paired with its opposite (ἄκων), as is the case in 1 Corinthians 9:17, to contrast doing something freely with

41. For further discussion and bibliography, see Wright, *Evil Spirits*; and Bell, *Deliver Us*.

42. To be sure, the passage is highly rhetorical, but the rhetoric simply underscores Paul's desire to persuade and does not signal that the content is to be overlooked or ignored.

43. There is almost no overlap, for example, with the issues addressed in Danielson's illuminating anthology, *Book of the Cosmos*.

44. For a sketch of the consensus argument, see Adams, *Constructing*, 174–84; and more recently Hahne, *Corruption and Redemption*, esp. 177–81. This paragraph and the two that follow draw heavily on *Our Mother*, 53–55.

doing it under compulsion.[45] Instead of drawing attention to the disposition or attitude of creation, then, the phrase serves to draw attention to the one who *subjects* creation, namely, God. The role of Romans 8:20, then, is to describe the subjection of creation and to reinforce the notion that creation was *acted upon* by God: "creation was subjected—not freely—but by the one who subjected it."

Second, the fact that creation is waiting for the children of God to be revealed and that 8:23 refers to the groaning of "we" prompts many interpreters to argue that Paul is distinguishing between creation and believers.[46] However, no clear distinction is made; the eagerness with which all of creation longs for the apocalypse of God's children does not preclude God's children themselves from being part of that same eager expectation.[47] Indeed, far from saying that the children are *not* part of creation's longing, 8:23 highlights their longing. Even with the fact that they have tasted the firstfruit (or perhaps precisely *because* they do), "we" long right along with (and indeed as part of) the rest of creation.

Third, other passages in Romans suggest that Paul understands humanity to be part of κτίσις. The most important is 1:23, where he introduces the charge of idolatry by asserting that humanity made images of "human beings, birds, four-footed animals, and reptiles" and exchanged those images for the glory of God. He then summarizes his accusation with the words, "they worshiped and served the *creation* [κτίσις] rather than the one who created" (1:25). In other words, the problem with humanity is precisely its refusal to acknowledge its standing as creature, as made by God. (And this is the sense in which humanity participates in the "not willingly" of 8:20, i.e., humanity did not wish to be subjected; in fact, humanity rebelled against its rightful place as creature.) The closing doxology of 11:33–36 corroborates this association of humanity and the rest of creation, as Paul calls on Scripture to convey the impossibility of understanding God's own wisdom and knowledge, concluding with the words "since from him and through him and for him are *all things*

45. See BDAG 313, LSJ 527. On the range of connotations of ἑκών, especially in early literature, see Rickert, *Hekón and Ekón*.

46. A related question concerns the relationship between the believing "we" and the rest of humanity, on which see Eastman, "Whose Apocalypse?" 263–77, who argues convincingly that the apocalypse of God's sons and daughters in Romans 8 anticipates the future rectification of all of humanity, Jew and Gentile alike.

47. In conversation, my colleague Shane Berg suggests the clarifying example, "The Senate awaits the revelation of the new majority leader." In this sentence, the "majority leader" is singled out, but the leader is nonetheless a member of the Senate.

[τὰ πάντα]."⁴⁸ There is here a unity of everything in its createdness and in its relationship to God that is hard to reconcile with the notion that Romans 8 separates humanity from the remainder of creation. Indeed, the "all" (πᾶς) of 8:22 may provide further indication of the inclusive connotation of "creation" in this passage, since (as noted previously) the word "all" repeatedly refers in Romans to the whole of humanity (see, e.g., 1:5, 7, 8, 16; 2:9–10; 3:9, 12, 19, 23; 5:18; 11:26, 32, 36; 15:11).

To be sure, even reading κτίσις as limited to non-human creation still indicates Paul's concern that the earth requires redemption, which can only come from God.⁴⁹ Reading κτίσις as I have done, however, serves to locate the "we" of 8:31–39 within a larger landscape of the salvation of all of God's creation.

CONCLUSION: THE COSMIC GRASP OF GOD'S SALVATION

The word *cosmos* in Romans takes on a slightly different nuance than in Galatians. Here, as we have seen, it can be used in a neutral way to refer to the whole human population and is not identified with the "present evil age" of Galatians 1:4b. Nevertheless, consistent with Martyn's analysis of Galatians, Romans too offers a picture of humanity as enslaved to powers that are set in opposition to God. What Paul sees in creation (both the human cosmos and the remainder of creation) is not its order or its wonder but its captivity to powers that endeavor to separate it from its rightful Lord. Although the death and resurrection of Jesus Christ defeated Sin and Death and inaugurated a reign of God's grace, all of creation continues to stand on tiptoe (to borrow from the translation of J. B. Phillips) waiting for the arrival of its redemption.

This conclusion is far more than the excavation of two first-century letters for what they might reveal about the convictions of their authors. What is at stake here is what we understand by salvation, specifically, who or what it is that requires saving.⁵⁰ As I read the contemporary discussion,

48. Less ambiguous and more to the point are the hymnic lines of 1 Cor 8:6.

49. Since this passage is sometimes invoked in discussions of ecology, I want to be clear precisely what I intend when I affirm that, for Paul, the redemption of the earth only comes from God. That is not at all to deny a role for human beings in care for God's creation; indeed, the solidarity Paul assumes here between human and non-human creation would seem to require such a role. But when Paul speaks about the subjection of creation and its need for redemption, he is not referring to the voracious destruction of the earth by humanity, a phenomenon he could scarcely have imagined.

50. To be sure, discussion of soteriology is not limited to the specific questions

whether in my classroom or in academic theological discourse, there seem to be two answers to that question. On the one hand, the answer is that what requires saving is the individual human being. Although he is commenting on Romans in particular, Douglas Moo's insistence on this point is indicative of this position: "The bulk of Romans focuses on how God has acted in Christ to bring the *individual* sinner into a new relationship with himself (chaps. 1–4), to provide for that *individual's* eternal life in glory (chaps. 5–8), and to transform that *individual's* life on earth now (12:1–15:13)."[51] On the other hand, the answer offered is that what requires salvation is not the individual per se but some corporate group of human beings, whether that group be understood as Israel or the church or some other group. For example, contemporary concerns about ethnic conflict motivate Philip Esler's reading of Romans as Paul's attempt to reconcile Jews and Gentiles into a shared new group that is "destined for salvation."[52] Assumptions about salvation tend to run along one of these two tracks, the individual or the corporate. With the help of Martyn's reading of Paul, we discover (or perhaps rediscover) that those alternatives are simply inadequate: what has been subjected and is in need of salvation is every individual, every human community, and the whole of creation.[53]

Perhaps even more radical is the implication of Martyn's work for our understanding of the need for salvation, the presenting problem. Over against the notion that the problem is limited to human actions or inactions (whether individual or corporate), we see in Paul a humanity that does what is wrong because it is has become captive to other powers.[54] And that captivity has rendered humanity incapable of repenting, seeking God's forgiveness, and resolving in future to do what is right.[55] Human-

---

addressed here. As John Webster has observed: "[N]o part of Christian teaching is unrelated to soteriology, whether immediately or indirectly" ("Soteriology," 16). Here I am simply highlighting two important soteriological questions that are at stake in Martyn's work.

51. Moo, *Romans*, 28 (emphasis original). Conventionally, this approach is identified with evangelical Christianity, but that identification is problematic in two ways: first, concentration on the individual believer is not limited to evangelicals; second, many evangelicals are quite aware of the problems of focusing exclusively on the individual. See Stackhouse, *What Does It Mean to Be Saved?*.

52. Esler, *Conflict and Identity*, 140.

53. On the latter in particular, see Creegan, "Salvation of Creatures."

54. See McFarland's review of important recent treatments of sin, all of which assume that human beings have the capacity to choose not to sin (*In Adam's Fall*, 11–18).

55. See Martyn's contrast between the "competent" and "incompetent" human agent in "Epilogue"; see also Gaventa, *Our Mother*, 113–36.

ity requires not merely repentance and forgiveness but liberation from its captivity and, indeed, new creation. Most characteristic of Martyn's exegesis is his relentless insistence that, for Paul, the initiative is God's.

In brief, what is at stake in J. Louis Martyn's reading of Paul is nothing less than the size and saving power of the gospel, which is to say the size and saving power of God.

9

"Christ Must Reign"

Ernst Käsemann and Soteriology in an Apocalytpic Key

Philip G. Ziegler

The first thing necessary for you is to be conquered by God; only as God's vanquished captive can you share in God's victory.[1]

INTRODUCTION

IN A CONTRIBUTION TO current debates in soteriology, Alan Spence weighs up the merits of the so-called victory model and asks whether it can provide an adequate paradigm for exposition of the Christian doctrine of salvation generally, and of Paul's account of salvation in particular.[2] N. T. Wright and Gustaf Aulén are called upon as advocates of the *Christus victor* doctrine. In Spence's judgment, Wright's recourse to the doctrine in his exposition of Paul's theology simply "does not do justice to the material before it," actively requiring him to neglect a whole range of crucial concepts such as forgiveness, mercy, guilt, and reconciliation.[3]

1. Vogel, "Shortened Course," 217.

2. Spence, "Unified Theory."

3. Ibid., 416. Spence concentrates almost exclusively on N. T. Wright's presentation of the case in *What St. Paul Really Said*.

Spence is also unpersuaded by Aulén's claim for the primacy and sufficiency of the "dramatic" model of salvation; once again, the inability of this discourse to capture the realities of enmity, forgiveness, reconciliation, and finally also grace itself tells decisively against it. As he explains, "Aulén never goes on to help us understand how the battle motif, so helpful in explaining the experience of human freedom and liberation, is able to shed light on the problems of guilt, judgment and animosity."[4] Spence's chief worry is that by construing salvation as rescue, victory models prove inadequate to express the personal transformation of the individual sinner required when human beings are acknowledged to be agents, rather than mere victims, of sin.

If one wished to press further into this matter and to engage Spence's critical conclusions concerning the limitations of the "victory model," a number of possibilities would be at hand. One could augment and complicate the assessment of N.T. Wright's exegetical project by drawing upon his wider corpus.[5] Similarly one could engage more fully with Aulén's theology and its sources in an effort to display its wider explanatory power and adequacy.[6] Alternately, one could look to more recent iterations of the *Christus victor* model that may do better justice to those "mediatorial concepts" that are at the heart of Spence's critical concern—J. Denny Weaver's much-discussed work would seem to recommend itself here.[7] Leaving such lines of inquiry to others however, this essay pursues another course. It turns to reconsider aspects of the theological legacy of Ernst Käsemann as a basis upon which to contend for the adequacy of a Christian doctrine of salvation whose central motif is the eschatological struggle and victory of God over Sin for the sake of his beleaguered creatures. My aim is to gesture toward an account of salvation that is christologically concentrated and apocalyptically charged, and to intimate something of the contours

4. Spence, "Unified Theory," 417; cf. 405, 416.

5. Wright's contributions to recent exchanges surrounding the doctrine of justification, for instance, would provide much directly relevant material. For a concentrated presentation, see his *Justification*.

6. Assessing the role of the *Christus victor* motif in Aulén's theology as a whole would involve careful analysis of his *The Faith of the Christian Church* and careful exploration of his reception of Luther himself on this score. For a recent reassessment of Aulén's own proposal from an evangelical perspective, see Ovey, "Appropriating Aulén?" For a detailed analysis study of the "salvation as battle" motif in Luther, see Rieske-Braun, *Duellem Mirabile*.

7. See Weaver, "Atonement," for a condensed example, and more fully his *Nonviolent Atonement*, especially chapters 2 and 3 on "Narrative Christus Victor."

of a Christian life concomitant with it. It is because apocalyptic conspires with Christology in a particular way in his work that Käsemann's soteriology can be shown to do justice to the concerns that animate Spence's criticism of the "victory model," not by diffusing but precisely by radicalizing its insights. In this way, I hope to make a modest contribution to what Carl Braaten has called a much-needed "recovery of apocalyptic imagination" in our day.[8]

J. L. Martyn—by whose work contributors to this volume have all be variously provoked and edified—has happily acknowledged the influence of Ernst Käsemann upon his own understanding of Paul's apocalyptic gospel of the invading grace of God in Christ, remarking that his account is "indebted above all to the works" of the great twentieth-century German pastor, exegete, and theologian.[9] Käsemann, for his part, also saw Martyn as one of the few in the English speaking world who could be relied upon to "step up for [him] from the trenches."[10] Käsemann's work elucidates the formative categories and logic of an account of salvation that takes with utmost seriousness the New Testament's witness to the apocalyptic form of the outworking of divine mercy. Käsemann was driven to acknowledge that the righteousness of God is "God's sovereignty over the world revealing itself eschatologically in Jesus,"[11] and took as his watchword Paul's declaration that Christ must reign until all his enemies have been put underfoot (1 Cor 15:25).[12] While vigorously defending the central place of justification in Christian theology, he fundamentally reconceives the doctrine by shifting the locus of divine salvation away from anthropology and onto cosmology, as the advent of God's righteousness means "God's power reaches out for the world, and the world's salvation lies in its being

---

8. See Braaten, "Apocalyptic Imagination." There is no question that Käsemann's own interest in "apocalyptic" had both exegetical but also substantive contemporary *theological* concerns motivating it. See Way, *Lordship of Christ*, 173.

9. Martyn, *Theological Issues*, 65 n. 36. Never in fact a student of Käsemann's, in the preface to the 1967 first edition of his *History & Theology* he simply calls Käsemann his "friend" (12). Writing in 1985, Robin Scroggs remarked that Käsemann's lasting importance would perhaps be as a *theologian* rather than as an exegete ("Divine *Agent Provocateur*," 260). For a valuable recent survey and analysis of Käsemann's legacy see Eckstein and Lichtenberger, *Dienst in Freiheit*.

10. In 1995 letter from Käsemann to Paul Zahl—see Zahl, "Tribute," 385.

11. Käsemann, "'Righteousness of God,'" 180.

12. Curiously, despite his regular invocations of 1 Cor 15:25f., Käsemann never published a detailed exegesis of the passage itself; see Way, *Lordship of Christ*, 138. Cf. Käsemann, "Primitive Christian Apocalyptic," 133.

recaptured for the sovereignty of God."[13] The categories of traditional "mediatorial" soteriology—e.g., grace, faith, forgiveness, repentance, etc.—are heavily inflected by this eschatological setting, as is the understanding of the Christian life to which it gives rise; so too are the fundaments of ethics and politics Christianly conceived. Theology takes its essential bearings in the present time of faith and obedience from the coming of the kingdom. This is a supremely practical, not theoretical, claim, since its truth is acknowledged and attested in a human praxis in which "Jesus of Nazareth is in fact our Lord and the Lord of the world."[14]

The stakes for Christian theology here are significant. In virtue of its decisiveness for Christian faith, life, and thought, Käsemann himself thought the matter of the apocalyptic gospel to be "at least as important as that of the historical Jesus, and ought perhaps even to take precedence over it."[15] In a notable understatement, Marytn once observed that if Käsemann's thesis concerning the eschatological character of divine rectification were correct, then "not a little of the discussion among systematicians will have to be changed."[16] And so we ask: what follows for an account of salvation when the *duellum mirabile* is allowed to frame the doctrine as a whole, i.e., when the apocalyptic struggle that God fights against the whole inimical dominion that holds humankind in bondage—a struggle whose turning point is Jesus Christ—provides its center of gravity?[17] As debates about the interpretation of Paul, the doctrine of the atonement, the scope of salvation and its relation to Jesus Christ continue in our day, we can expect that Käsemann's clear hearing of the eschatological gospel of salvation has much to teach us yet, not least by reminding us of the essential task and promise of such Christian theological labor, in which the Spirit "so binds the interpreter to the hearing of the Scripture that he cannot attempt translation into the world's different languages without returning to its substance, finding its heart in the midst of its variations, and thus acquiring criteria for discerning the spirits."[18]

---

13. Käsemann, *Questions of Today,* 182.

14. Käsemann, *Kirchliche Konflikte,* 216.

15. Käsemann, "'Righteousness of God,'"182.

16. Martyn, review of *Questions of Today,* 557.

17. Aulén uses the Latin phrase in his "Chaos and Cosmos,"157.

18. Käsemann, "Doctrine of Reconciliation," 62.

SAVED BY THE APOCALYPSE OF SOVEREIGN DIVINE LOVE

For our purposes, the account of human existence that Käsemann discerns to be ingredient in eschatological announcement of the gospel of God will be of great importance. It is this distinctive theological anthropology that ensures that the full range of soteriological concepts finally find a place within an apocalyptic description of the outworking of salvation. Yet, in keeping with the nature of the eschatological gospel itself, anthropology is subsequent to other more primary realities, namely the realities of God in Christ and of the fallen world. As Käsemann has it, the anthropology intrinsic to the apocalyptic gospel must be grasped as but "the projection of cosmology."[19] In order to understand this claim, we begin with one of Käsemann's programmatic statements on the matter. In the famous essay "On the Subject of Primitive Christian Apocalyptic," he writes:

> Man, for Paul, is never just on his own. He is always a specific piece of world and therefore becomes what in the last resort he is by determination from outside, i.e., by the power which takes possession of him and the lordship to which he surrenders himself. His life is from the beginning a stake in the confrontation between God and the principalities of this world. In other words, it mirrors the cosmic contention for the lordship of the world and is its concretion. As such, man's life can only be understood apocalyptically.[20]

Several key claims are made here. To be a human being—to have life in the body as a creature of this world—is to be irrevocably knit into the fabric of a larger reality, namely, "the world." This at first seemingly banal claim proves to be anything but. For, in the first place, it signals a polemical repudiation of modern characterisations of human beings whose chief currency is talk of individual autonomy and "self-reflexivity."[21] Such visions of autonomy are recognised as illusory when, with Paul, one understands a human "body" as "that piece of world which we ourselves are and for

---

19. Käsemann, *Romans*, 150. For more expansive discussions of Käsemann's anthropology see Zahl, *Rechtfertigungslehre Ernst Käsemanns*, 148–68; and Way, *Lordship of Christ*, 54–61, 154–63.

20. Käsemann, "Primitive Christian Apocalyptic," 136.

21. Käsemann uses the term "idealism" as a collective epithet for such anthropologies, signaling thereby both their indebtedness to a discretely modern European philosophical tradition and their contrast with other, "realistic" accounts of human existence—the latter a moniker he certainly claims for Paul's apocalyptic account of humanity embodied in and indeed by the world. This issue is central to his break with Bultmann's exegetical programme; see Käsemann, "What I Have Unlearned," 329–31.

which we bear responsibility because it was the earliest gift of our Creator to us."[22] To be a human being is to live in a particular world constitutive for individual existence. All humanity is always already *claimed* humanity.

Now, envisaged evangelically, human existence is held firmly within a specific understanding of the world as a field of contest between competing powers, and indeed, finally, as the site of a single contest between God and the anti-God powers of the fallen creation. It is precisely the force of Paul's witness in Romans 5:12f. to make plain that the antithesis of Adam and Christ represents a global confrontation of "alternative, exclusive and ultimate" spheres in which the "old world and a new world are at issue . . . there is no third option."[23] As Käsemann explains, Adam and Christ stand in an antithetical, if uneven, correspondence in which "both are bearers of destiny for the world. . . . These two—and basically these two alone—have determined the world as a whole."[24] So, as "specific pieces" of *this* world, human existence stands under one of two signs, that of the Creator or that of Sin; one has either Christ or anti-Christ as a lord. There is in such an apocalyptic vision of things no thought that human existence as such is or could ever be neutral vis-à-vis the eschatological either/or between the claim of God and his Christ and the sphere of Adam.[25] In working out the soteriological significance of such a view, just what it means to "have a lord" here proves decisive.

If, as Käsemann contends, the basic idea of Paul's anthropology is that "a person is defined by his particular lord," this is because as a "sphere of sovereignty" the world is simply the place wherein and from which human life is determinately claimed, formed, and animated.[26] The world of Adam—as a constellation of overlapping, fluctuating, and mutual contesting sovereignties that are variously and together in rebellion against

22. Käsemann, "Primitive Christian Apocalyptic," 135. Cf. Käsemann, "On Paul's Anthropology," 28: "We ourselves do not determine what we are. It is delusion to imagine that this is the case and presumption to rely on it."

23. Käsemann, *Romans*, 146.

24. Ibid., 153. On the development of Käsemann's use of the concept of Christ as a "bearer of destiny" see Way, *Lordship of Christ*, 167f.

25. "Man can never be 'neutral in himself' and is certainly not so in his corporeality, which is always already modified. An ontology that deprives him of this already-existing modification is order to observe him *per se* falls victim to an abstraction and no longer allows him the humanity of creatureliness" (Käsemann, "Paul's Anthropology," 20). Or again, "Whoever abrogates obedience to the Creator from then on lives for idols" (Käsemann, "God's Image," 114).

26. Käsemann, *Romans*, 250.

God—in this way defines humanity in Sin.[27] To be lorded over by these powers is not simply to suffer their oppression externally, though it involves that certainly. More than that, it means having been conscripted into their service. So Käsemann can describe Death as "a force which shapes the cosmos," and as "a curse in the texture of earthly life which ineluctably affects every individual"; the upshot is a human being is less the subject than the "object and projection" of his history, someone firmly "in the grip of forces which seize his existence and determine his will and responsibility at least to the extent that he cannot choose freely but can only grasp what is already there."[28] The lordship one suffers works itself inside the self, establishing a specific orientation within which life is lived, making us "of a piece" of that world of which we are part. One is thus "never an individuality but is always oneself *and* the world at any given time."[29] For the human creature is one who "radically and representatively for all others, submits to his lord"—in this case to the distorting and ruinous power of Sin—"becoming the instrument which manifests [its] power and [its] universal claim."[30] Thus women and men subjected to Sin are not merely its passive victims; they also become its active servants. To be lorded over by Sin is to have been engaged to be its representative, "member, part and tool."[31] This point will prove crucial. This apocalyptic vision does not conceive of our subjection within the sphere of Adam as a purely extrinsic fate and so fatalistically conceive of human existence as tragic. Since women and men *are* active sinners even under (and as a result of) the curse of Sin, "personal accountability can neither be eliminated nor isolated." This is because in our very existence "we are *exponents* of a power which transforms the cosmos into chaos," our lives actually "making a case" for the power that possesses us and in whose service we are enrolled.[32] This is why Paul characterised the guilt of sin not in terms of ignorance, but rather in terms of "revolt against the known Lord."[33]

---

27. Käsemann, "Paul's Anthropology," 27–28. Cf. Martyn, Comment 39, *Galatians*, 370f.

28. Käsemann, *Romans*, 141, 147.

29. Käsemann, "God's Image," 115.

30. Käsemann, "Paul's Anthropology," 28. Cf. Käsemann, *Romans*, 150: Paul speaks of "ruling powers which implicate all people individually and everywhere determine reality as destiny."

31. Käsemann, "God's Image," 115. Cf. Käsemann, *Romans*, 220.

32. Käsemann, *Romans*, 154 (emphasis added); Käsemann, "God's Image," 115.

33. Käsemann, *Romans*, 41, 42.

Now all this—which might be taken as a sketch of the architecture of an apocalyptic doctrine of original sin[34]—bears directly upon the description of salvation at the heart of the gospel of God. As noted above, Käsemann essentially construes the matter so: "God's power reaches out for the world, and the world's salvation lies in its being recaptured for the sovereignty of God."[35] Deliverance involves the "assault of grace upon the world of the body"[36] in order to effect a change of lordship, effectively translating the human being out from the sphere of Sin and idolatry into the sphere of Christ.[37] Exercising his right as Creator, God comes on the scene in Christ to wrest his complicit creatures from their servitude and plight under the false, yet all too real, reign of Sin. To talk of an exchange of lordships or transfer of spheres in this way is to evoke nothing less that the advent of the new creation, a gift whose only presupposition is the invading power divine grace itself.[38]

In Käsemann's account, the concepts of grace and righteousness overlap inseparably, as they each denote "under different aspects the same thing, namely the *basileia* of Christ."[39] Righteousness, for Käsemann, names "the rightful power with which God makes his cause to triumph in the world which has fallen away from him and which yet, as creation, is his inviolable possession."[40] While by "grace" we indicate not a disposition or attitude of God towards humanity—perhaps a "merely inscrutable or arbitrary love"—but rather the effective form of God's saving power. [41] As modalities of his lordship, these gifts of God are the very means by which he "subordinates us to his lordship and makes us responsible beings"; as gifts of *God*, they remain in his possession even as he gives them fully

34. So Käsemann writes, "Christianity has unjustly forgotten or at least diminished the theologically non-recindable, though haplessly described doctrine of original sin" (*Being a Disciple*, 232).

35. Käsemann, "'Righteousness of God,'" 182.

36. Käsemann, *Romans*, 213.

37. Ibid., 155: "The plus of grace consists in transfer from the sphere of death to that of life as resurrection power." Cf also Käsemann, "Paul's Anthropology," 28–29, where we read that hope lies in a "change of lordship and life in another world."

38. Käsemann, *Romans*, 154.

39. Ibid., 154, 158. Cf. "'Righteousness of God,'" 174, where Käsemann writes that there is an "indissoluble connection of power and gift within the conception of divine righteousness." Cf. Barth, *Römerbrief*, 196: "Grace is the kingdom, the lordship, the power and the rule of God over humanity" (as translated and cited by Way, *Lordship of Christ*, 42 n. 112.)

40. Käsemann, "'Righteousness of God,'" 180.

41. Käsemann, "Justice for the Unjust," 230.

and freely to us.[42] By the concrete exercise of his reign of righteousness and grace in Christ God rectifies the world, setting things to rights in accordance with his merciful deity.

Eberhard Jüngel expressly affirms the importance of Käsemann's insights when he asserts that contemporary theology must lay distinctive stress upon the fact that "God's righteousness is a power that penetrates into the fallen world in order to make over anew the world's unrighteous relationships."[43] Theology must credit the creative—or rather, re-creative—reality of God's simultaneous exercise of his right as God and the eschatological gift of his Son in the one act of salvation. In this one act of sovereign self-disclosure and gracious self-giving, both the deity of God and the humanity of man are revealed with saving effect: God's righteous mercy conquers and expels the false gods of the age, thereby securing for his beloved, threatened creatures that "other world," that new creation in which is constituted by the lordship of the Crucified One. Thus justification of the ungodly, Käsemann concludes, simply means "God's victory over the world that strives against him."[44] Salvation is had in Christ because in him is enacted the victory of God over the contentious world for its own sake.

Note that when salvation is understood along such lines as these—when it amounts to the lordly gift of "the God who brings back the fallen world into the a sphere of his legitimate claim . . . whether in promise or demand, in new creation or forgiveness, or in the making possible of our service"[45]—then, in a structural analogy with the reality of human captivity *and* active complicity with the aeonic power of Sin, human beings are at once those whom God rescues and, as such, those made new in and by his rescue. The victory God wins when Christ takes power over us is won *for us* even as it won *against us* insofar as we are exponents and instruments of that other false lord, i.e., insofar as we are ourselves "a piece" with the world vanquished and overturned. To speak of our redemption out from under the power of Sin is to speak therefore of a liberation whose form is

42. Käsemann, "'Righteousness of God,'" 174.

43. Jüngel, *Justification*, 64–65. Käsemann, while certainly admitting that justification involves the gift of righteousness to sinners, insisted vehemently that Paul primarily has in view, as the basis of this gift, God's own righteousness which rectifies the world. As Leander Keck wagers, "Käsemann's reconstruction of the morphology of this meaning has been criticized; nonetheless, when the dust settles he will be more 'justified' than not" (Keck, *Paul and His Letters*, 113).

44. Käsemann, *Romans*. 82.

45. Ibid., 29.

precisely that of judgment and forgiveness, for it involves the overcoming of enmity and the reconciliation of renewed creatures with the God who is in fact God. As liberation, salvation includes rather than bypasses personal sin: the gospel promises that God wills to wrest the earth out from "our egoism and our deep-seated indolence and hypocrisy," and that he does so by freeing us from the tyrannical powers that enslave us.[46] These are two aspects of the one rectifying movement of God's sovereign grace.

The world from which Christ sets us free is our world—a world for which we are responsible—in the radical sense that it has been constitutive of our very identities. We have been the very agents of its enmity towards God. It is for this reason that to be severed from that world is to have to die so as to be made alive; it is to have had the world "crucified" and to have been crucified to the world (Gal 6:14). To be translated out of that world is a profound act of salutary alienation, one for which defeat, judgment, and death are not exaggerated tropes. The exercise of divine righteousness "establishes his justice by being gracious," Käsemann argues, because God is ever putting an end to our illusions, for "God's truth is his lordship over the creature. It shatters as such our self-assertion and when accepted sets us in the power of grace. Grace is granted only from the Judge's hand."[47]

We can begin to see the upshot of this apocalyptic anthropology: to see that a person's reality is decisively determined by his or her lord, such that "the servant becomes like his master and shows this by his behaviour," has thoroughgoing consequences in soteriology.[48] It authorizes and makes sense of the strongest possible version of the victory model, in which salvation is strictly identified with having the lordship of Christ exercised over oneself, for one's own sake, as a consequence of God's eschatological revelation of his sovereignty in him. At the same time, because sinners are understood to be not merely insulated victims of the "world of Sin" but rather its settled inhabitants, actively habituated to its ways and means as subjects of in the service of its false gods, the soteriological motifs of enmity, guilt, judgment, forgiveness, and reconciliation all find a proper place within this account of salvation as divine victory, rather than simply falling out with it as a kind of alternate, possibly parallel "metaphor" for salvation. Käsemann himself in fact argues that while the juridical and cultic aspects of the reality of salvation are necessary implicates of its cos-

46. Käsemann, "What I Have Unlearned," 334.

47. Käsemann, *Romans*, 83. "The apocalyptic future brings new reality in the present through creative negation" (Braaten, "Significance of Apocalypticism," 491).

48. Käsemann, *Romans*, 43.

mological understanding, the converse cannot be said. Reconciliation—a motif particularly prominent in modern soteriologies—is itself best understood in an apocalyptic framework, Käsemann suggests.[49] Summarizing the point, he writes that the eschatological Christian gospel

> . . . is characterised by the open proclamation of the seizure of power by God and his appointed Saviour and by the verification of that proclamation in the union of both Jews and Gentiles in the Christian church. Heaven is no longer a closed realm hovering above the earth, and the world is no more the battlefield of every man against his neighbour and the arena of mutually exclusive sovereignties. The principalities and powers have been dethroned. If this picture is correct, reconciliation in this instance implies an eschatological, even an apocalyptic, phenomenon which is not primarily connected with, and cannot be appropriately conceived by the use of, either juridical or cultic categories. The eschatological and worldwide *regnum Christi* necessarily breaks the bounds of a community understood along merely juridical or cultic lines.[50]

Held firmly within this context, discourses of reconciliation—Spence's "mediatorial" motifs—serve to proclaim "God's solidarity" with humanity in Christ "as the basis for human solidarity" as well as to indicate the fact that "God aids and purposes to aid *his enemies* (and thus the whole world)."[51]

The capacity of Käsemann's apocalyptic soteriology to incorporate the breath of scriptural "models" and concerns is further confirmed when we attend to the description of the Chrsitian life that follows from such an account. Once again, what proves decisive is Käsemann's insight that "the ontological structure of anthropology remains determined by lordship as in the old aeon," though now in keeping with the truth of God's deity enacted in Christ.[52] What does it mean for us as "pieces of the world" that we should have *this God* as our Lord? What kind of existence arises when Christ takes possession of us, when he bears to us our destiny as the chil-

---

49. Käsemann, "Doctrine of Reconciliation," 53–56. Spence makes a contrary case for the sole adequacy of mediatorial model to encompass and explain the main lines of the others; see "Unified Theory," 417–20.

50. Käsemann, "Doctrine of Reconciliation," 55.

51. Ibid., 64, 63 (emphasis added). Cf. Martyn, *Galatians*, 336: "Before the advent of Christ humanity was an enslaved monolith; in Christ humanity is becoming a liberated unity."

52. Käsemann, *Romans*, 155.

dren of God? What does it look like for human beings to be crafted into representatives and exponents of the Lord of love? These are the questions to which the doctrines of sanctification and ecclesiology among others provide serviceable answers. A full exploration of these themes must await another occasion. But some brief indication of the direction in which Käsemann himself takes theological exposition of the Christian life will serve to secure the point at issue: namely, that his apocalyptic rendering of the *Christus victor* can do justice to the full range of soteriological motifs for which the New Testament makes Christian theology responsible in its service of the coherence and clarity of the proclamation of the gospel.

First, Käsemann insists that the apocalyptic inflection of Paul's doctrine of salvation takes it in a more, rather than less, realistic direction.[53] Rather than making the message of reconciliation into a utopian myth, understanding it apocalyptically ensures that attention is driven to the historical sphere of "concrete daily life and corporal community" where the gift and claim of salvation are in fact actualized. In this vein, Käsemann observes that talk of reconciliation keeps such close company in the New Testament with *parenesis* precisely because "cosmic peace does not settle over the world, as in a fairy tale. It takes root only so far as men in the service of reconciliation confirm that they have themselves found peace with God. The message of the reconciled world demonstrates its truth in the reconciled man, not apart from him or beyond him."[54] The same realism is echoed when Käsemann claims that "the earth is only liberated from enmity and chaos and made a new creation in so far as the service of Christ is carried on in her," not because our striving achieves it, but rather because faith knows that, beyond all human striving, women and men by grace receive and are made to bear "the divine work to a world which God has not forsaken."[55] Hence, though the gospel of salvation certainly "posits reality," whether this "remains a living reality" and whether Christians are preserved "in obedience" are matters forever "bound up with the actualization of the promise" in the actual lives of forgiven sinners in the church.[56] In short, because Christians most fundamentally *belong* to their Lord, their very existence is conscripted into the service of mak-

53. "The earth is constantly claimed also by false gods, about which only the naive can say, 'they are invisible.' Who is our Lord? And who should finally become our Lord? These are the central questions of existence" (Käsemann, "What I Have Unlearned," 335).

54. Käsemann, "Doctrine of Reconciliation," 56.

55. Ibid., 64.

56. Ibid., 177.

ing his lordship manifest. This line of exposition makes *discipleship* the primary category by which to understand the Christian life, as the only self-understanding available to disciples of the Crucified One "arises from the act of following," and not from any idea.[57]

Within such an approach, the biblical concepts of participation "in Christ" and of "union" with him become liable to distinctive hearing. They are heard now less as mystagogical descriptions of ontological ascent, and more as realisitic—even political—descriptions of our effective recruitment into Christ's cause and thus to his active service. As Käsemann argues, it is the work of such concepts in theology to give powerful expression to our incorporation under the lordship of the Crucified. They offer a condensed description of the state of the justified, where "justification" denotes that act by which Christ assumes his rightful claim and exercises his power over our lives, thereby binding us to him, securing our allegiance and enabling our witness and service by his grace. To be "in Christ" is therefore to "abide in the gift which we have received, and it can abide, living and powerful, in us" by the powerful activity of his Spirit.[58] There is an essential dynamism injected here into what can otherwise be taken to be static descriptions of a human position; our being in Christ is movement, because "the new Lord cuts us off from what we were before and never allows us to remain what we are at any given time, for otherwise he might be the First Cause but he would not be our Lord in the true sense."[59] As Zwingli once put it, participation "in Christ" occurs precisely in the faithful acknowledgement of him as the "captain" of our present existence

---

57. Käsemann, "What I Have Unlearned," 330; and *Romans*, 224. Cf., Käsemann, "Primitive Christian Apocalyptic," 134: "In the bodily obedience of the Christian, carried out as the service of God in the world of everyday, the lordship of Christ finds visible expression and only when this visible expression takes provisional shape in us does the whole thing become credible as Gospel message." Or again, "What is really at stake is this: we ourselves must become alert and, indeed, so must all who want to remain Christians . . . we have to remember that it is discipleship which is laid upon us all and nothing else. But in the same measure as discipleship takes hold, everything else follows of its own accord" (Käsemann, "Theologians and the Laity," 289–90).

58. Käsemann, "'Righteousness of God," 175. Here and elsewhere Käsemann lays great emphasis on the present work of the Spirit in the present outworking of Christ's lordship in the Christian life. The concepts of being drawn into the body of Christ and the effective exercise of Christ's lordship are mutually interpretative, and indeed finally identical, so that Käsemann can say that "by the Spirit Christ seizes power in us, just as conversely by the Spirit we are incorporated into Christ" (*Romans*, 222).

59. Käsemann, "'Righteousness of God," 176.

in this world.[60] All of this is in keeping with the construal of the Christian life as a gracious conscription to discipleship brought about by the fact that Christ has acted to take "total possession" of our lives such that we now stand in the "field of force" that is his effective reign.[61]

An apocalyptic account of salvation in Christ such as this stresses the radical objectivity and exteriority of God's saving acts: salvation is ever something that happens to us, it is something that befalls us *ab extra* despite ourselves. And yet, what is equally clear is that Käsemann's no less vigorous insistence upon the crucial agency of Christ and the Spirit in the actualization of salvation ensures that it is inescapably actual *for* us and catches us up in its outworking. If we ask about the contours of our discipleship—i.e., if we inquire into the form and direction of human existence held by the Spirit in the sphere of the power of the crucified Lord—we hear from Käsemann chiefly of freedom, witness, struggle, and resistance.[62] If the first two of these motifs reflect the present eschatological force of the exchange of lordships, the second two signal the patient orientation of Christian faith and life towards the future when Christ's lordship will be, as it were, fully apocalypsed. At present, during the time of Christ's own militant lordship—in the era during which he "must reign until he has put all his enemies underfoot" (1 Cor 15:25)—faith is beset and exercised precisely in trusting "in the love of Christ against all appearances"; its modes are often best captured in negative descriptions as refusals "to let discipleship be hindered" or repressed under pressure from the rearguard action of the defeated powers of Sin (Gal 5:1).[63] Our reconciliation with God engenders a new enmity with the world "according to the law of apocalyptic," because, as Käsemann writes,

60. "For Jesus Christ is the leader and captain whom God has promised and given to the whole human race" (article 6 of Zwingli's *Sixty-Seven Articles*, 36).

61. Käsemann, *Romans*, 219, 223. Cf., Käsemann, "What I Have Unlearned," 331: "What is proclaimed and should be taken with utmost seriousness is the Nazarene's path to world lordship, which becomes concrete and observable in the individual believer."

62. Käsemann, "What I Have Unlearned," 334: "Along with its preaching and ministering in our time, the church has to be the resistance movement of the exalted Christ in a world claimed by him and invited into his freedom." Cf. the concluding words of his autobiographical, "A Theological Review": "As a last word and as my bequest, let me call to you in Huguenot style: '*Résistez!*' Discipleship of the Crucified leads necessarily to resistance to idolatry on every front. This resistance is and must be the most important mark of Christian freedom" (in *Being a Disciple*, xxi).

63. Käsemann, *Romans*, 251.

Received blessing brands us, but it also sets us in conflict and contradiction. It places us before the need to persevere and in the possibility of relapse. It is not an irrevocable destiny which puts an end to the history of existence and the world. It gives free play to real history by making it the place, not of fallenness and doom, but of the assaulted freedom of faith and of the grace which is to be seized unceasingly in renunciation of the old aeon.[64]

In correspondence with the logic of the *Christus victor*, the overarching conceptuality of the Christian life here receives a decidedly *political* cast. Given the realism of Käsemann's apocalyptic hearing of the gospel, this is no mere trope. As Käsemann writes, Christ's "lordship over body and soul, heart and mind, disciples and demons, this world and the world to come, is a political fact."[65] Politics, in the normal course of things in the yet-unredeemed world, involves something like an all-too-human struggle to cast out demons by the power of other demons—i.e., the effort to check the exercise of power by the deployment of other powers.[66] But cleaved to the body of Jesus Christ as people who, in the power of Spirit, acknowledge that they have been set under his sovereign liberation and claim, Christians serve the extension of his reign. It is a reign different in kind from that of political powers (John 18:36), and is all the more real for being so. As Jesus announces to those who would assimilate his lordship to the patterns of this age, "But if it is by the Spirit of God that I cast out demons, then the kingdom of God has come upon you" (Matt 12:28). Accordingly, the Christian's political service to Christ's reign can and must be politics *by other means*. In several occasional works from later in his life, Käsemann proposed rather provocatively in this vein that Christian service in the world should be thought of as a form of *exorcism*.[67] This suggestion trades heavily upon the New Testament narratives and their apocalyptic grammar, a grammar within which concepts like

64. Ibid., 249, 156; cf. also 247: "The old aeon, rebellious, threatening, and perverted, is still present, so that Christians are under attack" and yet "in the Spirit God does not merely maintain his right. He also graciously brings [those he upholds] home and preserves them. In this way he manifests his love as Creator. This is the triumph of the assaulted."

65. Käsemann, "What I Have Unlearned," 334–35.

66. Perhaps the Niebuhrian account of justice as the achievable balance of competing human egoisms are matched under the conditions of sin may be open to such an exousiological redescription; see Niebuhr, *Nature and Destiny*, 252, 254.

67. See in particular the two essays, "Unrighteous World" and "Healing," in *Being a Disciple*.

freedom, liberation, and resistance come to serve as theological terms of art. To see the Christian life in terms of possession and exorcism, idolatry and iconoclasm, tethers the theopolitical rhetoric of the Christian life not only to the New Testament, but also crucially to the honoring of the first commandment. Further, it rightly emphasizes that the struggle to tell to the evangelical truth in and about the human situation is a struggle not just with error and ignorance, but finally also with powerful enrapturing superstitions and falsifications (Eph 6:12).[68] Understood in this way, Christian freedom names the power animating a discipleship whose form is a joyful, bold, and costly witness and whose hope is to serve Christ as the Lord of grace and to "bring him as such to others."[69]

A BRIEF EXCURSUS ON AULÉN

Some twenty years after the publication in 1931 of *Christus Victor*, Gustaf Aulén reprised and expanded the constructive element of that study in a concise essay entitled, "Chaos and Cosmos: The Drama of the Atonement."[70] Though the category itself never appears, the proposal is in close keeping with the hearings of Paul's *apocalyptic* gospel set forth by Käsemann, Martyn, and others in subsequent decades and may readily be supplemented and expanded by tapping this vein of New Testament theology. Aulén stresses that a properly evangelical soteriology can and must understand "atonement" only firmly within that "cosmos-encompassing dramatical perspective" which is "fundamental for all Christian thought."[71] The central motif of the biblical drama is the story of the love of God, militantly rampant against the "hostile powers" that bind and oppress humanity. In the New Testament these powers bear the particular names of Sin, Death, and the Devil, together with the Law and other creaturely powers themselves rendered inimical to God by the oppressive power of the same. The drama thus comprises a clash of antagonistic dominions whose catastrophic culmination is the confrontation in Christ of

68. See Käsemann, "Healing," 199–201.

69. Käsemann, "Healing," 204. Moreover, "it must be shown and proved that the gospel rids of demons, that it deserves to be called mother of Enlightenment and, in league with the Enlightenment, unmasks idols" (203). Cf. also *Romans*, 251: Christian freedom—"as an anticipation of the resurrection and the joy of conquerers"—is such that "even when inferno threatens on all sides, the Christian is stigmatized by the Lord who is present for him, and is set in *parhessia*."

70. Aulén, "Chaos and Cosmos." Cf. also §26 of his *Faith of the Christian Church*.

71. Aulén, "Chaos and Cosmos," 157, 156.

the grinding reign of "all the inimical domination" by the loving lordship of God. Such fearsome rhetoric as this is required, Aulén says, in order to "set forth in a concrete and active manner the constant, radical, and spontaneous opposition of the divine will of love to all that is opposed to it and therefore destructive."[72] Thus, as with Käsemann, the idiom of apocalyptic is acknowledged to give uniquely fitting voice to the dynamism, radicality, and effective scope of the outworking of God's loving will which is at the heart of the gospel.

In keeping with this emphasis, Aulén goes on to stress that the primary agent of salvation is ever God himself—it is God who comes low in the person of his Son to win the victory and reconciliation for beleaguered creatures. Indeed, to compromise the activity of God at this juncture would at once "deny the reality of the Incarnation" and "destroy" the gospel truth: as Luther had it, "to abolish sin, to destroy death, to take away the curse in himself, and again, to give righteousness, to bring life to light, and to give the blessing, *are the works of the divine power only and alone*."[73] This is true of the accomplished work of Christ; it is also true of the ongoing reality of the Christian life. For—as with Käsemann—Christian life is firmly set under the effective promise of the present and future activity of both Christ and his Spirit. In *Christus Victor*, Aulén argued that because Christ's victory over all creaturely enmity to God was an eternal one, it was ever a present as much as a past reality.[74] In later work he speaks more dramatically of the present time being one that is superintended by the "permanent work of the victorious Christ in his church" in and through the word of the gospel, a work "continuously realized in the present" and whose character is ever that of "self-giving, victorious and sovereign love."[75] On the other side of the turning point of the cross and resurrection, "the Spirit of God has the same hard work to do with every new generation and every new man."[76]

Aulén—again, much like Käsemann—recommends the apocalyptic discourse of *Christus victor* in part because of its power to demythologize our all-too-human common sense that sees us, wrongly and desperately, as the only agents on the field of history. For in the "classical" account of

---

72. Ibid., 160, 163.

73. Ibid., 158–59. The citation is from Luther, *Paul's Epistle to the Galatians*, 277 (Aulén's emphasis).

74. Aulén, *Christus Victor*, 150.

75. Aulén, "Chaos and Cosmos," 166; and *Faith of the Christian Church*, 216, 215.

76. Aulén, "Chaos and Cosmos," 167.

salvation, he writes, we hear afresh *"the old realistic message of the conflict of God with the dark, hostile forces of evil and His victory over them by the Divine self-sacrifice"*[77] Writing in the wake of the Second World War, he contends that "it would be rather striking if the thought of demoniacal powers, devastating in our world, would be unfamiliar to men in the present age," since his generation had "experienced beyond measure how such powers have swept over us like a pestilential infection; we know very well their might to poison and lay waste."[78] The apocalyptic "atmosphere" proper to the announcement of the gospel has an uncanny and unapologetic traction in our day, offering as it does an ancient and timely realism, and providing us with *"the metaphorical characterization of moral and cosmic realities which would otherwise defy expression."*[79] Apocalyptic concepts and categories are able to describe reality as we find it in the world of struggle at the frontline of the incursion of the kingdom; so too are they able to help us discern and to raise up "the cry of an enslaved creation and see the messianic woes taking place therein."[80] As Carl Braaten has observed, while other theological idioms are not incapable of giving voice to such truths, apart from perspective of a christological apocalyptic their expression is often obstructed and rendered "sterile or inactive."[81]

CONCLUSION

By way of an exploration of aspects of Käsemann's apocalyptic soteriology, I have sought to recommend the power of such a reading of the biblical witness to salvation. As the basic idiom of soteriology, an eschatological account of *Christus victor* is capable of articulating Sin's power and scope, but also the ever-so-much-greater power and scope of divine grace rampant in Jesus Christ. By embedding its theological anthropology firmly within an apocalyptic cosmology, it does justice to both the bondage and complicity of humans in Sin, and so includes rather than bypasses the reality of human enmity and guilt. So too, salvation comes upon us as liberation that, precisely because it translates the sinner from one sphere of lordship to another, gives radical evangelical substance to notions of forgiveness, justification, and new life. From this follows a compelling

77. Aulén, *Christus Victor*, 159 (emphasis added).
78. Aulén, "Chaos and Cosmos," 159.
79. Gunton, *Actuality of Atonement*, 66 (emphasis original); cf. 69, 80.
80. Käsemann, *Romans*, 251, cf. 250.
81. Braaten, "Significance of Apocalypticism," 499.

account of the Christian life as the politics of discipleship that honors the living, militant grace of Christ now come upon the church in the power of the Spirit.

Schooled in this apocalyptic gospel of radical and militant divine grace, theology is brought to acknowledge that Paul's claim that "Christ *must* reign" is, as Käsemann put it, "the nerve centre of the design and the firm ground which gives us confidence concerning our own destiny."[82] This confidence is that of the "wandering people of God,"[83] who testify, as has been confessed in our age, that "in the midst of a sinful world, with its faith as with its obedience, with its message as with its order, that it is solely his property, and that it lives and wants to live solely from his comfort and from his direction in the expectation of his appearance."[84] Liberation by Christ's lordship constitutes the church as the company of forgiven sinners who, in their creaturely obedience, deliver over to Christ "the piece of the world which they themselves are," in the firm hope that the day is coming when his reign will be manifest and "untrammelled."[85] In this hope, the apocalyptic imagination of Christian faith maintains and confesses in the teeth of all appearances that the crucified Nazarene is even now Lord. In so doing, it wins space for genuine human life whose cruciformity and freedom from idolatry justifies God.

82. Käsemann, "Primitive Christian Apocalyptic," 135.

83. The central theme of Käsemann's early study of the theology of the Letter to the Hebrews, *Wandering People*.

84. *Barmen Theological Declaration*, 311.

85. Käsemann, "Primitive Christian Apocalyptic," 135.

10

The Spirit and the Promise

On Becoming Aligned with the Way Things Really Are

Christopher R. J. Holmes

I

THE IMPRESSION I HAVE received over the years from fellow ministers in the Anglican tradition and in other Protestant traditions is that the Spirit is someone/thing who succeeds Christ, one who replaces Christ and who takes over as it were from him. After all, it is sometimes argued, Christ is not physically present, and so the Spirit comes on the scene in lieu of him, thereby compensating for his absence.[1] In Paul's account of the Spirit in Galatians, however, a thoroughly Christologized portrait of the Spirit emerges: the Spirit as one who is intrinsic to the person of Christ.[2] Indeed, the crucified, risen, ascended, and exalted Jesus Christ is absent in the mode of the body but present and active in the person of the Spirit. This has, I think, many implications for the shape of Christian existence. To live as a Christian is to be guided by the Spirit, subject to the workings of the Spirit of the *present* Christ, the Christ whose life is Spirit-filled.

1. A hasty reading of John 16:7 might suggest such.

2. I am indebted to Martyn's helpful turn of phrase, formulated with reference to J. Vos's study of the Spirit in Paul, namely "Paul's christologizing of the Spirit." See Martyn, "Epistemology," 108 n. 54.

Christ's presence is indeed a function of his identity, his person. To be Christ is thus to be present in a transformative way to all things, and to be *in* Christ is to be in one whose life is characterized by uninterrupted communion with the Father and the Spirit. The only Spirit that Paul knows is Christ's Spirit, the Spirit who abides in the Law-free gospel Paul preaches.[3] It is the coinherence in Paul's apocalyptic gospel of Son in Spirit and Spirit in Son that I will explore in this essay, with a view to its bearing for an account of the Christian life.

Fellowship with the gospel of the crucified Christ is fellowship with his Spirit whose coming is "*at hand* but not *in* hand."[4] The Spirit promises and has the power to bring about the kind of life that is in accord with the way things really are. Indeed, the Spirit conforms us to the real, the real being Jesus Christ. Christ's suffering and crucifixion establishes a new reality, a reality, Paul argues, that is profoundly expansive—"a new creation," Paul calls it.[5] Accordingly, the Spirit of Christ eclipses neither Jesus' agency nor our own, but rather can be said to be the active agent in guiding our lives into alignment with revelatory proclamation. Life in the Spirit is not a life bound by certain precepts and rules. Instead, it is a matter of crying, "'Abba! Father!,'" of being rendered transparent to the new creation effected at the cross.[6]

When Paul describes specific features of life in the Spirit in Galatians 5:25—6:10, his description is thoroughly anchored in Christology and so cannot be reduced to a series of vices and virtues. Said differently, exhortation or pastoral guidance, for Paul, does not take us into territory in which the gospel of the Crucified and the Spirit ingredient in it is no less present and at work. *Indeed, Paul advances a generative account of the Spirit as the Abrahamic blessing that grasps us through the gospel of the Crucified and so gives rise to forms of life consistent with the new creation.* I will unpack this thesis in three points. First, I argue that the Spirit is not outside Christ but is, rather, concomitant with his person. Second, Christian existence—life *in* reality—is a matter of being subject in everyday matters to the Flesh-curbing power of the Spirit. Reality has formative power for the here and now, displacing all that is not in agreement with the Christian community's baptism into Christ. Third and last, the Spirit's work in Galatians has

3. This raises interesting questions about the Spirit in the Old Testament.

4. Morse, *Difference Heaven Makes*, 122.

5. See Gal 6:15.

6. This line of thought is pursued in much greater detail in Holmes, *Ethics in the Presence of Christ.*

an eschatological horizon. The Spirit fosters a profoundly active hope for the rectification for which "we eagerly await" (5:5).[7]

II

The Spirit does not arrive on the scene after the proclamation of the Crucified. In Galatians 3:5, Paul asks, "Well then, does God supply you with the Spirit and work miracles among you by your doing the works of the law, or by your believing what you heard?" The gospel, for Paul, is "the Lord Jesus Christ, who gave [*eauton*] himself for our sins to set us free from the present evil age" (1:4). In Barth's words, ""It [the gospel] is always and everywhere the self-declaration of Jesus Christ, the Yes of the goodness of God towards man."[8] Included in the gospel of the Lord Jesus Christ is the Spirit. "God has sent [*exapesteilen*] the Spirit of his Son into our hearts" (4:6). The coming and presence of the Spirit is simultaneous with the coming and presence of Christ. Therefore, when Paul describes who the Spirit is and what the Spirit is doing, he cannot but refer to Christ's person and activity—especially Christ's cross. Commenting on Galatians 3:14, Barth notes "that the Spirit is the particular mode of the coming again and therefore the presence and action of Jesus Christ in the place and time between His resurrection and His final appearing."[9] Barth, following Paul, *christologizes* the Spirit to such an extent that he conceives of no other Spirit than the Spirit of the crucified Christ, who is the personal power of the new age, the new creation.

Speaking epistemologically, that is, in terms of how one can be said to *know* the Spirit, one cannot know what one has not truly heard. To know is nothing other than to hear the Spirit-spoken gospel of the crucified Christ. For it is in sharing in Jesus' suffering crucifixion that one knows, in a deeply participatory sense, the working of the Spirit. Just as the Spirit enables Christ to suffer faithfully unto death, so the Spirit mortifies in believers what is consistent with the old and vivifies them in accord

7. In this essay I use the term "rectification" instead of "justification" as a translation of *dikaiosunē*. This is because "the righteousness of God in Paul, as in the Old Testament, has the force of a verb. Therefore the noun 'righteousness' in English does not do the trick, nor does the very 'justification,' since they need to be the same word. The closest English equivalent is 'rectification' and 'rectify,' because—and this is crucial—God not only *declares* righteous but actually *makes* righteous" (Rutledge, *Not Ashamed*, 5).

8. Barth, *Church Dogmatics* (henceforth *CD*) IV/3/2:817.

9. Ibid., IV/3:351.

with the new. As J. Louis Martyn writes, "The Spirit is the down-payment of God's promise that our dying will be wholly swallowed up by life."[10] Or, to put it more immediately, the only Christ Paul speaks of in Galatians is a Spirit-dispensing Christ who, to be sure, slays the old but also raises from the dead and so guides people in their daily life in the way(s) of the new creation. God is the active agent in the bestowing of the blessing of Abraham, which is—principally—the Spirit, and so is the acting subject in leading the community into a "communal life of love, joy, peace, compassion, and the selfless service of one another (Gal 5:22; Phil 2:4)."[11] The community's becoming what it is in Christ is a function of the apocalypse of Christ's Spirit. The Spirit leads into—indeed, delivers into—reality. This is the blessing of Abraham. Or, in Barth's words, "To have the Holy Spirit is to let God rather than our having God be our confidence."[12]

Paul's Christology in Galatians is cruciform. The cruciform shape of his Christology is determinative of his account of the Spirit. As Martyn perceptively points out, the Spirit in Galatians is none other "than the Spirit of the *crucified* Christ."[13] That Paul's Christology is set more by the crucifixion than the resurrection in Galatians is important to ponder. This is not to suggest for a moment that Paul does not take with utmost seriousness the resurrection. Rather, it is to say that Paul would have the Galatian communities hear that the resurrected Christ is "revealed in the cross of the disciples' daily death, and *only* there."[14] Thus, Paul christologizes the Spirit with respect to a particular moment in the Christ-event, namely the cross. The Spirit delivers women and men into the real world, and that world is a world in which they, by the Spirit's power, learn to daily die. Life in the real world is a life oriented by the cross. "For you were called to freedom, brothers and sisters; only do not use your freedom as an opportunity for self-indulgence, but through love become slaves to one another" (5:13). Cruciform existence is, at its most basic, life in the Spirit of Christ, a mode of life that involves "daily death" in accord with Christ's cross.

If this is so, this first point about the Spirit not being subsequent to Christ needs further specification. That is to say, the Spirit is not subsequent

10. Martyn, "Epistemology," 93.

11. Martyn, "Leo Baeck's Reading," 61.

12. Barth, *CD* I/1:462.

13. Martyn, "Epistemology," 108 (emphasis added). Whilst the concentration on the cross is most intense in Galatians, different christological moments are privileged in other letters. For example, in 2 Cor 3:18 the work of the Lord Jesus who is "the Spirit" is understood in a distinctly eschatological fashion.

14. Ibid., 110.

to Christ Jesus' *cross*. The Spirit is revealed in the daily crucifixion of that which is, as far as the gospel is concerned, inimical to the real world. The Spirit comes with Christ to liberate in accord with his cross, which alone frees from tyranny. "God is creating a corporate people in Christ," but that people is marked by a cross, and this cross is effective in the creation of the "Israel of God" (6:16).[15] The promising gospel, resplendent as it is with the Spirit, begets a people for whom the power of the Flesh has been crucified. This is the "very *fundamenta*" of their existence.[16] Paul's description of the Spirit's work is a description never removed from Christ and so his cross.

If my description of the way in which Paul's Christologizes the Spirit be responsible, then it is fitting to appreciate the particular insight that Paul's cross-oriented Christology in Galatians evokes for a doctrine of the Spirit. Following Martyn, I would concur that Paul "is a theologian of the cross."[17] This is because Paul takes seriously Jesus' rectification of Jews and Gentiles through his faithfulness unto death. Christ's identity *is* secure as one "who gave himself" for us (1:4). In the Spirit, however, he continues to give himself; that is, he continues, because the Father has raised him from the dead, to rectify. To argue so is not to compromise the once for allness of his cross; but it is to say that, for Paul, there is a present state of affairs that results from Christ Jesus' self-giving unto death. Jesus—and not the Sinaitic Law—continually comes in the Spirit so as to be the guiding light for the daily life of the community. This is the promise that "Jesus Christ as the hope of all is present to us as the one who promises and is promised."[18] But the community can only faithfully adhere to what is real and promised because what Christ has done in the past has contemporary force. "There is one way out from the conclusion that all are under sin, but only one: the promise of the πίστις Ἰησοῦ Χριστοῦ (3:22)."[19] He relativizes any perceived gap between the "then and there" and the "here and now." The community is absorbed into and transformed by the world in which it actually can be said to live by virtue of Christ's cross.

In emphasizing that the Spirit is not subsequent to Christ's cross, I am suggesting that for Paul the Spirit as the Spirit of Christ is and remains the primary agent in clothing the community with Christ and in baptizing the community into him. Note again the aorist in 3:27: "As many of you

15. Martyn, "Abrahamic Covenant," 175.

16. Martyn, "John and Paul," 219.

17. Ibid., 226.

18. Barth, *CD* IV/3:351.

19. Ibid., IV/1:640.

as were baptized into Christ have clothed [*enedusasthe*) yourselves with Christ." The community is baptized into Christ, specifically Christ's cross, and so clothed with the cross of Christ. By believing what was before their eyes, namely Jesus Christ "publicly exhibited as crucified," God has supplied them with the Spirit of the crucified (3:1–5). "To be a Christian is *per definitionem* to be ἐν Χριστῷ," Barth writes.[20] If Barth is correct, and I would argue that he is, then the Spirit cannot be conceived as extrinsic to the cross. Rather, the Spirit's pattern of activity is set by the cross, indeed *generated* by the cross.[21] This leads us to the second point of the paper, namely the shape of Christian existence especially in relationship to Jesus' own experience of the Spirit.

III

Just as the Spirit draws its identity from Christ, so too does the Spirit draw its shape from Christ.[22] The Spirit is said to be one who is sent, who is apocalypsed. The Spirit, then, is not a kind of numinous presence, part and parcel of a realm impervious to anything beyond itself. The Spirit is a *revealed* or *apocalypsed* Spirit whose work is concrete but not able to be domesticated. In this regard, Barth writes: "There is no question of setting aside faith or the gospel, but rather of domesticating it, of integrating it into the well-know and natural view of man that his relationship with God is something in which he can and must help himself, that the grace of God is something which he can and must create and assure to himself by definite observances."[23] The Spirit, contemporary with Christ, invades the old order, the world of the Flesh, in order to deliver human beings and the whole cosmos from the "malignant powers that hold them in bondage."[24] The shape of the Spirit's work is indeed described, as is the case with Christ's, by the language of warfare, of battle. The Spirit crucifies those elements that would prevent Jews and Gentiles from living obediently in relation to

20. Ibid., IV/2:277.

21. This is not to shortchange the work of the Spirit in the ministry of Jesus. The pattern of Jesus' ministry is set by the Spirit.

22. In drawing its shape from Christ, the Spirit draws in shape from the Father too inasmuch as the Spirit proceeds from the Father and through the Son. Indeed, the Son eternally receives the Spirit from the Father and, in the economy of grace, breathes and sends the Spirit so that his children might receive from his Father the life that he eternally receives as the Son of the Father.

23. Barth, *CD* IV/1:640. He is commenting on Gal 5:3, 6, 11; 6:13, 15.

24. Martyn, "Leo Baeck's Reading," 53.

God's rectifying act in Christ. Not zealous observance of the Law but only the powerful working of the Spirit can liberate the community from the old world. "By his Law, the Law of this living One, he [Paul] has died to the 'Law'—the error of a justification of man by the fulfillment of another law than this—in order that he may now live for God."[25] Accordingly, only the Spirit can produce "a liberating community of mutual concern that is so radically novel as to be called the new creation."[26] And so, to talk about the shape of the Spirit's work is to talk about the bringing forth of the new creation's fruits whose content is Christ.

Even more specifically, the Spirit is ingredient in the covenant of promise. The Spirit is the *power* of the promised Abrahamic blessing. As the Christ's Spirit, the Spirit births circumcision-free communities. The Spirit destroys the power of Sin, something the Sinaitic Law could not do. Just as Christ and his faithfulness rectifies, so too does the Spirit continue to rectify. The daily life of the church is a life that is *"made what it is by the advents of Christ and his Spirit."*[27] Or, in Barth's words: "The Christian life begins with a change which cannot be understood or described radically enough, which God has the possibility of effecting in a man's life in a way which is decisive and basic for his whole being and action, and which He has in fact accomplished in the life of the man who becomes a Christian."[28] The Spirit who sustained Jesus in the doing of his Father's will even unto the point of suffering death is the same Spirit who sustains the church as it seeks to live in accord with the indicative—with what *is*. Therefore, Paul's hortatory sections in Galatians presuppose the presence of the Christ who in the Spirit rectifies.[29] Indeed, his rectification is contemporary in the Spirit. The Spirit just is the rectifying presence of Christ. "It is the Spirit of the Son, drawing its characteristics from him."[30] Said differently, the Spirit is the particular *hypostasis* of God who is not only the active agent in Christ's ministry but in Christ's ongoing ministry through his children who are learning to die daily.

25. Barth, *CD* IV/1:638.

26. Martyn, "Part II," 88.

27. Martyn, "Part IV," 233.

28. Barth, *CD* IV/4:9.

29. The "hortatory" sections to which I am referring are 5:13–24 and 6:1–9. Regarding the former, note that "all of the verbs in the weighty sentences of vv. 17–24 are in the indicative mood." 5:13–24 is not, for Martyn, so much "parenetic and hortatory as pastoral." Paul's pastoral guidance is rooted in a description of the way things really are, and so can be appropriately expressed *via* imperatives.

30. Martyn, *Galatians*, 391.

It is by the Spirit's power that the community lives. "If we live by the Spirit, let us also be guided by the Spirit" (5:25). To live by the Spirit is to live by Christ. This is something the Christian community is exhorted to do. Indeed, it can do so because "God has graciously created an addressable community."[31] Indeed, as Martyn notes, all of the verbs in 5:25—6:10 are imperative and hortatory.[32] The two are consonant. "But if you are led by the Spirit, you are not subject to the law" (5:18). Life led by the Spirit is life in promise of the covenant—Jesus Christ—and not life in the Sinaitic covenant. One is no longer subject to the Law as the Law too has been taken captive by Sin. The Law is that to which one cannot submit as it is impotent when it comes to curbing the desires of the Flesh. Therefore, it cannot be a reliable guide for Christian behavior. The only reliable guide for Christian behaviour is reality. Reality, for Paul, has one reference point, and that is "Jesus Christ and God the Father, who raised him from the dead . . . the Lord Jesus Christ, who gave himself for our sins to set us free from the present evil age" (1:1, 4). This is "the standard."[33] Commenting on Galatians 6:16, Martyn writes: "The standard is the *real world* that has now been made what it is by the event of God's gracious invasion via his Son and the Spirit of his Son. In short, the standard is not a 'should' but rather an 'is,' a cosmic announcement couched in the indicative mood in order to *describe* the real world."[34]

Paul would seem, then, to have the Galatians experience the Spirit as Jesus did. Jesus' life was lived by the Spirit, the Spirit being proper to every moment of his earthly ministry. Paul would have the life of the Galatian community be subject to the Spirit's sanctifying activity in a manner analogous to Jesus' own experience of the Spirit. In 5:13–24, the Spirit does not guide the Galatians's activity in accord with a series of "dos" and "do nots." Rather, the Spirit places them (and us) into the world in which we actually live, meaning that when Paul discusses the everyday life of the church he, in 5:13–24, addresses the subject in a fundamentally descriptive way.[35] The world after Christ's crucifixion is one that—if it is true to its having been redeemed—shares the characteristics of his own life, that is, a world in which the Spirit is constantly working to make the world permeable to Christ's kingdom. To live by the Spirit is to live as Christ lived, that is as

31. Ibid., 536.
32. See ibid.
33. Ibid., 567.
34. Ibid.
35. See Martyn, "Daily Life," 258.

one in whom the Spirit he receives from his Father is always active. Thus, exhortations such as those found in Galatians 5:25—6:10 are not then exhortations in the general sense. Rather, "with the imperative Paul calls on the Galatians steadily to be what they already are."[36] The exhortations are fundamentally descriptive. Paul is pointing to patterns of life that bear the mark of the Spirit's invasion of "the territory of the Flesh."[37] That Paul even would think of offering such guidance as in 6:5—"For all must carry their own loads"—is indicative of how different the world is *post Christum*. The Galatians are free, "and that [as such] they can make use of the freedom in which they have been made free in Christ (Gal 5:1)."[38] The Galatians are made by the Spirit's working into an addressable community, a community capable of bearing one another's burdens and so fulfilling the "Law of Christ."[39] The specific guidance Paul offers is thus guidance that takes as its basis the Spirit's working to create ears and so hearers where none existed before, ears that hear in a way that agrees with the way the world is *post Christum*.

Just as Jesus' life is one of uninterrupted obedience to the Father by the power of the Spirit, so too can the life of the Galatians churches be such, albeit in a more provisional sense. The Law of Christ, unlike the Sinaitic Law, does produce the righteousness it promises, for it is uttered by God himself.[40] It creates, as was mentioned a moment ago, a community that is capable of doing things like bearing their own loads.[41] The Galatians are people of the promise spoken into being by God's promises to Abraham, the promise that has come and is at work in Christ. Jesus Christ is the promise's singular seed, the proclamation of whom births circumcision-free churches among the Gentiles. The Spirit is the primary actor in his defeat of the Flesh and so too in our efforts to resist the Flesh. To be in Christ Jesus is to be in his Spirit, who does in us what it did in him whilst he was physically present. In Barth's words, "The ἐν Χριστῷ εἶναι is the *a priori* of all the instruction that Paul gives his Churches, all the comfort and exhortation that he addresses to them. They, too, live in

36. Martyn, *Galatians*, 535.

37. Martyn, "Daily Life," 259.

38. Barth, *CD* IV/2:532.

39. This is a reference to Gal 6:2. "Law" is capitalized following Martyn's translation. Christ is indeed "the decisive event in that [the Law's] history." See Martyn, *Galatians*, 558.

40. See Martyn, "Communal Discord," 277. Following Martyn's lead, I capitalize Law (and also Sin and the Flesh).

41. See Gal 6:6.

the flesh, in the world. But as Christ gave Himself up for them, it is not only for Himself but for them that He lives in them, enfolding them and ruling them."[42]

To think of the daily life of the Christian community (or the Christian person) as a field removed from the activity of the Christ's Spirit, or to think of Christ's life in isolation from the Spirit, is to relapse into a false gospel. There is guidance for the particular shape of a Spirit-filled life in which faith works through love. Paul shows in 5:13–24 "that his gospel does provide guidance for daily life."[43] Indeed, a pneumatologically charged account of the life of the Christian community is not short of specifics concerning the shape of community life. But that guidance's orientation is always vertical in origin and only then horizontal in orientation. It is to see that guidance's source is the Spirit who always comes anew, whose fruits are as described in 5:21–22 those of the "liberating new creation."[44] These fruits are called into existence by the crucifixion of the old age. This old age still enslaves as is evidenced by the Galatian communities desire to embrace circumcision and so the Sinaitic Law as part and parcel of life in Christ and the Spirit. However, the old age has been crucified by Christ, Paul avers, the Christ whose cross is radically generative of a new form of daily life, the shape of which can be described in very specific ways. Daily life for the Galatians is now a matter of seeing, indeed of living "bi-focally."[45]

To live bifocally is to receive new criteria of perception—criteria indicative of the real world. The gospel—God's stepping on the scene—generates criteria of perception that enables the Christian community to see things as they really are. Thus, Christ's advent can be said to be the victory over Sin and the Flesh. But the Galatian communities, as is the case with us today, cannot *see* and inhabit the reality of this victory without bifocal vision, vision which Paul's apocalyptic gospel supplies. Indeed, seeing bifocally is a matter of waking up to the real world, and so of sowing to the Spirit who calls faith into existence. (6:8) This is a faith that is created *ex nihilo* by the preaching of the Spirit-bestowing cross of Christ, the ultimate act of grace, which re-creates a world shorn of opposites (see 3:28) that begins to live like Jesus lived and lives, and so to live a life transparent to the activity of the Spirit, who is the only "antidote to the Impulsive Desire

42. Barth, *CD* IV/2:277.

43. Martyn, *Galatians*, 27.

44. Martyn, "Paul to Flannery O'Connor," 284.

45. Ibid.

of the Flesh."[46] This is but to live by faith, for faith rather than establishing what is the case recognizes what is the case.

Christian life is a matter of living "a human life of divine character in something like the way Jesus did."[47] What is of divine character about the way in which Jesus lived is the qualitative difference as concerns his union with the Spirit with whom he communed and who anointed him. What is qualitatively different is that the Spirit is Jesus' by nature, whereas it is ours by grace. The Spirit is not ingredient in us in the same way that it is in Jesus: "The Holy Spirit never becomes his [the Christian's] spirit but is always the Spirit of God."[48] The Spirit is Christ's by virtue of who Christ is. And yet, the same Spirit, the Spirit *of* Christ, gathers the Lord's disciples "into abiding union with Christ."[49] This union is an active union, one in which we are formed "according to the image of God that is the second person of the Trinity."[50] To be formed according to "the image of God [is] to take on Christ's identity."[51] Because Paul seems unable to conceive of Christ without the Spirit, to take on Christ's identity is to take on *his* Spirit. Indeed, in Christ's rectifying action we are attached to him—the divine image—and so live by his life: that is, by his faithfulness, by his cry of "'Abba! Father!'"[52] (4:6). Commenting on 2:19 and following, Barth writes: "The fact that I live in the faith of the Son of God, in my faith in Him, has its basis in the fact that He Himself, the Son of God, first believed for me, and so believed that all that remains for me to do is to let my eyes rest on Him, which really means to let my eyes follow Him. This following is my faith."[53] The primary fruit of becoming attached to Christ is indeed the "'Abba! Father!'" (4:6). With such a cry "human nature is made to be open to divine influence, to be more fully itself by way of it."[54] Jesus does pray and cry out to his Abba throughout his ministry and passion. But in so doing throughout his days, his person does not change. To be open to his Father, to live as his Father's image even unto death, is possible because his identity is eternally sure as the Son of the Father.

46. Ibid., 21.

47. Tanner, "Creation and Salvation," 61.

48. Barth, *CD* IV/3/2:942.

49. Torrance, *Trinitarian Faith*, 221.

50. Tanner, *Salvation*, 63.

51. Ibid., 66.

52. The language of "attachment" is not original to me. It is present throughout Kathryn Tanner's *Christ the Key*.

53. Barth, *CD* II/2:559.

54. Tanner, *Salvation*, 69.

This is important to reflect on, for it helps us to see the generative nature of the Spirit's work not only in Jesus' life but in our lives as well. The work of the Spirit in Galatians is that of giving to us what we do not have by nature but what Jesus has by nature: the Spirit as his own. "He [the Word] gives to his humanity what he has by nature insofar as he is God," Tanner writes.[55] That includes of course *his* Spirit. But it also means that he shares his obedience to the Father's will, which "'is part of his nature,'" with humanity.[56] Because the Spirit is intrinsic to the person of the Word, the Spirit "is also secure, irrevocable, in the humanity united to that Word."[57]

Life in the real world is "*made what it is by advents of Christ and his Spirit.*"[58] The Christ's Spirit, in particular, generates fruits that are reflective of his Kingdom and testify to reality. These fruits, rather than being capacities that the community can generate of its own accord, are what humanity is made to share in, inasmuch as it is reworked by the Spirit's power. The doing of good, for example, is proper to the Spirit and so proper to Christ.[59] The presence of the cry of the Spirit in us does not eclipse our humanity but rather perfects it in agreement with the good. To be sure, the world (the old cosmos) has been crucified; however, what is included in that "No" is a profound "Yes," the form of which is the human being able to be more fully herself. Paul, therefore, in Galations 5–6 is not advocating moralism. When Paul writes that "you who have received the Spirit should restore such a one in a spirit of gentleness" (6:1), he is not exhorting the Galatian communities to act in abstraction from the Spirit. Such guidance may sound rather pedestrian to us, but such a course is entirely in keeping with what now *is*. Leaving a brother or sister in a transgression is to let them fall prey to the old, to what has been crucified. Therefore, Paul offers such pastoral guidance, because the presence of the Spirit among them is a creative and renewing presence, a concrete presence. Indeed, Paul is not evacuating the agency of the community; walking or living by the Spirit does not mean the abandonment of our efforts. Rather, together with us, "the Spirit directs our lives as we attempt to direct our own."[60] In seeking to do good, to restore one "detected in a transgression," the Galatians will find themselves subject to the Spirit's direction. (6:1)

55. Ibid., 74.

56. Ibid., 74 n. 18. She is drawing from Gregory of Nyssa's *Against Eunomius*.

57. Ibid., 74.

58. Martyn, "John and Paul," 223.

59. Gal 6:9–10.

60. Tanner, *Christ the Key*, 297.

The way in which the Spirit works as a distinct *hypostasis* within the Godhead is analogous to Christ's other self. The Law, for Paul, is impotent, and so unable to overcome the old order. "For through the law I died to the law, so that I might live to God. I have been crucified with Christ" (2:20). The reality of Paul's being crucified is achieved in him and the Christian community by the Spirit, "the Spirit who is as [Christ] himself, through whom it is Christ himself who acts and speaks."[61] Christ acts in us to accomplish in the Spirit the crucifixion of all that is antithetical to the new. What Christ through his faithful death crucified, is what he crucifies in us by his Spirit. In this connection, Barth states:

> To be "with Christ" is to take part in His history, so that in His history that of the community and all its members has already happened, and has therefore to find in His history its model and pattern, to see itself again in it; the result being that the community and its members necessarily cease to be what they are if they are guilty of any arbitrary deviation from His history. This "with Christ" determines their past and present and future; their whole history.[62]

"Having started with the Spirit, are you now ending with the flesh?" (3:3). Only the Spirit, and not circumcision, is capable of subjectivizing the deliverance actual in Jesus' cross. This is just what the Spirit does, and is the key to understanding the generative power of the indicative mood. Tanner writes, "And humanity is only more fully itself with being thoroughly reworked by divine power. Refashioned by divine power, humans are more fully human in knowing the truth and choosing the good as they were meant to."[63] The Spirit's work in curbing the Flesh is humanizing work. "So then, whenever we have an opportunity, let us work for the good of all, and especially for those of the family of faith" (6:9). The Spirit engenders the doing of such good precisely because the Galatians have been rendered by the Spirit and addressed in the Spirit of Christ as a people capable of doing good. The world has been reworked entirely by the apocalypse of Christ. Exhortation is a matter of living by the fruit-bearing Spirit, who enables humanity to be more fully itself, which is a matter of being crucified with Christ and of being clothed with Christ.

To be informed by Jesus' faithful reliance upon the Spirit he receives and bestows, rather than by a Law-observant reading of Scripture, is to

61. Torrance, *Trinitarian Faith*, 226.

62. Barth, *CD* IV/2:277.

63. Tanner, *Christ the Key*, 297.

be alive to God's effective action in the here and now over and against the Flesh. This is, again, the positive moment as regards the Spirit's work. The Spirit as described by Paul in Galatians "invades" but only so as to "establish:" to be invaded is to be baptized into the Christ who crucifies the Flesh and so establishes the new order. Whereas the Teachers privilege the negative moment, what still must be—faith in Christ *and* Law observance—the Spirit establishes Jews and Gentiles in God's rectifying deed manifest in his Son's advent and death. This is determinative of what will be, disclosive of God's future come among us. In Barth's words, "God is *Spirit*, and therefore He truly awakens man to freedom. . . . He treats him, and indeed establishes him, as a free subject. He sets him on his own feet as His partner." What will be points us to the eschatological horizon of the Spirit's' work in awakening "man to freedom," which brings me to my third and last point.[64]

IV

Life in the Spirit is one of sowing to the Spirit.[65] There is, in short, an eschatological dimension to life in the Spirit. The Galatian community eagerly awaits the day when what is—the new creation—will be universally manifest. This is "the hope of righteousness" (5:5). This righteousness is present, birthing circumcision-free communities who are saved by Jesus' faithfulness. But as the Galatians look to the past, they are pointed to the future by the one who is present, but present only in the mode of promise.

Here we begin to really see, then, the difference between the Spirit as the Spirit of Christ and the Spirit's indwelling of Christian (or the Galatian) communities. The future that God holds out for those who have faith kindled into flame by the gospel is something decisively new. It is surprising to hear Paul say this, given that Paul has "constantly said that the human scene—indeed, the cosmos itself—has already been changed by God's rectifying deed in Christ's advent and death."[66] What differentiates Christ's experience of the Spirit from our own is that his life is one that is lived on the horizon of what has always been. Throughout his ministry and passion he receives the Spirit who has always proceeded from the being of the Father through him, whereas the Galatian community hopes not for what has always been but for the universal manifestation of the

64. Barth, *CD* IV/3/2:941.

65. See Gal 6:8.

66. Martyn, *Galatians*, 472.

new thing that is already on the scene because of Jesus' defeat of the powers. The Spirit is not simply part and parcel of the Christian community's domestic life. The Spirit is, rather, a gift—the one who grasps them in a way that approximates and will approximate what has always been the case with Christ. What has always been the case with Christ is that the Spirit is "inherent in him as he is in God the Father and as the Father is in him," something which cannot be said in any straightforward way of the Christian community.[67]

In the case of the Galatians, "God's deed of rectification—accomplished in Christ—is still finding concrete form in the daily life of the church, as the church expands into the whole of the world."[68] The Galatian communities have a future that is "presided over by God," a future that is finding concrete form.[69] Fellowship with and leading by the Spirit—which will result in eternal life—is a matter of promise and expectation for the Galatians. The promise is not proper to them but something they receive in faith even now. In the case of Christ, however, such union with the Spirit is eternally his by nature. His descent and ascent in the Spirit attests to what is the case with respect to his nature. Christ, therefore, does not hope for rectification like we do. In Torrance's difficult but important words, "The Spirit is not outside the Word but being *in* the Word he is *in* God through him."[70] The communal fruits that the Spirit bears are true to Christ's nature, for the Spirit inheres in him and he in the Spirit, and so together they are in the Father and the Father in them. The Christian hope is that the community might ever-increasingly be formed by and share in those fruits that are for Christ not a matter of promise but of nature; that what he is be found in them.

V

In this essay, I have argued that *paraenesis* is a function of reality, that is, a Christology that is inclusive of the apocalypsed Spirit. A rightly proportioned Christology is one that emphasizes the different moments of the Christ-event in a way that agrees with Scripture itself. In Galatians, we have a Christology that is heavily oriented by the cross. Likewise, we have a portrait of the Spirit as the prevenient one who realizes and subjectivizes

67. Torrance, *Trinitarian Faith*, 201.

68. Martyn, *Galatians*, 478–79.

69. Ibid., 479.

70. Torrance, *Trinitarian Faith*, 235.

Christ's cross in the life of the Christian community. Thus, we get a pneumatology that is distinctly cruciform in shape in that the only Spirit at work is the Spirit who inheres in the Crucified.

One of the important implications of this is that we do not get a sense in Galatians that the Spirit's work is best understood in a redemptive historical sense but rather in a radically christological sense. Christ and the Spirit are not hidden potentials within "sacred history." Rather, they come upon history. In coming upon history, Christ and his Spirit do not abolish the body, culture, or history. Rather, they redeem it. This is why Paul insists upon the non-circumcision of Gentiles. The Gentiles as Gentiles are redeemed through Christ's crucifixion and resurrection, and they are thereby liberated into a new human agency and a new history through union with Christ in the Spirit.[71] The Spirit by whom we live is *the* promised Abrahamic blessing. The promise is inclusive of the Spirit, who is of a different origin than the Law, which "was ordained [*diatageis*] through angels by a mediator" (3:19). The promise is the *reality* of the covenant, the covenant that brings blessing to all. Indeed, *the* offspring of the promise, unlike the Law, grants the power to resist all that is opposed to the promise. He through his Spirit brings about a people of promise who can be truly said to live by faith and so fulfill the only law there is: the law of Christ's love. Put somewhat differently, "He [the Christian] cannot escape His [Christ's] law. Therefore it only remains to live in faith in Him."[72]

To conclude, life in the Spirit is life that is not unconcerned with moral particulars. The fact that the Galatian communities can respond to those particulars is the form of Paul's pastoral guidance, especially in 5:25—6:10; they can do so because they are being acted upon by the same power that enabled Jesus to give of himself even unto death. This the Law cannot do: it cannot overcome the Sin it would deliver from. Paul, however, presents the Law of Christ. This Law is the Law of a living person—"its living quality," as Barth says—who is always the agent of his own presence and who realizes in us what he is.[73] As one filling all things, Jesus is present through the person of the Spirit, rectifying the community in relation to

---

71. I am indebted to Doug Harink at this point. His incisive comments on an earlier draft of this paper have helped me to better see the extent to which the Gentiles' very non-Jewishness is redeemed through Christ's crucifixion and resurrection.

72. Barth, *CD* IV/1:638.

73. Ibid., IV/3/2:818.

what is real—the new creation.[74] Indeed, he is already forming the world in such a way that the future hope of rectification is present and at work.

74. Christ's *plērōsis*, that is his ascent "so that he might fill [*plērōsē*] all things" is not present in Galatians as it is in the so-called cosmic Christologies and heavily realized eschatologies of Ephesians and Colossians. See Eph 4:10.

11

"Discerning the Body" at the Apocalyptic Standpoint

A Feminist Engagement with Martyn's Thought

Jodi L. A. Belcher

APOCALYPTIC INTERPRETATIONS OF PAUL seem to have little in common with feminist discourse. The overarching cosmological vision of apocalyptic contrasts with feminist interest in contextuality and particularity. An emphasis on "discontinuity"[1] in apocalyptic thought clashes with feminist attention to identity formation through complex racial, ethnic, sexual, class, national, colonialist, and able-bodied dynamics. Finally, apocalyptic war rhetoric and imagery of divine invasion pose obstacles for feminists committed to struggles against violence, especially sexual violence inflicted upon women and girls;[2] for survivors of abuse, as well as for colonized people, a God portrayed as "invading" may sound like anything but good news. With different starting points and aims, not only do apocalyptic discourse and feminism seem to have little room for

---

1. Käsemann, "Paul's Anthropology," 9–10.

2. Ernst Käsemann and J. L. Martyn both incorporate this rhetoric. In "Paul's Anthropology," Käsemann says, for example, "The world is not neutral ground; it is a battlefield, and everyone is a combatant" (23). Martyn characterizes God's action as "invasion" and an "apocalyptic war" on "anti-God powers" in several writings, including "Paul to Flannery O'Connor" (see 281–84).

constructive dialogue, but also little to compel those involved in these different modes of thought to engage one another.

In spite of their incongruities, the trajectory of feminist theory is remarkably instructive for examining the apocalyptic interpretation of Paul put forth by J. Louis Martyn. When juxtaposed with Martyn's work, feminist theoretical discourse illuminates the unmistakable similarity between the structure of Martyn's thought and the logic of feminist standpoint epistemology. Feminists' subsequent critiques of standpoint epistemology likewise bring into focus the significant problems intrinsic to the standpoint epistemological infrastructure of Martyn's thought. Finally, the feminist turn to the embodied subject, exemplified by "strategic essentialism,"[3] elucidates a constructive way to reframe Martyn's epistemological approach through a turn to the body and its relationship to knowledge in Paul's writing.

In this essay, I place Martyn's work in dialogue with feminist theory in order to argue that Martyn's apocalyptic interpretation of Paul relies on a standpoint epistemology and, as a result, the conceptual and practical flaws in standpoint logic equally undermine Martyn's thought. Because these problems impede discerning the truth about God's work in the world within Martyn's apocalyptic framework, I propose a turn to Paul's emphasis on the body in order to reorient Martyn's epistemology and thus

---

3. This idea of strategic essentialism is briefly described by Gayatri Chakravorty Spivak, in an interview with Ellen Rooney, as a contextually specific mobilization of essentialism for "a situation," which entails "persistent critique." Strategic essentialism for her is a process of negotiation because she believes essences are unavoidable but the uses to which they are put also always require interrogation. A turn toward strategic essentialism is not a way of escaping the essentialist/anti-essentialist debate in feminism; rather, for Spivak, it seems to be a way of illuminating the fact that all the positions within that debate are actually non-neutral, strategic negotiations of essences. See Spivak with Rooney, "In a Word."

Both Spivak and Elizabeth Grosz read the work of Luce Irigaray on sexual difference as a kind of strategic essentialism. Irigaray often gets characterized as simply an essentialist because she seems to affirm genuine material differences between men and women based on their bodies—even though her brand of "essentialism" is not a biological overdeterminism. However, Spivak and Grosz see in Irigaray a significant critique of patriarchy that refuses to abandon bodies—especially female bodies—to patriarchal construction and commodification. For Grosz's discussion of Irigaray, see Grosz, "Bodies and Knowledges."

In the context of this paper, a turn to the body like that found in certain strategic essentialists—like Irigaray and Grosz, among others—is not an attempt to escape epistemology. My goal is to highlight the significance of the body for knowledge production and to think through the relationship between the body and knowledge.

engender the discernment at which Martyn's thought cannot otherwise arrive.

I begin by comparing the feminist standpoint epistemology in the work of Sandra Harding to the structure of apocalyptic in Martyn. Then I show how feminist critiques of standpoint epistemology's power dualism, parsing of identities, and circularity also apply to Martyn's thought. I conclude by examining body and epistemological language in 1 Corinthians 11:17–34 and 12:12–27 to demonstrate that "discerning the body"[4] in all its complexity matters for reading and reflecting theologically on Paul.

MARTYN'S APOCALYPTIC AS STANDPOINT EPISTEMOLOGY

The Power of Knowing Where You Are: Epistemology from a Feminist Perspective

The present world is not all right. It is full of injustice. Every day people exploit, marginalize, violate, and oppress others. These injustices are not simply localized, discrete instances, but they are systemic, woven into the fabric of political, economic, social, and cultural institutions and structures. Through such systems, persons are situated in hierarchical relations of power, in which certain people are attributed power to dominate others' positions of powerlessness. Those with power thrive and benefit from the disempowering exploitation of the powerless, who have little to no share in the goods produced from their labor and sacrifice. What is more, the systems of this world operate insidiously to veil their structural injustices from those located higher in the hierarchical arrangements, so that the oppressors remain "oblivious"[5] to the oppression of others to which they contribute as they maintain their

---

4. 1 Cor 11:29.

5. I am using this word to suggest something different from unintentional ignorance. Instead, I am drawing upon the way Mary McClintock Fulkerson defines the term in *Places of Redemption*. Although her work is not advocating a standpoint epistemology, it highlights "obliviousness" as what could be called a structural problem for the church. "Obliviousness," for her, is "power-related willing-to-not-see," in which the ways "the/my production of 'difference'" and marginalization of others take place are "repress[ed]" by the agents involved in this othering. Obliviousness is a "social phenomenon" that is felt "viscerally," and as she notes, it is best understood as a "reflexive"—rather than an overtly "intentional"—operation. A characteristic example of "obliviousness" to which she points is the claim of white persons to not see the race of non-white persons. In this case, not only is race effectively attributed only to those who are not white, but also the need to claim not to see demonstrates that one has already differentiated between oneself and "the other." See Fulkerson, *Places of Redemption*, 15–22.

powerful situations. The only people who can see and understand the truth of this unjust world are the powerless, the exploited, the marginalized, the oppressed—those who live and die under the weight of the hierarchical, exploitative systems of this world. Their victimized position gives them "epistemic privilege,"[6] a unique vantage point to know the world as it really is. In fact, their special access to this knowledge paradoxically bestows on the powerless a form of power unavailable to their "blind"[7] oppressors: an epistemological power that can be the source of their liberation from oppression right in the middle of their structural powerlessness.

This tale narrates the logic of "standpoint epistemology," which claims that a person's non-neutral locatedness matters for what and how she or he can know.[8] Because knowing subjects differ from one another in their situations within the world, these differences inevitably shape how they acquire knowledge of the world. They give subjects particular epistemological standpoints, through which subjects gain certain insights about the world and remain oblivious to other truths. A person's standpoint, in fact, determines how accurate one's knowledge of the world can be. Contrary to modern Cartesian rationalism, standpoint logic asserts that objective knowledge is not the product of a presumed neutral stance or thought process but is the result of a highly "interested"[9] stance. The paradox of standpoint epistemology—at least when considered from one point of view—is that true, objective knowledge is more readily attained from

6. This phrase is used by Bat-Ami Bar On to characterize the central feature of feminist standpoint epistemology, which Bar On finds most problematic in her engagement with this epistemological perspective. See Bar On, "Epistemic Privilege."

7. Sandra Harding quotes Nancy Hartsock in her description of feminist standpoint epistemology, who links power-imbued social perspectives with an inability to see "the real relations of humans with each other and with the natural world." Harding is critical of Hartsock's idea of "real relations," but she agrees with Hartsock's argument that access to true knowledge of social reality is inhibited by being located in a position of social dominance. See Harding, "Standpoint Epistemology."

8. Harding, "Standpoint Epistemology," 54–55.

9. I am borrowing the language of Mary McClintock Fulkerson in *Changing the Subject* to illuminate the logic of standpoint epistemology. "Interest" is a concept she deploys in discussing "liberationist epistemology" to underscore the particular biases and involvement of the subject in knowledge production. As she says, "Knowledge is not *tainted* by interest: it *is* interest" (*Changing the Subject*, 25, emphasis original). For her, interest does not necessarily enable or limit access to objectively true knowledge, as advocates of standpoint epistemology would argue, but the concept is helpful for exposing what looks like a paradox within standpoint logic, insofar as certain forms of subjectivity engender objectivity.

hierarchically lower or disempowered positions than from socially, economically, or culturally powerful loci. Situations of domination preclude true knowledge, but situations of powerlessness engender it. As Sandra Harding notes, the difference lies in the ability "to generate the most critical questions about received belief," which the powerful typically lack and the powerless possess because of their divergent standpoints.[10]

Standpoint epistemology became an important tool in feminist discourse in the 1970s for authorizing feminist challenges to patriarchy.[11] It provided a way to critique, for example, the so-called natural hierarchical ordering of male over female, because it attends to the sociocultural structures that maintain male privilege and power by subjugating and marginalizing females. The logic of standpoint epistemology has enabled feminists within this philosophical trajectory to expose the biases and oversights of men's supposedly objective knowledge claims about the world.[12] With the aid of standpoint epistemology, women have turned their situations of marginalization and exploitation into sources of power and privilege in patriarchal societies because, through their experiences, women acquire true insight and knowledge into the sexist infrastructures they encounter every day in this world. Rather than submitting to patriarchally determined accounts of reality, they can resist patriarchal orderings of the world by unveiling the false assumptions on which those accounts depend, and narrate the truth about social reality from their standpoint as women. In this way, women's subjugation becomes the ground of their epistemological authority and power of resistance.

Because feminist standpoint epistemology problematizes knowledge produced by men, it interrogates men's status and role in discerning truth when women's experience is the privileged source of knowledge. According to the movement identified as "radical feminism," the very positing of such a question further subjects women to patriarchy, but for proponents of standpoint epistemology like Harding, critical, objective knowledge of reality is not female-exclusive. As she notes, feminist standpoint epistemology is rooted in the philosophical work of men who were located in social positions of power: Hegel, on the one hand, who developed the idea of the master/slave dialectic, and Marx and Engels, on the other hand, who conducted the critical class analysis of capitalism.[13] According to Harding,

10. Harding, "Standpoint Epistemology," 55.

11. Ibid., 54.

12. For a discussion of this critical function of feminist standpoint epistemology, see Solberg, *Compelling Knowledge*, 25–35.

13. Ibid., 59, 62.

men too can share in discovering the truth of the world; their point of entry for epistemological inquiries, however, must be from women's experience. She says,

> The activities of those at the bottom of . . . social hierarchies can provide starting points for thought—for *everyone's* research and scholarship—from which humans' relations with each other and the natural world can become visible. This is because the experience and lives of marginalized peoples, as they understand them, provide particularly significant *problems to be explained* or research agendas.[14]

The involvement of both women and men in the pursuit of knowledge can potentially "maximize objectivity,"[15] uncover knowledge that is "for marginalized people" and not solely for the "dominant" to use,[16] and even transform relationships between men and women by "chang[ing] our patterns of belief."[17]

Women also need to implement a similar approach for epistemological inquiries at the margins, according to Harding, because they are located in different positions through the intersections of race, ethnicity, class, nationality, sexuality, and other identity structures amid patriarchal social systems. All women do not share the same experiences and knowledge perspectives. In order to gain the most holistic and truthful understanding of the world, different voices are crucial. In fact, the complex composition of standpoints often locates individual women in conflicting spheres simultaneously, and for Harding these "contradictory social position[s]" are what actually yield "feminist knowledge."[18] The path to the truth lies in inhabiting the spaces of contradiction within one's own experience—as a man or woman—while also attending to the differences between standpoints among different women and men. The burden for those positioned in "dominant groups," to whatever degree, is, as Harding says,

> to listen attentively to marginalized people; it requires educating oneself about their histories, achievements, preferred social relations, and hopes for the future; it requires putting one's body on the line for 'their' causes until they feel like 'our' causes; it requires critical examination of the dominant institutional beliefs

14. Ibid., 54, emphasis original.

15. Ibid., 52.

16. Ibid., 56.

17. Ibid., 60.

18. Ibid., 66.

and practices that systematically disadvantage them; it requires critical self-examination to discover how one unwittingly participates in generating disadvantage to them . . . and more.[19]

Through full-bodied engagement with one another in dialogue, study, and activism, women and men in all their differences can open one another's eyes to see the world as it really is. By doing the work of standpoint epistemology, they may be able together to confront the world's structural injustices and discern possibilities for redress and change.

This brief description of feminist standpoint epistemology provides a basic outline of the major intellectual moves many feminists make in responding critically and constructively to historically male-dominated epistemological accounts of reality. Harding's work is particularly illustrative for two reasons: first of all, it exemplifies the rigor and nuance with which standpoint epistemology can be articulated and developed in feminist discourse; second, these nuances in Harding's thought resonate remarkably with Martyn's interpretation of Paul. Their uncanny similarities will surface by trekking through the terrain of apocalyptic in Martyn.

Making Sense of Apocalypse Now: Martyn's Standpoint Epistemology

"Apocalypse" commonly refers to a cataclysmic event so dramatic, powerful, and all-encompassing that the entire world comes to an end. It signifies a rupture of order, a destruction of the familiar, and a halting of life, so that nothing remains the same. What—if anything—lies on the "other side" of apocalypse is utterly incomprehensible, unforeseeable, and unintelligible for the world prior to the event. Under these terms, apocalypse would appear to be relegated to a future possibility.[20]

When Paul surveys the world around him, however, he boldly writes, "Apocalypse now!"[21] According to Martyn, Paul sees the world already brought to its end in the person of Jesus Christ, and "apocalypse" is the most viable way to express the cosmic revolution that Christ has

19. Ibid., 68.

20. In *Apocalypse Now and Then*, Catherine Keller describes what she calls an "apocalypse pattern" as involving the "[expectation of] some cataclysmic showdown in which, despite tremendous collateral damage (the destruction of the world as we know it), good must triumph in the near future with the help of some transcendent power and live forever after in a fundamentally new world" (11).

21. Martyn, "Paul to Flannery O'Connor," 281.

instigated. In him, Martyn says, God has "powerfully step[ped] on the scene,"[22] "invading" this world as a declaration of war on the powers that held the whole world captive to their destructive and divisive operations.[23]

God's "plan of attack" on these "anti-God powers"[24] nevertheless takes them all by surprise because God displays God's power at the moment of Christ's powerlessness on the cross.[25] Christ's crucifixion is the paradoxical event in this war that has forever dethroned the powers of Sin and Death and thereby set the cosmos free to new life. In Christ, the world ruled by anti-God powers is no more; a "new creation" takes place.[26] This strange divine apocalypse, according to Martyn, is the good news for the world that Paul's letters proclaim in "present tense": "Today is the day of salvation!"[27]

For Paul's audience, this startling announcement—that the apocalypse has already occurred, that new creation is a present reality—may induce a sense of cognitive dissonance.[28] The "real world" looks like anything but new creation; anti-God powers still appear to rule the day as divisions, destruction, violence, and death continue to structure human life. Martyn recognizes the significance of this problem, in which the truth of God's apocalypse in Christ seems implausible from all appearances. The solution that Martyn essentially develops in interpreting Paul is a standpoint epistemology. This framework for knowledge allows Martyn to hold

---

22. This is how Martyn translates 1 Cor 1:18: "For to those who are perishing the word of the cross is *foolishness*, to those of us, however, who are being saved, it is *God powerfully stepping on the scene*" (Martyn, "Gospel and Scripture," 217–18). He also describes God's action as "stepping on the scene" in "Epilogue," 180. Finally, in "Paul to Flannery O'Connor," Martyn says that "the *One* who has been on the other side rips the curtain apart, steps through to our side, altering irrevocably our time and space" (282); an identical sentence also occurs in "Twice-Invaded World," 124.

23. Martyn, "Paul to Flannery O'Connor," 282–84.

24. Martyn, "Epilogue," 179–80.

25. Ibid., 287–89.

26. Martyn, "Twice-Invaded World," 124–27.

27. 2 Cor 6:2; Martyn, "Paul to Flannery O'Connor," 280–83.

28. I am using this phrase in a colloquial sense to refer to the experience of confusion induced by an announcement that claims to be true but does not seem to represent reality accurately. Alexandra Brown incorporates the technical psychological term of "cognitive dissonance" positively into her discussion of the relationship between perception and human ethical transformation in the context of Paul's letters. Cognitive dissonance for her is not a problem but a crucial step in transforming human perception and action. See Brown, *Cross*, 157–69.

together a present-tense new creation with a present-tense experience of enslavement to anti-God powers without one invalidating the other.

The key standpoint, for Martyn, on which Paul's message of good news hangs is the crucified Christ. His death is "the absolute epistemological watershed"[29] that puts into "crisis"[30] the way of thinking that perceives new creation and present enslavement simply as mutually exclusive, opposing realities. Both realities concur paradoxically in the crucifixion of Jesus Christ because, in his powerlessness and humiliation, Christ breaks the power of Sin and Death, crucifying these anti-God powers by being crucified himself. Martyn describes the scene in this way: "On a real cross in this world hangs God's own Messiah, the Lord of glory! How can that be anything other than an epistemological crisis?"[31] The crucified Jesus is the Lord who inaugurates a new creation, a new age, where—and when—the anti-God powers appear to be most victorious: in his death. True apocalypse takes place in Christ, the one "who has been crucified,"[32] because he unveils the paradoxical way in which God has acted to liberate the world.[33]

Since Christ crucified constitutes the apocalyptic standpoint at which new creation concurs with the world's enslavement, the issue of access to this standpoint becomes crucial. For Martyn, "the cross of Christ means that the marks of the new age are at present hidden *in* the old age"[34]; therefore, the only way to perceive this otherwise imperceptible new creation is to start from Christ's standpoint—which is to say, to be in Christ. Those who live in Christ, specifically "in the cross,"[35] see and know the truth of God's apocalypse because they are made a part of the new creation right in the middle of the enslaved world. Their simultaneous location in both realities grants them what Martyn calls "bi-focal vision,"[36] a dual perspective through which those in Christ "see *both* the enslaving Old Age and God's invading and liberating new creation"[37] at once. Bifocal vision opens their eyes to see the world apocalyptically, as a cosmic power struggle begun by

29. Martyn, "Epistemology," 108.

30. Ibid.

31. Ibid.

32. 1 Cor 1:23 (my translation).

33. Martyn, "Paul to Flannery O'Connor," 284.

34. Martyn, "Epistemology," 110.

35. Ibid., 108.

36. Martyn, "Paul to Flannery O'Connor," 284.

37. Ibid.

God in Christ against anti-God powers, while also perceiving the "ultimate outcome" of this struggle to be God's victorious reign.[38]

Because access to this mode of perception requires a particular situation within the world—rather than detachment, neutrality, or a bird's-eye view above and beyond the fray—those in Christ with bifocal vision perceive not only the dual truth of the world but also the dual truth of themselves and their own standpoint in the world. In Christ, individuals become a "new-creation community,"[39] which Martyn describes as the "new human agent" fashioned by God that is "corporate, newly competent and newly addressable."[40] This agent, enlivened by the Spirit, stands in the middle of the struggle—"in the front trenches"[41]—where it serves not as a "passive puppet"[42] but an active "combatant."[43] In this agent's action, God is active and "participat[ing]"[44] to bring to fruition the fullness of God's new creation. Moreover, the struggle occurs right in the middle of this agent's life because its formation by God is not yet complete; this corporate agent is "at the same time a sinner and rectified."[45] The agent stands and fights in "the juncture of the ages,"[46] as Martyn says, but the juncture is also in the agent. Bifocal vision, then, enables the corporate human agent to perceive its eschatological identity in God, as well as its enslavement, and thereby to discern how God is at work in its present communal life in both the old age and the new creation.

Such discernment entails living *kata stauron*: in the cross of Christ. For Martyn, this takes shape in several interrelated ways. First, cruciform life involves "the disciple's daily death,"[47] which, within Martyn's framework, suggests the bringing to an end of one's situation of enslavement, as well as the destruction of one's "carefully ordered . . . world"[48] and way of seeing and knowing that is bound up with one's situation in the old age. It

---

38. Ibid., 283.
39. Martyn, "Epistemology," 109.
40. Martyn, "Epilogue," 180.
41. Ibid., 182.
42. Martyn, "Daily Life," 260.
43. Ibid., 262.
44. Martyn, "Epilogue," 182.
45. Martyn, "Paul to Flannery O'Connor," 296.
46. Martyn, "Epistemology," 107.
47. Ibid., 110.
48. Martyn, "Paul to Flannery O'Connor," 296.

also involves living by the "power of the cross,"[49] which may include sharing in Christ's situation of powerlessness by occupying positions within the world that are deemed weak and foolish, rather than positions deemed powerful, strong, and wise by an old-age estimation.[50] Finally, cruciformity is participation in the new-creation community that is led by the Spirit, in which the Spirit's fruit-bearing work becomes manifest in the everyday life of the community[51] and members of the community turn to and "serve the neighbor who is in need."[52] None of these things may look glamorous, dramatic, or particularly effective against the backdrop of an enslaved world, but for those in Christ, in the thick of the apocalyptic struggle, cruciformity is the difference between life and death, liberation and enslavement, discernment and dissonance.

Conclusion

Through this series of conceptual moves, Martyn's apocalyptic thought effectively displays its reliance upon a standpoint epistemology infrastructure. For Martyn, as for standpoint epistemologists like Harding, the world is not an arena of harmonious order or neutral territory, but the site of struggle between different powers, in which injustice, oppression, and destruction seem to reign. Within this world of struggle, for Martyn—just as for Harding—location is everything, because only from a particular situation or vantage point can one recognize and understand the truth of the world. Indeed, for Martyn as well as for Harding, the vantage point for knowing the world as it really is lies in the space of contradiction, because in such spaces a person can gain access to two pictures, two realities, simultaneously and thus perceive the whole truth of reality. Being situated in a space of contradiction may involve occupying a position that looks like powerlessness from one perspective, but, for both Martyn and Harding, such a perspective remains oblivious to the form of power present

49. Martyn, "Epistemology," 109.

50. An example of this is found in "Paul to Flannery O'Connor," in which Martyn contrasts the power of the "leaders of the white community" during the Civil Rights struggle as "Old-Age power" with the power of the black community, "the unconditional grace in the cross of Christ," which, as Martyn says, "is powerful enough to keep the black community walking on sore feet every day, instead of riding the segregated buses" (289). From the perspective of the white community, the black community might have appeared to occupy a position of powerlessness and even foolishness, but such a perspective fails to see the power in that apparent "powerlessness."

51. Martyn, "Daily Life," 258–59, 261–65.

52. Martyn, "Epistemology," 109.

precisely in the powerlessness of a contradictory space. Finally, those who see and know the truth of the world from their particular vantage point can also discern their place within the struggle and engage with others in the fight for a new world.

The shared structure of Harding's standpoint epistemology and Martyn's apocalyptic interpretation of Paul does not remove the differences in content between them; Martyn, after all, is involved in a distinctly theological project. Nevertheless, because Martyn's thought operates according to a standpoint epistemological framework, some of the problematic issues accompanying that framework also afflict Martyn's apocalyptic theology. A critical analysis of standpoint epistemology will uncover the problems and indicate a helpful way of correcting them.

APOCALYPTIC "TO WHOM?"[53]: A CRITICAL ASSESSMENT OF STANDPOINT EPISTEMOLOGY IN MARTYN

The Elusive Quest for Knowledge "for Marginalized People"[54]

The strength of standpoint epistemologies like Harding's is their recognition that location affects what and how one knows. The major flaw in standpoint logic, however, is its failure to attend to the complex and fluid relationships between locations, knowers, and knowledge production "on the ground," so to speak. The nuances of Harding's standpoint epistemology enable her to reflect on these relationships a little more deftly than other standpoint theorists, but her thought still falls prey to a fundamental contradiction, which the work of Bat-Ami Bar On helpfully illuminates. On the one hand, it cannot recognize the "taint"[55] within its own judgments about marginalization and power, and on the other hand, it cannot verify the objectivity of the knowledge produced by starting from "the marginalized." As a result, Harding's work, along with that of other standpoint theorists, obscures the power dynamics of concrete social

---

53. This quotation is taken from the title of Luce Irigaray's essay "Equal to Whom?" and is meant to suggest a parallel rhetorical interrogation of apocalyptic. For Irigaray, equality is not a neutral concept but is determined from a normative, patriarchal stance, so the question poses a challenge to equality as the standard or ideal toward which feminism aims. Similarly, this section calls into question the conditions under which apocalyptic is produced.

54. Harding, "Standpoint Epistemology," 56.

55. Bar On, "Epistemic Privilege," 94.

relationships and fails to accomplish its aim of engendering knowledge "for marginalized people."

Harding's standpoint epistemology falters, first, because it revolves around a dichotomy between the dominant social group and the marginalized group. Although Harding does not employ these categories to affirm "a single center"[56] of social power in the world—because she understands multiple social groups to be marginalized and multiple groups to be dominant—she uses them formally, presupposing a center in relation to which a margin can be identified. Her notion of "start[ing] thought from marginalized lives"[57] is predicated upon determining whose lives are marginal, which requires a prior center. Marginal identity, therefore, as Bat-Ami Bar On critically notes, is derived from and dependent on a central identity that serves as the standard or stable axis around which social organization takes place.[58] The dichotomy of center/margin is not a neutral division but a power-laden one, effected by the center through the authorization of that center. Harding's appeal to this dichotomy is not simply descriptive but "performative,"[59] because it enacts a dichotomous structuring of power that circumscribes a center as the site of power and the margin as powerlessness. Consequently, the quest for objective knowledge about social reality begins with an unquestioned subjective mapping of that reality from a position of power.

The application of this formal dichotomy to social reality introduces another problem: it results in "cumulative"[60] or parsed identities. In a social reality organized around multiple centers of power and multiple forms of marginalization, many situations are mixed loci in which persons and groups occupy neither a purely dominant nor a purely marginal position. For Harding, such "heterogeneous"[61] and even "contradictory" situations

56. This is a problem that Bar On identifies in the work of other proponents of feminist standpoint epistemology. See ibid., 90.

57. Quoted in Harding, "Standpoint Epistemology," 50.

58. Bar On, "Epistemic Privilege," 90.

59. I am pointing to Judith Butler's understanding of performativity here, which can apply not only to embodied performance and activity—which she discusses in *Gender Trouble*—but also to discourse; indeed the two are not so easily separated, according to Butler. Drawing upon Foucault, she defines "performativity" most basically as "the reiterative and citational practice by which discourse produces the effects that it names" (Butler, *Bodies That Matter*, 2).

60. Bar On, "Epistemic Privilege," 90.

61. Harding, "Standpoint Epistemology," 65.

are what produce "new knowledge"[62] amid a multiply stratified social order, because persons in such situations occupy positions in both dominant and marginalized groups simultaneously. In order for her to privilege contradictory situations, however, Harding assumes that such situations can be clearly identified as contradictory, which requires presupposing that they can be parsed into layers of power according to specific identity components, like gender, race, class, sexuality, and nationality. In effect, a person's identity must be seen as a "cumulative" combination of isolatable features to be deemed contradictory, like a poor (powerless) white (powerful) heterosexual (powerful) woman (powerless) in the U.S. (powerful), for instance. This implicit parsing prevents Harding from recognizing two complex features of social reality. First, lived experience and experiences of marginalization are not so readily compartmentalized as purely racial or gendered or classist, because particular identity "combinations" are always already inseparably interrelated and entangled for concrete persons and social realities. Second, the complex constitution of a situation, in which power and powerlessness are inseparable, may be precisely the source of a person's or group's marginalization. Moreover, by privileging contradictory positions for the production of new knowledge, Harding effectively shifts methodologically from starting from "the marginalized" to starting "from multiple lives that are in many ways in conflict with each other, each of which itself has multiple and contradictory commitments."[63] This shift reifies marginalized identities as marginal in the quest for true knowledge.

A third problem in Harding's standpoint theory is the circularity entailed in putting its method into practice. Harding's thought begins by assuming social division between dominant and marginalized groups, through which those in marginal positions gain what Bar On refers to as "epistemic privilege,"[64] the capacity for critical insight into social reality. Standpoint epistemology then prescribes a method of starting from the lived experiences of the marginalized. In order to implement this method, according to Harding, "members of dominant groups [must] make themselves 'fit' to engage in collaborative, democratic, community enterprises with marginal peoples,"[65] which entails members of the dominant group identifying fully with the marginalized.[66] For this to occur, however, a

62. Ibid., 66.
63. Ibid.
64. Bar On, "Epistemic Privilege," 85.
65. Harding, "Standpoint Epistemology," 68.
66. See ibid.

change in "social relations"[67] is necessary; the dominant group must enter into a different relationship with the marginalized in order to attain true knowledge of social reality. If social relations change, though, then the social reality also changes, which means that the goal of knowing the "prior" social reality that is structured by the dominant/marginalized dichotomy cannot be achieved. The prescribed process of knowing changes both the subject (knower) and object (social reality) of knowledge, so that the objective knowledge at which one aims within one social reality is not the knowledge at which one arrives through the alteration of that social reality. The truth inevitably eludes the knower because knowledge production through this method is unmistakably subjective, bearing the marks of time and space. Harding's theory, therefore, is caught in a circular method that undercuts the practical fulfillment of its epistemological project.

For these three reasons—power dualism, parsed identities, and methodological circularity—Harding's standpoint epistemology cannot yield knowledge for those with which it is most concerned: the marginalized. In fact, through these problematic conceptual moves, Harding's thought unwittingly obscures the concrete identities and situations of those characterized as marginal by those in positions of dominance. As a result, the agency of the marginalized becomes commodified by and for the dominant in the following ways: the marginalized must comply with the construal of their identity as "marginalized" and powerless; they are to supply the "problems to be explained or research agendas"[68] for knowledge projects; they must accommodate the attempts of dominant group members to "make themselves fit" for starting from the marginalized; and they are to stay outside of knowledge production itself. Their only opportunity to participate actively in the knowledge process is to critique the final product of knowledge, which unfeasibly demands that the marginalized occupy a bifurcated identity as both powerless objects of knowledge and subjects with the power to assess knowledge.[69] As Bar On rightly con-

67. Ibid.

68. Ibid., 54.

69. This final issue—serving as the critical voice to hold knowers accountable—emerges unwittingly through Harding's discussion of objectifying objectivity in knowledge production. She argues for the need for "strong reflexivity," in which "the subject as well as the object of knowledge [is] a necessary object of critical, causal—scientific!—social explanations" ("Standpoint Epistemology," 71). She does not want the subjects and objects of knowledge to be cast in two different molds and thus calls for knowers—that is, scientists and observers—to be interrogated as well. However, in distinguishing scientists from the objects of knowledge in the process of knowledge production, Harding maintains a divide between those who know and those who

tends, marginal identities and experiences thus become "idealized" and "valorized" according to the two extremes of utter powerlessness, on the one hand, and their ability to "resist," on the other hand.[70] At every turn, "the marginalized" are constructed to serve the utilitarian needs of the dominant in knowledge production. Harding's standpoint epistemology, therefore, secures knowledge for "the marginalized" only insofar as those identified as marginalized submit to this power-laden designation and "reinscribe the values and practices used to socially marginalize [them]."[71]

In light of these problems in Harding's work, the pressing question for us is how the same difficulties apply to the structure of Martyn's apocalyptic interpretation of Paul. To address this issue, a comparative critical evaluation of Martyn's apocalyptic standpoint epistemology is in order.

Apocalyptic Contradictions

The epistemological structure of Martyn's apocalyptic interpretation succumbs to the fundamental contradiction inherent in standpoint theory. Like Harding, Martyn effectively assumes a problematic power dualism upon which his understanding of apocalypse is founded. Like Harding, Martyn's privileging of a contradictory standpoint for accessing true knowledge results in abstracted, parsed identities. Finally, Martyn too advocates an epistemological method that becomes trapped in practical circularity. For Martyn, unlike for Harding, however, these structural problems significantly complicate divine-human relationship as well as social relations.

Martyn's characterization of God's apocalyptic invasion, first of all, employs a power dichotomy between God and the anti-God powers of Sin and Death. His rhetoric—God's entrance from the "outside," God's "powerful" action in the powerlessness of the crucifixion, God's "war" on the anti-God-powers[72]—discloses this dichotomy by conveying how powerful the anti-God powers are in relation to God. Their stronghold in and over the cosmos rivals God's power to the extent that they pose a viable threat

---

are known; the work of objectifying the objectifiers—the scientists—then effectively becomes the burden of critique placed on the first objects of knowledge, the marginalized. Throughout the process of knowing, then, the marginalized are barred from being knowers.

70. Bar On, "Epistemic Privilege," 91–94.

71. Ibid., 96–97.

72. Martyn, "Paul to Flannery O'Connor," 282–85.

to God. As God's declaration of war indicates, the anti-God powers assume the power to dictate the terms of engagement between themselves and God, by which they even normatively determine God's standpoint, so that God's subsequent action serves to legitimate their claim to power. The dualistic logic of Martyn's apocalyptic interpretation, therefore, installs the anti-God powers as the powerful center in relation to which God occupies the margin. It presumes that God recognizes and authorizes their centrality in order to challenge it by divine invasion. This apocalyptic framework shores up the power of anti-God powers and limits the power of God by relativizing it to that of the anti-God powers.

This dualism generates the additional problem of abstracted, parsed identities. Because God's apocalypse in the crucified Christ effects a juncture of the ages, in which the old age and new eschatological age intersect, present cosmic reality is marked both by the reign of anti-God powers and by the reign of God. Within this contradictory space of present reality, Christ's identity, along with the identity of those who are in him, becomes split by the power dualism. Christ on the cross reveals the dual reign of God and the anti-God powers at once, which means that, on the one hand, he unveils God's victory over anti-God powers in the new age, and on the other hand, he reveals the anti-God powers' victorious reign over the old age. In demonstrating the power of both God and the anti-God powers, however, Christ also effectively figures the disproportionate power between them. Christ is no longer God's deeper victory beneath the apparent victory of the anti-God powers, as Martyn interprets the crucifixion; rather, Christ crucified signifies the deeper victory of the anti-God powers beneath the apparent paradoxical victory of God. Christ's identity, therefore, becomes bifurcated in the cross, precisely from the standpoint of the juncture: he liberates the cosmos only by conceding the enslaved world to the anti-God powers and beginning a new age for God to rule; and, because the crucifixion locates him in both ages at once, he must concede himself as well to enslavement in the old age in order to be liberator in the new age. The crucifixion nails him forever to the contradictory identity of being simultaneously the liberator and the one in need of liberation. Thus the power dualism between God and the anti-God powers installs an unbridgeable rift in Christ's identity.

Consequently, the new-creation community, which subsists in Christ, also acquires a bifurcated identity. As both "sinners" and "rectified," as Martyn says, inhabiting both the old and new ages at once, those in Christ are both enslaved to the anti-God powers and part of a new human agency brought about by God's apocalypse. Their existence consists of being "morally incompetent,"[73] powerless agents while also being a new "corporate," morally "competent" and "addressable" agent in whom the Spirit of God is active.[74] This contradictory human existence, however, requires a denial of concrete, embodied life in all its ambiguities, complexities, and limitations because it necessitates two concurrent yet opposing forms of agency, which cannot take place within an actual human life. Such an abstraction—however it may be conceived and applied to embodied human life—devalues the body and neglects the bodily constitution of the situations of enslavement and liberation.[75] As a result, the bifocal vision attained by those in Christ at the juncture reinforces the power dualism that attributes normativity to the anti-God powers and abstracts human identity—"sinner" or "rectified" or "rectified sinner"—from embodiment. The corporate agent's bifocal vision thus obscures the particular situation that it is supposed to perceive: present reality at the juncture.

Finally, Martyn's apocalyptic logic ensnares his thought in a circular epistemological "method," so to speak, for discerning the truth of the present, in which apocalypse has occurred and cosmic enslavement seems to persist. For Martyn, "epistemology at the turn of the ages" begins from the situation of being in Christ, which involves being part of the new-creation community within the old age. Communal life at the standpoint of the cross is shaped by "daily dying," inhabiting positions of powerlessness, weakness, and foolishness similar to Christ's, and "knowing and serving the neighbor who is in need." For this kind of cruciform life to occur, however, the community must retain its old-age existence in order to be the new creation community, specifically in order that the community's old-age life may be continuously put to death. The community's new-age, new-creation existence is thereby continually forestalled. Additionally, the agent responsible for the community's cruciformity is caught in an internal conflict in shaping the community's life. Either the

73. Martyn, "Epilogue," 177–78, 180.

74. Ibid., 180–82.

75. This abstracting move could take place in a variety of ways. It could install a classic body/mind split, so that agency is associated primarily with the mind and the body is consigned to the old age. It could also take the form of an outer/inner division within a person, linking agency to all that is internal to oneself (heart, mind, soul, spirit, conscience, etc.) and thereby individualizing and separating oneself from others. Conversely, it could even translate into a personal/social distinction, in which personal agency is circumscribed as morally incompetent and the social body is the locus of new creation, responsible agency; in order to be an agent, then, the personal would have to be abandoned for the sake of the social.

community must enact the practical contradiction of putting itself to death daily, or God must continually oppose the community in its old-age existence in order to affirm the community as the new creation.[76] Cruciform life, therefore, like Harding's notion of becoming "fit," requires a practical circularity that circumvents true perception of reality: it denies new creation in order to negate the old, and neither the human nor the divine agent can actually accomplish the task of conforming communal life to the standpoint of the cross.

Within Martyn's apocalyptic interpretation, then, these three problems—power dualism, bifurcated identities, and methodological circularity—obstruct the fundamental purpose of Martyn's idea of bifocal vision: to see what God is presently doing in the juncture among us. The standpoint-epistemological structure of Martyn's thought actually makes such discernment more difficult because the roles that it constructs for the various players in the apocalyptic "drama" remain distanced from "the rough and tumble"[77] of present reality. First, God is not allowed to be God as long as both God's power and presence are determined by anti-God powers functioning as "directors"; God is scripted into an off-stage part, located outside the enslaved world and beyond present reality, only gaining the "artistic freedom" to reign in the eschatological new age that cannot arrive. The power of God cannot consist of anything other than competition with that of the anti-God powers, which means that God can only be present where they are absent. This apocalyptic logic has no way to entertain the possibility of God being present with God's creation through it all—through enslavement and deliverance and thus right in the middle of present reality.

Similarly, human beings are conscripted into a conflicted role inherent to the contradictory space of present reality, in which human agency is grounded in epistemology—that is to say, in being a knower by means of bifocal vision. Because this role is played under the direction of the anti-God powers, human access to bifocal vision is always already thwarted by human complicity with the anti-God powers' determination of knowledge production. The role into which humans are cast also demands an unfeasible abstraction from embodied life, which places human agency in

76. Based on Martyn's argument in his "Epilogue" essay, I conjecture that he would dismiss the former possibility—of human beings bearing sole responsibility for daily dying—and may also find the latter highly problematic. Nevertheless, the logic of his thought implicitly commits him to one of these options.

77. Martyn uses this language in a couple places to argue that apocalyptic is in fact "on the ground," "Epistemology," 109; "Twice-Invaded World," 127.

a competitive relationship with the body. Because human beings are thus unable to perceive the truth of reality or to escape embodiment, they are barred from agency.

The concurrence of these problematic implications for God and for human beings is not coincidental; the strictures placed on God bear directly upon the division between human agency and embodiment. This correlation takes center stage in the role given to Christ, in whom, according to Martyn, God "steps powerfully on the scene" and a new human agent is created. However, insofar as God is not free to be God and human beings are denied agency, Christ's identity becomes "emptied of its power."[78] Who he is essentially is confined to the cross—spatially and temporally—and thus he cannot effect liberation for the cosmos and bring about new creation. Like "the marginalized" for Harding, the crucified, dead body of Jesus is idealized and valorized as the presumed apocalypse of salvation from the standpoint of the juncture, which in turn fuels an idealization and valorization of cruciformity for those who are in Christ. Both forms of valorization have a masking effect, not only hiding the power attributed to the anti-God powers and distancing those who are in Christ from Christ's body, but also cloaking the bodies of those in Christ from one another. At the juncture, those who are in Christ cannot recognize how the anti-God powers' operations structure bodily life through competitive social divisions—which assign privilege to certain bodies and identities by devaluing others—nor recognize their complicity in such divisive structures. Cruciform life becomes an insidious means for sanctioning the non-neutral social order, in which those devalued by the anti-God powers' structuring of bodily life are all the more subjugated under the guise of liberation. Martyn's apocalyptic interpretation, therefore, is unable to elaborate how Christ saves and how that salvation is incarnated for embodied human beings involved in social arrangements.

Ultimately, this standpoint-epistemological infrastructure places significant limitations on Martyn's reading and theological reflection on Paul's letters. Martyn's apocalyptic interpretation cannot articulate a coherent, present-tense apocalypse of God for people in the concrete world because his epistemological assumptions overlook the complex relationship between the agent(s), process, and object of knowledge. Martyn's interpretation thus divorces knowledge and its production from both the crucified Christ and the body.

78. 1 Cor 1:17.

When we turn to Paul's first letter to the Corinthians, however, we see a contrasting epistemological orientation. Paul's use of epistemological language there is inextricably tied to embodied life. In order to understand how Paul approaches knowledge and knowing, we must examine his emphasis on the body. Therefore, like the feminist move toward strategic essentialism, which turns affirmatively to the body to challenge its objectification, I want to shift now toward embodiment and its relationship to knowledge in 1 Corinthians. By highlighting the pivotal role of the body in shaping and producing knowledge within this letter, I will provide a constructive corrective to Martyn's problematic epistemology and demonstrate that an apocalyptic interpretation of Paul unequivocally needs the body.

"DISCERNING THE BODY": A CONSTRUCTIVE RESPONSE TO MARTYN'S APOCALYPTIC FRAMEWORK

The long letter of 1 Corinthians communicates that, for Paul, the body matters for life in Christ. The letter itself marks Paul's bodily absence from the church in Corinth, even as his words recall and re-present his body to the church.[79] Within the content of the letter, Paul addresses several issues pertaining directly to personal, material bodies, including eating practices, sexual relationships, and marriage and celibacy. In conjunction with this, he also focuses on the church as a body, devoting attention to the unity of its different members as he discusses divisions, conflicts leading to lawsuits, spiritual gifts, and practices of prophesying and speaking in tongues. Certainly not least of all, Paul highlights the body of Jesus, crucified and resurrected, in whom the members of the church have been joined together by God.

Throughout Paul's comments on these body matters, he employs a semantic field that can be broadly characterized as epistemological. In exhorting the church to unity, Paul calls members to be "restored/made complete in the same mind [*noi*] and in the same purpose/will [*gnōmē*]" (1 Cor 1:10). Paul describes God's call and salvation through the crucified Christ in terms of "wisdom" (*sophia*) and "foolishness" (*mōria*) (1:18–31).[80] In multiple places, Paul invokes a common interrogative

79. See, for instance, 1 Cor 2:1–5; 4:9–21; 5:3–5; and 9:1–27.

80. Paul continues to deploy these words in chapters 2 and 3 to speak of God's revelation of God's mystery through the Spirit, as well as to emphasize the contrast between God and the "wisdom of this world" (3:19).

refrain, "Do you not know [*ouk oidate*] . . . ?" as he draws attention to the church's identity and the problems with some of its practices.[81] He contrasts "knowledge" (*gnōsis*), which "puffs up" (8:1) and "will be abolished" (13:8), with "love" (*agapē*), which "builds up" (8:1) and "never fails" (13:8), while also correlating love with being "known [*egnōkenai*] by [God]" (8:3; cf. *epegnōsthēn* in 13:12). In addressing the issue of eating food sacrificed to idols, Paul directs church members to the differences in "conscience," or "understanding" (*suneidēsis*), among them and indicates how neglect of those differences can be destructive to members in this particular practice (8:7–13; cf. 10:23–29). Finally, Paul uses the language of examination (*dokimazetō*) of oneself and discernment (*diakrinōn*) of the body to instruct the church on eating and drinking together in the assembly (11:28–29).

As this array reveals, these epistemological terms do not function univocally in the letter, either simply to advocate or reject knowledge, wisdom, and understanding. Neither, however, do they serve to promote a bifocal vision; Paul's response to the question of eating sacrificed food makes this clear, because Paul allows different members of the church to maintain different understandings of the situation—even if one of those ways of understanding sacrificed meat is an "old-age" mode of thinking and perceiving, according to Martyn's logic. What Paul's epistemological language does convey is that knowledge, wisdom, and understanding depend on the body. This dependence goes deeper than simply affirming a concrete context for epistemology to take place, as if the body forms a backdrop to the main event of knowledge production. The body is the source, end, and means of epistemology for Paul in 1 Corinthians: knowledge is grounded in the body, is for the sake of the body, and can only be

---

81. These are the nine occasions of this phrase: "Do you not know that you are God's sanctuary . . . ?" (3:16); "Do you not know that a little leaven leavens the whole mixture?" (5:6, in the context of the church's boasting over a situation of sexual immorality); "Do you not know that the saints will judge the world?" (6:2), "Do you not know that we are to judge angels . . . ?" (6:3), and "Do you not know that the unrighteous will not inherit the kingdom of God?" (6:9, in the context of church members bringing one another to court "before the unrighteous"); "Do you not know that your bodies are members of Christ?" (6:15) and "Do you not know that the one joining himself to a prostitute is one body?" (6:16, in the context of the bodily harm produced by fornication); "Do you not know that those who are employed in the temple service get their food from the temple . . . ?" (9:13, in the context of Paul's abstinence from certain rights as an apostle); "Do you not know that the ones who run in a race all indeed run, but one receives the prize?" (9:24, to implore the church to run to win, which may mean letting go of certain rights/freedoms).

had bodily. Paul's use of epistemological rhetoric, then, does not primarily aim to instill information in the church at Corinth;[82] rather, it turns church members to bodies: the body they are together in Christ through the Spirit, the particular bodies of members in their differences, and the body of Jesus, the crucified and risen Lord, in which they share.

A portion of the letter that especially brings this to light is Paul's critical discussion of the church's eating and drinking together in 11:17–34, coupled with his subsequent characterization of the church as a body in 12:1–31 (specifically vv. 12–27). Paul once more addresses the issue of division in the church at Corinth, which revolves around social status differentiations in this section of the letter.[83] According to 11:17–34, divisions (schismata) have become manifest in the church's gathering together to celebrate the Lord's Supper as "each one takes one's own supper first in the eating, and one suffers hunger and [another] one is drunk" (11:21). The likely scenario is a meal arranged and distributed in accordance with Greco-Roman social hierarchy, in which those of higher standing receive the best places at the table and choice portions of food and drink, while those of lower standing occupy lesser positions—perhaps even in a different area in the home—and are given less—or nothing—to eat and drink.[84] The coming together of church members in Corinth has instantiated social stratification and thus, ironically, produced division.

From Paul's perspective, by adopting this social practice at their gatherings, the church is effectively no longer sharing the Lord's Supper (11:20),[85] because members thus demonstrate their failure at "discerning

82. On a couple occasions in 1 Corinthians, Paul does deploy the phrase "I do not want you to be ignorant . . ." (10:1; 12:1). In the first case, he then proceeds to rehearse the story of Israel in the wilderness, and in the second, he reminds church members of their former idolatry and then points to the role of the Spirit in confessing Jesus as Lord. In neither instance does Paul seem primarily concerned with conveying information; rather, Paul begins his discussions of eating food sacrificed to idols in chapter 10 and of spiritual gifts in 12 with this phrase in order to point the church to who it is in relation to God and to the reality of God's presence in their embodied activities of eating and worshipping God together.

83. Differences in social status are arguably the source of most—if not all—the conflicts and problems within the church at Corinth. Many commentators emphasize the role of status differences for division in chapters 11 and 12; see, for instance, Hays, *First Corinthians*, 193–203, 212–16; Horsley, *1 Corinthians*, 157–73; and Thiselton, *First Epistle*, 850–53, 900. For an elaboration of social differences as the crux of the church's problems, see Martin, *Corinthian Body*.

84. Hays, *First Corinthians*, 196–97; Thiselton, *First Epistle*, 860–62; see also McRae, "Eating with Honor."

85. Thiselton, *First Epistle*, 859–63.

the body" (11:29). The phrase "discerning the body" (*diakrinōn to sōma*) evokes several meanings in this passage, all of which inform one another and must be held together to understand Paul's criticism and exhortation. First, "discerning the body" points to the preceding verse, which calls a person to "examine oneself and thus let one eat of the bread and drink of the cup" (11:28). In eating the Lord's Supper, a member of the church must discern his or her personal body, which includes, as 11:34 suggests, the basic act of recognizing one's hunger and "eat[ing] at home."[86]

The phrase implies a second association for "body," which appears earlier in 11:24 and 11:27 in connection with the "Lord Jesus" (11:23). Paul responds to the church's situation by recalling Jesus' words "'This is my body that is for you'" (11:24), and then deems anyone who "eats the bread or drinks the cup of the Lord unworthily" as "liable to the body and the blood of the Lord" (11:27). "Discerning the body," therefore, also entails recognizing Jesus' body as the church eats and drinks.[87] The coming together of the church to share the Lord's Supper requires acknowledging that this is the *Lord's* Supper, in which their eating and drinking serves to "proclaim the death of the Lord until he comes" (11:26).

This embodied proclamation enacted in the church's meal indicates a third dimension of "discerning the body," which emerges through 12:12–27: attention to the church as a body. Paul's metaphorical use of "body" to characterize the church in its spiritual gifts in chapter 12 actually demonstrates what it means to discern the body that is the church. On the one hand, it underscores both the interdependence and difference between the members that constitute the church body.[88] Just as no member can claim

---

86. Both Hays, (*First Corinthians*, 203) and Martin (*Corinthian Body*, 74–75) view Paul's instruction to eat at home as directed toward those of higher social standing rather than toward those who have been left to hunger (11:21), who are presumably of lower social standing. Therefore, "discerning the body" in this first case could be seen as more applicable to the socially higher members of the church. Even so, I do not wish to designate this first dimension of discernment as only applicable to those of higher status and thereby close off the significance it may have for those of lower status as well.

87. I am not trying to argue for or against a sacramental theology here. Such recognition in the context of this passage does not require a doctrine concerning eucharistic elements. This dimension of discernment simply involves attending to the fact that this meal is not just another meal; the church's gathering together for the Lord's Supper evokes and proclaims Christ—his death, his risen life, his lordship, and his imminent return. See Thiselton, *First Epistle*, 891–94, for more on this particular christological point of recognizing what is "different" about participating in this meal.

88. Here I am drawing upon Hays, who helpfully delineates these two points of "diversity and interdependence," as he says (*First Corinthians*, 213–16).

to have no need of another member within the body (12:21), neither can a member, by virtue of one's difference from others, conclude that one does not belong to the body (12:15–16). Discernment involves recognizing the deep relationships that members share with one another, in which both their mutual dependence and particular differences concur.

On the other hand, as Dale Martin argues, Paul's description of the church body presents a rhetorical critique of Greco-Roman use of the body metaphor to depict social organization, which served to promote the maintenance of social hierarchy.[89] In contrast to Greco-Roman hierarchical ideology, Paul declares the apparently "weaker" members of the body to be "necessary" rather than dispensable (12:22), those considered "dishonorable" to be clothed with "more abundant honor," and the "unseemly/shameful" to have "more abundant elegance/grace" (12:23), while the "elegant/graceful" are not afforded the same or greater honor or grace (12:24). The church body has been arranged by God in a way that runs counter to Greco-Roman social hierarchy, "giving more abundant honor to the lacking/inferior [member]" (12:24) rather than to those of higher social standing. God's strange reversal does not function simply to invert Greco-Roman social hierarchy, according to Paul, but it enables members to "care the same for one another" without "division" (12:25). Discerning the body that is the church, then, requires recognizing that God's formation of the church body actually makes the members into a body—rather than a stratified society—in which mutual care takes place and hierarchical social divisions have no place.

Finally, Paul identifies the church with "the body of Christ" (12:27), which essentially connects the interdependence, difference, and mutual care among church members to participation in Christ. They are joined to one another as they are joined to Christ as members of his body, living in and through him. Therefore, to discern the body is to recognize that the interdependence, differences, and mutual care among members of the church are the shape of "union with and participation [in] Christ."[90]

In light of these three dimensions of Paul's phrase—attending to one's personal body, the body of Jesus, and the body that the members of the church form together in Christ—one final meaning of "discerning the body" surfaces by reading 11:17–34 with 12:12–27: recognizing the particular bodies of other members of the church. Within the church body, differences between members are not to be dismissed but affirmed.

89. Martin, *Corinthian Body*, 92–96.
90. Hays, *First Corinthians*, 213–14.

At the same time, those differences are not cause for division, particularly for privileging the socially higher and denigrating the socially lower, but for unity, interdependence, and mutual care. As church members come together to share the Lord's Supper, their participation in Christ entails recognizing that all are to share in the meal together without anyone eating and drinking to the exclusion of anyone else. This bodily event of eating and drinking together requires the church to discern the bodily effects that its divisive meal practice has had on particular members' bodies, because members' dependence on one another as the church means that every member's body matters for the life of the church body. The Lord's Supper is not to be an occasion for dividing bodies from one another, but for "receiv[ing] one another," as Paul says (11:33). Discerning the body, therefore, means affirming the particular differences of members' bodies in the act of eating the Lord's Supper together as one body.

This cursory treatment of 1 Corinthians 11:17–34 and 12:12–27 reveals how Paul's use of epistemological language throughout the letter is oriented to the body—the particular bodies of church members, the body that they constitute together as the church, and the body of Christ to which they have been joined and in which they share in coming together to eat the Lord's Supper. Discernment begins and ends with bodies, and the only way to discern "the body" is bodily, as one is in one's personal body, together with other particular bodies, performing the bodily act of eating the Lord's Supper, forming one body in Christ. The purpose of epistemology for Paul, then, particularly in the context of 1 Corinthians, is not for those in Christ to arrive at disembodied knowledge or an accurate vision of the world, but to abide in embodied solidarity.

Consequently, the intricate relationship between the body and epistemology in 1 Corinthians provides a helpful starting point for redressing the structural flaws in Martyn's apocalyptic interpretation. First, it serves to connect both knowing and the body to human agency. Second, it brings together embodied human agency and participation in the incarnate Christ, so that human life in present reality involves embodied communion with an embodied Christ in solidarity with other embodied agents. The body becomes vital for living in Christ and thus for relating to God who is in Christ. Third, it removes competition between different personal bodies and the body that they form as a community in Christ, because attention to particular bodies directly correlates with attention to the communal body.

PART TWO: Apocalyptic and Christian Doctrines

By establishing these connections, the body-epistemology relationship functions to dismantle the series of contradictions installed in
present reality under Martyn's apocalyptic schema, and it opens the way
for an alternative understanding of apocalyptic in Paul. Instead of total
destruction and new creation, which reveals God's impotence and denies
embodiment in the crucified Christ, apocalypse can be the revelation of
God's persistence to abide with bodies, vividly declared in the embodied
life, crucifixion, and resurrection of Jesus.[91] The love of God's bodily solidarity with embodied human beings is the power strong enough to nullify
Sin and Death, because, as Christ demonstrates, God refuses to abandon
or relinquish any body. Whether "dispensable" or "indispensable," judged
"dishonorable" or deemed "honorable," poor or rich, living or dead, all
bodies matter to God. Apocalypse in this alternative mode does not mark
the end of the world or inaugurate a war fought through daily dying, but
it points to God's steadfast affirmation of concrete, bodily life, moment by
moment, which invites embodied human beings to abide with God and
with one another in mutual care for their differences. An apocalypse of
this kind can truly turn the world upside down.

CONCLUSION

In this essay, I have presented a critical philosophical analysis of Martyn's
apocalyptic interpretation of Paul. By juxtaposing the work of feminist
theorist Sandra Harding with that of Martyn, I have argued that Martyn's
Pauline interpretation rests on a standpoint-epistemological framework.
As a result, the problems that beset standpoint epistemologies like Harding's also plague Martyn's apocalyptic reading of Paul. To address these
problems in Martyn's work, I have proposed an approach to Pauline
apocalyptic that focuses on the body and its significance for epistemology, anthropology, Christology, and ecclesiology. As I have demonstrated
through a brief investigation of 1 Corinthians 11:17–34 and 12:12–27, the
body is vital to Paul's epistemological language and thus requires attention
for a full engagement with Paul.

My hope in writing this essay is to further conversation in apocalyptic Pauline interpretation around one of its major lacunae: the significance

91. In using the language of abiding, I have in mind Paul's comments on love in 1
Cor 13, specifically vv. 7 and 13, with the related words for "endure" (*hupomenei*) and
"remain" (*menei*). I am also thinking of Paul's statement in 1 Cor 6:13: "And the body
is not for fornication *but for the Lord, and the Lord for the body*" (my emphasis).

of the body in God's redemptive action in Christ. By emphasizing the relationship between epistemological language and bodies in Paul, I hope that more attention may be given to how Pauline interpretation can speak to bodily differences, like sex, gender, race, sexuality, culture, age, ability, and others, and to the relationship between such differences and power dynamics in contemporary Christian communities. Finally, I hope that apocalyptic Pauline interpretation may continue to engage with feminist theory and discover additional ways in which feminism can contribute positively to apocalyptic thought.

12

In Christ, There Is No Opposition

Cross, Resurrection, and Baptism in the Apocalyptic Paul[1]

J. David Belcher

According to the old baptismal hymn in Colossians 1:13, to forgive means to be rescued from the power of darkness and transferred into the kingdom of his beloved Son. What is really perilous is to live and die as though the kingdom of Jesus Christ began only in heaven, as though we did not already belong to his kingdom today and in the body. Mussels close up when one takes hold of them. When the Nazarene came to us, heaven opened over us, and it remains open over us because, as at Pentecost, God's Spirit continually allows us to hear that the Father says "Yes" to his children, to me and to all he created and calls to himself. There is only one life-threatening sin, that is, to refuse to be totally open to the One who speaks his "Yes" to us and allows us as members and witnesses of his kingdom on earth to become something to the praise of his glory.

—ERNST KÄSEMANN[2]

---

1. I was in the middle of revising a draft of this paper during the final weeks of the season of Lent as I also began preparations on a sermon I was to preach on Good Friday. The difficult, prayerful work of shaping that sermon—not only for Good Friday, but in the middle of the Great Triduum, the concluding "threefold day" of Holy Week—has had a profound impact on the shape of this paper as well.

2. Käsemann, *Being a Disciple*, 224.

I

IN THE OPENING LINE of his article for the *Festschriften* presented to Ernst Käsemann on his seventieth birthday, Leander Keck remarks that "Paul was, and remains, a disturber of the peace."[3] No doubt, as Keck signals in the closing line of the same article, this is something he learned especially from Käsemann.[4] In fact, one might argue that a central—perhaps *the* central—aim of Käsemann's work on Paul is to uncover the offense (*skandalon*) of Paul's gospel, specifically the foolish Word of the cross (*logos ... tou staurou*; 1 Cor 1:18).

This was also, of course, the stated goal of Käsemann's teacher, Rudolf Bultmann, who claimed in his debate with Karl Jaspers that the entire purpose of demythologization is "to make the stumbling block [*skándalon*] real."[5] Yet, Käsemann understood his own recovery of Pauline polemics to be at odds with Bultmann's anthropological proposal. Specifically, Käsemann argued that Paul's polemical theology of the cross is inseparable from his further conviction of the primacy of "apocalyptic" in the proclamation of the Word.[6] Thus, where Bultmann linked the proclamation of the Word to the *present* eschatological event of the human decision of faith, Käsemann insisted that the Word always encounters us in the earthly, this-worldly event of the cross that points to its *future* eschatological fulfillment. Significantly, then, Käsemann did not reject Bultmann's existentialism,[7] but corrected his reduction of eschatology to a non-apocalyptic eternal now, qualifying both Bultmann's individualist

3. Keck, "Justification," 199.

4. The last lines of the article read: "We have deliberately restricted ourselves to the nexus of the justification of the ungodly and ethics in order to show that for Paul ethics is not a matter of paraenesis for the justified but rather the justification of the ungodly transforms the ethical situation of the doer with respect to the obligatory good and its ground, and with respect to the doer himself and his fellows. That this transformation of the ethical situation occurs precisely in this context is the offense of the gospel; here the point at which Paul's ethics becomes significant is identified. That this was revolutionary was perceived already by Paul; that it remains so is understood by Ernst Käsemann" (ibid., 209).

5. Bultmann, "Case for Demythologization," 71.

6. The primary texts where Käsemann lays out his theology of the cross, and with which we will deal below, are: Käsemann, "Primitive Christian Apocalyptic"; "Saving Significance"; "For and Against."

7. Consider, for instance, Käsemann's claim that Paul's "self-understanding is apocalyptic" or his statement that "Apocalyptic, finally, is the disquieting question which not only moves the apostle but apparently faces every Christian, a question bound up with his task and his existence: who owns the earth?" ("Saving Significance," 24–25).

understanding of "existence" and his "presentative" eschatology with an apocalyptic theology of the cross.[8]

The following paper investigates this fundamental link between apocalyptic and the critical, polemical theology of the cross, focusing especially on the way this trope appears and is modified in Käsemann and his followers, particularly J. Louis Martyn.[9] My claim is that the polemical deployment of the theology of the cross as the ethical norm for Christian discipleship works at cross-purposes with its intention. By actively dividing the cross from Christ's resurrection within the life of the church, these thinkers transform the cross into a transcendental ideal meant to regulate both theological discourse and the ecclesiastical arrogance of the church, effectively separating the life of discipleship from participation in the resurrected life of Jesus. While Käsemann utilized this separation in combat with the Enthusiasts,[10] it ironically prevents the cross from having any concrete historical significance, contrary to Käsemann's own purposes. The solution to this problem, I propose, is a thoroughly sacramental understanding of baptism, which can maintain both the positive link between Christ's cross and his resurrected life for the church's life and the gospel's this-worldliness. Because the polemical theology of the cross is internal to the account of apocalyptic, the future of apocalyptic theology itself requires a coherent account of apocalyptic detached from the polemic.

8. Jürgen Moltmann uses the phrase "presentative eschatology" as a descriptor for Bultmann's project. See Moltmann, *Theology of Hope*, 160–61.

9. I have included sections on both Paul W. Meyer and Charles B. Cousar below for two reasons. First, because both Meyer and Cousar attempt to modify Käsemann's polemic and yet accept the central tenet of the polemic itself—namely, that the cross is a critical norm for discerning the authenticity of Christian witness—they help us to see the impossibility of working *from within* the polemic to modify it. As we will see below, it is the oppositional nature of the polemic's central tenet that creates all the difficulties. Secondly, Martyn is very much indebted to both Meyer and Cousar and attempts to weld their own modifications of Käsemann onto his rereading of apocalyptic in Paul. Because Martyn retains Käsemann's oppositional approach to apocalyptic, however, he ends up repeating and in some sense amplifying the problem bequeathed by Käsemann.

10. "In Romans 6, Paul has even separated present participation in the Cross from future participation in the Resurrection; he discerns the reality of the new life solely in the *nova oboedientia*" (Käsemann, "Primitive Christian Apocalyptic," 125).

Ernst Käsemann

According to Ernst Käsemann, Paul's theology of the cross is polemical in nature. What is more, it *must* be polemical, otherwise it "loses its original meaning."[11] A non-polemical theology of the cross always runs counter to the Reformation centrality of the cross, specifically Luther's claim that "the cross alone is our theology."[12] For Käsemann, the theology of the cross stands firmly in this Reformation tradition, opposing any theology that diminishes the cross *in any way*.[13] The polemical nature of the theology of the cross thus gives it a sharp either/or character:

> The advocates of a theology of the resurrection and of the facts of redemption do not generally wish to set aside the theology of the cross; they want to give it a place in a wider context. But this is to overlook the fact that we are thereby levelling down the theology of the cross and giving it a merely relative importance; and this means, primarily speaking, denying it altogether, if we take account of its original intention. For we cannot say *crux nostra theologia* unless we mean that this is the central and in a sense the only theme of Christian theology. The statement is rhetorical if the cross is only one, or even the most important, link in a chain. Whether we like it or not, the cross will then be overshadowed by the resurrection and the facts of redemption.[14]

---

11. Käsemann, "Saving Significance," 35. By "original meaning" Käsemann refers to Paul's meaning as recovered *through* the Reformers, particularly Luther: "It must be asserted with the greatest possible emphasis that both historically and theologically Paul has to be understood in the light of the Reformation's insight. Any other perspective at most covers part of his thinking; it does not grasp the heart of it" (ibid., 32).

12. "*CRUX sola est nostra Theologia.*" Luther, *Op. in Ps.*, Ps 5:11, in D. *Martin Luthers Werke* 5:176.32–33 (hereafter *WA* with volume, page, lines). All translations are mine unless otherwise noted. Cf. also the relationship Luther posits between the cross and glory: "But we ought to glory in the Cross of our Lord [*Nos autem oportet gloriari in Cruce domini nostri*]" (*WA* 5:178.32).

13. "Anyone who limits the significance of the cross for Christianity and the world obscures God's truth and the offence that attaches to grace. He inevitably falls into the realm of superstition, even if he is supporting a theology of resurrection" (Käsemann, "For and Against," 74).

14. Käsemann, "Saving Significance," 48. On "facts of redemption," see Cousar, *Theology of the Cross*, 14. Käsemann clearly does not understand "polemics" to be merely "rhetorical"! The polemical nature of the theology of the cross for Käsemann requires that it be deployed unreservedly and without limit.

And if the polemical theology of the cross is "the central and . . . only theme" of theology, then a theology of the resurrection can be nothing more than a *theologia gloriae*.[15]

The main example of such a theology of the resurrection/glory is represented by those he dubs "Enthusiasts" (*Schwärmerei*)—who are clearly not only Paul's Corinthian opponents, but also those contemporaries who relinquish the polemical nature of the theology of the cross. Enthusiasts espouse a "sacramental realism" that presumes "complete redemption" has already occurred, "in that by baptism a heavenly spiritual body has been conferred and the earthly body has been degraded to an insubstantial, transitory veil." Paul, however, according to Käsemann, refuses to grant any ground to such a realized eschatology, and, while he "associates sharing in the Cross with sharing in the Resurrection," he does so only by building in a "remarkable caveat in the shape of an eschatological reservation."[16] Baptism thus "equips for" participation in the resurrection, but because such participation is entirely futural, baptism "does not itself convey this gift." Baptism grants a share in "new life," but this life is only that of the *nova oboedientia*, which is specifically *not* Christ's resurrection life, but a life of voluntary, obedient movement into the suffering of the cross.[17] In this sense, "for the time being," Christ's resurrection is "the great exception, in which we can participate by hope alone."[18] While the cross and resurrection remain indivisibly united *for Christ*, creatures experience Christ's resurrection only by sharing in his cross.[19]

While few if any of Käsemann's contemporaries actually claimed that a renewed "theology of the resurrection" signified that the baptized are walking around even now in resurrected, spiritual bodies, Käsemann's polemic is nonetheless directed against Enthusiasts of his own time.[20]

15. "A theology of resurrection that does not become a theology of the cross is bound to lead, as the Corinthian example shows, to wrong-headed enthusiasm, and therefore to another form of the theology of glory against which the Reformation fought" (Käsemann, "For and Against," 82).

16. Käsemann, "Primitive Christian Apocalyptic," 126. "Sacramental realism" here is clearly a reference to Albert Schweitzer and his mechanical "*ex opere operato*" view of sacramental dispensation.

17. Ibid., 132.

18. Ibid., 134.

19. "As in 2 Cor 13:4 the power of the resurrection which is in fact at work in them asserts itself initially by setting them contrariwise (*sub contrario*) under the shadow of the cross and makes this in a special way the mark of the new life" (Käsemann, *Commentary on Romans*, 166).

20. Thanks to Joel Marcus for conversations on some of these questions.

Specifically, he is attacking those in the *Evangelische Kirche* who hold to "a theology of the resurrection which takes precedence over, and is isolated from, a theology of the cross," since the latter inevitably leads "to a Christian variation of a religious philosophy in which the imitation of Jesus and the lordship of Christ lose all concrete meaning."[21] The real target of Käsemann's polemical theology of the cross, then, is the otherworldliness of the enthusiastic rejection of the cross: "A Christianity which is supremely conscious of participation in the glory of its Lord flees from the lowliness in which it is set on earth and in which alone it can be of benefit to the exalted one."[22] The theology of the cross grounds creatures firmly on earth, cutting off the "bourgeois transcendence" of a realized eschatology that is really only concerned with maintaining the *status quo*.[23]

Thus, for Käsemann, the polemical purpose of the theology of the cross is to root creatures deep into the soil of this world under the sovereignty of Jesus Christ. This is why he refuses to allow the reduction of the cross to a "historical affair," as with the Enthusiasts, because this inevitably makes the cross just one "link in a chain," where resurrection succeeds and surpasses the cross.[24] The cross cannot be "simply one chapter in a book of resurrection dogmatics." On the contrary, the resurrection is "one aspect of the message of the cross."[25] In consequence, the theology of the cross shifts the entire register of baptism from present glorification and otherworldly abstraction to solidarity with Christ in his cross here on earth: "As Luther rightly says, standing on God's way is moving back and forth; it

21. Käsemann, "Saving Significance," 57.

22. Käsemann, *Romans*, 339.

23. Käsemann, "For and Against," 73, 75. And cf. Käsemann, *Romans*, 232: "Grace relates us more deeply to the earthly because it thrusts the community as a whole and each of its members beneath the cross where extreme assault and victory coincide. In opposition to the enthusiasts Paul had to go back to Jewish apocalyptic to present it thus. . . . The Gentile-Christian enthusiasm of a radically realized eschatology has finally gained the upper hand in church orthodoxy too, and in so doing has obscured the theology of the cross." For a helpful summary of Käsemann's understanding of the earthly, and the social conditions driving his polemic here, see Käsemann, *Being a Disciple*, 237.

24. Cf. Käsemann's rejection of Cullmann's (and by proxy Stendahl's) *Heilsgeschichtlich* theology for making the justification of the ungodly only one causal event in a chain of events rather than the center of salvation history; "Justification and Salvation."

25. Käsemann, "For and Against," 68, reiterating the famous claim in his earlier essay "Saving Significance," where he said, "Here the theology of the resurrection is a chapter in the theology of the cross, not the excelling of it. Since Paul all theological controversy has radiated ultimately from one central point and can hence only be decided at that point: *crux sola nostra theologia*" (59).

is always beginning afresh. Whereas enthusiasts proclaim a metaphysical change of nature, Paul is concerned about the lordship of Christ which must be confirmed and passed on by every Christian and which stands in sharp opposition to the powers that rule the world."[26] This is why the cross cannot simply be a historical event of the past for Käsemann, since the cross "remains set up on earth as a sign of divine truth and of the offence that it causes to the world," and in this way always serves as "faith's foundation and archetype" [*Grund und Urbild . . . des Glaubens*]."[27] The cross thus becomes elevated to a critical ideal, a transcendental *Urbild*, so that the theology of the cross equally becomes a polemical method for regulating all theological discourse, even that of the resurrection.[28]

26. Käsemann, *Romans*, 363. This "beginning afresh" is for Luther always associated with baptism. See n. 75 and n. 65 below. Luther recounts false opinions of his day regarding the relationship between baptism and penance, all of which, he says, are rooted in a "dangerous saying" (*verbum illud periculosum*) of St. Jerome, "either badly put or badly understood," which said, "Penance [*poenitentia*] is called the second plank after shipwreck [*secundam post naufragium tabulam*]," as though, Luther comments, "baptism were not penance" (*quasi baptismus non sit poenitentia*). The medieval tradition of Luther's day understood postbaptismal sins to be a betrayal and destruction of baptism, requiring the additional act of penance to return to a state of grace: "Therefore, when one has fallen into sin, she despairs of the first plank, or the ship, as if it was lost, and begins only to lean on and put her trust in [*niti et fidere*] the second plank, that is, penance." On the contrary, Luther claimed that we never get beyond our baptism: "Wherefore, while we rise up again [*resurgimus*] from our sins, or repent, we are doing nothing other than [rising up again] to the power and faith of baptism, from which we departed, and turning back to the promise we were then given [*revertimur et ad promissionem tunc factam redimus*], which we deserted through our sinning. For the truth of the promise once made always endures, extending its arms to receive us back upon our return." Martin Luther, *De capt. Bab.*, in *WA* 6:527.10–17; 528.13–17.

27. Käsemann, "For and Against," 74, 73. I have modified the English based on the German in Käsemann, "Für und wider eine Theologie der Auferstehung," 99. It is significant to note here that the cross functions for Käsemann in much the same way that Jesus does in Schleiermacher's system, as an "archetype" (*Urbild*), which thus always has a critical, transcendental character. In this way, the cross is a check and balance, a regulative ideal for the Christian life. The Christian life is thus a "reflection" of rather than an "imitation" of Jesus, since Jesus is "exemplar, not example" (this is equally reflected in the difference in prefixes in the German, between *Urbild* and *Vorbild*). See Davis, "Apocalyptic, Typology, and Metaphysics," 8–9, and Hans Frei's description of Schleiermacher in "David Friedrich Strauss," 247.

28. Here we can recall that it was Bultmann who made the authentication of the *kerygma* the central element of his theological project, a point on which Käsemann follows his teacher.

Paul W. Meyer

Paul W. Meyer's important article "The This-Worldliness of the New Testament" follows up on Käsemann's influential recuperation of the theology of the cross, specifically taking up his emphasis on the this-worldliness of the message of the cross.[29] However, while Käsemann refused to reduce the cross to "a historical affair," Meyer claims that it is precisely the New Testament's assertion of the irreducible historical event of Jesus' public crucifixion that is the answer to the primary obstacle to a coherent theological interpretation of the New Testament, namely, "otherworldliness."[30] In one sense, Meyer's focus on the historical event of the cross lays the groundwork for Martyn's later reconception of apocalyptic in terms of the event of the cross.

The force of his argument derives from his engagement with Martin Buber's claim that Jesus could not possibly have been the Messiah because we continue to live in an unredeemed world. According to Meyer, Buber's point is that the Christian confession of Jesus as the Christ "links the Messiah with redemption, and both of these to the transformation of the world into another, or its supplanting by a new order," thereby construing this link in "unambiguously otherworldly terms." This is simply the nature of Jewish eschatology in which Buber was steeped, says Meyer, where redemption and the coming of the Messiah are inseparable from the end of history. Buber's challenge is thus helpful in that he calls Christianity to take seriously the present condition of the world.[31] What Buber fails to account for, however, is the way in which, in the New Testament, Jewish

29. Meyer, "This-Worldliness."

30. The problem Meyer seems to be isolating is clearly related to the diminishment of the historical significance of Jesus' crucifixion, as in Bultmann, who denied any significance to the historical events as such, grounding the "rise of faith" instead in the proclamation of the "inseparable unity" of cross and resurrection as *saving*. The proclamation of the *kerygma* is thus the condition for the emergence of faith, the condition of possibility for grasping the existential significance of Christ's cross. This always takes place in a decision of faith and thus the historical event of the cross has little significance in and of itself (the historical event could not be reconstructed at any rate such that it could serve as a basis for faith). What is significant for Bultmann is not the historical events themselves, but the "eschatological event" by which a human person makes a decision of faith, *within history*, and so appropriates the saving significance of those events for present existence. See Bultmann, "New Testament and Mythology," esp. 32ff.

31. Those who failed to heed Buber's challenge were burying their heads in the sand, refusing to recognize the way that an "otherworldly" gospel is contradicted by "their experience of life." See Meyer, "This-Worldliness," 8ff.

eschatology itself "passed through a crucible fired by a public act not only available but also inevasible to every onlooker and every inquirer—the crucifixion of Jesus of Nazareth." Thus, the fundamental claim of the New Testament is that the Messiah "*has* come in an *unredeemed* world," and consequently eschatology "has irreversibly become 'this-worldly.'"

While he thus breaks from Käsemann and Bultmann by rooting the this-worldly character of the New Testament in the "sheer historical given-ness of the crucifixion as a public event," like Käsemann, Meyer believes that the this-worldliness of the cross never allows us to set it aside as we move beyond it to the glory of the resurrection.[32] He claims, in fact, that in order to understand the significance of the resurrection in its proximity to the cross for the early Christians, we must "think about the crucifixion of Jesus *as if* there had been no resurrection."[33] As with Käsemann, Meyer's point here is anti-enthusiastic in that it specifically targets the otherworldly elements of enthusiasm. For, just like Käsemann, Meyer sees in the cross, precisely *in* its "sheer historical givenness," a critical norm by which to judge the authenticity of Christian proclamation.[34] In fact, it is the *resurrection* that elevates the cross to be "the paradigm, the clue, the source of the disclosing impact that is sedimented in various ways within our New Testament." In this way, the resurrection is for Meyer, as for Käsemann, that which "makes the crucifixion (or, more exactly, the One who was crucified) normative for Christian faith."[35] The crucified Christ

32. Ibid., 14. I believe that Meyer is actually criticizing the latent Bultmannian elements in Käsemann, specifically the way in which a theology of the cross is raised to a hermeneutical *method*, while he otherwise completely agrees with Käsemann's exegetical and theological conclusions.

33. Ibid., 12, emphasis original. Meyer, clearly following Käsemann's critique of Walter Künneth, says, "Theological reflection and personal piety tend to leap ahead to seize upon the resurrection as the Christian answer to the historical givenness of the crucifixion and to its massive and devastating impact" (ibid.). See Künneth, *Resurrection*, which famously claimed that the cross and resurrection stand together "in the relation of riddle and interpretation," where the "very raising of the theological question is conditioned by the answer of the resurrection" (151).

34. Cf. Meyer, "Faith and History Revisited," 25: "Of course the resurrection is appealed to by all branches of New Testament theology as the authorizing warrant for Christian confession and preaching. But what if one were to understand the resurrection as God's elevation of that public and indisputable historical reality of the cross to the status of the critical norm by which the authenticity of the distinctive Christian message to the world is to be established? Not as the wiping out of the crucifixion but as its confirmation and finalization?"

35. Meyer, "This-Worldliness," 17; and, "In short, the crucial issue in our understanding of the resurrection is what it means in relation to the one whom all the world knows to have been crucified" (13).

is, once again, just as for Käsemann, the archetype, the shape, pattern, and ideal for the Christian life.

Charles B. Cousar

Cousar's incisive investigation of the death of Jesus in the letters of Paul is in many ways a lengthy engagement with Käsemann's theology of the cross, and he follows both Käsemann's and Meyer's emphasis on the this-worldly character of Paul's theology. However, Cousar attempts to correct the one-sided polemic in Käsemann. For Cousar, Käsemann hamstrings the theology of the cross by making it *entirely* polemical, which prevents him from seeing the wider use of the theology of the cross in all its variety in Paul's letters. This does not mean there is no room for the polemic—in fact, he thinks there is. Especially in "the West" and in North America in particular, Cousar thinks that we tend to blunt the edge of the theology of the cross, replacing it instead with political and economic triumphalism rooted in a certain theology of the resurrection. In such a context, the polemical use of the theology of the cross is still absolutely necessary. However, he also finds a positive emphasis on the resurrection in Paul that Käsemann's polemics tend to obscure. "[O]ne has to recognize," Cousar remarks, "that it is not the resurrection of Christ itself that feeds triumphalism, but a misguided theology of the resurrection." Thus, Cousar brings a much-needed balance to Käsemann's polemical emphasis on the theology of the cross, effectively decentering it while continuing to lay claim to its full force as a polemical tool.[36]

What is worth noting, however, is the way that Cousar interprets the resurrection in Paul as a "promise (*only* a promise, but a *real* promise) of the future." While Cousar is directing the reader to the "positive aspect" the resurrection plays for baptism and the Christian life in Paul's letters beyond Käsemann's polemical emphasis on the "eschatological reservation," he recovers Käsemann's own positive view of the resurrection by casting it in terms of the promise of a future reality—one that is real now *as* promise.[37] Echoing Käsemann's own anti-enthusiastic sentiments, Cousar

36. By "decentering" the theology of the cross, I am referring to Meyer's claim that the theology of the cross cannot and must not be the center of the New Testament message, though it can help illuminate its actual center, namely, the historical event of the cross. See Meyer, "This-Worldliness," 16–17. Cousar follows Meyer on this point; *Theology of the Cross*, 185 n. 14.

37. Cf. Jürgen Moltmann's appropriation of Käsemann's conclusion that baptism is participation in Christ's cross and not his resurrection life in the formulation of his

notes, "Baptism, however, is not a gateway into a heavenly existence, where one communes immediately with the exalted Christ, removed from the trials and anguish of earthly life." Instead, Christ's resurrection is, as in Käsemann's exegesis of 1 Corinthians 15, the firstfruits of the "resurrection of the dead" and not simply an isolated event of the resuscitation of a dead person, such that it functions for the Christian life now only as promise and hope for future reality. Like Moltmann, however, Cousar still goes further than Käsemann when he adds, "The phrase 'newness of life' itself ([Rom] 6:4) contains an eschatological quality, albeit proleptically, denoting the extraordinary vitality of union with Christ. The future so impinges on the present as to give it a distinctive buoyancy . . . union with Christ leads to the service of righteousness, sanctification, and its end, eternal life."[38]

Therefore, Cousar follows Käsemann very closely and refuses to blunt the edge of the theology of the cross, especially in engagement with his North American context, while he also submits Käsemann's polemics to a more balanced modification grounded in the positive reality of the resurrection within Paul's letters. For Cousar, instead of forcing a sharp alternative between *either* a theology of the cross *or* a theology of the resurrection—though Cousar himself certainly gives more ground to the former than the latter[39]—one must approach the cross and resurrection by recognizing "in the Pauline letters repeated elements of a narrative Christology."[40] As he notes, "The crucifixion is repeatedly appealed to as the foundation and norm of the Christian life," and yet the "whole story" is assumed whenever one element is mentioned, and thus the positive reality of the resurrection equally applies to the Christian life.[41]

---

own "theology of hope." Like Käsemann, Moltmann's theology of hope is explicitly framed in terms of a future reality that is *real* now only in the mode of promise. Moltmann, however, gives a much more positive reality to hope and promise than does Käsemann, where our present "hope" is grounded in the transformation of the cosmos in Christ's resurrection. The latter is itself the reality that undergirds and continues to transform our own present embodied existence within the unfolding new creation in this cosmos. See Moltmann, *Theology of Hope*, 155–65, and esp. 160, where he recasts Käsemann's "theology of the cross" as an "*eschatologia crucis.*"

38. Cousar, *Theology of the Cross*, 103.

39. As Cousar says, Paul's "accent falls" much more on the statement that "the one who is risen is the crucified one" than the reverse, that "the crucified has been raised" (ibid., 106–7).

40. Here Cousar appeals directly to Richard B. Hays' dissertation study on the narrative substructure of the *pistis Christou* trope in Galatians. See Hays, *Faith of Jesus Christ.*

41. Cousar, *Theology of the Cross*, 107.

Like Meyer and Käsemann before him, however, we still see in Cousar the claim that the cross serves as a critical norm for discerning the authenticity of Christian proclamation and witness. As he says, "Paul constantly reminds his readers that the risen Christ is none other than the crucified one, whose wounds cannot be removed by exegetical surgery. The crucifixion of Jesus is not only a past, datable, verifiable fact in the church's memory, but also an ever-present reality to guide and determine the church's life."[42] According to Cousar, especially within a Western context where the theology of the cross has been set aside for the triumphalism of a theology of the resurrection, the cross serves as a constant, critical rupture of all claims of security and possession of the gospel.[43]

J. Louis Martyn

In many ways, J. Louis Martyn both continues this line and brings it to its proper fulfillment. While he continues the polemical emphasis on the *theologia crucis* in Paul, he does so by way of a creative redeployment of "apocalyptic" focused completely on Christ's rectifying death on the cross. According to Martyn's forceful rereading of Paul, the "whole of the apocalyptic theater takes its bearings from the cross," since "the crucifixion of Jesus Christ *is itself* the apocalypse, after which nothing can be the same."[44] Thus, building on Meyer's "this-worldly" thesis, the cross for Martyn is the moment on which Paul's entire narrative Christology hangs.[45] He likens the cross-event to a volcanic explosion that has blown apart *this* cosmos

42. Ibid., 4.

43. "[T]he message of the cross functions as the norm and point of critique of the church's quest for identity" (ibid., 183, emphasis original); and "The church whose theology is shaped by the message of the cross must itself take on a cruciformed life if its theology is to carry credibility" (186).

44. Martyn, "Paul to Flannery O'Connor," 285, emphasis added.

45. See Cousar, *Theology of the Cross*, 107, on Paul's "narrative Christology" as a correction to Käsemann's one-sided polemic; and see Martyn, *Galatians*, 166 and 166 n. 209. Martyn, "Twice-Invaded World," at 127 and n. 29, cites Käsemann's famous dictum that, "The theology of the resurrection is a chapter in the theology of the cross, not the excelling of it." In the footnote to the passage, however, Martyn urges the reader to see the "explication, enrichment, and correction of Käsemann in Cousar, *Theology of the Cross*." Thus, Martyn seeks to draw on the balance Cousar has brought to Käsemann's relentless polemic. What we have seen above, though, is that Cousar is correcting Käsemann on *exactly* this point! The upshot is that, at any moment, any *positive* stance one takes while deploying polemic is also threatened by its perpetual movement of negation.

enslaved to Sin and has "scattered the pieces into new and confusing patterns."[46] As such, the cross is nothing short of *the new*. So strong an association does Martyn make between the dawning of the new creation and the death of the cosmos in Christ's cross that not even Christ's resurrection can "divert [Paul's] glance from the cross."[47]

Naturally, this association of the dawning of the new creation in the cross also affects Martyn's treatment of the Christian life. As he explains, "[A]lthough for Paul the cross and the resurrection constitute an indivisible whole, the pattern of the church's daily life is set far more by the cross than by the resurrection."[48] The reason for Paul's cruciform emphasis, says Martyn, is that the eschatological life of the new creation community is life in the Spirit, who is "specifically the Spirit of the crucified Christ," and "permanently bound up with the real and earthly event of Christ's crucifixion." Those incorporated into Christ by the Spirit in baptism will likewise live entirely by that same cruciform event. Even the "marks of the resurrection are hidden and revealed in the cross of the disciple's daily death, and *only* there."[49] While it is certainly true that Martyn presupposes the reality of the resurrection,[50] he nonetheless polemically emphasizes the

46. Martyn, "Apocalyptic Gospel," 256. Here we might make a comparison with Carl E. Braaten's early article, "Significance of Apocalypticism." There he claims that, in apocalyptic, "the world becomes historical through the process of dualization . . . the mediation of mutually antagonistic forces. A Christian interpretation of history is impossible without the dualistic element in apocalyptic, namely, the dialectical differentiation of all reality into this present evil age and the new world of promise to come. The new world that is coming is mediated through a negation of the world. In more abstract terms, negativity is the *movens agens* of the creative process; in symbolic terms, the cross is the symbol of death as the way of salvation, and the resurrection is a symbol that the negation of life can be the medium of the transcendent future" (491).

47. Martyn, "Apocalyptic Gospel," 259.

48. Martyn, "Paul to Flannery O'Connor," 296 n. 23.

49. Martyn, "Epistemology," 110, 109, emphasis original. Cf. Käsemann, *Romans*, 219: "The Spirit points us back to the cross of Christ as the place of salvation. He [*sic*] thus continually actualizes justification, sets us unceasingly in the sphere of power of the Crucified, and is . . . the earthly presence of the exalted Lord. If the motif of union is to be used at all, it must be precisely understood as incorporation into the lordship of the Crucified."

50. Consider, e.g., Martyn's statement that "There is, to be sure, a fundamental reversal on Easter morning" ("Twice-Invaded World," 127), and note that Paul and the Teachers in Galatians both presuppose the reality of Christ's resurrection, which is not under dispute (Martyn, *Galatians*, 85).

cruciform pattern of the daily life of the church. Resurrection life in the church can be nothing more than the cross-shaped pattern of that life.[51]

As did Käsemann, Martyn rejects a certain theology of the resurrection that "replaces" or "reverses" the cross. Here Martyn stresses that the problem with Paul's opponents in 1 Corinthians, those "Enthusiasts" who lay claim to present resurrection life in the Spirit, is not simply with the way they cut off eschatological expectation, but with their "inflexible determination to live somewhere other than in the cross."[52] Building upon Meyer's engagement with Buber, Martyn also says that Paul's claim that the apocalypse takes place on Christ's cross serves as the only real response to Buber's challenge that we live in an unredeemed world. Though the world all around the Enthusiasts remains "unchanged," they continue to bury their heads in the sand, believing they have been granted the fullness of eschatological blessings. Thus, they fail to recognize the epistemological crisis brought about by the cross. It is only possible to proclaim good news in the midst of the numerous crosses that continue to populate this unredeemed world, Martyn claims, if one first recognizes that, "while [the cross] is in one sense followed by the resurrection, it is not replaced by the resurrection." In other words, *because the cross alone shows us the real world*, Christ's cross only retains its significance in this world if it ruptures all claims to participation in Christ's resurrection life in the present.[53] The

51. Cf. Martyn, "Twice-Invaded World," 127–28: "Christ's resurrection does not leave the cross behind, making the crucifixion merely a way station on the journey to glory. 'The theology of the resurrection is a chapter in the theology of the cross, not the excelling of it.' Seen through resurrection lenses, the cross itself remains the event of God's weak power, the event in which power is, in fact, transfigured and thus fundamentally redefined [. . .] Born in the resurrection that consistently refers to and interprets the crucifixion, born precisely in the midst of God's weak power enacted daily in God's strange war of liberation, God's new creation is nothing other than the new community, the cross-bearing church in the here and now."

52. Martyn, "Epistemology," 102. Martyn follows Käsemann's identification of Paul's opponents in 1 Corinthians as "Enthusiasts." The Enthusiasts are those members of the Corinthian community who have been misled by the pseudo-apostles into thinking that they possess the fullness of the Spirit and thus can know their world completely by the Spirit (*kata pneuma*). Thus, the Enthusiasts believe they are the recipients of "ultimate eschatological blessings in the midst of a world that appears to be unchanged" (Martyn, "Epistemology," 102).

53. I am quite certain Martyn would retort that the second clause in this sentence need not follow from the first, and also that it is contrary to his intentions to separate Christ's resurrection life in the present from the reality-disclosing cross. I think this is indeed true of much of what Martyn says, for instance, about the daily life of the church in the Spirit, or about the unity of the baptized with Christ. My point here is that the polemical insistence on linking apocalyptic with the cross *alone* ends

cross serves quite literally as a "reality check" in this unredeemed world. The only possible "theology of the resurrection," then, is one that permanently roots the Christian life in the cross, as Martyn himself concludes, again following Meyer: "God's resurrection of Jesus is the event that takes us back to the cross, making and keeping Christian faith and life inevasibly this-worldly."[54]

Two distinct features of Martyn's apocalyptic theology of the cross are immediately apparent. First, by directing the focus of Pauline theology on the cross and *away from* the resurrection, Martyn places his own interpretation of Pauline apocalyptic within the Käsemannian line emphasizing the polemical nature of Paul's *theologia crucis*. Second, notwithstanding this continuity with Käsemann, however, he also makes an important modification of the latter by associating apocalypse *not* with the future, imminent end, but with the explosive cross of Jesus Christ. It is precisely this latter move that makes Martyn's a forceful *re*reading of apocalyptic in Paul's letters.

When Martyn brings these two elements together, we are left with an account of *God's own act* to rectify the cosmos in Christ's cross that is itself "polemical":

> *Paul's* rectification polemic against the Teachers in [Gal.] 2:16 is nothing other than a reflection of *God's* rectifying polemic against his [*sic*] enemies. . . . It is thus *God's* polemical act in Christ that causes Paul's doctrine of rectification to be polemical, and that means that one cannot minimize the latter without doing the same to the former. . . . At root, [Paul] was sure that his call to be an apostolic soldier was a reflection of God's identity as *the* soldier, intent on making things right. It is God's declaration of war against all the forces enslaving the human race that formed the foundation of Paul's militant doctrine of rectification.[55]

---

up compromising even these most positive claims, as we will see in the concluding section.

54. Martyn, "Personal Word," xxii. This is from Martyn's introduction to a collection of essays by Paul Meyer that serves as a kind of brief intellectual biography framed in terms of his personal interaction with Meyer over the years. While he is summarizing Meyer's essay "This-Worldliness" here, I believe my exposition of Martyn's casting of the relationship between cross and resurrection shows this to be a claim entirely consistent with his own.

55. Martyn, "God's Way," 155–56.

Not only, then, does Martyn follow Käsemann's claim that the *theologia crucis* must be polemical, but he provides the basis for *justifying* the perpetual deployment of the polemic by transposing Paul's apocalyptic "militant doctrine of rectification" back onto God's act. While I do not believe that such a move can be sustained,[56] it shows an important qualification of Käsemann's polemic that has proved to be very influential for an apocalyptic theology of Paul. Once passed through the crucible of Martyn's apocalyptic rereading of Paul, all theological discourse falls under the shadow of the interrogatory mark of the cross. Thus, Martyn is still able to maintain that the cross stands in this world as a critical norm, holding all other discourses in check, only now by the rupturing, volcanic explosion of God's own act that has scattered the former pieces of theological knowledge into new and confusing patterns.

II

We must take note of two features of this apocalyptic polemic of the theology of the cross. First, the overwhelming centrality of the cross *always* functions to hold a certain theology of the resurrection in check. Whether priority is given to the decision of faith at the proclamation of the Word of the cross (Käsemann), or to the sheer historicity of Jesus' public crucifixion (Meyer, Cousar), or to the cross's apocalyptic significance as God's own act rupturing the cosmos (Martyn), the cross is set up as a regulative ideal that is meant to guard the this-worldliness of Christian discipleship from otherwordly pretentions to resurrection life in the present, unredeemed world. Second, a crucial element of Käsemann's polemic is its focus on the sacrament of baptism, both in his rejection of the Enthusiasts' "sacramental realism" and in his own constant appeal to baptism as a participation in Christ's death that roots believers at the foot of the cross in this world, and thus under Christ's sovereignty until he comes again. In this way, while baptism does not feature prominently in all of the above figures as it does for Käsemann, the relationship between baptism and the church's ongoing cruciform life is indeed central to the apocalyptic polemical theology of the cross. These make up the basic elements of the polemical theology of

---

56. Either in the sense that God's own act could be called "polemical," a term referring specifically to disputation, discourse, and rhetoric, or in the sense that *Paul's* polemic can be explained by a form of causal regress to God's polemic—and this latter point is something that I learned from Martyn himself! See esp. Part 1 of Martyn, *Theological Issues*.

the cross, then. Essentially, the historical event of the cross is a tool for cutting down otherworldly and moralistic theological discourses, while baptism is a tool for cutting down the triumphalism of ecclesiastical arrogance and presumption.

As we have seen above, the central purpose of the polemical use of the theology of the cross is to prune and cut back otherworldly abstractions, "theological" and "moral" alike, in order to ground all Christian ethics in the sign of the cross in this world. The consequence of this essentially prophylactic function of the polemic, though, is the insertion of a dividing line between Christ's cross and his resurrection for the life of the church.[57] While Käsemann unabashedly claims that Paul's doctrine of baptism in Romans 6 has "separated present participation in the Cross from future participation in the Resurrection," he does not consider what affect divorcing these inextricably united realities will have on his discourse. Specifically, proponents of the polemic do not recognize the way that this division cuts off a positive account, not only of the reality of Christ's resurrection, but of redemption itself for the life of the church in this world, because it perpetually exposes any such an account to the rupture of the cross.

In part, as Barry Matlock has concluded with regard to Käsemann's work, this is simply the nature of the polemic: "[S]o sharp is the theological tension and so fine the theological balance of what Käsemann is always driving at—so fragile the conditions of perpetual protest, recurrent reform—that, by nature, the moment it is grasped it is in danger of becoming that which it despises." Ironically, the polemic itself breeds the "self-subversion" of its own discourse.[58] While the purpose of the polemic is to ground the gospel in the ambiguities of this-worldly reality, the oppositions that form the very essence of its discourse bring even that central purpose under the question mark of the cross. That is, because any positive, this-worldly account of the church's life must be measured according to the cross, the apocalyptic, polemical theology of the cross actually submits concrete social reality to an abstraction above and outside that reality established in order to govern it.

What is imperative to recognize here is that the division of the cross from the resurrection makes the cross into an abstraction—which is to say

---

57. Gustavo Gutiérrez offers a helpful word of caution towards such protective dialectics: "It is those who by trying to 'save' Christ's work will 'lose' it" (*A Theology of Liberation*, 104).

58. Matlock, *Apocalyptic Paul*, 237 n. 61.

that the cross cannot actually be separated from the resurrection. By cutting off the church's life from Christ's resurrection life, the polemic actually loses any true account of the mystery of the redemption of the world—which consists of the unity of Christ's cross and resurrection, living and active in Christ's body through the power of the Holy Spirit.[59] Without a positive account of Christ's resurrection for the life of the church, then, the polemic has no way of saying how the cross is concretely significant for Christian discipleship in this world.

We can see this dilemma most clearly in Käsemann and Martyn's theologies of baptism. For both Käsemann and Martyn, baptism keeps the daily life of this-worldly discipleship rooted in the cross, and thus baptism is premised on the division of cross from resurrection for that daily life. Yet here, in its central, positive account of daily life in the Spirit, the polemic yields internal contradictions that compromise a coherent account of this-worldly discipleship.

For instance, Käsemann's invective against the Enthusiasts places baptism not only in the middle of the battle between "otherworldly" and "this-worldly" forms of Christian discipleship, but at the dividing line between Christ's cross and resurrection in the church's life. He makes an important point, commenting on 1 Corinthians 15:20–28, when he stresses, against the Enthusiasts' otherworldly understanding of baptismal participation in the resurrection, that for Paul the resurrection is not about our reanimation but about Christ's sovereignty.[60] Thus, he insists, baptism

59. The Second Vatican Council's return to the sources (*ressourcement*) for the renewal (*aggiornamento*) of the church referred to the reality of Christ's redemption, living and active in the church through the Holy Spirit, as "the paschal mystery." See *The Constitution on the Sacred Liturgy* 1.5 ("[Christ] achieved his task principally by the paschal mystery of his blessed passion, resurrection from the dead, and glorious ascension, whereby 'dying, he destroyed our death, and rising, restored our life'") and 1.6 ("Thus by baptism [persons] are grafted into the paschal mystery of Christ; they die with him, are buried with him, and rise with him"), in Flannery, *Vatican Council*, 1:3, 4. On this connection in Paul, in addition to Rom 6:1–5 and Gal 3:26–29, cf. 1 Cor 5:7b-8 with 1 Cor 11:23–26; 15:3–5. My use of "paschal mystery" in what follows refers specifically to the unity of Christ's cross and resurrection, living and active within the life of the church through the power of the Holy Spirit, who is the very presence of the living Lord Jesus Christ in his body. In this way, it also refers to the unity of the sacraments, baptism, and the eucharist.

60. Resurrection for Paul "is not primarily oriented towards the reanimation of the dead or any such thing, but towards the reign of Christ. Because Christ must reign, he cannot leave his own in the grip of death. Conversely, his own are already engaged today in delivering over to Christ by their bodily obedience the piece of world which they themselves are; and in so doing they bear witness to his lordship as that of the

places us between the "two poles" of Christ's *regnum* in this world, "his Resurrection and ours."[61] Because "Christ alone is risen," we only have "in the Spirit the reversionary expectation of the Resurrection and proclaim this by the new obedience of our lives" through daily dying and taking up our cross.[62]

This anti-enthusiastic polemic creates a conflict, however, when he pits the futural note of eschatological reservation in 1 Corinthians 15 against Paul's understanding of our participation in Christ's resurrection life through baptism in Romans 6:4ff. Essentially, Käsemann's exegesis of the former overdetermines his exegesis of the latter.[63] Whether or not Paul is engaged in an anti-enthusiastic polemic in Romans 6 as Käsemann argues is quite debatable, but his polemic hinders him from seeing the difference for Paul between the baptized actually being raised from the dead and their participating in Christ's resurrection life. The sharp, absolute character of the polemic forces a black-and-white either/or between our bodily resurrection through baptism, on the one hand (otherworldly enthusiasm), and our participation only in Christ's cross, on the other (eschatological reservation). Thus, Käsemann ties his exegesis in knots by separating the "newness of life" in Romans 6:4b from present participation in Christ's resurrection life, failing to recognize the parallel structure of Romans 6:10 and 6:11.[64] The more coherent interpretation is that we

---

Cosmocrator and thus anticipate the ultimate future of the reality of the Resurrection and of the untrammeled reign of Christ. The apocalyptic question 'To whom does the world belong?' stands behind the resurrection theology of the apostle, as behind his parenesis which centres round the call to obedience in the body" (Käsemann, "Primitive Christian Apocalyptic," 135–36).

61. Ibid., 134.

62. Ibid., 133.

63. This is especially the case in Käsemann, "Primitive Christian Apocalyptic."

64. In a remarkable fashion, Käsemann claims, "Verse 11 is not to be taken with v. 10" (*Romans*, 170). Instead, he says, v. 10 is to be read in light of v. 8b "in such a way that out of the *sun Christō* the destiny of the prototype is indicated to which we are destined to be conformed" (ibid.). The point, in other words, is to indicate our future eschatological conformity with Christ, since, through baptism into his death, his destiny has become our own. Certainly v. 10 should not be separated from what precedes it, and yet the clear parallel structure between vv. 10 and 11 simply will not stand up to Käsemann's reasoning: "v. 10: For [in that] he died to sin [*apethanen tē hamartia*], he died once for all, but in that he lives, he lives to God [*zē tō theō*]. v. 11: So you also, account yourselves to be dead indeed to sin [*nekrous men tē hamartia*] but living to God [*zōntas de tō theō*] in Christ Jesus." Likewise, we can agree with Käsemann when he adds that "vv. 9f. do not emphasize *the fact* of Christ's resurrection as such but the life of the Ruler who is no longer threatened by death" (ibid., emphasis

participate even now in Christ's resurrection life, which, though not our own bodily resurrection, is nonetheless the proleptic anticipation of that bodily resurrection through incorporation into Christ's own life.

We see a similar conflict in Martyn's interpretation of Paul's theology of baptism in Galatians 3:26–29. According to Martyn, baptism is crucifixion with Christ (cf. 6:14–15).[65] Because Christ's death on the cross put

mine). However, Paul clearly associates this point *with* Christ's being raised from the dead: "v. 9: Knowing that Christ, being raised from the dead [*egertheis ek nekrōn*], no longer dies, death no longer has dominion over him [*ouketi kurieuei*]." Thus, Christ's "living to God" is *entirely* through his being raised from the dead. Or, put otherwise, his life is itself his *resurrection life*. Thus, the clear parallel structure between vv. 10 and 11 indicates our own share in Christ's resurrection life. The point Paul is making, then, is not that "newness of life" is only life in the cross, but that our life is *in Christ*, who has put death to death and now lives to God. Thus, our new life, "walking according to the Spirit" (Rom 8:4–5), is itself in and with the living, resurrected Christ's life. Moreover, Käsemann makes the claim that the verb *peripatēsōmen* (*might walk* in the newness of life) in 6:4b should be interpreted as an "eschatological future" in conformity to the future indicatives in vv. 5b and 8b: "Hence one is forced to say (with Bultmann [. . .]) that Paul modifies his tradition, differentiating between the already risen Lord and believers. As in 2 Cor. 13:4 the power of the resurrection which is in fact at work in them asserts itself initially by setting them contrariwise (*sub contrario*) under the shadow of the cross and makes this in a special way the mark of the new life" (ibid.). While Käsemann is correct in his rejection "of mystical union with Christ" (ibid., 167) in baptism, involving an ontological change of the human nature, he fails to note the clear connections Paul is drawing throughout this passage between Christ's life, *through his resurrection from the dead*, and our own "new life." Paul Meyer offers a more reasonable approach. Speaking about the future indicative in v. 5b, he says, "The solidarity that already exists between Christ and the individual in death must be followed by a solidarity in life as well. Since the latter still lies in the future, this solidarity has become a shared destiny. Verse 8 repeats this result as a flat indicative assertion about the future resurrection (like 1 Cor. 15:22). But significantly, here in v. 4 this future indicative is deflected into a statement of God's purpose for men and women in the present: 'The reason why we were buried with him through this 'baptism into death' is that, just as Christ was raised from the dead through the Father's glory, we also might [now] live a new life.' What shall be, already ought to be; hope and ethical obligation are simply two sides of the same future given to each individual in Christ. Verse 11 draws the bottom line: 'So you also should consider yourselves dead to sin and alive to God in Christ Jesus'" (Meyer, "Romans," 182; brackets original). Here I should point out that my agreement with Meyer's exegesis of this passage highlights the problem in his elevation of the cross to a critical norm all the more. That is, in order to affirm what he says here, the presuppositions that undergird the polemical insistence on the cross as a transcendental ideal must be released.

65. Martyn, "Apocalyptic Antinomies," 119: "In baptism all of the Galatians *were crucified with Christ*. They all suffered the consequent loss of the world of religious differentiation, the world, that is, that had as one of its fundamental elements the antinomy of the Law/the Not-Law. For crucifixion with Christ means the death of the cosmos of religion, the cosmos in which all human beings live" (emphasis original).

to death the cosmos under the control of Sin—that is, the cosmos defined according to pairs of opposites such as Law/Not-Law[66]—Paul's reminder to the Galatians that at their baptism these antinomies were declared non-existent (3:28) calls attention to the *loss of the cosmos* they experienced in baptism.[67] Moreover, it is the nonexistence of the cosmos defined according to the antinomies that "causes one to participate in Christ's death (cf. 2:19)."[68] Baptismal crucifixion with Christ is at once incorporation into Christ himself, who is the new anthropological unity in which the opposi-tions characterizing the cosmos enslaved to Sin no longer exist. Martyn in fact says that the "newly created unity" of the body of Christ through bap-tism is so "fundamentally and irreducibly identified with Christ himself as to cause Paul to use the masculine form of the word 'one.'"[69] Thus, "baptism is a participation both in Christ's death and in Christ's life; genuine, escha-tological life commences when one is taken into the community of the new creation in which unity in God's Christ has replaced religious-ethnic differentiations."[70] This latter point is consistent with Martyn's claim that

66. The Galatians had been convinced by the Teachers that true descent from Abraham, and thus inheritance of the Abrahamic blessing, required law observance, which meant getting on the right side of the antinomy of "Law/Not-Law." The Gala-tians would have been familiar with the prevalent view, Martyn says, that the world had as its basic building blocks pairs of opposites, essentially dividing God's good creation against itself. Thus, Martyn associates the view of the cosmos as constituted by elemental pairs of opposites with the incursion of the power of Sin into the cosmos, convincing the cosmos' inhabitants of this illusory reality. Significantly, then, Paul does not refer to the demand for *non*–Law observance in response to the Teachers' demand for Law observance, but declares the opposition between Law and Not-Law itself to no longer exist: "For neither is circumcision anything nor is uncircumcision anything. What is something is the new creation" (Gal 6:15). See Martyn, "Apocalyptic Antinomies," 118–19.

67. "As persons who were acquainted with some form of the tradition of elemental, oppositional pairs, the Galatians heard in the baptizer's words a list of the oppositional elements that had ceased to exist. In that declaration they suffered the *loss of the cos-mos*, as though a fissure had opened up under their feet, hurling them into an abyss with no dimensions" (Martyn, *Galatians*, 571).

68. Ibid., 376.

69. Ibid., 377. And similarly cf. the use of "sons" in Gal 4:6: "Drawing on baptis-mal traditions, Paul again takes the Galatians back to the moment of their baptism (3:26–29). It was there that they heard the performative words announcing their in-corporation into Christ, God's Son (3:27), their adoption into God's family as God's sons (3:26), and their receipt of the Spirit of the Son. . . . He uses the word 'sons' inclusively in order to draw the link between God's Son and God's family, the members of which are sons by being incorporated into the Son" (ibid., 391).

70. Ibid., 382–83.

Christ's cross and resurrection "constitute an indivisible whole," as we saw above.

However, when Martyn speaks about the daily baptismal life of the Christian church, participation in Christ's life is conspicuously absent. Instead, he says that daily life in the Spirit is always "daily dying" because the Spirit conforms the baptized to the Crucified One. Yet, if this daily dying is *itself* "Christ's life; genuine eschatological life," how is it that the baptized participate not only in Christ's death, but also in his life? Ultimately, the polemic prevents Martyn from supplying any account of participation in Christ's life, though his exegesis demands it, instead reducing Christ's life *to* his death for the Christian life.

A potentially more detrimental example of the persistence of the polemic on Martyn's exegesis is the way he imposes opposition back onto the anthropological unity in Christ in his account of the new creation. While, on the one hand, he asserts that there are no more opposites in the new anthropological unity in Christ, on the other, he says that the new creation is characterized by *new* oppositions. While the idea that the unity of the new creation opposes opposition itself is not *prima facie* problematic, the claim that the new creation is itself *made up of* new pairs of opposites controverts Martyn's own exegesis of baptismal unity in Christ in Galatians 3:28. Essentially, fidelity to the polemic causes Martyn's account of the new creation to repeat the *illusory* oppositional picture of reality imposed by Sin.

Whereas in Käsemann the polemical division of cross from resurrection for the life of the church overly dictates his exegesis of Paul's baptismal theology, in Martyn the commitment to the polemic works against his own exegetical conclusions. In this sense, while Martyn's exegesis of Paul's baptismal theology actually offers a way out of the inherent deadlock of the division of cross from resurrection, in the end his commitment to Paul's *theologia crucis* keeps his own theological conclusions about the baptismal life within the confines of the polemic.

What the polemical theology of the cross, by its nature, cannot provide, then, is a coherent, positive account of the Christian life rooted in and flowing from the indivisible unity of Christ's cross and resurrection. And yet, this is precisely what we find in Paul's theology of baptism. In Galatians 3:26–29, as Martyn correctly sees, Paul directs the Galatians to their actual baptisms by repeating parts of the liturgy in order that they might better grasp the truth of their incorporation into and unity with

Christic.[71] Likewise, in Romans 6:1–11 Paul says that in baptism we have been buried with Christ in his death so that we might also walk in the newness of life (Rom 6:4). By directing the Romans to the reality of the concrete event of their having been plunged into and raised out of the water[72] as itself a true union with Christ himself in his death and resurrection, he urges them now to live from out of that reality: "So you also must consider yourselves dead to sin and alive to God in Christ Jesus" (Rom 6:11). In both instances, the indicative reality of baptismal incorporation into the paschal mystery,[73] Christ's saving death and resurrection, *is itself* the newness of life in Christ, what Paul in Romans 8:4 calls "walking according to the Spirit."[74]

Thus, as the union of the life of Christ's body, the church, with the reality of Christ's redemption of the world in his death and resurrection, baptism is the beginning of Christian discipleship, which sets us, through the Spirit, on the Way that is Christ himself. For this reason, the *whole life* of the body of Christ is a remembering of baptism. Martin Luther grasped this point well when he famously claimed that, as the new beginning that marks the entirety of the Christian life, baptism is a daily return to Christ's saving cross and liberating resurrection. "For whatever life we live, it should be baptism and the fulfilling of the sign or sacrament of

71. Ibid., 375. Cf. Käsemann, *Romans*, 219: "If the motif of union is to be used at all, it must be precisely understood as incorporation into the lordship of the Crucified," commenting on Rom 8:3.

72. While Käsemann claims that "only pious imagination can link . . . burial with Christ to going under the water" (*Romans*, 164), as Everett Ferguson has shown, there is a potential connection here between the ritual action of Christian baptism with Christ's burial and resurrection: "The theology stated here [in Rom. 6:1–11] can be advocated without a physical likeness in the action of baptism, and many believers have divorced the theology from their practice in the administration of baptism. However, the description of baptism in terms of death, burial, and subsequent walking (after a rising) in a new life is certainly consistent with an immersion, and the likeness of the action to a burial may even have suggested the analogy. Even if one should not move from Pauline theology to the ritual of baptism, one might wonder if Paul moved from the ritual practice to his theology. Hence, Paul's use of the word 'likeness' (or 'form,' *homoiōmati*) in verse 5 may be understood accordingly" (Ferguson, *Baptism in the Early Church*, 157). Also cf. Søren Agersnap, *Baptism and the Newness of Life*, 268–71.

73. See p. 21 n. 59 above.

74. With a proper understanding of the paschal mystery, the classic dilemma between the "indicative" and the "imperative" in Romans 6 is no dilemma at all. See Agersnap, *Baptism*, 30ff. On this point, cf. the discussion of the Bultmannian phrase "Become what you are" and its implications for the indicative/imperative in Käsemann, *Romans*, 173ff.; and Martyn, *Galatians*, 535 and n. 184.

baptism, since we have been liberated from all else and handed over once for all to baptism, that is, to death and resurrection."[75] Jonathan Trigg has helpfully coined the phrase "baptism's present tense" to express Luther's understanding of baptism as the entirety of the Christian life: "That baptism cannot be confined to the beginning of life under the covenant but *is* that covenant; or that it is not just the entrance to a new life, but continues to determine that life throughout its length; these aspects of Luther's view of baptism further underline its 'present tense.'"[76] Similarly, Paul in both Romans 6 and Galatians 3 directs the baptized *to* the truth of the new reality in their baptism in order that they may now so live. For Luther, as for Paul,[77] then, the reality of Christ's saving death and resurrection is living and active throughout the believer's entire life through God's action in baptism.

For Paul, all of this takes place because of the activity and power of the Holy Spirit, who is the very indwelling presence of the living, resurrected, and crucified Christ in his body, the church (Rom 8:1–17; 1 Cor 12:12–13). The Holy Spirit in Paul's letters is "the Spirit of the living God," "life-giving" (2 Cor 3:3, 6), the manifestation of hope (Rom 5:1–5; 8:18–27; Gal 5:5), the seal and pledge for future heavenly life (2 Cor 1:22; 5:5), and is therefore the firstfruits of the eschatological future that Christ's resurrection has opened up for "the children of God" incorporated into him through baptism.

By no means, then, does Paul's account of baptism as participation both in Christ's cross and his resurrection remove the "eschatological reservation," as Käsemann fears. For instance, in 2 Corinthians 1:19–22 Paul tells the Corinthians, "For the Son of God, Jesus Christ, whom we proclaimed among you . . . has always been 'Yes.' For as many of God's promises as there are, in him they are 'Yes.' For this reason it is through him that we say the 'Amen,' to the glory of God. But it is God who is establishing us with you in Christ and has anointed [*chrisas*] us and sealed

75. Luther, *de capt. Bab.*, in WA 6:535.24–26. "Quicquid enim vivimus, Baptismus esse debet et signum seu sacramentum baptismi implere, cum a caeteris omnibus liberati uni tantum baptismo simus addicti, id est, morti est resurrectioni." And see p. 7 n. 26 above.

76. Trigg, *Baptism*, 45.

77. The significance of the association I am making here between Luther and Paul relates to Käsemann's claim that fidelity to the Reformation, and especially Luther, requires the deployment of the polemical *theologia crucis*. I do not believe that this claim can be sustained with careful attention to Luther's corpus, especially his baptismal theology. I point to some of this briefly in the footnotes in the discussion that follows.

[*sphragisamenos*] us and has given the down payment of the Spirit in our hearts."[78] Alongside the proclamation of Jesus Christ, in whom all of God's promises are fulfilled, baptism seals[79] and establishes us in Christ's body, marks us as belonging to him even now through the gift of the Spirit, who dwells in our hearts as the downpayment of God's eschatological kingdom.[80]

Paul's clear eschatological thrust is thus wed to his further conviction that we have been taken into Christ's own body through the Spirit in baptism (1 Cor 12:13), and the same Spirit continues to dwell within our embodied lives in this world here and now. Gustavo Gutiérrez reaches the same conclusion, asserting that for Paul the "spiritual body" in 1 Corinthians 15:44 is not "something mysterious or impalpable that can exist only after death." Rather, it is "an already present reality, provided that by the power of baptism we live even now the resurrection of the Lord and are journeying toward the fullness of a life we already possess in an inchoative way."[81] In this way, while still clinging to the expectant future of the libera-

78. I have altered the NRSV here. On the connection of this text with baptism, I direct the reader once again to the epigraph to this paper from Käsemann. That Käsemann could (as indeed all of our polemicists do in a number of places) speak at times in ways that undeniably indicate present participation in Christ's resurrection life highlights the problem I have been tracing here all the more. That is to say, *his own polemical criteria* require him to place even such statements as these under the critical mark of the theology of the cross.

79. Though the association of baptism with *chrisas* and *sphragisamenos* is not explicit here, there are parallels in the deutero-Pauline epistles and in the early, extra-canonical apostolic literature that suggests a strong case for such an association. Cf. Eph 1:13–14; 4:30 with Col 1:11. See also 2 *Clem. ad Cor.* 6.9–13 and 7.6–8. Käsemann agrees: "[T]he possibility has to be seriously considered that 'to seal' in 2 Cor 1:22; Eph 1:13; 4:30 belongs to the fixed vocabulary of baptism" (*Romans*, 115). Cf. also idem., "Pauline Doctrine," 113, and "God's 'Yes' to All," 224–25.

80. Luther, in a sermon from 1519, makes the association of baptism's present reality with its eschatological significance: "This plan, as has been said, begins in baptism, which signifies death and the resurrection at the Last Day. Therefore so far as the sign of the sacrament and its significance are concerned, sins and the man are both already dead, and he has risen again; and so the sacrament has taken place. But the work of the sacrament has not yet been fully done, which is to say that death and the resurrection at the Last Day are still before us" (*Ein Sermon vom dem Heiligen Hochwirdigen Sacrament der Tauffe*, in WA 2:729.32—730.2; English translation: *Luther's Works*, 35:32).

81. Gutiérrez, *We Drink*, 63, 66. Cf. idem, *Theology of Liberation*, 104: "Temporal progress—or, to avoid this aseptic term, human liberation—and the growth of the Kingdom both are directed toward complete communion of human beings with God and among themselves. They have the same goal, but they do not follow parallel roads, not even convergent ones. . . . While liberation is implemented in liberating historical events, it also denounces their limitations and ambiguities, proclaims their fulfillment,

tion of the whole cosmos, Gutiérrez can speak without hesitation of the church as the "extension of the incarnation."[82] Baptism unites us to the indivisible unity of Christ's cross and resurrection *because* it unites us to Christ's very person through the gift of the Holy Spirit.[83]

In contrast to Paul's baptismal theology, in which the baptismal life is joined with Christ's cross and resurrection through the Spirit's present activity in the church, the polemical theology of the cross makes baptism a means for regulating the authenticity and purity of the church's life, much as did certain Anabaptist and other radical wings of the Reformation.[84]

---

and impels them effectively towards total communion. This is not an identification. Without liberating historical events, there would be no growth of the Kingdom. But the process of liberation will not have conquered the very roots of human oppression and exploitation without the coming of the Kingdom, which is above all a gift. Moreover, we can say that the historical, political liberating event *is* the growth of the Kingdom and *is* a salvific event; but it is not *the* coming of the Kingdom, not *all* of salvation. It is the historical realization of the Kingdom, and, therefore, it also proclaims its fullness. This is where the difference lies. It is a distinction made from a dynamic viewpoint, which has nothing to do with the one which holds for the existence of two juxtaposed 'orders,' closely connected or convergent, but deep down different from each other." Cf. also Bonhoeffer, *Ethics*, 37.

82. Gutiérrez, *Theology of Liberation*, 69. Käsemann, "Corporeality in Paul," 47, claims, "The apostle did not at all mean that Christ is absorbed in his church as the idea of the *Christus prolongatus* (the extended Christ) suggests," and then goes on to root both baptism and eucharist in the *signum Crucis* alone. While he thus rejects a simplistic notion of Christ being "absorbed in his church," note, however, that later in the same essay he places strong emphasis on Christ's body, the church, as itself the earthly rule and existence of the exalted Christ: "Paul understands the Body of Christ primarily as the earthly rule of the exalted Christ, thus as the presence and communication of Jesus in the world after his departure from earth" (ibid., 50). And, "In [the Body of Christ] the Exalted One is revealed as its true Lord. The bodily service of his servants in fellowship with every creature is the demonstration and *realization* of the claim and promise of the One whose resurrection in 1 Corinthians 15:25 is interpreted as a worldwide revolutionary and explosive event: 'Christ must reign'" (ibid., 51, my emphasis).

83. Martyn is right when he says that there is in Paul a "christologizing of the Spirit," but this is incomplete insofar as he identifies the Spirit only with Christ's cross. See Martyn, "Epistemology," 108 n. 54. Also, cf. the very Käsemannian remark in ibid., 108: "For until the parousia, the cross is and remains the epistemological crisis, and thus the norm by which one knows that the Spirit is none other than the Spirit of the crucified Christ."

84. Here we do well to remember that Luther criticized the Anabaptists' baptismal theology for denying the Word of promise by separating it from the external element to which it is joined in their insistence on right understanding and practice (adult profession of faith, illegitimacy and invalidity of infant baptism, separation from the rest of the church for its failure to maintain purity, holiness, and discipline, and so

Cousar's application of the polemical theology of the cross to the Western, triumphalistic church demonstrates this point well: "The church whose theology is shaped by the message of the cross must itself take on a cruciformed life if its theology is to carry credibility," since "*the message of the cross functions as the norm and point of critique of the church's quest for identity.*" However, by dividing Christ's cross from his resurrection for the life of his body in this world, and elevating the former to a critical norm by which to govern the authenticity of that life, the polemic effectively divides the church's life from the Holy Spirit, who actively brings us into the exalted Christ's presence. Because the Spirit is the Spirit of Christ, who brings us through baptism into unity with Christ's body in which there is no opposition, the polemical sacrifice of one integral part of the paschal mystery sacrifices it altogether. The actuality of Christ's cross is inseparable from his resurrection.

What is thus necessary is an account of the fullness of the mystery of salvation revealed in the paschal mystery—the unity of cross and resurrection with the life of Christ's body, the church, through the power of the Holy Spirit—and that demands a more fulsome account of believers' participation in Christ's life with God through baptism. What is required, then, is an exposition of the sacramental nature of baptism, which is nothing less than this very reality itself, living and active through Christ's Spirit in the church. While Paul does not use the terms "sacrament" or "mystery" with reference to baptism,[85] he does maintain what we could call a "sacramental bond" between Christ's cross and resurrection and the baptismal life of the church (where the "baptismal life" includes the celebration of

---

forth). The denial of the Word, as we saw above, is Käsemann's main charge against the Enthusiasts (n.b.: Luther uses the epithet *Schwärmerei* for the Anabaptists, the same term Käsemann gives to the Enthusiasts in Corinth.) Moreover, Luther likewise said that the Anabaptist relinquishing of the Word was not only common to the papist *ex opere operato* doctrine, but made the Anabaptist baptismal theology a reinstatement of *ex opera operato* efficacy. See the account in Trigg, *Martin Luther's Baptismal Theology*, 78 and n. 71. That the polemical theology of the cross would leave a position such as Käsemann's in close company with an Anabaptist understanding of baptism, given his deep indebtedness to Luther's own theology of the cross, is thus highly ironic. See Luther, *Annotationes D. M. in Priorem epistolam ad Timotheum*, in WA 26:15.21–24, and *Promotionsdisputation von Johannes Macchabäus Scotus* (February 3, 1542), in WA 39/2:172.5–15.

85 Cf. Paul's use of *mystērion* in 1 Cor 2:7; 4:1; 13:2 and the deutero-Pauline usage in Eph 5:32.

the eucharist[86]). In this way, he sees baptism as a sign that bears the reality it signifies by the addition of the Word of divine promise.[87]

The Pauline theology of baptism presented above sketches the outline of such a sacramental account, but it is only a beginning. A Pauline, apocalyptic, sacramental theology of baptism will unflinchingly locate the beating heart of redemption, the paschal mystery, firmly in this world, that is, in the middle of the irresolvable tension between the present reality of eschatological hope through the gift of the Holy Spirit and the ambiguities of this-worldly existence in which we now see in a glass dimly (1 Cor 13:12). What it will not do, however, is separate the positive, concrete social reality of life in the Spirit from the fullness of the mystery of Christ's redemption of the world. The institutional, ecclesiastical nature of the church's existence in this world shows us a face of the church that is oftentimes ugly and even reprehensible. And against the church's sinful tendencies, in those times and places where the church too often colludes with the powers of Sin and Death rather than with those who are crushed beneath the weight of oppression and systems of domination, the critical theology of the cross can still be useful. For all that, however, the sins of the church in this world do not drive it outside of the grace and activity of the Spirit, who is the presence of the living God.[88] The church remains the

86. The eucharist is not isolated from, but is an ever-deepening of the reality into which we are incorporated at baptism. As a "remembering" (*anamnēsis*) and a "proclaiming [*katalleggete*] of Christ's death until he comes" (1 Cor 11:24–26), it is at once a remembering and proclaiming of our baptism, such that the unity of baptism and Eucharist in the life of the church leads us ever deeper into the mystery of Christ's redemption of the world.

87. I am drawing on St. Augustine's description of the sacrament as a "visible word." When the word or divine promise is added to the element, the latter becomes a sacrament since it is joined with the word and bears its reality and truth. "'Now you are clean because of the word which I have spoken to you.' Why does he not say, 'you are clean because of the baptism whereby you were washed,' but says, 'because of the word which I have spoken to you,' unless the word cleansed in the water? Take away the word, and what is the water except water? The word is added to the element, and it becomes a sacrament, also itself as if a visible word [*Accedit verbum ad elementum, et fit sacramentum, etiam ipsum tamquam visible verbum*]" (Augustine, *Tract. Ev. Jo.* 80.3.1–5; CCSL 36: col. 0278). Luther follows Augustine quite closely for his own conception of sacrament. See especially Luther, *Grosse Katechismus*, in *WA* 30/1:214.14–17. See also Luther's comments throughout Johannes Scotus Maccabaeus' doctoral disputation, in *WA* 39/2:154–84. "Where the Word is, there is the church. This is just" [*Ubi est verbum, ibi est ecclesiam. Das ist recht*] (*WA* 39/2:176.8–9).

88. Cf. the rather perverse claims of the abandonment of the church by the Spirit in Radner, *End of the Church*, and Reno, *In the Ruins*.

body of Christ even in the middle of its sometimes compromised life. That certainly does not mean either that Christ's life is also compromised with Sin or that the church's life is beyond the threat of trial and temptation (our Lord taught us to pray, "Save us from the time of trial and deliver us from evil!" and we pray this daily). Rather, it means that God has determined that the church, as Christ's body, is one of those "bodily places" on earth where God wills to be found.[89]

Our investigation of the joining of apocalyptic with the polemical theology of the cross has produced rather ambivalent results as to the future possibility of an apocalyptic theology. What I believe is clear, however, is that an apocalyptic theology cannot continue under the rubrics of the polemic, which separates it from the concrete life of discipleship. If apocalyptic is to fulfill its original purpose, that is, to direct us to Jesus Christ's liberating apocalypse into *this* world, then it will also require the incorporation of the positive significance of the liturgical life of the church, and especially baptism, into its discourse. For it is in Christ's body through the power of the indwelling of the Holy Spirit that the fullness of the paschal mystery is living and active, even now. Any future apocalyptic theology should thus be able to say with F. D. Maurice's paraphrase of Luther: "Believe on the warrant of your Baptism, You are grafted into Christ,

---

89. Luther offers this sentiment in his *Genesisvorlesung*, commenting on Gen 28:17: "For God so governs us that, wherever [God] speaks with us here on earth, the approach to the kingdom of heaven is open. This is indeed remarkable consolation. Wherever we hear the word and are baptized, there we step into [*ingredimur*] eternal life. Where is such a place to be found? On earth, where the Ladder that touches the heavens stands: where Angels descend and ascend, where Jacob sleeps. It is a bodily place [*locus corporalis*], but here is ascent to heaven without material ladders, without wings and feathers. Faith speaks thus: I am going to the place where the word is taught, where the Sacrament is offered, where Baptism is administered. And all these things, which are done in my sight in a bodily place, are heavenly and divine words and works. That place is not only ground or earth, but is something more splendid and majestic: undoubtedly the kingdom of God and the gate of heaven . . . do not seek a new and foolish entrance: but in faith look with astonishment [*intuere*] at the place of the word and the Sacraments. Direct your steps there: where the word resounds and the Sacraments are administered: And there write the title: GATE OF GOD. Whether that should be done in the temple and public assembly or in the bedroom, when we are comforting and lifting up the sick, or when we absolve the one who sits with us at table [*assidentem nobis in mensa absolvimus*]: there is the gate of heaven. As Christ says, 'Where two or three are assembled in my name there I am in the midst of them': There is the house of God and the gate of heaven throughout the whole of the world, wherever the word with the Sacraments is taught purely" (*WA* 43:599.1–22). The whole of the passage that follows (up through 43:602.5) is relevant. Cf. this rich passage with the epigraph from Käsemann quoted at the beginning of this paper.

claim your position. You have the Spirit, you are children of God; do not live as if you belonged to the devil."[90]

---

90. "This was [Luther's] invariable language, with which he shook the Seven Hills" (Maurice, *Kingdom of Christ*, 1:323).

PART THREE

Apocalyptic and
the Church's Witness

13

Sentences and Verbs
Talking About God[1]

Fleming Rutledge

IN THE YEAR OF the four-hundredth anniversary of the King James Version, writer after writer, critic after critic, commentator after commentator all said the same thing—the power of the language of the KJV, along with Shakespeare, shaped not only the English language but the entire Western tradition in its English-speaking countries. Edward Rothstein, the very fine culture critic for *The New York Times*, who happens to be Jewish, went so far as to say that the KJV—its content, but also the way it entered the language—gave a powerful boost to the emphasis on freedom and moral responsibility that characterizes the Western tradition in its English-speaking form.[2]

Stanley Hauerwas, in his 2001 Gifford Lectures, drew upon Karl Barth's conviction that the form of our speech is intimately related to our understanding of God. Hauerwas draws attention to Alan Torrance's work *Persons in Communion*, in which Torrance suggests that Wittgenstein's understanding that language creates and conditions thought illumines and reinforces Barth's point.[3]

---

1. An unpublished version of this article was presented as a lecture at Wycliffe College in the University of Toronto, October 5, 2011.

2. Rothstein, "400 Years Old and Ageless."

3. Hauerwas, *With the Grain*, 173 n. 1, citing Torrance, *Persons in Communion*. Hauerwas also directs us to McDonald, *Strange New World*.

297

Richard Mitchell was the editor of *The Underground Grammarian*, described in *Time* as "the most inflammatory broadsheet to come out of Philadelphia since Tom Paine published *Common Sense*." Mitchell wrote:

> The real purpose of language is to talk about the world you can't see . . . if we fail to master the tools, then difficult, important ideas go out of public discourse. We live meager, pinched lives, all of us, because we speak and write a meager, pinched language.[4]

How then do preachers today talk about the world we can't see? Very few of us today have the gifts, the training, or the background in reading to create sentences that are anything like those in the KJV or the old *Book of Common Prayer*. But all of us can learn the difference between a weak sentence and a strong one. All of us can develop a sense of the power of verbs. Most important, all of us can learn to make God the subject of the sentence.

The American writer Annie Dillard was asked by someone at a lecture, "How do I know if I can be a writer?" She replied, "Do you like sentences?"

Preachers should like sentences, or should at least understand the power of a sentence. A good storyteller knows the power of a sentence, more by immersion in the tradition than by academic learning. African-American preaching, notable for its rhetorical power, was largely shaped by the cadences of the King James Version with its vigorous use of verbs. Attention paid to verbs and to their placement in sentences will yield results not only literary but, more important, theological.

Take for instance this resounding sentence from the KJV and RSV of 1 Corinthians 15:22:

> For as in Adam all die, even so in Christ shall all be made alive.

Compare that sentence with this flattened one in the New Revised Standard:

> For as all die in Adam, so all will be made alive in Christ. (NRSV)

The point to note is that in the first version the verbs "die" and "be made" are postponed until the *end* of the two clauses; whereas in the second version not even the all-powerful name of Christ can save the sentence from dying off at the end. This can be further underscored by the fact that although the juxtaposition of the names Adam and Christ is indeed central

4. Mitchell, "Glassboro, NJ," 5.

for the worldview of the apostle Paul (as we know from Rom 5:12–21), in the stronger sentence even these crucial names are syntactically subordinate to that final "*all* be made alive." Thus, in the weaker sentence ("all will be made alive in Christ"), not only is the force of the verbs reduced, but the emphasis on "all" is also reduced because it has been moved away from the words "made alive"—and, as a result, the two names, Adam and Christ, lose some of their force as well. Ending the sentence with the verb "to be" and its outcome, "made alive," gives the reader or hearer a hint of the power of God that raises the dead and calls into existence the things that do not exist (Rom 4:17). "For as in Adam all die, even so in Christ shall all be made alive."

Here is another illustration, from Isaiah 9:6:

> For to us a child is born, to us a son is given. (RSV; KJV has "unto")

In the NRSV the sentence reads,

> For a child has been born for us, a son given to us.

In this example, the shift of the verbs from the ending to the beginning of the two clauses, and the change in the tenses, weakens *not only* the power of the verbs *but also* the "for us" and "to us." For forcefulness, there is no comparison between "to us a child is born" and "a child has been born for us." "For us" takes on more weight when the verb is held back to the end of the sentence.[5]

Why are we talking about sentences? These are subtle matters, perhaps, but they shape the way we think. Alterations in syntax indicate alterations in our concepts. The 1928 Episcopal *Book of Common Prayer* and its antecedents provided this form for godparents as they vowed to support their godchild in the faith:

> I will, God being my helper.

In the new *Prayer Book* (1978), the response is,

> I will, with God's help.

We can understand that the revisers wanted to modernize and simplify the sentence, but in the process they have removed the verbs about willing

---

5. Take for instance a sentence from the great prose stylist Cormac McCarthy: "Most of those buildings still standing were at the farther end of the town and toward those he rode" (from *The Crossing*, 137). How much weaker the sentence would be, and how much would be lost in the way of suggestion and portent, if it read "he rode toward these."

and being from God so that only the human being gets a verb. This greatly diminishes the power of the word "helper."

Well, what's at stake here? We can illustrate by the way Augustine poked fun at Pelagius. Pelagius said that by the help of the Holy Spirit we can "more easily" resist evil. "Now why," asks Augustine slyly, "did he insert the phrase 'more easily'? . . . He wants it, of course, to be supposed that so great are the powers of our nature, which he is in such a hurry to exalt, that even without the help of the Holy Ghost the evil spirit can be resisted—less easily it may be, but still in a certain measure . . ." More seriously, he continues, "The addition of the words 'more easily' tacitly suggests the possibility of accomplishing good works even without the grace of God."[6] Thus Augustine illustrates the potency of words arranged in a sentence.

Pelagius's theme, "the powers of our [human] nature," is the subject of most preaching and popular religion today. Movies and books are frequently advertised with a favorite motto—"the triumph of the human spirit." The meretriciousness of this phrase can readily be illustrated by its use to promote Roman Polanski's movie *The Pianist*. This superb film depicts life and death in the Warsaw Ghetto during the Nazi occupation of Poland. Its depiction of the "human spirit" is anything but triumphant.[7] Our addiction to our own supposed powers leads us perpetually to sentimentalize and romanticize human possibility rather than acknowledge our desperate predicament.[8] This tendency, in turn, subtly or not so subtly encourages the making of sentences that have human capacity as their subject and God as their object. Thus we have the current enthusiasm for "spiritual journeys," with the human religious search as the controlling metaphor. Barth's clarion call is still widely ignored; instead of kerygmatic sermons announcing that God has made the journey to us, we prefer to speak of our own spiritual journeys toward God.

Take for instance the story of the events on the road to Emmaus in Luke 24. A characteristic sermon on this passage will dwell on the metaphor of the journey—"we are all on our own roads to Emmaus." The

6. Augustine, "Treatise on the Grace of Christ," 28.27–28 (emphasis added).

7. Even less "inspirational," yet even more arresting, is the true story upon which the film was based, *The Pianist*, by Wladyslaw Szpilman. The story of this stunning little book is remarkable; it first appeared in Polish in 1949, then was suppressed by the Stalinists and did not reappear until after the fall of the Berlin Wall in 1989.

8. The German officer struggling with his conscience whose diary forms the most impressive portion of *The Pianist* is brutally detained and swallowed whole by the Red Army.

preacher will typically continue with illustrations of disillusionment and despair similar to the situation of the disciples, and will exhort the listeners to expect and hope for wonderful things to happen along the road, even when the circumstances are dire. Perhaps the preacher will ring the changes on the words "but we had hoped" (v. 21), encouraging us to remember our own hopeless moments. The congregation is urged to watch for the stranger with the message, to look for the moment of grace in a meal, to take heart from opportunities for fellowship and renewal along the way.

There is nothing really wrong with this sort of evocative exhortation, but it is not the same thing as the explosive *kerygma*. Very rare nowadays is the sermon that takes note of the two key verses, "their eyes *were kept* from recognizing [Jesus]" (v. 16) and "their eyes *were opened*" (v. 31). The passive form of the verb in both these sentences directs us to the powerful hidden action of God that withholds and then reveals according to God's own purposes. The subject here is not the religious journey or spiritual growth of the disciples. The acting subject is *God*. The mystery and sovereignty of the ways of God are thus brought to the forefront. In the typical sermon, however, this is more often overlooked than not. Not only in preaching but in all forms of communication in the churches, a sense of a living, acting, intruding God who appears without warning and seizes human beings *against* their own sense of possibility and inclinations is missing.[9]

Missing also from the typical Emmaus sermon is the christological content of the passage. The progression of revelatory statements is overlooked when the preacher is not working out of the surrounding context. Just prior to the Emmaus story we read: "Was it not necessary that the Messiah [*Christou*] should suffer these things and enter into his glory?"(v. 26) and "The Lord [*Kurios*] has risen indeed, and has appeared to Simon!" (v. 34). Following the Emmaus story are the Lord's farewell words: "These are my words which I spoke to you . . . that everything written about me in the law of Moses and the prophets and the psalms must be fulfilled. . . . Thus it is written, that the Christ should suffer and on the third day rise from the dead. . . . And behold, I send the promise of my Father upon you; but stay in the city, until you are clothed with power from on high" (vv. 44–46, 48–49) When the chapter is understood *in its entirety*, it becomes clear that human spiritual insight is not the active agent in the

9. Until recently, this lack of divine agency in sermons was less characteristic of African-Americans, but some of their preachers have now been exhibiting a turn toward personal "spirituality"—both the word and the concept.

post-resurrection events, but divine revelation; and the transformation in the disciples recounted in Luke's book of Acts is that wondrous "power from on high."

Now to be sure, Luke's *kerygma* shifts more easily into a focus on human response and human "spiritual journeying" than even Matthew's, let alone John's or Paul's.[10] J. Louis Martyn would not permit any discussion of the passage just quoted to proceed without attention to the omitted verse 47: "repentance and forgiveness of sins should be preached in his [the Christ's] name to all nations, beginning from Jerusalem." No one influenced by Ernst Käsemann will fail to note that Luke's characteristic emphasis on repentance and forgiveness cannot in itself constitute the fullness of the *kerygma*.[11] Käsemann's groundbreaking interpretation of *dikaiosune* has been greatly enhanced and made applicable through the work of Martyn, who has done more than anyone to spread awareness that "rectification" is a better word for *dikaiosune* in English than "justification." This corrective is badly needed in preaching and teaching the Christian faith. Christopher Hitchens was on to something when he opined that forgiveness is immoral; there is a widespread tendency among Christians and their critics alike to speak almost exclusively of God's mercy and forgiveness, with no corresponding theme of judgment and "making right what has been wrong" (Martyn's theme).[12]

10. The older view of Matthew's Christology as weak and underdeveloped has been driven from the field by the work of Jack Dean Kingsbury, Dale Allison, and others. Today, the emphasis seems to be on the *narrative* structure of Matthew—the *entire* structure, including the genealogy, the birth narratives, and the passion-resurrection narrative. Matthew's framing was ignored in the five-books-of-the-Pentateuch interpretation that dominated Matthean studies in the mid-twentieth century. These crucial portions that frame Matthew reveal the evangelist's intention to display Jesus of Nazareth not merely as an ethical teacher and healer but as Messiah and Son of God, the one to whom "all authority in heaven and on earth has been given" (28:18). In the words of Peter's confession, "You are the Christ, the Son of the living God." When Matthew is read through in its entirety, it is easy to see the high Christology in the opening verses, the concluding verses, and various other points in between. This is what the more literary and canonical developments in biblical studies have done for preachers.

11. This recognition found its way into England via Edwin Hoskyns, who, unlike most English scholars, was influenced by Barth. Reginald Fuller, a student of Hoskyns, wrote (and often said) that forgiveness was too weak a word to convey what God had done in Christ.

12. A clergy discussion group was assigned the task of coming up with a single sentence that described the gospel message. Their consensus was, "We're all sinners but God loves us anyway." This was not a group of rustic unsophisticates, but graduates of mainline seminaries. The current motto of "no exclusion" is even more blind to the necessity for the divine corrective.

The foundation of Christian forgiveness is the confident certainty that, as Abraham Lincoln said, "the judgments of the Lord are true and righteous altogether."[13] God will exercise that judgment in order to reclaim and reorder his *kosmos*. The depth of Lincoln's theological thinking in the crucible of the Civil War is nothing short of miraculous. His writing during that period illustrates the way that biblical thought can shape and inform leaders in the most dire and intractable conflicts. In early 1864 he wrote a letter to a Kentuckian newspaper editor, Albert D. Hodges, to explain why, having promised not to interfere with slavery, he was moving toward Emancipation:

> In telling this tale I attempt no compliment to my own sagacity. I claim not to have controlled events, but confess plainly that events have controlled me. Now, at the end of three years' struggle the nation's condition is not what either party, or any man devised or expected. God alone can claim it. Whither it is tending seems plain. If God now wills the removal of a great wrong, and wills also that we of the North as well as you of the South, shall pay fairly for our complicity in that wrong, impartial history will find therein new cause to attest and revere the justice and goodness of God.

The thing to notice here is the way Lincoln makes God the chief mover in all that he says, including the oblique "events have controlled me." God is the acting subject throughout, yet this does not in the least remove the necessity for wise human leadership. Indeed, it is precisely human leadership in its most admirable form that Lincoln exercised. There is no better place to study sentences than in the works of Lincoln, who saw himself as one with the people of both North and South in the hands of the God whose judgments are good and righteous altogether.[14]

We can illustrate further from Matthew's Gospel. Let us take as an example a sermon recently preached on Matthew 11:25–28:

> At that time Jesus declared, "I thank thee, Father, Lord of heaven and earth, that thou hast hidden these things from the wise and understanding and revealed them to babes; yea, Father, for such was thy gracious will. All things have been delivered to me by my Father; and no one knows the Son except the Father, and no one knows the Father except the Son and any one to whom the Son chooses to reveal him.

13. Lincoln, Second Inaugural Address.
14. Ibid. See especially White, *Lincoln's Greatest Speech*.

The preacher took the reference to the wise and understanding versus the babes as an opportunity to tell a number of stories about himself when he was younger and quite stuck on himself. He illustrated the way that he had been embarrassed on occasion when he thought he knew all the answers and it turned out that other people whom he considered his inferiors were more discerning than he. These were disarming stories and the congregation was clearly amused by them. The preacher then continued with an appeal to the hearers to be less certain of their own opinions, to be more humble, to listen with more respect to the "babes." There was nothing in this sermon that could not have been said in a completely secular or generically religious setting. Not one word in this sermon alluded to the great "Johannine" christological declaration. Thus the news of the action of the Father in delivering all things to the Son was unheard that day. The gracious will of the Father was unmentioned.

It is very difficult to retrain patterns of thought. Many students of preaching today have scarcely ever heard any types of sermons other than the ones just described. Moreover, current practices in education lead them to put their own stories at the center of their understanding of the world. Recent studies of language show a sharp increase in the use of the words "I" and "me"—in popular music, for example. Many analysts of American culture have observed that in the last fifty years there has been a notable shift toward self-referential thinking.

However, this tendency to make the self the autonomous agent is as old as Adam, perhaps especially in matters of religion. In Paul's letter to the Galatians, the apostle seems to make a conscious move to correct his own thinking. He interrupts himself as he dictates, recasting his sentence, exchanging the object for the subject:

> Formerly, when you did not know God, you were in bondage to beings that by nature are no gods; but now that you have come to know God, *or rather to be known by* God, how can you turn back again to the weak and beggarly elemental spirits . . . (Gal 4:8–9)

Paul's move in this sentence, so easy to pass over, is of crucial importance (it would be interesting to know if he made it on purpose, for emphasis). The Galatians' "knowing" *of God* is subordinate to God's primary and precedent "knowing" *of them.* Another example that comes readily to hand is 1 John 4:19: "We love, because he first loved us." God's intimate, prevenient knowledge of us is described in radical terms in Psalm 139:

O Lord, thou hast searched me and known me! . . .
Thou knowest me right well;
my frame was not hidden from thee,
when I was being made in secret,
intricately wrought in the depths of the earth.
Thy eyes beheld my unformed substance;
in thy book were written, every one of them,
the days that were formed for me,
when as yet there was none of them.

When God's preexistent and complete knowledge of us is deemphasized in favor of our vaunted capacity for knowing God, we are in danger of usurping the place not only of God as Creator but also as Redeemer and Lord. We have substituted our own religious searching for the primary, unique story of God's search for us. A story is told about Beethoven that nicely suggests our almost ubiquitous tendency to shift from the power of God to human potential. Once when a composer showed Beethoven a score on which he had written, "Finished with the help of God," Beethoven wrote under it, "Man, help yourself!"[15] This neatly illustrates the typical movement of sermons and Bible studies on both ends of the ecclesiastical spectrum. The agency and initiative of *God* in creating a new reality is set aside in favor of energetic participation in social programs on the one hand and fervently individualistic piety on the other. It's the great American gospel of "God helps those who help themselves."

So complete and so pervasive is the use of verbs in sermons to make us the subject and God the object that even the most willing student of homiletics finds it difficult to grasp the nature of the problem. We need to learn to reverse our typical way of framing the subject-object relationship in speaking of God, but it is not easy. I can say with certainty that without immersion in the theocentric teaching of J. Louis Martyn in the days when he and Paul L. Lehmann were colleagues at Union Theological Seminary in New York, I would never have fully grasped the significance of the divine agency. Even though I had been immersed in the Bible from early childhood, I had never fully grasped the shift in thinking and in verbalizing that kerygmatic preaching requires. Indeed, it was almost ten years after I earned my degree that I fully appropriated my professors' teaching. There were several turning points in my own preaching when I had to be corrected for inconsistencies in my presentation. The crowning moment

15. From Jan Swafford's notes on the Ninth Symphony in the Tanglewood Music Festival program, August 2009. It is both amusing and instructive to recall that Karl Barth preferred the humanity of Mozart to the didacticism of Beethoven.

as I remember it was in 1982, seven years after I began my ordained ministry, when Joel Marcus, a student of Martyn's at the time, pointed out to me that in a sermon I had misinterpreted a passage—making the gracious action of Jesus subsequent to and dependent upon the repentance of a disciple.[16] After that, the subject-object relation became firmly lodged in my thinking, but it took half a lifetime of training. My point in mentioning this is to show how deeply ingrained is the habit of focusing on human agency, even in the case of a person who was raised with the Scriptures and the traditional Episcopal liturgy.

Lehmann used to say, "God is up to something in the world." The whimsical mode of expression was deceptive; he was mounting a frontal attack on anthropocentric ways of understanding the biblical story. In this, he was distinguishing himself from those in both academy and church who shared his passion for social justice but, in their focus on various sociopolitical strategies, had lost sight of the divine agency. Similarly today, although the theme of the kingdom of God is frequently the center of attention in the mainline churches' messages, the predominant notion is "building the kingdom," with ourselves as the active agents. This is equally true of the current enthusiasm for being "missional"; much emphasis is put on what used to be called "outreach," but there is a gap in the center where the *kerygma* should be. Thus we fail to acknowledge not only the *prior*, but also the *continuing* activity of God in planting signs within history of his coming reign. In the 2000s, for instance, it has become popular in the Episcopal Church in the United States to speak of helping God realize God's "dream." This notion of a God who is "dreaming"—not acting—is almost absurdly unbiblical. The God who raised up Moses and Elijah and Cyrus of Persia in spite of themselves is not a "dreamer"; God is the Holy One of Israel who delivers his people with a mighty hand and an outstretched arm.

It should be emphasized that the current enthusiasm for helping God realize God's dream (or, more biblically, build God's kingdom) is well intended. Indeed, "faith without works is dead," and the churches have much cause to repent, in view of our frequent collaboration with the powers and principalities. In view of the fact that an apocalyptic interpretation of the New Testament has moved to the foreground in our time, we might have expected a favorable reaction to it from groups within the church who have a high level of concern about global, social, and political

16. Joel Marcus is now professor of New Testament and Christian Origins at Duke Divinity School.

developments, because apocalyptic theology fits particularly well with these commitments. This embrace of apocalyptic by the church has often not been the case, however, for a very specific reason.

What is this reason? It is the centrality of *the divine agency*, without which the apocalyptic theology so powerfully recovered from the New Testament by Käsemann, Martyn, and many others cannot be grasped.

Lesslie Newbigen writes this sentence:

> The author of our salvation is God.[17]

This declarative sentence, in its very simplicity and directness, delivers a jolt of syntactical energy that would have been missing if the verb and the name of God had been placed at the beginning, thus: "God is the author of our salvation." Even so, it is insufficiently clear to most Christians that this plain statement calls for a wholesale overhaul of even the most sincere believer's thinking, because at the same time that one is nodding assent to the statement, one is already putting "but" at the end: the author of our salvation is God, "but we must believe," or "but we must repent" or "but we must become missional." We are locked into an "if-then" way of thinking rather than "because-therefore."[18] Paul's "because-therefore" way of speaking can be illustrated by a passage in 1 Corinthians:

> Do you not know that a little leaven leavens the whole lump? Cleanse out the old leaven *that you may be* a new lump, *as you really are unleavened.* For Christ, our paschal lamb, has been sacrificed. (5:6–8, emphasis added)

Another way of describing this typical "because-therefore" mode of Pauline address is familiar to many a seminary student: "Become what you already are!" The formulation has often been invoked, but not so often implemented in preaching. We are not convinced of that "already are." Does this not leave us with nothing to do? How strange it is that we are more attracted to the injunction to clean out the old leaven than we are to the declaration that it has already been accomplished by the Lamb of God! Many gifted preachers have never quite gotten this straight; the "if-then" pattern is hardwired into us and the "because-therefore" dynamic has not displaced it. A great many sermons therefore direct their appeal to those "powers of our nature" that Pelagius was "in such a hurry to exalt."

The missing ingredient in so much preaching and teaching today is the nature of Sin, which J. Louis Martyn has taught us, following not only

---

17. Newbigen, *Sin and Salvation*, 56.
18. I owe this formulation to Philip Ziegler.

Paul but also the Gospels with their portrayal of Jesus' exorcisms.[19] Sin cannot be understood as an inventory of individual misdeeds. Sin is an irresistible, autonomous, malignant power from which we must be delivered by another, greater power. Lesslie Newbigen is particularly clear in his Pauline-Augustinian discussion of this matter:

> We have seen . . . that man is unable to extricate himself from sin. Like an animal trapped in a clever snare, mankind trapped in the snare of sin struggles to free himself, but the more he struggles, the more the snare fastens its grip on him. His efforts to be free of sin are themselves infected by sin and drive him deeper into sin. Because sin is a corruption of man's will, even when he wills to be free from sin he is driven deeper into sin. . . . Man can never by his own power or will extricate himself from the grip of sin; only God can extricate him. And God has done it. That is the good news which we preach.[20]

This clear exposition of our incapacity is not what we ordinarily hear in mainline churches today. If we talk of sin at all, we prefer to think with Pelagius that God can help us to resist sin "more easily." We are used to thinking that we are quite capable of "making good choices" as the current lingo has it—"with God's help," of course.[21] The idea that we are helpless in the grip of Sin is always going to be deeply offensive to those who cherish the idea of "free will." Most Americans remain resistant to any suggestion that we cannot accomplish whatever we set our minds to. Indeed, despite the insights of analytic psychology, of which Dorothy Martyn is such a gifted expositor, most people continue to use the language of choice and decision making, as though our ability to make good choices were

---

19. John's Gospel has no exorcisms per se, but it could not be more clear about the confrontation between Jesus Christ and "the ruler of this world" (John 12:31; 14:30; 16:11).

20. Newbigen, *Sin and Salvation*, 56.

21. Notice how, in Cranmer's *Prayer Book*, we pray, "We humbly beseech thee, O heavenly Father, so to *assist* us with thy grace *that* we may continue in that holy fellowship and do all such good works as thou hast prepared for us to walk in" (prayer following Communion; online: http://justus.anglican.org/resources/bcp/1549/Communion_1549.htm). Here, the word "assist" has a very different impact because of the word "that," which clearly indicates that without God's grace going before us, we are not capable of doing those already-prepared good works. "For by grace you have been saved through faith; and this is not your own doing, it is the gift of God—not because of works, lest any man should boast. For we are his workmanship, created in Christ Jesus for good works, which God prepared beforehand, that we should walk in them" (Eph 2:8–10).

indisputable.[22] We say of a person, "She made bad choices," as though it were a simple matter to reject drugs, or liquor, or bad company. Thus we reduce Sin (singular) to sins (plural), thereby encouraging a reductive view of sin as discrete, willful action.

We are forced, then, to an unsatisfactory conclusion: either such sins are deliberate choices and therefore deserving of condemnation, or they are infinitely forgivable. *Neither* of these options is commensurate with Paul's great vision of the conquest of the powers in Romans 5–8, for Paul uses neither the language of "free choice" nor "forgiveness." Instead of forgiveness, which he rarely mentions, Paul speaks of the *dikaiosunē theou*, the righteousness of God that is capable of calling into existence the things that do not exist—namely, a community whose righteousness is the very mirror of God's own.

If this is true, then we can see that *both* the left *and* the right in the churches are building on the wrong theological foundations. The "liberal" churches eschew all talk of sin and emphasize human participation in kingdom-building, "missional" activity, making God's dream come true.[23] The conservative-evangelical constituency typically argues as though the divide between social activism and individual salvation were the key point of disagreement, not recognizing that that the distinction is a false one in the first place. The real test lies elsewhere: *do we have a God who is actively shaping events in the world, or not?*

Paul Lehmann's partnership with Martyn took place in the late 60s and early 70s, when apocalyptic theology was opening up at Union

---

22. See Dorothy Martyn, *Beyond Deserving.* The title of one of J. L. Martyn's lectures at Union Theological Seminary in the early 70s was "The Myth of Man the Decision-Maker."

23. It can be argued that the sins of racism, anti-Semitism, classism, and all the other isms, plus homophobia and environmental degradation, are regularly denounced in liberal pulpits. The problem here is that the congregations to whom these sermons are addressed are already, for the most part, committed to the positions espoused in the preaching. This is quite different from hearing sermons in which all—including the preacher—are implicated: "even our righteous deeds are like filthy rags" (Isa 64:6); "all human beings, both Jews and Greeks, are under the power of sin" (Rom 3:9). Preaching that challenges the closely held views of a congregation is truly rare. Even in the great days of William Sloane Coffin, his self-selected listeners could be counted on to support him. After 9/11, it became more personally costly than ever before for a preacher to raise questions about America's conduct of war. No doubt this partly accounts for the deafening silence from the churches on both the left and the right when widespread prisoner abuse and "extraordinary rendition" by the United States became known.

Theological Seminary.[24] No theologian writing in English in the latter half of the twentieth century was more oriented toward socioeconomic issues or more geopolitically involved.[25] In spite of this, he was regarded with suspicion by those who ordinarily would have been partners with him in these commitments. Why was that? It was because he was an unabashed believer in the divine agency.[26] In this regard he was, like Karl Barth, not only greatly learned but also at heart a man of childlike trust. Many of his students and colleagues were baffled by this combination of intellectual sophistication and Abrahamic faith.[27]At the same time that Martyn was leading seminars in which students were being retrained to make God the subject of the verb, Lehmann was insisting that a *theological* ethics begins with the discernment, by faith, of God's activity in the world. Social action is a form of witness to what *God* is doing; it never claims to be righteous in itself. This has tremendous implications for preaching.

The controlling vision in apocalyptic theology is that of the intervention of God in human history to reclaim his creation for himself. Indeed, since the *kosmos* is in bondage to a power that seeks its undoing, it is more accurate to speak of God's *invasion*. In an important essay, "World without End or Twice-Invaded World," J. Louis Martyn sets out the two-part story: God's good creation was *invaded* by powers hostile to his purposes, and then God in the person of his Son *invaded* this "territory held largely

24. Raymond E. Brown was also offering a new appreciation of New Testament apocalyptic in his courses at Union at that time.

25. The title of one of Lehmann's books, *The Transfiguration of Politics*, gives the general idea. Some would say this particular book is dated, since it deals with the upheavals of the late 60s, but his imaginative readings of Scripture and his theological daring, fully grounded in the tradition yet fully engaged in current events, is as lively and pertinent as ever.

26. Christopher Morse, in an essay about Lehmann's work, notes that this was precisely the problem that Lehmann faced from the left (Morse, *Explorations*, 11).

27. There were, to be sure, other discomfiting traits, like his elaborate syntax and sharp skewer. But the key issue, *theologically*, was Lehmann's *thoroughly Reformed emphasis on the pre-eminence and prevenience of God* (Latin *praevenere*, meaning "to go before"—we might say "proactive," today). A useful comparison can be made with *Faith Works*, a book about Christian activism by the estimable Jim Wallis, leader of the Sojourners community. The book is filled with wonderful examples of, and good counsel about, Christian social activism, but there is a strange vacuum at its heart; God is scarcely mentioned, and hardly ever as the subject of any verbs. Is this because Wallis is trying to reach an audience of nonbelievers? In any case, it is the most *anthropo*centric, least *theo*centric work that one could imagine coming from a prominent Christian and self-identified evangelical.

by the Devil," defeating Satan on the very ground that he illegitimately occupies.[28]

And yet there continues to be resistance to this narrative. The cherished contemporary notion of "self-esteem" is lurking here. Numerous analysts have raised questions about this preoccupation, wondering if concentration on "self-worth" has not in fact produced a singularly unmoored, narcissistic, perpetually dissatisfied society. In any case, the failure of the churches to grasp the nature of Sin as an autonomous power has greatly weakened our ability to preach the gospel to those who are striving for "self-actualization," because without any grasp of our essential helplessness, we are thrown back on our own devices—which is precisely the way that we, with our exaggerated assessment of our own powers, prefer to have it.

Simon Gathercole of Cambridge University wrote an assessment of the so-called New Perspective on Paul for non-specialists in *Christianity Today.* He agreed that there is merit in the warnings of the of the New Perspective scholars against caricaturing Judaism as lacking in grace. However, he insisted, there is nevertheless much testimony from the time of Paul to indicate that "many of Paul's contemporaries seem to have believed that obedience was possible *without* a radical inbreaking of God." Here is the crux: for Paul, Gathercole writes, "salvation was impossible without the earth-shattering events of the Cross, Resurrection, and Pentecost." Obedience to the covenant was not possible without "mighty acts of God." The "flesh" (*sarx*) is not only powerless to obey; it actually wars with God (Rom 8:7).[29]

Preachers must therefore find grace-filled ways to speak of *sarx* and its bondage to Sin without needlessly alienating congregations. It is easy

---

28. Martyn, "Twice-Invaded World," quoting Flannery O'Connor, *Mystery and Manners.*

29. Gathercole, "What Did Paul Really Mean?" He continues to show that *faith* is defined (following Rom 4:18–22) as *"being fully persuaded that God had the power to do what he promised"* (ibid., 6). It is "God who justifies the ungodly (4:5), who creates out of nothing (4:17), and who raised Jesus from the dead (4:24). Utterly all-powerful, he wields that power to bring righteousness where there was none, creation where there was none, and life where there was none. That's the God we believe in" (6). This is exemplary. He continues (note the subject-object relation): "God is the sole operator in salvation. . . . It is not that we have accomplished some successful law-observance that needs to be topped off by God to make a full quota . . . God acts so that it is obvious to all that he alone does the whole saving work (Rom 11:6)" (7). My only disappointment with this article is that Gathercole missed an opportunity to define *dikaiosunē* explicitly as rectification.

enough to find examples of the way that the power of Sin is able to undo even our best efforts. It is not difficult to find illustrations. A phenomenal bestseller in the 2000s was *Three Cups of Tea*. Its much-admired, widely celebrated author founded an agency in Afghanistan to carry out his insights into what was needed there. He was invited to speak to diplomats and legislators. When a 60 *Minutes* investigation disclosed serious discrepancies in both finances and facts, there was much wailing and gnashing of teeth among his many admirers.[30] Yet we should not be surprised at this. The saying "no good deed goes unpunished" is remarkably apt when seen in the light of the power of Sin. Every honest humanitarian agency will admit that very often its best efforts are undone by implacable malign forces at work in human nature and in the created order. The great challenge in preaching about Sin is to do it in a cosmic context of prevenient grace, with God's rectification of all things as the center and circumference. Thus in the words of the *Book of Common Prayer*, we may have confidence that, in submission to God, a miracle of his power can actually make it possible to speak of "all our works begun, continued, and ended in thee."[31]

In closing, if I were to suggest just one area in which J. L. Martyn's work needs to be supplemented, it is in the theology of the Old Testament. The revelatory testimony of the Hebrew people displays for us the lordship of the Holy One of Israel in the time before the Son was called *kyrios*. It is confounding that so much interpretation of the Scriptures continues to make human activity and human religious imagination the subject of passages like this:

> I am God, and there is no other; I am God, and there is none like me, declaring the end from the beginning and from ancient times things not yet done, saying, 'My counsel shall stand, and I will accomplish all my purpose. . . . I have spoken, and I will bring it to pass; I have purposed, and I will do it'" (Isa 46:9–10)

I have long believed that if a preacher were to set aside three months, say, to preach through Isaiah 40–55, it would radicalize his or her understanding of the subject-object relationship. It would be very difficult to continue to put human potential at the center of such an extended period of exposition. One might begin doing so out of habit, but week after week

---

30. Particularly poignant was the anguish (not too strong a word) of the columnist and humanitarian Nicholas Kristof ("Three Cups of Tea, Spilled").

31. Not incidentally, Martyn taught us to avoid the word "possibility," in connection with the agency of God, at all costs! I believe that this usage illustrates a *theological* way to use it.

the divine agency that is the *subject* of Deutero-Isaiah would assert itself. The human being appears in these chapters largely as the maker and worshipper of impotent idols. The potency is all the Lord's, who declares,

> Lift up your eyes to the heavens, and look at the earth beneath; for the heavens will vanish like smoke, the earth will wear out like a garment, and they who dwell in it will die like gnats; but my salvation will be for ever, and my deliverance will never be ended. (Isa 51)

> I, I am the Lord, and besides me there is no savior . . .
> I am God, and also henceforth I am He;
> there is none who can deliver from my hand;
> I work and who can hinder it?" (Isa 43:11, 13)

But lest we should think that there is nothing for human beings to do except stand agape at the majestic deeds of the Lord, there is indeed an identifiable, active, historical human being in Deutero-Isaiah. Cyrus of Persia is not a passive recipient of spiritual illumination; indeed, he does not appear to be "spiritual" at all, but is rather a man of action:

> I stirred up one from the north, and he has come, from the rising of the sun, and he shall call on my name; he shall trample on rulers as on mortar, as the potter treads clay . . .

> Thus says the Lord to his anointed, to Cyrus . . . "I will go before you and level the mountains . . . that you may know that it is I, the Lord, the God of Israel, who calls you by your name. . . . I gird you, though you do not know me, that men may know, from the rising of the sun and from the west, that there is none besides me; I am the Lord, and there is no other." (Isa 45:1–6)

Who is the kingdom-builder here? Who is the subject, and who the object? Who is the actor and who the acted-upon? Is it not the Lord who stirs up one from the north? Is it not the Lord who goes before his servants to part the Red Sea? Is it not the Lord who sets great movements in motion to serve his eternal purposes? And is it not the human being who, willingly or not, is taken up into the will of God and thereby liberated from the powers? Is it not the human being who is raised up by the Lord who clears his path before him?

Now, finally, I will admit that all this talk of sentences and verbs may give the wrong impression. Very few people are blessed with exceptional literary or rhetorical gifts, and most students of preaching today cannot be expected to rise to standards of eloquence that were commonplace in earlier centuries. But there is no one who, in declaring the gospel message, cannot learn to make God the subject of active verbs. It is a form of trusting in the God who speaks. None of us can be John Donne, but we can all make a sentence like this: "The author of salvation is God." We can all learn to avoid sentences like "We are all on a faith journey" and declare instead, "God has sought us and found us." We can all be retrained to make the righteousness of God the active agent in our illustrations from life, being freed by the great good news that our works are already prepared for us to walk in, for we are *God's* workmanship (Eph 2:10). We all can apply ourselves to conveying the thrilling message that the Lord God is on the move whether we join him or not, for if we are not climbing aboard his train he will pass us by, calling a Cyrus and setting him in motion as an agent of his purposes.

The Holy One of Israel, the triune God, is at work reclaiming peoples, nations, principalities, powers, the realm of the flesh, and the entire *kosmos* for himself. The proper work of the Lord's people is to follow the path that he has already blazed ahead of us and to rejoice in the movement of the Holy Spirit among us, for as the Apostle writes,

> . . . for though we walk in the flesh, we do not wage war after the flesh: For the weapons of our warfare are not worldly, but mighty through God to the pulling down of strongholds." (2 Cor 10:3–4)

14

Baptism at the Turn of the Ages

Joseph Mangina

Baptism thus implies a *break*. Christ invades the realm of Satan and lays hold of those who belong to him, thereby creating his church-community [Gemeinde]. Past and present are torn asunder. The old has passed away, everything has become new. The break does not come about by our breaking our chains out of an unquenchable thirst to see our life and all things ordered in a new and free way. Long ago, Christ himself had already brought about that break. In baptism this break now also takes effect in my own life.

—Dietrich Bonhoeffer, *Discipleship*[1]

I

CHRISTIAN BAPTISM IS AN eschatological act. This much is clear through its origins in the practice of one John "the Baptizer," who summoned Israel to repentance in light of the coming Judgment. Just as the Eucharist and eschatology is a firmly established theme in the theology of the Lord's Supper, so the link between baptism and eschatology is something contemporary theologians tend to take for granted.

---

1. Bonhoeffer, *Discipleship*, 207 (emphasis original). I am grateful to Robert Dean for bringing this quotation to my attention.

But is baptism also an apocalyptic act? Much depends on how we understand that highly contested term, which can denote everything from Darbyite dispensationalism to the 9/11 attacks to the effects of global warming. The present essay takes as its point of departure the work of J. Louis Martyn, a scholar who, more than anyone else, has opened our eyes to the apocalyptic Paul. Though Martyn wisely does not offer any succinct definition of "apocalyptic," his distinctive use of the word emerges clearly in his *Galatians* commentary and other writings. Martyn notes the usual translation of the verb *apocalyptō* as "to reveal" or "to unveil," only to dismiss it, at least as far as Pauline thought is concerned. The metaphor of pulling back a curtain is far too passive for Paul's God:

> The genesis of Paul's apocalyptic—as we see it in Galatians—lies in the apostle's certainty that God has *invaded* the present evil age by sending Christ and his Spirit into it. There was a "before," the time when we were confined, imprisoned; and there is an "after," the time of our deliverance. And the difference between the two is caused not by an unveiling, but rather by the coming of Christ and his Spirit.[2]

The created cosmos has—temporarily and inexplicably—fallen out of God's hands. It has become enslaved to alien, malign powers.[3] In response, God invades the captive world to set it free. And the site of that invasion is the cross. In the "thoroughly real event of Christ's crucifixion, God's war of liberation was commenced and decisively settled, making the cross the foundation of Paul's apocalyptic theology."[4]

Note the words "decisively settled." Although the war is still going on—the Galatian *ekklesia* are themselves combatants in it—the tide of battle has turned; "Jesus is victor." Thus Martyn writes that "in an anticipatory but altogether real sense, Christ's advent is [the] victory, even if its victorious character can be seen only in the bifocal vision of apocalyptic."[5]

Despite his pervasive use of military imagery, Martyn is almost equally enamored of the metaphor of drama. Indeed, his great commentary opens with a list of *dramatis personae*.[6] The main actors include Paul, the Teachers—Martyn's almost Orwellian term for the circumcision party

---

2. Martyn, *Galatians*, 99 (emphasis original).

3. Ibid., 105.

4. In support of this point, Martyn tellingly cites the work of his mentor Ernst Käsemann, in particular the latter's *Perspectives on Paul*.

5. Martyn, *Galatians*, 105. On "bifocal vision" see Martyn, *Issues*, 279–97.

6. Martyn, *Galatians*, 13–15.

who occasioned the crisis in Galatia—the False Brothers, and not least the Galatian Christians themselves. All of these come alive in the course of an exposition that is at once historical, theological, and thoroughly dramatic. Martyn has an uncanny ability to draw the reader into the unfolding action that is Galatians. Nor are we allowed to forget for one moment the one who is both the author of the drama and its chief character, the God who comes powerfully "onto the scene" for the deliverance of human beings (Gal 4:4, 6).

If the advent of the gospel has the form of a drama, what role has baptism within it? We thus revert to the theme of this essay. Paul mentions baptism only once in Galatians, but when he does so, the appeal is powerful:

> For you are—all of you—sons of God through the faith that is in Christ Jesus. For when all of you were baptized into Christ, you put on Christ as though he were your clothing. There is neither Jew nor Greek; there is neither slave nor free; there is no "male and female"; for all of you are One in Christ Jesus. And, if you are Christ's, then as a result of that, you are seed of Abraham, heirs in accordance with the promise.[7]

While much of Galatians is taken up with the interpretation of Scripture, here we find Paul commenting on a piece of Christian liturgy. At the heart of this passage stands a traditional baptismal formula, reflected also in 1 Corinthians 12:13 and Colossians 3:9–11. Paul refers to baptism in order to re-enforce the larger point he is making about the Galatians' identity. By the coming of Christ and of faith—for Paul, this constitutes but one divine action—the Galatian Christians are *already* "sons of God." As evidence of this, Paul cites the time when the Galatians were baptized, putting on Christ "as though he were your clothing." The unity with Christ thus effected is all the divine sonship they need. They have nothing to gain, and everything to lose, by yielding to the Teachers' imprecations that they be circumcised.

Both in the *Galatians* commentary and in *Theological Issues*, Martyn devotes a great deal of attention to the pairings Jew/Greek, slave/free, and male/female that appear in the baptismal formula of Galaitians 3:28. He cites multiple ancient sources that describe the world as constituted by such binary opposites, for which he coins the term "apocalyptic antinomies."[8]

---

7. Gal 3:26–29, Martyn's translation (*Galatians*, 6).

8. See Comment 40, "Not Jew and Gentile, but One in Christ," in *Galatians*, 378–83. At a more conceptual level, see the essay "Apocalyptic Antinomies."

Representing the common sense of the old aeon, these structures or orders of creation have come to seem natural for Jew and pagan alike. For Paul, however, these ways of organizing reality no longer pertain for those who have "put on" Christ. Persons previously identified as Jews and Gentiles "have been made into a new unity that is so fundamentally and irreducibly identified with Christ himself as to cause Paul to use the masculine form of the word 'one.' Members of the church are not one *thing*; they are one *person*, having been taken into the corpus of the One New Man."[9]

Baptism, then, is of a piece with what might be called Paul's "apocalyptic realism." In the cross of Christ is enacted the mutual "crucifixion" of the self and the world—the corrupt passing aeon. While the structures of the latter persist for a while, they have no power to constitute reality. Rather, reality is constituted by God's apocalyptic act in Jesus Christ: "For neither is circumcision anything nor is uncircumcision anything. What is something is the new creation."[10] The *ekklesia* is the social form this new creation takes in the present, and baptism a person's entry into it.

But is this apocalyptic realism compatible with a sacramental realism? More simply, is baptism a "sacrament"? It would be anachronistic to foist on Paul later definitions of sacrament, whether as "means of grace" or as "a sign that effects what it signifies." Indeed, contemporary theological discussions of sacrament tend to resist making any such general notion determinative, insisting instead on the particularities of such rites as baptism and the Supper.[11] While this is a useful caveat, we should also not lose sight of the analogous relation that obtains among such actions, and that led them to be grouped together in the first place. If 1 Corinthians 10:1–5 is any indication, Paul already tended to baptism and Eucharist as the same "kind of thing," the first representing Israel/the church's Passover-like deliverance, the second being the manna and the water that sustains her in the wilderness.

To belong to Christ, in other words, is to belong to his people, and to belong to his people entails being baptized and sharing the spiritual food and drink of the Eucharist. To be sure, these actions are not ends in themselves. They are instrumental to the creation of a people that lives beyond the determinations of the present age (Jew/Greek, slave/free, male/female; in light of 1 Cor 11:17–34, one would surely have to add rich/poor to this list). Yet it is equally the case that the church as God's apocalyptic

9. Martyn, *Galatians*, 377.

10. Gal 6:15, Martyn's translation; Martyn, *Galatians*, 10.

11. See Fahey, "Sacraments."

"beachhead" lives by just such actions. Thus Martyn writes that "Paul sees in baptism the juncture by which the person both participates in the death of Christ (Rom. 6:4) and is equipped with the armor for apocalyptic battle (1 Thess. 5:8–10; 1 Cor. 15:53–54; Rom. 13:12)."[12] It is both a dying to the old self and an empowerment by the agency of God's own Spirit.

In scholastic theology, any given sacramental action could be analyzed into three distinct moments. There is the *sacramentum tantum*, the pure sign considered in itself. There is the *res tantum*, the ultimate reality or grace to which the sign directs us, that which it "signifies." Hovering between these two is the *res et sacramentum*, in which sign and reality—miraculously but truly—coincide. It is this third moment that describes the realm of the sacramental in the proper sense. Here a bath is more than just a bath; it is a cleansing from the effects of original sin. Here bread is more than mere bread; it is the life-giving body of the Lord.

What now if we transposed these scholastic categories into the idiom of apocalyptic? The *res tantum* would clearly be the new creation, the ultimate deliverance of the cosmos from every evil, the time when "God will be all in all."[13] The scope is cosmic, the implied soteriology more *Christus victor* than Anselmic in character.[14] The *sacramentum tantum* would—in the case of baptism—be simply the water rite itself, as the portal of entry into the life of the new age. It is whatever action Paul performed over Crispus, Gaius, and the household of Stephanas.[15]

As for the *res et sacramentum*, this would be nothing other than the irruption of the eschatological goal into the midst of the present aeon. "If anyone is in Christ"—that is, if anyone has "put on Christ as though he were their clothing" in baptism—"new creation!" Far from being simply a future reality, the new creation is here, and the church is evidence of it. This is the "enthusiastic" moment in Paul noted earlier, though it exists side by side with the understanding that the old aeon has not totally lost its hold. If this were not the case, Paul would not have had to write his at times tender, at times imperious letters to the all-too-human churches under his care. The gospel has come to Galatia, but the Galatian church is quick to abandon it for the old religious ways. The body of Christ exists in

12. Martyn, *Galatians*, 376.

13. 1 Cor 15:28.

14. Though the distance between these two can easily be exaggerated. One theologian who combines both elements is the Orthodox writer David Bentley Hart. See his vigorous defense of Anselm against some of the typical objections in *The Beauty of the Infinite*.

15. 1 Cor 1:14–16.

Corinth, but the rich in that community show their contempt for the body by the way they treat the poor.

Given this enduring imperfection, can we even speak of a coincidence of sacramental sign and reality? Yes, because while there is undoubtedly a human agency at work in baptism and the Supper, the power of these actions resides elsewhere. It is God who acts in baptism, God who graciously clothes believers in the garment of Christ. In the language of Reformation theology, the reliability of the sacraments is a function of the Word, of the divine promise that attaches to particular objects and actions in the church's life. Christians obey the mandate—"do this!"—so that they may receive the promise.[16] The content of the sacrament is none other than the content of the gospel itself. It is the Pauline proclamation of Christ crucified, but now as rendered in the language of material and bodily reality, a visible emblem of the new age planted in the midst of the old.

Paul does not often speak of baptism in his letters; but when he does, it is usually to underscore the gospel's perfect-tense character. It is as if he needed to remind his readers that their world—the world as such—has been irrevocably changed by Christ's coming. In Romans, baptism into Christ's death serves to underscore the absurdity of sinning "that grace may abound." In Galatians, putting on Christ means the end to enslavement, whether to the Law or to the taken-for-granted structures of human society. In 1 Corinthians, we have evidence that Paul himself baptized, although this fact is an occasion of some awkwardness for him, as people may use it as evidence that he is "their" special apostle.[17] Paul thus roundly insists that "Christ did not send me to baptize but to preach the gospel, and not with words of eloquent wisdom, lest the cross of Christ be emptied of its power."[18] Read in context, even this disclaimer testifies to the power of baptism. The Corinthians were baptized not in Paul's name, but *in the name of Christ*.[19] Therefore they belong to the body of this One New Man; and therefore they may not allow the social divisions characterizing the old aeon to tear them apart. The church is the gospel's social corollary, and baptism its apocalyptic portal.

---

16. For an exquisite analysis of the sacraments in light of these Reformation categories, see Jenson, *Visible Words*. By contrast, Aquinas employed the language of instrumental causality to account for the human role in sacraments. See *Summa Theologiae*, 3.62.1.

17. See 1 Cor 1:14–16.

18. 1 Cor 1:17.

19. 1 Cor 1:13.

II

Baptism is an apocalyptic act. That is the basic point of the picture just sketched of the role of baptism in Paul. But baptism is also a ritual action, a rite of entry into the visible and historical community known as the Christian church. It is not only divine, eschatological, and invasive, but also human, historical, and prone to corruption. Baptism has a history. This history is not other than the church's own history, its expansion from the tiny communities planted by Paul in the eastern Roman Empire, to the centuries-long experiment known as Christendom, to our present reluctant or enthusiastic embrace of a church that is once again missional.

The present essay cannot seek to recount the complex history of baptism.[20] Instead, I will rehearse a parable that attempts to catch up many features of that history: the famous baptism scene in Francis Ford Coppola's movie *The Godfather*. This example has the advantage of being both artistically powerful and culturally iconic. It can serve as an emblem of the problems that ensue when the church and its baptism becomes an established religious practice. It will also, I hope, suggest the ways in which baptism resists its own subversion, and so testifies to the grace of God at work in it.

The scene in question occurs at the very climax of *The Godfather*, as Michael Corleone (played by Al Pacino) prepares to make his decisive move against the other four Mafia families in New York City. Michael's father, Don Vito Corleone (Marlon Brando,) has recently died of a heart attack—a surprisingly natural ending to a life marked by such violence. Michael now heads the Corleone family. His first formal act in his new role is to serve as sponsor at the baptism of Michael Rizzi, the infant son of his sister, Connie. It is a solemn occasion, both because the baptism of a child is an important event in the life of the community and because it marks Michael's assuming of his father's mantle. From now on he will be, quite literally, "the godfather."

The baptismal liturgy depicted by Coppola is the traditional Tridentine rite, spoken in Latin. It involves the placing of salt on the infant's tongue, signifying preservation from corruption, as well as an exorcism, performed by the priest's blowing three times on the child to drive out the "unclean spirit." The liturgy also involves a confession of faith in God the Father, God the Son, and God the Holy Spirit, and—as the negative

---

20. At least on the Protestant side, perhaps no one has mastered the relevant literature like Bryan Spinks, in his series of books treating the history of baptism.

corollary of this—a renunciation of the devil. Since the infant Michael cannot speak for himself, his godfather answers the questions on his behalf:

> Michael Francis Rizzi, do you renounce Satan?
> *I do renounce him.*
> And all his works?
> *I do renounce them.*
> And all his pomps?
> *I do renounce them.*
> Michael Rizzi, will you be baptized?
> *I will.*[21]

So the baptism proceeds; so the requirements of God and the church are fulfilled.

Yet even as Michael Corleone utters these solemn words, another drama is unfolding, as his lieutenants move ahead with their plan to execute the heads of the other mob families. The victims are gunned down as they go about their everyday lives. One is shot while getting a massage; another is in bed with his girlfriend; another is haggling with a policeman over a parking ticket, the cop being in fact a Corleone assassin. The camera repeatedly cuts back and forth between the baptism and these scenes of bloodshed, the one a liturgy of life, the other of death. The effect is unnerving. As viewers we know that those killed are not "nice" people, and yet we respond with an instinctive human sympathy. No one should have to die this way.

The meaning of Michael Rizzi's baptism may be sought at multiple levels. At one level, it is an episode in the story of Michael Corleone, whose descent into a life of corruption is the primary theme of *The Godfather*. At the outset of the story, Michael's life is full of promise. He is a college graduate and war hero, and is engaged to marry a lovely young WASP (Fay, played by Diane Keaton). He was not supposed to go into the "family business." But fate—and Michael's own decisions—would dictate otherwise. By the time he comes to stand at the baptismal font, Michael has been a killer many times over. Nor is his work quite finished. Having finished off his rivals, he immediately turns his attention to traitors within the Corleone circle, including his brother-in-law, Carlo Rizzi, father of the baptized child. Carlo will be dealt with as ruthlessly as were Michael's other enemies.

---

21. Jones, *Annotated Godfather*, 222ff. The screenplay does not contain the actual text of the baptismal rite, but simply notes that the priest "speaks Latin." For this I have consulted the film itself.

In light of all this, it is hard to see Michael's role in the baptism as anything but a willful act of self-damnation. He confesses faith in the Trinity, at the same time that he is engaged in a way of life completely at odds with such faith. He professes to reject "Satan and all his pomps and all his works," even as he carries out Satan's bidding. It is part of the brilliance of Pacino's performance that he is able to convey the awfulness of this moment. Michael speaks the words quietly, soberly, yet with resolve. Here is a man who knows exactly what he is doing. He does not flinch even at blasphemy if it serves the consolidation of his power.

But is it really true that Michael knows exactly what he is doing? Do any of us? Michael undoubtedly "knows" that he is a bad Catholic, and that whatever slim hope of heaven he may have had died long ago, on the floor of a restaurant in the Bronx.[22] Nevertheless, the baptismal service is not really interested in the sponsor's good or bad opinion of himself. The sponsor is but a surrogate. Michael speaks not as Michael Corleone here, but as Michael Rizzi. Whatever Michael may have "intended" when he agreed to become his nephew's godfather, the role in which he is cast has hijacked his identity, in ways that he himself does not quite understand. Even if Michael accepts damnation for himself, we can imagine him willing a different destiny for his godson—as his own father had once willed a different destiny for him. The understated sobriety of Pacino's performance perfectly reflects the ambiguities at work here.[23]

In saying this, I do not mean to absolve Michael of responsibility for his actions. Nor do I wish to suggest, sentimentally, that participation in his godson's baptism will save him. Murder is murder. What I do wish to say, however, is that Michael's story cannot be reduced to that of a heroic, clear-minded willing of good or evil. His freedom is real, and yet at the same time it is an engaged freedom, inseparable from contingent events and relationships. For instance, it was only his brother Sonny's death that thrust Michael into his unexpected role as head of the family, and that death in turn was the outcome both of Sonny's character and of external forces. The mystery of human freedom is worked out in unpredictable ways across time. Michael could in principle inhabit the role of godfather

22. I am referring to Michael's first act of murder, the killing of a rival mob leader and his policeman bodyguard. This action set off a vicious war among the Mafia families of New York City.

23. The analysis in this paragraph is indebted to comments made by Chad Pecknold in response to an earlier draft of this essay. Pecknold's own reflections on the concept of "intention" may be found in "Beyond Our Intentions."

simply by acting as a benign *paterfamilias* to the Corleone clan. By the time the story ends, the title has become something far more sinister.

Yet we are not done with the unfathomability of intention. Whatever Michael's intentions may be—indeed, whatever the intentions of the screenwriters—the event of baptism itself introduces a wild card in the form of divine action. The primary agent in any baptism is God. It would be wrong to say that God simply ignores or overrules human agency. The various human participants all come to this scene with their personal agendas, some good, others perhaps less good. God's intention does not so much overrule as *outrun* these various agendas, causing something to come about that no human power could achieve on its own. "If anyone is in Christ—new creation!" This declaration applies also to Michael Rizzi. He has been baptized into the triune Name. He has been delivered from the domain of darkness and transferred to the kingdom of God's beloved Son.[24]

These are, to be sure, extraordinary affirmations. Stuck in the assumptions of late modernity, we are inclined to say that Michael Rizzi will be a "real" Christian only when he has made his own decision of faith, when he claims for himself the promises others have made on his behalf. Let us imagine for a moment that this occurs. Suppose young Michael grows up, repudiates the Corleone family business, and becomes a model husband and father. He believes the church's teaching and lives a life full of faith, hope, and charity. Will he then need to be rebaptized? Surely not. However contested the practice of baptism may be, the conviction that it is unrepeatable has remained steadfast throughout the church's history. Why is that?

The cultural anthropologist might say that, as a typical rite of passage, baptism is among those journeys made only once in life. And of course there is a grain of truth in this answer. The church is a human community. It would be odd indeed if it did not obey some of the general laws and patterns governing human social interaction. But viewed theologically, baptism's unrepeatability is grounded in the decisiveness and singularity of God's action in Jesus Christ. Christ has died to Sin, once for all.[25] This is the very act by which he has conquered the powers of Sin and Death. Baptism is the sign of a believer's participation in this event. As Christ (with finality) has died to Sin, so we (with finality) have died with Christ,

---

24. Col 1:13.
25. Rom 6:10.

an action that marks the apocalyptic cancellation[26] of the old self and its ways, and the birth of a new self "alive to God in Christ Jesus."[27]

But now we return to the crux of the problem: how can this *eschatological* identity be conferred by a *religious* act such as baptism? The issue is sharply posed in the writings of J. Louis Martyn. In good Barthian fashion, he defines religion as the "various communal, cultic means—always involving the distinction of sacred from profane—by which human beings seem to know and to be happily related to the gods or God." As such it must be seen as "the polar opposite of God's apocalyptic act in Christ." The church as religious organization attempts to make itself as different from the world as possible. While the church is indeed distinct, writes Martyn, the distinction in question is not religious but apocalyptic. He quotes Bonhoeffer with approval: "God has founded his church beyond religion."[28]

"Beyond religion"—but does this mean "without religion"? Surely Martyn would not make the mistake of reading this remark of Bonhoeffer's in such a flat, undialectical way. Oddly, to reject religion as such would mean giving it too much importance. It would amount to taking one's stand on one side of the apocalyptic antinomy religious/secular or sacred/profane. It would mean becoming a theologian of the secular city. While such a reading of Bonhoeffer did flourish for a while in the 1950s and 1960s, the trend mercifully did not last for long. Bonhoeffer's goal was not to valorize secularity in the abstract, but to announce God's freedom to claim the profane, unbelieving world as his own, no less than the world that had been defined by Christendom.

If we take this insight and apply it to the baptism of Michael Francis Rizzi, the results are intriguing. There is no doubt that the baptismal service depicted in *The Godfather* is a cultic act. It is a liturgy, performed using archaic language and gestures, by a member of a professional clerical class. The odor of sanctity hovers over the whole proceedings. Only we must not imagine that we can escape the religious determination of baptism by gathering at the riverside for a revival service. Religion is not dispensed with quite so easily. We can alter the particular terms of the observance—and this may well be a good and necessary thing—but we cannot escape some element of the cultic, at least not without dissolving baptism altogether.

26. The verb Paul uses in Rom 6:6 is *katargeo*, which he uses elsewhere to speak of God's overturning or dissolution of the present world order; cf. 1 Cor 1:28; 2:6; 15:24, 26.

27. Rom 6:11.

28. Martyn, *Issues*, 80, citing Bonhoeffer, *No Rusty Swords*, 118; cf. Bonhoeffer, *Letters and Papers*, 168.

The question, however, is whether a baptism has been performed here at all. And if it has—if Michael Rizzi has been transferred out of the domain of darkness into the kingdom of God's Son—then we can honor the grace that originates beyond the church and the world, and that is sovereign in respect of both. Like the sacraments more generally, baptism has an odd double character. In one sense they are clearly acts "of" the church, performed by human actors following a more or less determinate script. As human actions they may be performed well or poorly. Some pastoral practices serve the integrity of baptism, others subvert it; some eucharistic liturgies show forth the divine grace, others obscure it. One of the primary motivations for theological reflection on the sacraments is the desire to perform them more faithfully. In Pauline terms, we seek to insure that it is the *Lord's* Supper we celebrate and not some self-aggrandizing meal of our own.[29]

But if sacraments are in one sense acts of the church, in another sense they are prior to the church, just as the Word itself is. Thus Hans Frei writes that it is "proper to say that they [Word and sacrament] constitute the church rather than the church them."[30] This is a Protestant way of putting the matter, yet one that is not, I think, incompatible with a Catholic ecclesiology. The sacraments do not float in midair; they are part of the fabric of the church's existence, "ordinary means of grace." They are ordinary in the sense that God has appointed them as a reliable means of laying hold of the gospel—we may even say, laying hold of God. Yet while the church is the steward of the divine mysteries, she does not control them.[31] Lurking not far below the surface of the human and historical is the divine grace that breaks forth upon church and world in surprising ways. In, with, and under the human forms of sacramental activity, the apocalypsing of God that took place once for all in Jesus Christ becomes an "apocalypse now."

This is good news for Michael Rizzi, and for us. No doubt we can identify much that is imperfect about his baptism. Or—since he is after all a fictional character—there is much that is imperfect about the baptisms performed in our own churches. I will leave it to readers to provide particulars from their own experience. At the same time, we can be grateful that the power of the sacraments does not depend upon our "getting things right," but on the reliability of God's promise, by which the new creation irrupts into the midst of our solemn assemblies.

29. 1 Cor 11:20.

30. Frei, *Identity*, 159.

31. 1 Cor 4:1.

III

Reflection on the nature of baptism and its relation to the gospel inevitably raises questions concerning proper baptismal practice. How shall we baptize? Perhaps more to the point, *whom* shall we baptize? Who should be admitted to candidacy, and what are our expectations concerning their preparation and catechesis? These are important questions, but also difficult ones in this awkward time following the end—though not quite the absolute disappearance—of Christendom. The churches seem especially anxious at present to show that they are not just churning out "nominal Christians."

As evidence for this awkwardness, we may turn to the baptismal rite in the American *Book of Common Prayer* (1979), a work that embodies much that is best in the modern liturgical movement.[32] A notable feature of this service is the so-called Baptismal Covenant. Here the whole congregation joins the candidates and sponsors in confessing the apostolic faith as expressed in the Apostles' Creed. The use of this creed in a baptismal context is of course ancient. The rite goes on, however, to pose a further series of questions to both the candidates and community:

- "Will you continue in the apostles' teaching and fellowship, in the breaking of bread, and in the prayers?

- Will you persevere in resisting evil, and, whenever you fall into sin, repent and return to the Lord?

- Will you proclaim by word and example the Good News of God in Christ?

- Will you seek and serve Christ in all persons, loving your neighbor as yourself?

- Will you strive for justice and peace among all people, and respect the dignity of every human being?"[33]

In each case, the prescribed answer is "I will, with God's help."[34]

A major impulse at work in the liturgical movement was to restore to baptism something of the dramatic, boundary-crossing character that

32. This rite has been taken over, essentially unchanged, by the *Book of Alternative Services* (1989) of the Anglican Church of Canada. It is therefore the service in which my own children were baptized.

33. *Book of Common Prayer* (1979), 304–5.

34. How weak this is, compared with the old prayer book's affirmation, "God being my helper"! I am grateful to the Rev. Fleming Rutledge for pointing this out.

PART THREE: Apocalyptic and the Church's Witness

marked Christian initiation in the early centuries.[35] It can be charitably understood as a nod to our post-Christendom reality, in which Christians are once again being made rather than born. The church is to regain its countercultural identity through clear specification of the way of life being assumed by the baptized.

Unfortunately, this well-intentioned effort seriously misfires. The unrelenting emphasis in this liturgy is on human promise-making, at the expense of God's singular action in Jesus Christ. In Reformation theology, the logic of promise works the other way: it is on account of *God's* initiative that the candidate is inducted into the kingdom. Moreover, the actual content of the human undertakings made here is problematic. Striving for justice and peace, respecting human dignity—these high, humanitarian aspirations are as generic as they are idealistic. It is not clear what they are doing in a Christian baptismal liturgy. While following Jesus undoubtedly requires that we reflect critically on the virtues of our host society, they seem badly out of place in the baptismal liturgy, whose focus needs to be on baptism's theological and christological basis. Only in the light of Christ can we grasp the true contours of "justice" and "peace."

Unfortunately, this strongly horizontal dynamic is by no means limited to the baptismal covenant, but extends to other parts of the liturgy. It is already evident in the opening Examination of the candidates, with its drawn-out acts of renunciation and adhesion: "Do you renounce all sinful desires that draw you from the love of God? . . . Do you turn to Jesus Christ and accept him as your Savior?" These echoes of modern revivalism seem jarringly out of place here. Is not baptism more about God's turning to us than about our turning to God? There was wisdom in the austerity of the older Prayer Book rite, which, after a relatively simple renunciation of Satan and his pomps, plunged worshipers directly into the deep waters of the Creed. Other traditional liturgies show similar restraint at this point, including the Latin Tridentine rite we examined earlier.[36]

I do not simply mean to heap opprobrium on the 1979 American service, which is not without its moments of eloquence. There is grace enough to go around, even amid the flurry of human promise-making. Moreover, the liturgy has the virtue of reminding us that even those who

35. Bryan Spinks has a good account of the origins of this language in his *Reformation and Modern Rituals and Theologies of Baptism*. While Marion Hatchett points to various modern antecedents for the Baptismal Covenant—confessing Christ as Savior, for instance, goes back to the 1928 American *BCP*—he does not comment on the use of the concept "covenant" itself. See Hatchett, *American Prayer Book*, 273–74.

36. This pattern is still found in the 1978 *Lutheran Book of Worship*.

have been "marked as Christ's own forever"—one of the rite's happier formulations[37]—must still reckon with the devil and the powers at his disposal. Those who have been marked as Christ's own are Satan's target. The references to the devil, and the allusions to the Pauline principalities and powers, reflect an awareness of what J. Louis Martyn calls the "three-actor drama," in which not only God and humans, but also the anti-God forces are among the *dramatis personae*. This language is at least a gesture toward a more vertical and theological understanding of what happens in baptism.

In the ancient liturgies, the devil was not only spoken ill of, he was summarily dismissed, as in the Tridentine rite we examined earlier. Cranmer's first Prayer Book of 1549 retained the exorcism. By 1552 it had disappeared, a victim of the Protestant desire to strip away medieval accretions and superstitions. Reformed sacramentology was to be a return to essentials. Yet what could be more essential to baptism than the public display of Satan's kingdom overthrown? Roman Catholic and Orthodox liturgies have always retained the exorcism in some form, although in the *novo ordo* Catholic rite it has been greatly simplified. It is worth asking whether the churches of the Reformation might not want to retrieve it, precisely as a token of the conviction that something actually *happens* in baptism. Certainly in Luther, a robust sacramental realism was central to the doctrine of justification. When assaulted by the devil, he appealed to his baptism—*baptismus sum*—as a powerful sign that the evil one no longer had claims in this area. Luther had been "marked as Christ's own forever." Satan and his minions could therefore be gone.

Yet if the exorcism had a negligible impact on the historic Anglican rite, the same cannot be said of the Flood Prayer, which until quite recently appeared in successive versions of Prayer Book liturgy. Borrowed by Cranmer from Luther, who was himself echoing patristic and medieval sources, the *Sintflutgebet* brilliantly evokes the Old Testament types of baptism. It celebrates God "[destroying] by floods of water the whole world for sin," the deliverance of Noah and his family, as well as the drowning of Pharaoh's armies in the waters of the Red Sea. These are potent apocalyptic images, well grounded in both parts of the canon of Scripture. Yet the destructive elements in the imagery sit uncomfortably with the writers of modern liturgies. In subsequent versions of the Prayer Book, the reference to the drowning of the Egyptians would be eliminated,

---

37. *Book of Common Prayer*, 308.

while the American editions of both 1928 and 1979 omit any reference to the flood. We are made of less stern stuff than our forebears.[38]

Given this clutch of typological references, one might expect the central christological content of the prayer to be baptism into Christ's death, following Romans 6:3–4. This would, of course, be entirely consistent with central themes of the Reformation. Instead, the prayer takes a surprising turn—to Jesus' own baptism by John in the Jordan. In Cranmer's version:

> . . . by the baptism of thy well-beloved son Jesus Christ, thou didst sanctify the flood Jordan, and all other waters, to the mystical washing away of sin . . .[39]

The prayer moves, in other words, not directly to the baptizand's dying and rising with Christ, but to the instrumental role of water in this dying and rising. Note that the water here is not blessed or sanctified, in so far as God has already sanctified this element by Christ's own baptism. Nevertheless, the presence of a sacramental imagination at this point is unmistakeable. In neither Luther nor Cranmer do we find a distinction between Spirit baptism and water baptism, of the sort so vigorously promoted by Barth in his later *Tauflehre*. Baptism is baptism. The physical washing is the mystical washing, the believer's entry into God's kingdom and her incorporation into the body of Christ. Thus, the prayer goes on to affirm that the candidate, "being delivered from [God's] wrath, may be received into the ark of Christ's Church," living a life "steadfast in faith, joyful through hope, and rooted in charity . . ." Baptism is never merely an action of the individual, but involves his or her entrance into a community and its very particular way of life.

But can the concept of sacramental imagination be rhymed with the apocalyptic imagination? I would argue that not only can they be, but they *must* be rhymed in order to avert theological disaster looming on both sides. To take them in order: the temptation that awaits any sacramental theology is clearly that of a kind of religious immanentism, in which the

38. The Flood Prayer had disappeared already by the time of the 1928 American *BCP*, whose biblical warrants for baptism are almost entirely drawn from the New Testament (Jesus welcoming the little children in Mark 10, birth "by water and the Spirit" in John 3, and the baptismal commission in Matthew 28). To its credit, the 1979 *BCP* at least seeks to retrieve the tradition of thinking about baptism typologically, in relation to the Old Testament.

39. Quoted from the 1552 version, as reprinted in the Everyman's Library edition of *The First and Second Prayer Books of Edward VI*, 395 (spelling modernized). The more familiar 1662 version reads: "by the Baptism of thy well-beloved Son Jesus Christ in the river Jordan, didst sanctify Water to the mystical washing away of sin . . ."

church is not merely the steward of the means of grace but their master. By engaging in the proper cultic actions, by the meticulous observation of "days and months and seasons and years,"[40] the community has in itself the capacity to make things right. Surely Paul's letter to the Galatians is the sufficient refutation of such a theology. The Word of the cross does not conform to the expectations of humans, whose captive minds cannot think beyond the form or master plot of this present aeon.[41] If we are not saved by Torah observance, surely we are not saved by human sacramental activity simply as such. This would be to turn the sacraments into magic, which they most decidedly are not.

By obvious contrast, the temptation that awaits any self-consciously apocalyptic theology is that of dualism: the world having fallen out of God's hands altogether, it must be retaken or invaded from without. In a full-blown dualism, the coming new creation would be a replacement for rather than a transformation of the first. We would then read the Pauline verb *katargeo* in a purely negative sense. On this view God the Redeemer—the loving Father of Jesus Christ—cancels the work of the bungling Creator, thereby "bring[ing] to nothing the things that are."[42] This would be the proverbial act of "destroying the village in order to save it." It goes without saying that in this conception Israel and the Jews are likewise dispensable, anchored as they are in creation and history and the flesh.

Impaled on the horns of this dilemma, we must ask ourselves if we have posed a false alternative by defining our key terms in an abstract way. Just as sacrament need not mean sheer immanence, so apocalyptic need not mean a creation-denying dualism. At one level, we may say each requires correction by the other. Sacrament needs apocalyptic as a reminder that it is God, and not the church, that effects the world's salvation. The gospel is not about the perpetuation of things as they are, whether by religious or other means. It is about God's gracious overturning of the structures and certainties of the present age. The church is but a steward of the mysteries that proclaim this good news.

Similarly, apocalyptic needs sacrament as a reminder that God continues to care for and preserve his creation, despite the destructive work of Satan and the powers. The latter's "occupation" of the world is *de facto* but never *de jure*. That being the case, creaturely reality remains available and disposable to God, a medium of divine action and presence. In fact,

40. Gal 4:10.

41. 1 Cor 7:31.

42. 1 Cor 1:28.

this is to state the matter much too weakly. As the Creator, God is interior to the reality of creatures, moving them without violence to the ends he has appointed. It is true that, *from the perspective of their enslavement to the powers*, humans may well experience the divine apocalypse as an invasion—a reclaiming of territory temporarily ceded to the Evil One. But the metaphor may be pressed only so far. "The earth is the Lord's and the fullness thereof." God's apocalypsing in Christ is the confirmation and vindication of this truth. It is a conviction Paul himself fully shared.[43]

It is no surprise, then, that the waters of baptism should be so polyvalent and complex. Water is a created element, necessary for sustaining life (and the newer baptismal liturgies tend to stress this aspect).[44] Water also kills, however; one can drown in it. Thus the references to the flood and the exodus in Luther's baptismal prayer. In recent literature, this destructive character of baptism was a major theme in the fiction of Flannery O'Connor, rightly identified by J. Louis Martyn as a writer marked by apocalyptic vision.[45] In O'Connor's fiction, including her story "The River" and the great novel *The Violent Bear It Away*, baptism is figured in an actual event of death by drowning. Baptism is death because it spells the crucifixion of the old self, the necessary prelude to entering the kingdom.

Yet if baptism is a death, it is also important to bear in mind that it is a death that takes place *in Christ*. It is God's gracious turning to the world in Christ that lends baptism its significance. In Bonhoeffer's language, baptism belongs not to those things that are last but to those that are next to last. It belongs to the present age of faith and hope, which will ultimately yield to the new creation, marked by the abiding reality of love. Baptism *qua* sacrament has only a penultimate character.

But as a joining to Christ, and as an act of entry into his body the church, baptism marks the beginning of a person's participation in that which is ultimate. "If anyone is in Christ—new creation!" This reality is apocalyptic in the sense that it is the divine, trinitarian life intruding into the midst of the present age. It is for this reason that the scene of Christ's baptism in the Jordan has always been one of the great icons of the Trinity.

43. Ps 24:1, cited in 1 Cor 10:26.

44. Thus, the waters of the womb and the Spirit's hovering over the waters in Genesis have become favorite themes in baptismal prayers. Such references to creation are hardly out of place in a trinitarian liturgy, so long as they do not overshadow the central *second*-article content of baptism: the forgiveness of sins, justification, incorporation into the body of Christ.

45. See Martyn's essay "Paul to Flannery O'Connor."

At the center of the icon stands Jesus himself. The Spirit descends upon him, dove-like, an apocalyptic intrusion from heaven. A voice proclaims, "This is my beloved Son." The new life of the Christian proceeds out of this trinitarian fullness. It is worth noting that in this episode as portrayed in the Synoptic Gospels the devil and the powers are nowhere to be seen. Only afterwards does the Spirit drive Jesus into the wilderness to do battle with Satan.

A robust theology of baptism will be one that does not lose sight of this trinitarian ultimacy, while at the same time giving the penultimate its due. In so far as baptism belongs to the historical life of the church, reflections on its liturgical enactment will never be out of place. Liturgies of baptism in the church's history display the most astonishing variation, though at their core they come down to something quite simple: washing in water in the triune Name, an act of incorporation into the body of Christ. We should, of course, seek to be as faithful as possible to baptism's mandate and promise, reforming our practice where this seems necessary. There are good and less good ways of heeding the mandate. At the same time, we should be wary of thinking that we can "fix" baptism by confecting the proper liturgy—the most ancient, the most contemporary, or the most relevant. Precisely in that baptism finds its ultimate origin in the divine grace and truth, it does not need to be fixed by us. As we saw earlier, even so compromised a baptism as that of Michael Francis Rizzi cannot help but testify to the overflowing grace of God in Jesus Christ.

Baptism, then, is a sign erected at the turning of the ages. Christ himself is that turning; this is the Pauline gospel Martyn has taught us to hear afresh. Through Christ's death and resurrection, the cosmos itself has been decisively altered. But surely Paul's preaching would never have taken hold had it been merely an abstract message about "the cosmos." It took hold because of its transformative effect in the lives of particular persons, Jew and Greek, male and female, slave and free, drawing them into a new and unexpected form of human community. By the Word of God and the waters of new birth, these lives were now bound to each other "in Christ." Before we give thought to reforming baptism, we might well pause and simply give thanks for it. That a Christian has been baptized should never be less than a cause for astonishment.

15

Apocalyptic and Imminence

A Response to Christianity's Cultured Defenders[1]

Nathan R. Kerr

Church fellowships that imagine they are indispensable and whose thinking revolves about earthly and eternal survival will have to be told that God allows us all to die, that great churches have gone under, that only the bourgeoisie with its claim to ownership and permanence confuses the resurrection of the dead with its own survival. What is indispensable for our Lord is only that we follow him and shoulder the cross rather than shifting it back to the neighbor or stranger, only to make it heavier there. Put stiffly, but in genuinely evangelical fashion, the Crucified inspires all prophecy that has any right to genuine authority. It is not, as occurred in early Christianity according to 3 John, interchangeable with hierarchy, nor, contrary to 2 Peter 1:20, to be reduced to the message of the printed Scripture and needing official church interpretation. The Crucified is its legitimation at all times, and still is today. But the Crucified should not be made an edifying altar painting. He is present among the least.

—E. Käsemann[2]

1. I want to thank Halden Doerge, Craig Keen, Peter Kline, and Ry Siggelkow for their many contributions, through much reading and writing and conversation, to this essay. It would not and could not have been written without them.
2. Käsemann, *Being a Disciple*, 305.

I

It was Ernst Käsemann who famously claimed that apocalyptic "was the mother of all Christian theology," and described "primitive Christian apocalyptic" as the expectation of an imminent Parousia, as faith in a Christ whose promised coming brings with it "a radical reversal of the earthly state of affairs."[3] To live by way of such faith is indeed to live "at the turning of the ages"[4] that occurs in the singular apocalyptic event that is Christ's cross/resurrection. It is to live with a certain and determined *urgency*, to live *kata stauron* and thus to be thrust into the thick of God's apocalyptic struggle with the powers and principalities of this world that is passing away, in the trust that God's rectifying justice is already becoming manifest amongst those who, in obedience to the call to be "crucified with Christ" (Gal 2:19), live and work in constant expectancy of God's coming new creation. And so, to confess Jesus Christ as the coming Son of Man and to live in the expectation of the imminent Parousia is to respond to "the call to die as a follower of the Crucified" and precisely thereby to enter into a eucharistic way of life by which the eschatological messianic banquet is celebrated in the midst of the struggle for the coming reign of God.[5] Anyone who has not felt the shortening of time that comes with this imminent expectation, and who has not thereby been struck with the urgency to struggle on behalf of the coming *basileia*, must be forced to ask whether it is in fact the gospel apocalypsed in the cross of Christ that she has heard. She is forced to ask whether she has not come to hear and to live according to another—false—gospel altogether.

Yet already in the New Testament, as Käsemann demonstrates with respect to 2 Peter, there is a slackening of this imminent expectation, and with it a settling down of the church into an earthly-historical existence by which she might go on surviving for further generations.[6] There occurs, as J. Louis Martyn notes also as happening amongst the false teach-

---

3. Käsemann, "Beginnings,"

4. Martyn, "Epistemology."

5. Käsemann, "Beginnings," 105, 88–89.

6. For what follows in this paragraph, see Käsemann, "Apologia." As David Congdon rightly notes in his contribution to this volume, Käsemann is here in these essays making a historical point about early Christian apocalyptic and the developments that began to occur with the so-called delay of the Parousia. And yet, Käsemann also clearly understands the perennial challenge of the gospel to be that of continuing to live in the expectation of the imminent reign of God, in a way that refuses to "historicize" apocalyptic or to "existentialize" it in the pattern of Bultmann.

ers of Galatia, "a reversal of the order of tradition and apocalypse,"[7] such that revelation itself ceases to be understood as an apocalyptic event and comes rather to be seen as an object that is to be received on the basis of a particular traditioning process. As such, the apostle comes to be seen not as that one who by the immediacy of Christ's apocalypse is a messenger of the gospel, but rather as "the guarantor of the tradition."[8] Witness to the resurrected Christ comes to be interchangeable with witness to ecclesiastical tradition's own *historia sacra*; and the ecclesiastical institution comes to be seen as the mediatrix of salvation and so is itself conceived as "the bearer of the eschatological action of God."[9] Apocalyptic paraenesis is replaced by education into a particular Christian cultus. Ontology and metaphysics come to dominate the theological task, insofar as the gospel is said to require a religious construal of reality that would render this world habitable. Early christological titles such as *kyrios* and *soter* come no longer primarily to characterize the one whose cross and resurrection has brought about the liberation of an enslaved cosmos, but rather indicate fundamentally the ontological preeminence of the God of the Christian cultus. To be sure, whereas its author understands and defends the apocalyptic reality of Christ's activity and the apocalyptic existence of the disciple as portrayed for us by the earliest New Testament writers,[10] 2 Peter nevertheless represents a development within Christian theology whereby apocalyptic expectation is subsumed within a traditioning process that removes the imminence of the *basileia*. Eventually, apocalyptic will come to be entirely conditioned by a given ecclesiastical history, replete with its own interior cultus and culture.

I begin with this précis of early Christian apocalyptic, as understood by Käsemann and as developed by Martyn, because I am convinced that perhaps the most pressing question that Martyn's work leaves for theology is that of what it means to live today at the turning of the ages, as disciples who follow Jesus along the *via crucis* and who live in expectancy of the *basileia's* imminent coming. What does it mean to say that the church "is constituted by the imminent kingdom of God and not by any kind of great or small historical dominion?"[11] What does it mean to understand

7. Martyn, *Galatians*, 150.

8. Käsemann, "Apologia," 177.

9. Ibid.

10. See, e.g., the beginning of 2 Peter 3, where the author warns against those who scoff at the delay of Christ's promised coming. For an excellent reading of 1 and 2 Peter from an apocalyptic perspective, see Harink, *1 & 2 Peter*.

11. Barth, *Church Dogmatics* (*CD*), III/4:488.

the ecclesial life apocalyptically? I begin by examining the ecclesiology of one contemporary theologian in particular, Robert Jenson. My aim will be to show how Jenson's insistence that the church *is* a culture conditions the gospel in such a way as to foreclose on apocalyptic imminence in the name of stabilizing a given ecclesiastical culture.[12] Alternatively, I shall suggest that to retrieve the exigence of apocalyptic imminence for the church today, we shall have to account for its concrete social location amongst "the least" of society—those who are suffering and crying out and dying under the weight of the powers of this world. Taking as my point of departure Jesus' itinerancy in Mark's gospel, I will suggest that it is finally here, as Jesus lives and works and ultimately is crucified with "the least" (*oi eschatoi*) at the margins of society, that the turning of the ages occurs. It is these ones for whom the kingdom is imminent, and it is from these ones that the church will emerge to live and to work and to hope for the coming *basileia* of God.

II

I begin with Robert Jenson's ecclesiology because I take it to be perhaps the most sophisticated articulation of a particular trend within contemporary "postliberal" theology, viz., the conviction that the very truth of the gospel depends upon a very particular ontological construal of the church as its own objectively discernible culture.[13] It is precisely this conditioning of the gospel by the insistence upon a locatable Christian culture, I shall argue, that forecloses on the kind of expectation of an imminent *basileia* that arises in faithfulness to the apocalypse of Jesus Christ.

In his *Systematic Theology*, Jenson is concerned to hold together what are for him two indispensable theologoumena for any doctrine of the church. The first is that the church is constituted by the good news of the gospel and just so is a gathering that is founded upon the apocalyptic event of Christ's resurrection and exists by anticipation of the promised end. As such, "the church is neither a realization of the new age nor an item of the old age. She is precisely an event *within the event* of the new

---

12. I have been greatly aided in my understanding of Jenson on the objectivity of God and culture by two unpublished papers: Flett, "Spirit"; Kline, "The Real Absence."

13. I am speaking here of Anglo-American postliberalism, mostly associated with George Lindbeck and Stanley Hauerwas, and within which I include both John Milbank and Jenson.

age's advent."[14] The second is that the church (in continuity with Israel) is the one elect culture with which God has chosen to identify Godself in God's self-revelation,[15] and thus the church—*as* this culture—must be considered "in its own proper entity, in which it is in God's intention antecedent to the gospel."[16] As such, "'Church' and 'gospel' therefore mutually determine each other," in that the gospel is both constitutive of and perdures in the historically continuous form of linguistic custom we call "the church." [17] While both theologoumena are ingredients in his doctrine of the church, Jenson very strategically proceeds from the latter to the former in constructing his ecclesiology, for it is only as the church in its actual historical existence is identified with the "objectivity" of the gospel's truth *pro nobis* that any concrete content can be adduced from the gospel that is apocalypsed to us in Jesus Christ.

When Jenson comes to treat the content of that gospel which is "apocalypsed" to Paul and the apostles, he means to refer to a very particular kerygmatic reality: the identity of Jesus as "the Risen One"—viz., that this human being, who was crucified, has been raised and so identifiable as "God."[18] One of the chief worries that haunts Jenson's writings throughout, however, is that unless we can speak of the resurrected Son as objectively identifiable and externally available to us as the historical reality of the salvation event prior to any subjective hearing of it, then the objective content of what we call the gospel will not finally transcend that which we subjectively intend in its hearing.[19] Were the risen Jesus not present to us as an actually existing historical object—a *body*—in which he subjectively intends himself and us in him, and which we are called in turn to intend as historically embodied subjects, the resurrected Jesus would remain "imprisoned in history" and so historically locatable only with respect to some remote past (as in modern historicism[20]), or worse

14. Jenson, *Systematic Theology* (*ST*), 2:171.

15. Ibid., 1:59–60.

16. Ibid., 2:168.

17. Ibid., 1:5.

18. Ibid, 1:194–206.

19. Ibid., 1:154.

20. It is at this point that Jenson critiques both the position of Bultmann, for whom Jesus is famously raised into the kerygma and thus presently available to us only in the timelessness of an "existential moment of decision" (ibid., 1:165–71), and that of Barth, whose "'I-Thou trinitarianism'" reproduces itself economically as a subject-object dialectic in which the objectivity of the risen Son ultimately denudes the subjectivity of our human response (ibid., 1:153–56).

yet, with respect to some equally remote, ever-deferred future (as in post-modern nihilism). Those familiar with Jenson's theology will recognize immediately the dilemma here. It is the subject/object dualism of German idealism, which Jenson resolves by recourse to the "Domination and Slavery" passage from Hegel's *Phenomenology of Spirit*. As Jenson summarizes it, "If in the meeting between us you are a subject of which I am an object but are not in turn an object for me as a subject, you enslave me. Only if I am able to intend and so grasp and respond to you as you intend and grasp me can our relation be reciprocal."[21] If, therefore, the risen Jesus is to be an object for me in a way that does not imprison him in history, and I am to be free subjectively to receive and to reciprocate the love of the risen Jesus for which I am the object, there must be some mediating third that frees these parties for the recognition of oneself in the other.

That mediating third, for Jenson, is "the church with her sacraments"; in the loaf and the cup and the community gathered around them the Spirit frees the resurrected Jesus to intend himself in a concrete historical object, and frees us in turn to intend ourselves as the historical actuality of Christ's factual embodiment. And so Jenson:

> Where does the risen Christ turn to find himself? To the sacramental gathering of believers. To the question "Who am I?" he answers "I am this community's head. I am the subject whose objectivity is this community. I am the one who died to gather them." And again: "I am the subject whose objectivity for this community is the bread and cup around which she gathers." The church with her sacraments is the object as which we may intend Christ because she is the object as which he intends himself. The relation between Christ as a subject and the church with her sacraments is precisely that between transcendental subjectivity and the objective self . . . the church is the risen Christ's Ego.[22]

Herein lies the key point: Jenson's entire conceptual labor regarding that which is "apocalypsed" to Paul and the apostles has arisen over an anxiety to *locate* the risen Jesus in such a way as not to "imprison" him within the historicity of a resurrected "history."[23] And this leads him to describe the

21. Ibid., 2:214.

22. Ibid., 2:215.

23. "'Even Jesus had to be liberated from history.' This liberation is of course primarily the Resurrection. But had there been no Pentecost, had Jesus risen into the eschatological future while we were simply left behind, had he no present-tense actuality within the church's moment, he would still be for us an item of mere memory, imprisoned in history. That it is not so is the church-founding work of the Spirit, who

risen Christ's body as exhaustively present and so directly available to us in the eucharistic communion that is the church. "We must learn to say: the entity rightly called the body of Christ is whatever object it is that is Christ's availability to us as subjects; by the promise of Christ, this object is the bread and cup and the gathering of the church around them."[24] "[Christ] needs no other body to be a risen man, body and soul. There is and needs to be no other place than the church for him to be embodied, nor in that other place any other entity to be the 'real' body of Christ."[25] (Here the suspicion arises that what Paul preached in apocalyptic-christological terms about the new creation has been converted to a function of ecclesiology, and that the church has become the decisive eschatological event.)

The critical issue here is not with the identification of the church with the body of Christ; any honest reading of Paul cannot deny that the Eucharist involves us in Jesus' death and so incorporates us "in Christ." The problem with Jenson's account is that he has read into this Pauline motif a particular ecclesiological ontology that is developed in response to the anxieties over where objectively to "locate" the risen Jesus, given the fact that the awaited Parousia did not happen. And this has led him so to identify the risen Christ with the church as to arrogate to the church that which belongs to Jesus alone in the singular event of his cross and

---

'unites the Head with the Body of Christ.' The liberation of Jesus is accomplished not only by the Resurrection but also by the Spirit's liberation of a community to receive and be his actuality within the present time of this age" (ibid., 2:181).

24. Ibid., 1:205.

25. Ibid., 1:206. Here is a good place to address the charge of ecclesiological docetism that Jenson has leveled against me in his review of my book, *Christ, History, and Apocalyptic*. Jenson's concern is that apart from identifying the risen body of Christ *with* the church we end up "with a remarkably disembodied Christ." But this is a conclusion that can only be drawn when one allows Christology and ecclesiology to merge into one another, to the extent that Jesus of Nazareth's own historicity is reduced to a series of "evangelical events" that can be read as prefiguring his truly salvific embodiment as risen into the church. The concern to avoid a certain kind of ecclesiological docetism thus runs the risk a very real *christological* docetism, in which Christ's risen body cannot really and concretely be affirmed as the risen body of Jesus *the Nazarene*, the transfigured but no less wounded and concretely singular body of the Crucified One. In all his concern to counter Bultmann's existentialism, Jenson simply inverts the problem, creating another version of the *Christus praesens*, now thought not in terms of "existential event" but of "Christian culture." Whereas for Bultmann Jesus is raised directly into the kerygma, for Jenson he seems to be raised directly into the church. In neither case does the question of the resurrection of Jesus of Nazareth's *body*—the question of an *actual* empty tomb—pose any problem of real significance. See Jenson, review of *Christ, History and Apocalyptic*. My thanks to Ry Siggelkow for working out these thoughts with me.

resurrection.[26] And so, Jenson can say that the church, in its Spirit-enacted identity with the risen Son, constitutes a communion that can be "identified as the 'objectivity' of the gospel's truth *pro nobis*"; in its identity as the eucharistic *totus Christus*, the church herself is constitutive of the new reality by which the world is transformed and reconciled to God—"the active *mediatrix* of faith."[27] That is, the church itself, "in its structured temporal and spatial extension would be seen as the *Bedingung der Möglichkeit* ["condition of the possibility"] of faith."[28] Thus we see how Jenson's concern for the objectivity of the gospel has led him to identify the church, as it subsists antecedently to any human response, as constituting the basic salvation-historical reality necessary for faith. For it is precisely "the loaf and the cup, the bath and the rest of the gospel's factual churchly embodiment," that constitute God's own objectivity for us.[29]

III

Jenson's identification of the church "in its structured and spatial temporal extension" with God's objectivity leads him to define the church in history as a culture: "the church *is* a culture."[30] Jenson defines a culture as follows:

> By a definition that seems plausible, a culture is a group of deliberate human practices and artifacts that mutually and independently of the momentary intents of their users make a functioning system of signs. The church—with her strikingly odd meal and bath, with her particularist holy writings, eccentric forms of leadership and counter-cultural discipline, and

---

26. As to the objection that this entails an absorption of Christ into the church, Jenson will insist that Christ is other from the church, in the mode of the eucharistic elements' otherness from the congregation: "Within the gathering we can intend Christ as the community we are, without self-deification, because we jointly intend the identical Christ as the sacramental elements in our midst, which are other than us" (*ST*, 2:213) But this is to say that Christ is other from the congregation only within an encompassing sameness that is the church's Eucharistic culture, thereby repeating the logic that otherness only ever appears within the self-conscious representation of the self-as-other to itself. Christ then appears as other to the church only as a representation of the church's self-as-other to itself. My thanks to Peter Kline for this way of putting the matter.

27. Jenson, "Where the Spirit Went," 303.

28. Ibid., 303.

29. Jenson, *ST*, 1:13.

30. Jenson, "Election and Culture," 49.

with a hundred other distinctive gestures and habits—of course always fit this definition.[31]

We might thus say that a "culture" is constituted by those particular modes of cultic practice, moral behavior, and communal formation that a particular people constructs out of the given nature that is presented to it in history. And it is as its own forms of cultic practice, moral behavior, and communal formation take shape as a historically embodied *Christian* culture that the church presents to us the objectivity of the gospel and so the very condition of the possibility of faith.

What makes Jenson's position so radical is that he goes on to identify the culture that the church *is* as the mediatrix of God's own triune being. In a reprisal of the German idealist logic whereby the Spirit acts as the "liberating" agent between subject and object, both immanently and economically, Jenson makes the point that God is in Godself a culture:

> What it is to be God is given in the Father's eternal begetting of the Son and enlivening through the Spirit, in the Spirit's eternal liberating of the Father and the Son for one another, in the Son's eternal self-giving to the Father in the Spirit. Thus the triune God is nothing *but* culture, and just so is infinite culture, culture setting nature and transforming it and just so setting nature and so on in an eternal act.[32]

But God is not this culture abstractly. The culture that God is in Godself is not independently available apart from the church's own culture. Thus, the axiomatic move that Jenson makes at every turn in his theology: to emphasize that God's identification with Godself in God's historical act finds its objective concretion in God's act to establish and maintain the church's own culture. Thus, faith in the church amounts to "faith in the Spirit's presence and rule in and by the structures of the church's historical continuity."[33] The christological upshot of this is clear. Just as the Spirit works in history to constitute the culture that the church is, the Spirit at one and the same time liberates Christ for identification *with* this culture. Once again the idealist logic sketched above dominates:

> If the church is the body of Christ, that is, if the church is the availability of Christ in and for the world, and if this body of Christ, the church, is a culture, it follows then that Christ is a

31. Jenson, "Christian Civilization," 155.

32. Ibid., 160–61.

33. Jenson, *ST*, 1:25.

culture. And the sense of the "is" in "Christ is a culture" will be the sense in which each of us must say that he or she "is" his or her body.[34]

Here the identification of Christ with the church's culture is complete: "As Christ is the church, he is in that same or a related sense a culture, the culture the church is."[35]

Thus we see how Jenson's identification of Christ's resurrected body with the eucharistic *totus Christus* leads to an entirely *heilsgeschictlich* understanding of Christ as salvifically present to us in the development of the church's own historically determined culture. It only remains for us to show how, in thus abstracting the eschatological reality of Christ from the singularly apocalyptic event in history of his cross and resurrection, Jenson forecloses on the imminent expectation of the coming reign of God at the heart of New Testament apocalyptic. That is to say, there is in Jenson's account of the risen Jesus' identification with the church's culture a particular understanding of God's immanence to history that eschews apocalyptic imminence by placing the church in a directly telic relation to the final end, or Parousia. Let me try to unpack this.

We noted above that Jenson's ecclesiology of the eucharistic *totus Christus* involves him in an identification of the risen Christ's body with the church *without remainder*. "There is and needs to be no other place than the church for [the risen Christ] to be embodied, nor in that other place any other entity to be the 'real' body of Christ."[36] At that point I noted the suspicion that the singularly christological event of new creation had thus become a function of ecclesiology, such that the eschaton comes to be ecclesiocentrically located with respect to the church's culture. That suspicion is borne out when we turn to consider what Jenson means by the promise of eschatological fulfillment. There he describes the eschaton as the fullness of creation's "inclusion in the triune life," which is determined by created being's final encounter and identification with the risen Jesus.[37] As Jeremy Ive aptly comments, "The future is to be known as that which is and can be centered on him."[38] As such, the future that awaits us is that "of a new heaven and earth patterned according to the personality of the risen

34. Jenson, "Christ as Culture 1, " 325.

35. Ibid., 325.

36. Jenson, *ST*, 2:206.

37. Ibid., 2:317–19.

38. Ive, "Jenson's Theology," 149.

Jesus."[39] But it is precisely at this point that the teleological foreclosure on apocalyptic imminence occurs. Insofar as the body of that risen Jesus is locatable and identifiable *nowhere else* than in the eucharistic communion that is the *totus Christus*, we need look no further than the development of the church's own culture in history in order to identify the teleological coordinates by which the world's incorporation into the kingdom will finally be brought about.

Thus, we see that for Jenson to speak as he does of the church as "an event *within the event* of the new age's advent," or as "a moment in the coming of the Kingdom," and so "the gate of the Kingdom's present tense with God"—the "gate of heaven"—is for Jenson to characterize the church as that place in history whereby God anticipates, and so *possesses*, "the created future's presence—*as* future!—with God."[40] Jenson continues: "The creation is liberated to its End and Fulfillment by God the Spirit; heaven is the telos of this dynamism insofar as it is a teleology within creation itself."[41] To this we need only to add the conclusion to which Jenson's identification of Christ's risen body with the church leads him: "Heaven is where God takes space in his creation to be present to the whole of it; he does that in the church."[42] So, in the end, it is God's objective identification with the given development of a particular Christian culture via the economy of the risen Son and the liberating Spirit that opens to us the future of the kingdom and secures our teleological movement into that future. Here again, Ive's commentary is helpful: "The church . . . as the body of Christ, constitutes within itself, by virtue of that identity as *totus Christus*, the new reality by which the whole universe is to be transformed."[43] As possessing within herself the *telos* by which alone creation is opened toward and moved to its fulfillment and end, the church's work is to be nothing less than the cultivation of "the ultimate cultural action of new creation" itself. The church does this by incorporating the world itself into her own construal of reality—which alone locates the one truly "habitable

---

39. Ibid., 149.
40. Jenson, *ST*, 2:121.
41. Ibid., 2:121.
42. Ibid., 1:206.
43. Ive, "Jenson's Theology," 151.

world" in history[44]—by way of the enculturation of that world into its own distinct modes of cultic practice, moral behavior, and social formation.[45]

So where does all of this leave us? In the end, Jenson's ecclesiology is a rather sophisticated form of what Donald MacKinnon diagnosed as "ecclesiological fundamentalism," in which an "unyielding commitment" to ecclesiastical history as inherently self-justifying is maintained precisely for the sake of upholding the Christian culture that history has bequeathed to us and developing it into the future.[46] Such ecclesiological fundamentalism almost always brings with it an espousal of "the cause of conservatism," not only in relation to the church but the broader culture as well,[47] in the hopes that the development of Christianity's own high culture might give warrant for and perhaps coincide with the growth of the civil society into a "Christian civilization." And so, for the sake of maintaining the church's high culture as such, we find in Jenson a derogation of the beats of rock and early jazz as unable to attain to the more highly cultured rhythms of Beethoven, for the precise reason that the latter's art was more clearly "shaped and driven by a cultural memory of Christian eschatology and devotion"[48]; we find a derision of those liturgical efforts of "Roman Catholic" and "Norwegian-Lutheran" congregations to abandon the organs and recruit a band in order to "try to swing with African-America songs"[49]; we find lament over the revisionist history of the "chattering classes" in which "the Pilgrims have become heartless exploiters of the original Americans and the Founding Fathers a conspiracy against blacks"[50]; we find in the gospel's promise a vision of the end in which the best of America's hopes and dreams of "economic freedom" will be fulfilled and with this an affirmation of the modern capitalist free market as morally and politically necessary to securing ourselves against economic and social tyranny[51];

44. The phrase "habitable world" is used by Hauerwas in relation to the practices of Christian culture in *With the Grain*, 214. I am using it here to sum up the argument of Jenson in "How the World."

45. Jenson identifies such enculturation, via catechesis into the church's cultic practices, as the very task of mission in our time. See Jenson, "Catechesis for Our Time." For a critique of Jenson's understanding of mission here see Kerr, "In Solidarity"; see also Flett, "Spirit."

46. MacKinnon, *Stripping of the Altars*, 9.

47. Ibid., 9.

48. Jenson, "Christian Civilization," 158, 163.

49. Jenson, "Christ as Culture 3," 200.

50. Ibid., 200.

51. Jenson, *ST*, 2:314–17.

and the storied vision of reality that this great tradition of Christian culture tells us is proffered as the last best hope for the world's own narratival coherence.[52]

At last, we cannot now refrain from acknowledging the apparent upshot of this particular mode of ecclesiological fundamentalism: its cumulative effect appears to be one long apologia on behalf of white, Western American cultural Christianity. To this way of thinking church, I can only insist that we must finally once and for all say "No!" To the extent that postliberal narrative theology insists on the maintenance of a discretely "Christian culture" as consistent with the gospel apocalypsed to us in the event of Christ's cross and resurrection, in a way that forecloses on the imminence we find at the heart of early Christian apocalyptic, we must take leave of its mode of ecclesiological construction. And to the extent that a new way of thinking church will emerge, it will have to be borne out of the very struggle for the kingdom that emerges out of the crucified Nazarene's own solidarity with those "little ones" (*ta eschata*) at the margins of culture, the very ones who are oppressed and despised in the course of our attempts to cultivate "high culture" for its own sake, the ones whom Jesus in Mark's gospel unflinchingly identifies with as "the least." This will require a rethinking of apocalyptic imminence at precisely this point. The rest of this essay will be an attempt to do just that.

IV

We have seen how the foreclosure on imminence and the loss of apocalyptic urgency arise in part as the result of an anxiety over where precisely to "locate" the risen body of Jesus, and of the felt need to construct a given ecclesiastical culture with which this risen Christ might be identified, so as objectively to guarantee his presence to the world in the church as the condition of possibility of faith. Thus, Christ is no longer present to us in his apocalyptic singularity, but rather via the teleological outworking of the church's own high culture. In the remainder of this essay, I should like to return to the question of what it might mean to live in expectation of the imminent Parousia by suggesting that the coming *basileia* Jesus proclaimed is in Mark's gospel given a concrete social location—the turning of the ages "begins with the little ones at the margins (*ta eschata*)," and it is from within this marginal "space" that the imminence of the *basileia*

---

52. Jenson, "How the World."

is announced and expected.[53] My concern is not to offer an alternative ecclesiology or to work out an alternative theory of the Eucharist. Nor am I concerned with any particular attempt to locate the risen body of Jesus. I will only take it as a given that where the resurrected Jesus appears to his disciples he appears precisely in his singularity as the crucified Nazarene. Thus to confess and bear witness to the resurrected Crucified One is precisely to *follow* him as "he is going ahead of you into Galilee" (Mark 16:7).

That, of course, is where Mark's gospel rather abruptly ends. But it is a gospel that begins no less abruptly. Already in the Mark's opening cry of the coming kingdom there is a kind of repetition of its ending. "Now after John was arrested, Jesus *came to Galilee*, proclaiming the good news of God, and saying, 'The time is fulfilled, and the kingdom of God has come near; repent, and believe in the good news'" (1:14–15). Here at the outset the one who is to be re-surrected arrives on the scene to announce a particular kind of *in-surrection*—a "standing out into," if you will, the disruptive coming of a *basileia* that the marked-off cultural territories of this world will be unable to accommodate. Already, by submitting to John's baptism of repentance in the wilderness and by proclaiming the gospel to the second-class citizens of Galilee,[54] Jesus has set himself to the work of transgressing and subverting the carefully disciplined cultural borders—both political and religious—of his day.[55] Jesus stands to face the religious and political elite, and right in the midst of their territory casts out demons (1:21–28); he not only touches the ritually unclean, but he heals them as if oblivious to the purity codes and Sabbath norms that forbid it (1:41; 3:1–5); he defies social practices of exclusivity by eating

---

53. This connection was first brought to my attention by Vítor Westhelle, and in what follows I will be expounding in conversation with Mark's gospel the suggested implications of this connection. See Westhelle, *Church Event*, 82–83.

54. We should note here the significance of two crucial coordinates of the Roman-Palestinian landscape of Mark's gospel: the wilderness and Galilee. On the one hand, the wilderness (*eremos*) would have marked off the most utterly desolate and uninhabitable of regions, where there is no possibility of life. Brigands would hide, and rob, and kill there—and be hunted down and killed there as well. On the other hand, Galilee is the region where the most massive oppression in all of Israel happened. It was oppressed both by the Romans and by the Jerusalem temple elite, who sent their emissaries (scribes, Pharisees, etc.) to extract what they could from the Galileans. Both the wilderness and Galilee would thus have designated places of severe marginalization and oppression, but also death. My thanks to Craig Keen for conversations on the significance of the wilderness and Galilee in Mark. See also Myers, *Binding the Strong Man*, 125–26, 53–54.

55. See ibid., 122–26.

with those deemed sinners and misfits (1:15–17). And he does all of this in such a way as to bring the very ones responsible for policing those cultural borders to conspire together to kill him (3:6).[56] Far from there being any accommodation or even transformation of the highest of high cultures of Jesus' day, there is in his announcement of the imminent *basileia* a rather urgent cry of insurrection against them.

Jesus' lived life is thus precisely an apocalyptic contest with the cultural powers of his day. What is particularly significant about the way Jesus challenges these powers is that he refuses to set himself *against* these powers as if a rival among them contending for the same limited resources of this world. No, the coming of God's reign, as Jesus is so clear to point out, is the coming of that which is decisively *new* (cf. 2:21–22). The word "new" (*kainos*) has significance as a term that would have almost certainly evoked the expectations of an "eschatological re-creation."[57] With this point, we begin to get something of an indication of what it might have meant to acknowledge this coming *basileia* as *imminent*. For one, this newness is clearly one that comes directly from outside the world's system of power, in a manner that is to open a way of living without that system. As Christopher Morse has shown, the imminence of the *basileia* "does not approximate, or conform to, any state of affairs that may be said to be already in hand, or in place. . . . No antecedent form of this world can accommodate the heavenly *basileia's* coming."[58] Imminence signifies that the newness of the *basileia* comes always in a way that evinces no obvious conformity to what has preceded its coming in this world: "What is imminent is not immanent."[59] But secondly, as referring to the coming eschatological re-creation, the imminence of the *basileia* would have been understood in terms of a decisive future *adventus*, the distinctive arrival of that new creation in which our bodies will be made new. And so, even as Jesus pronounces that the *basileia* is "at hand" or has "come near" (1:15), it has not come near in such a way as to be historicized as some goal towards which the cultures of this world are decisively moving, nor has it come near as some existentialized event of subjective decision that is to be actualized in each new moment. No, the kingdom has come near in such a way as to open up a space within which we might even now work free of

56. Ibid., 117.

57. Myers, *Binding the Strong Man*, 159.

58. Morse, *Difference*, 21–22.

59. Ibid., 54.

this world's systems of power in expectancy of the very real and decisive *adventus* of a future new creation.

Of course, the imminence of the kingdom is to be *expected* as *lived*. It is to be *lived* in the way of Christ's cross, and it is to be *expected* as the future transfiguration of our bodies in the resurrection from the dead. Thus, Jesus not only with urgency finds himself proclaiming the coming of God's *basileia*, but—perhaps contrary to even his own best laid plans—*performing* it.[60] As one who refuses to be arranged by and among the closed and territorial systems of this world, Jesus has from the beginning of his very ministry nothing left to *do* with respect to these systems—except *to die*. Jesus is *already* the Crucified One—preveniently—and he lives out this cruciform life as one who lives every moment in expectancy of his coming resurrection. And he calls those who are to follow him to live in exactly the same way. (This point will become even clearer momentarily.) But here we should not miss the significance of the conjunction of the imminent expectation of a new *basileia* with Jesus' obstinate refusal of the dominant cultural powers of this world. Almost at every turn in Mark's gospel, Jesus' subversive refusal of these cultural powers coincides with his turning to those embodied persons whom these very powers have left with nothing—except *to die*. And so over and over again in Mark's gospel Jesus turns aside from the rich and powerful—the cultured elite—to those who have been given him from the margins—those whom Mark identifies as "the crowd" (*ho ochlos*) and to whom Jesus will refer almost interchangeably as "the little ones" (*ton micron*) or "the least" (*hoi eschatoi*). And he does so in such a way as continually to subvert cultic and cultural custom.

One poignant example of this occurs in Mark 3, where, just after confronting the religious and political elite, Jesus finds these very crowds pressing in upon him. Instead of withdrawing, Jesus turns to this crowd, letting the diseased touch him and touching them in return—healing them and expelling demonic spirits (3:10–11). After withdrawing for the express purpose of appointing his apostles (who were themselves numbered among the crowd), he returns immediately to feast in his home *with those of the crowd* (2:19–20). And here, in Galilee, surrounded by the cultural powers of the scribes and of kin, he rebukes both, and turns for the first time to address the crowd itself as what could only be described as a new sort of community of discipleship (3:34–35). And while this new community is no doubt distinct from those cultures that have been built

---

60. Keen, *After Crucifixion*, 183. I am grateful to Craig Keen for allowing me access to the unpublished manuscript of his book; all page references refer to that manuscript.

up on the labor and the lives of those among this crowd, this community will be commanded to live in such a way as finally to forbid "the erection of exclusive and rigid social boundaries around the community of faith."[61] In utter contrast to the kind of logic that identifies through separation and exclusion—by which alone a discrete culture can build and maintain its own identifiable core or interior—Jesus refuses this logic for the sake of solidarity with those who are most threatened by extinction in the building up of discrete cultures, those who have no standing before imperial powers and their religious functionaries, those who are most despised and rejected by the high-cultured of their day and so targeted for imprisonment, banishment, and ultimately death.

So much, then, for confusing this community with the establishment of anything like the kind of "church" that we might identify as its own "Christian culture."[62] Barth was right in observing "that the acts of Jesus have no direct connexion with cultural activity,"[63] if by that we take it to mean that there is no direct causal connection between the cultures that we seek to build up in this world and the irruptive coming of God's *basileia*.

But this does not mean that we are not to speak and to think, to make music and to sing, to live and to work, to throw seeds onto dirt and to thrust hands into the soil in the hopes that those seeds will die and bear fruit—in other words, to do all those activities that are, straightforwardly, the most basic of "cultural" acts. In fact, what is perhaps most strikingly significant about Jesus' turning to the outcast, the sinner, the sick and the dying—the *dead*—in Mark's gospel is that Jesus turns to them in order to *eat and drink with them*. By way of this simple act of "eating and drinking" with those cast aside as nought by the cultured powers of this world, Mark comes to situate the force of Jesus' apocalyptic struggle with these powers *eucharistically*, by placing at the center of this struggle the prevailing image of the messianic banquet—that feast of pure thanksgiving that is to be the way of life when God's new creation arrives in its fullness. For Jesus to be cast aside in solidarity with the oppressed and marginalized of his day, and there to *eat and drink* with them, is for Jesus to engage in a concretely and excessively celebratory act of thanksgiving and praise that testifies to

---

61. Myers, *Binding the Strong Man*, 262. Myers is here commenting on Mark 9:38–41.

62. It is interesting to note in this regard that the word *ecclesia* nowhere appears in Mark.

63. Barth, *CD*, III/4:486.

the way in which life is to be lived *free from the need of the powers* of this world, as a life lived *free for the coming shalom of God*. But herein lies the real subversive force of this eucharistic act: Jesus turns to eat and drink with these ones by turning *immediately* to the cross and to the coming new life to which Jesus' dead body is to be opened in the event of the resurrection. And he turns to this cross always with the simple command "Follow me!"

And here we return to the theme of imminence, and the way in which the expectancy of the coming *basileia* is bound up with Christ's crucifixion and resurrection. In chapter 8, at what might be called the midpoint of Mark's gospel, the particular significance of this eucharistic act of eating and drinking in relation to the coming kingdom is brought forth explicitly. Mark 8:1–26 recounts the second of Jesus' miraculous feedings. These feedings do not occur by any means among the cultured of society. These feedings occur, rather, as Craig Keen describes it,

> not in the walled, secure *polis*, home of the well-nourished, well-housed, and well-respected ruling elite; nor in the productive *chora* around the city, agricultural land directly and indirectly from which the goods of the city's aristocracy come; but in the *eremos*, the wilderness, the non-productive, empty land, the resourceless, barren, dangerous land, land out of the dark caves and pits of which might at any moment emerge those murderers and thieves who for a little while survive by preying on wayfarers like hyenas, desperate children abandoned by their desperate parents, nobodies whom enforcers of the peace hunt down and kill, the scum among whom Mark's Jesus is explicitly counted on Good Friday.[64]

Here we witness the kind of radical subversion of culture that can only come as the work of one's hands is abandoned to the extravagant unpredictability of God's four thousand. Here, these hungry ones who have worked for the bread by which alone they live abandon that work and that bread in faith to something they know not what, but which they have learned to expect will come as radically *new*. And what happens is not the result of or continuous with the work they have been doing all along, but is rather the gift of new life, of manna in the wilderness. And they eat, eucharistically, in thanksgiving.

And yet just as this happens, just as the cultured religious elite press upon Jesus looking for a sign and the disciples, bewildered, look for ways

---

64. Keen, *After Crucifixion*, 188–89.

to name him, to situate him in relation to the language this cultured religious elite have taught them, there occur in the words of Jesus the pronouncement of a very *new* day indeed, the *newness* of the *basileia*, the "turning of the ages" that happens only in cross and resurrection: "Then he began to teach them that the Son of Man must undergo great suffering, and be rejected by the elders, the chief priests, and the scribes, and be killed, and after three days rise again. He said all this quite openly" (8:31–32). And then, just as this act of solidarity with the crowd is what will take Jesus to the cross in imminent expectation of the new life into which his crucified body will be raised, so Jesus calls out to the crowd, whose eating and drinking have bound them in solidarity to him, and turns their attention to the coming Son of Man with the words, "If any want to become my followers, let them deny themselves and take up their cross and follow me. For those who want to save their life will lose it, and those who lose their life for my sake, and for the sake of the gospel, will save it" (8:34–35). Those of the crowd who with their bodies have believed in him and followed him, who in faith have just taken the manna of *new* bread, are called down the same road. They are called to live and to work and ultimately to die with this Jesus in the expectancy that their crucified bodies also will, with the force of an imminent coming that no amount of time passed could ever be said to delay, be raised into new life.

This is what it means to live and to work in imminent expectation of a coming *basileia*. It is to live and to work subversively with those little ones at the margins, to live and to work in the way of Christ's crucifixion and so unto death, in the hope that in our death, as in his, the "curtains" of religious and political high culture that serve only to separate and oppress will be torn from top to bottom, so that the dawning of that *new* day will even *now* be given to be lived—with urgency!—as we yet cry out from these margins in expectancy of the future transfiguration of our bodies in the resurrection from the dead.

V

So where does this leave us with respect to the question with which we began, the question of what it means to be a church that lives, today, at the turning of the ages, in urgent expectation of the *basileia's* imminent coming? Most certainly, it must mean to get behind that Jesus who is going ahead of us into Galilee and who withdraws constantly into the wilderness—the most oppressed of this world's places and the most marginalized of this world's non-places. It must mean to think of the poor, the imprisoned, the migrant, and mentally ill as inhabiting an *eschata* on which the turning of the ages is to come. It must mean to dwell with the marginalized who are barely hanging onto life. It must mean to move into solidarity with those who have no standing before the imperial and cultural powers of this world, those most despised and threatened by extinction, those most clearly targeted for arrest and expulsion. It must mean to live, and to speak, and to work along the way with these people. It must mean to throw our fingers into dry and infertile soil with poor migrant farmers and to turn over the seed—to do so not under the dictates of Monsanto, but in faith in the promise of God that if this seed dies it will indeed bring forth much fruit. It must mean to sing and to dance and to laugh and to cry with the imprisoned—to do so not under the auspices of the Corrections Corporation of America, which has learned how to turn the system of criminal justice to a quick profit, but rather to do so in the hopes of learning how to live outside the reach the long arm of the law. It must mean to clothe the naked, to feed the hungry, and to house the homeless—to do so not for the sake of teaching these ones how to play the world as it now stands to their own advantage, but for the sake of freely eating and drinking with these ones in ways that cannot be reduced to the market logics of property and ownership. The church as it is, as we have come to imagine it, will perhaps without doubt, there at the margins, meet its end. But if it is there, in genuine solidarity with the *eschatoi* of this world, that the church meets its end, then it is there that it will be opened *by these very ones on the margins* to an imminent expectation of *new life*, a coming resurrection. And out of that very solidarity and expectation will be born the struggle for a life so extravagantly free that no established culture—not even the highest of high ecclesiastical cultures—shall ever come to contain it.[65]

The question now facing theology today is this: Do we have a way of speaking of ecclesial life that waits and works toward—stands out into—a coming resurrection? Can theology itself hold itself open to the challenge of thinking and writing and speaking from the margins in expectation of this imminent *basileia*?

65. Westhelle, *Church Event*, 116–18.

16

The End of Sacrifice

An Apocalyptic Politics

Stanley Hauerwas

MARTYN AND YODER ON APOCALYPTIC

JOHN HOWARD YODER, AS Douglas Harink has suggested, would have found Lou Martyn's account of Paul's apocalyptic gospel supportive of his reading of Paul.[1] Like Martyn, Yoder did not think Paul's "gospel" to be first and foremost about us. Rather, as Martyn suggests, Paul's gospel is centered on "God's liberating invasion of the cosmos. Christ's love enacted in the cross has the power to change the world because it is embodied in the new community of mutual service."[2] Thus Yoder and Martyn, in quite similar ways, contend Paul understood that in the cross and resurrection of Christ a new creation has been enacted, bringing an end to the old age and inaugurating a new time characterized by the reign of God as King.[3]

Sometimes when I am reading Martyn I almost forget I am reading him and think instead that I am reading Yoder. Many of Martyn's sentences could have just as easily come from Yoder. For example, commenting on Paul's view that God had dispatched the Spirit of Christ into the believers'

1. Harink, *Paul*, 147.
2. Martyn, "Apocalyptic Gospel," 246.
3. Martyn, *Galatians*, 22.

hearts to make them soldiers for Christ, Martyn writes: "The martial, cosmic dimension of Paul's apocalyptic applies, then, to the church and for that reason Paul can speak of the church itself both as God's new creation and as the apocalyptic community called to the front trenches in God's apocalyptic war against the powers of the present evil age."[4] Yoder, who emphasized the significance of the principalities and powers for understanding what it means to live at the same time in two times, could have easily written that sentence.[5]

Pauline apocalyptic, according to Martyn, expresses itself through antinomies. An old cosmos has suffered death and a new order has been born.[6] The new order has replaced the divisions of the old order—Jew and Greek, slave and free, male and female—by the establishment of a new unity in Christ. The new order is characterized by opposition between Spirit and the Flesh as well as between Christ and the Law. Though Paul does not employ dramatic apocalyptic language to characterize these new antinomies, Martyn suggests they constitute an antinomy characteristic of apocalyptic because they intimate a cosmic battle.[7]

Yoder would not disagree with Martyn's understanding of Pauline apocalyptic, but I will suggest that he would emphasize more than Martyn has done that a crucial apocalyptic antinomy is that between church and world. Martyn quite rightly suggests the central question of Paul's apocalyptic gospel is "What time is it?"[8] As I hope to show, time is the heart of the matter for Yoder, who believes that Christ's triumph over the powers has created a new age, a new aeon that simultaneously exists with the old aeon. These two aeons have political expressions, one in the world, the other in the church.[9]

As complementary as Martyn's and Yoder's understanding of apocalyptic may be, by calling attention to Yoder's understanding of the church/world dualism, I hope to show he is able to display the political significance of apocalyptic in a manner that is absent in Martyn's work. Douglas Harink observes that the focal concern of Martyn's later work has been that of divine and human agency. As a result, Martyn has not given attention to the political aspects of Paul's thought.[10] By contrast, Yoder's

---

4. Ibid., 102.

5. Yoder, *Christian Witness*, 8–9.

6. Martyn, *Theological Issues*, 111–23.

7. Ibid., 120–21.

8. Ibid., 121.

9. Yoder, *Christian Witness*, 8–11.

10. See ch. 2 above, Harink, "Partakers of the Divine Apocalypse," 91–92.

thought is political all the way down, and so it's my contention that Martyn's case would be stronger if he had read Yoder.[11] But such a statement is hardly helpful, so to move from a more constructive place I'll reframe my argument by suggesting that for contemporary readers Martyn's work can be tested and complimented by reading him in conversation with Yoder.

Before turning to Yoder, however, I want to call attention to Harink's suggestions about how Martyn's work might be developed politically. For Harink quite rightly observes that there is a politics—a politics that is perhaps underdeveloped—in Martyn's understanding of the three-actor moral drama that constitutes Paul's understanding of the human situation. Besides divine and human agency, there also exist anti-God powers whose agency is apparent in their ability to deceive and enslave. Harink suggests that in most accounts of Christian ethics the role of these powers, particularly as corporate agents, is ignored, which often means that the church as a political entity and agent is also lost.

Harink argues that, just to the extent that Martyn develops an account of the church as a corporate agent capable of countering the powers by fulfilling the law of Christ, he has begun to make explicit the politics inherent in Paul's apocalyptic gospel. What Martyn has not done, according to Harink, is suggest how this newly created agent called the church enacts this political witness among the nations. Harink thinks the way forward is to develop an account of how the messianic community even now participates in the kingdom of God in a manner that avoids the "wreckage of worldly political history." Accordingly this cruciform community will not be caught up in "locating those points of worldly-political leverage from which it might launch the next 'conservative' effort to keep things as they are, or the next 'progressive' movement in order to 'advance toward' or 'bring about' the kingdom of God or at least a 'higher' stage of history."[12]

That certainly seems right to me, but surely more needs to be said about what *kind* of politics the church represents amid the "wreckage of worldly political history." In an attempt to develop the "more" I want to direct attention to the significance of sacrifice as a central political reality. I may well test the patience of my readers in the development of this theme because I cannot deny that the argument I try to make is anything but straightforward. I begin by suggesting that Yoder's church/world dualism, a dualism that depends on the central claim of the lordship of Christ, can be seen as an important supplement to Martyn's account.

11. As far as I can tell Martyn never enters into conversation with Yoder's work.
12. Harink, "Partakers of the Divine Apocalypse," 95.

In order to develop the political significance of Yoder's account of what it means to see history from an apocalyptic perspective I will call attention to Peter Leithart's criticism of Yoder in *Defending Constantine: The Twilight of an Empire and the Dawn of Christendom.* For Leithart rightly contends that the heart of the political revolution that the church represented was to be "the end of sacrifice." I hope to show that Leithart's account of the political significance of sacrifice not only illumines Yoder's politics but helps us see how these issues remain relevant in our world.

YODER ON CHRIST THE KING

In his presidential address to the Society of Christian Ethics in 1988, "To Serve Our God and to Rule the World," John Howard Yoder took as his text Revelation 5:7–10. He explained that the apocalypse was not his theme for that occasion but the text from Revelation was crucial for what Yoder argued to be the main task of Christian ethics, that is, "to see history doxologically." To see history doxologically, according to Yoder, does not mean that Christians should try to usurp the Emperor's throne or to pastor Caesar prophetically, but rather "to persevere in celebrating the Lamb's lordship and in building the community shaped by that celebration."[13] Christians see history doxologically because they are convinced that they participate in God's rule of the cosmos.

Yoder observes, however, that apocalypse is only one of many modes of discourse the believing community uses to discern what such a rule entails. But apocalyptic language is particularly appropriate to express what it means for God is to be praised as the ruler of the world. Yoder's emphasis on the lordship of Christ as central to apocalyptic suggests a subtle but quite important difference with Martyn's account of apocalyptic. As I suggested above, in spite of the similarities between Martyn's and Yoder's accounts of apocalyptic, Yoder's stress on the lordship of Jesus Christ means the political character of the kingdom of God is evident in the tension established between church and world. To see Jesus "sitting at the right hand of the Father" not only indicates Jesus' role in the cosmic victory in which he is put in charge of history by becoming sovereign over the principalities and powers, but also that Jesus "sits at the right hand of the Father" is a declaration of his rule of the world.[14]

---

13. Yoder, "To Serve," 130.

14. Ibid., 132–33.

This way of stating the significance of apocalyptic allows Yoder to avoid Martyn's language of "invasion" and intervention. Of course Yoder does not disavow God's agency, but observes that what was novel about the Christian understanding of God's "intervention" was that the God who "intervenes" in Christ is the one God whose "intervention" is not unusual because that is the way God works. According to Yoder, what was unique about New Testament eschatology is that instead of several gods using the world as their playground, the Christians maintained that there is one God who uses the world as the theater of divinely purposeful action. The God who is the Father of Jesus Christ has always wanted to gather a people to operate in fellowship with God and one another. History has an end and we are it.[15]

Everything Yoder writes is informed by his conviction that Jesus is "sitting at the right hand of the Father," but perhaps his most concentrated account of what it means for Jesus to be so enthroned is developed in his course in Christian doctrine, published after his death as *Preface to Theology: Christology and Theological Method*. In *Preface to Theology* Yoder develops his Christology in terms of the three-fold offices of prophet, priest, and king. I suspect he thought that by doing so he was staying closer to the language of the Bible and, just as important, the people of Israel. Yoder suggests, therefore, that when Jesus says, "I am the king, but the servant kind of king," he fulfills the hope of the Jews, who had learned through bitter experience that earthly kings are, to say the least, a mixed blessing.[16]

If, as Yoder maintains, the lordship of Christ is at the heart of apocalyptic then the political implications are immediate. Indeed, that way of putting the matter is misleading. It is not a matter of working out the "implications," but rather the politics of apocalyptic simply *is* the existence of a people who refuse to acknowledge the claims of worldly rulers to be kings.[17] Moreover, because the one who is Lord has triumphed on the cross, his followers refuse to use the violence of earthly rulers to achieve what are allegedly good ends.

15. Yoder, *Preface to Theology*, 256.

16. Ibid., 245.

17. Anathea Portier-Young's account of the beginnings of apocalyptic literature supports Yoder's claim that the kingship of God necessitates a literature of resistance to empire. For empires not only exercise power over the world by force, but through propaganda and ideology. "Empire manipulated and co-opted hegemonic social institutions to express and reinforce its values and cosmologies. Resisting imperial domination required challenging not only the physical means of coercion, but also empire's claims about knowledge and the world. The first apocalypses did precisely this" (*Apocalypse Against Empire*, xxii).

Nonviolence is obviously a central commitment defining the kind of politics Yoder thinks is required to acknowledge the lordship of Christ, but it is equally important that nonviolence not be isolated as the defining feature of apocalyptic politics. Nonviolence is but one aspect of the conviction that history is determined not by kings and empires, but by the church. Nonviolence is, therefore, but an expression of a more determinative ecclesiology. The church's first duty to the societies in which she finds herself is, therefore, the same duty she has to her Lord. That means the church's witness to the lordship of the Crucified One cannot let "local obligations" to one state lead her to treat those in another state as an enemy. Any attempt, for example, "to justify war for the individual Christian citizen, after it has been judged incompatible with the ministry of the church, is a refusal to be honest with the absolute priority of church over state in the plan of God."[18]

Accordingly, Yoder makes the extraordinary claim that the church knows better than the state what the state is to be and do. The church may well be a moral stimulus to help a society and state to be better, but the church does not exist to enable the work of the alleged "wider" society. Rather "it is for the sake of the church's own work that society continues to function."[19] The meaning of history is to be found in the existence of the church.

Apocalyptic politics is based on the confidence that God uses the power structures of this world in spite of themselves for God's purposes. Christ carries out the purposes of the One who is sovereign by ruling over the rebellious structures of the universe.[20] That rule is hidden but made visible through the servant church. The place of the church in the history of the universe is the place where Christ's lordship is operative. This is where it is clear he rules, as well as the kind of rule he exercises. He is the Suffering Servant whose rule is decisively revealed on a cross. The church makes history not through domination but through being the servant of a crucified Lord.[21]

That the gospel is to be preached to the ends of the world is why time does not stop. What it means for Christ to be King is that he rules over history to give the church time to preach the gospel. Yoder is quite well aware that strong metaphysical claims are correlative of this understanding of

18. Yoder, *Christian Witness*, 17.
19. Ibid., 13.
20. Yoder, *Preface to Theology*, 247.
21. Ibid., 248.

the role of the church. That God gives the church time to witness to the lordship of Christ means that God is not timeless. That does not mean God is not eternal, but rather that eternity is not *not* temporal; eternity is temporal. Put differently, God is "more temporal than we are, who is ahead of us and behind us, before us and after us, above us in several directions, and who has more of the character of timeliness and meaningfulness in movement rather than less."[22]

Yoder's view of God's timefulness expresses his contention that "the cross and not the sword, suffering and not brute power determine the meaning of history. The key to the obedience of God's people is not their effectiveness but their patience (John 13:10). The triumph of the right is assured not by the might that comes to the aid of the right, which is of course the justification of the use of violence and other kinds of power in every human conflict. The relationship between the obedience of God's people and the triumph of God's cause is not a relationship of cause and effect but cross and resurrection."[23] This relation between cross and resurrection, moreover, is the most determinative mode of seeing history doxologically.

Yoder's well-known criticism of the Constantinian settlement is but the expression of this understanding of the apocalyptic character of the gospel. The fundamental problem that beset the church when Constantine became a member, a problem Yoder recognizes was beginning well before Constantine, was how becoming established changed the self-understanding of the church. Under the influence of Constantinianism the church no longer understood herself to live simultaneously in two times. Eschatology became an ideal relegated to the future rather than a reality that transforms the character of time.

As a result the church no longer thought she stood in the obedient line of the true prophets witnessing to the reality of God's kingdom. Rather the church now has a vested interest in the present order tempting her to use cultic means to legitimize that order.[24] Consequently, it is now assumed that everyone is Christian, so that Christian ethics no longer is the exploration of what makes us faithful disciples, but rather is an attempt to develop an ethic that is workable for all of society. For it is now assumed that the church exists to serve society and as a result the apocalyptic presumption that society exists to serve the church is lost.

22. Ibid., 276.

23. Yoder, *Politics of Jesus*, 232.

24. Yoder, *Original Revolution*, 65.

Yoder's understanding of Constantinianism is nuanced and complex, but hopefully I have said enough to suggest how Yoder's emphasis on the lordship of Christ for determining the apocalyptic imagination is a politics.[25] It is a politics, moreover, that I should like to think is compatible with Martyn's understanding of Paul's apocalyptic gospel in Galatians. For, as I suggested above, Martyn also thinks the questions "What time is it?" and "In what cosmos do we actually live?" to be apocalyptic questions.[26] I now want to try to show how the answer to those questions represents a profound challenge to the sacrificial politics of the world. Ironically Peter Leithart's defense of Constantine provides the categories I need to show why Yoder's understanding of apocalyptic politics is so important.

LEITHART ON SACRIFICE

In his book *Defending Constantine*, Peter Leithart develops a helpful critique of Yoder's politics. His critique is helpful because Leithart's criticisms, I hope to show, help us better appreciate the significance of Yoder's eschatology. I need to be clear. I am not particularly concerned with Leithart's defense of Constantine's integrity as a Christian. As Leithart recognizes, Yoder's critique of Constantinianism has little stake in questions surrounding the authenticity of Constantine's "conversion." Much more interesting is Leithart's suggestion that Yoder failed to appreciate how Christianity fundamentally transformed Rome by Constantine's outlawing of sacrifice.

That Constantine outlawed sacrifice—a law he enforced, according to Leithart, haphazardly—was significant because sacrifice was thought essential to Roman social and political life. That sacrifice was considered essential to a good politics was an unquestioned assumption in the ancient world. For example, Leithart calls attention to Celsus's contention that religion has to do with culture and political traditions, with support of the city or state, and is expressed primarily through the act of offering sacrifices.[27]

Leithart develops a strong case that sacrifice was at the center of Roman life. It was so because Romans assumed sacrifice was the chief religious act that allowed them to communicate with the gods and keep the

25. For the best analysis as well as criticism of Yoder's account of Constantianism see Sider, *To See History Doxologically*, 97–132.

26. Martyn, *Galatians*, 104.

27. Leithart, *Defending Constantine*, 40

gods happy. Moreover, sacrifice disclosed the secrets of the future by reading the entrails of slaughtered animals. Political decisions by the senate
were determined by sacrifices, as were imperial decrees. Soldiers sacrificed
to the gods prior to battle with the hope of insuring their success. Particularly important were the sacrifices made to or for the emperor to acknowledge him as Lord, Savior, or Deliverer. Because Christians believed there
was another King, they refused to sacrifice to the emperor, which invited
the Romans to sacrifice Christians not only for entertainment but for the
good of the empire.[28]

One of the reasons Christianity proved to be so offensive to Romans,
according to Leithart, was that it could not be a civic religion in the Roman
sense because it was a religion without sacrifice.[29] That is why, Leithart
argues, we should not miss the significance that after Constantine's triumph and having established himself as Caesar, he refused to enter the
Capitolium and sacrifice, as was required, to Jupiter. After his defeat of
Maxentius, Constantine made clear, Leithart argues, that a new political
theology was being established, that is, one without sacrifice.[30]

Through his refusal to sacrifice to the pagan gods Constantine gave
political expression to Christ's triumph over the "elementary things of this
world." According to Leithart, by renouncing sacrifice Constantine created a new political reality. In effect Constantine "secularized" political life
by showing that the state would no longer be the agent of salvation.[31] By
bringing an end to sacrifice, Constantine brought an end to Rome because
now Rome depended on a more determinative civic polity, i.e., the church.

---

28. Ibid., 327–28.

29. Ibid., 40. Leithart's assertion that Christianity is a religion without sacrifice is
overstated. Later in the book he will qualify that claim. He may be right that Christianity could not supply the kind of sacrifice that sustained the civic culture of Rome, but
sacrifice remained at the heart of Christian worship. Leithart refers a number of times
to Stroumsa's *The End of Sacrifice*. I think Stroumsa gets it right when he observes that
in some aspects "early Christianity represents a transformation of Judaism that opens
new horizons, but it seems in other ways to mark a conservative return to Israel's sacrificial system. While the rabbis gathered in Yavneh in 70 succeeded in transforming Judaism—without admitting doing so, and perhaps also without admitting it completely
to themselves—into a non-sacrificial religion, Christianity defined itself precisely as
a religion centered on sacrifice, even if it was a reinterpreted sacrifice. The Christian
anamnesis was the reactivation of the sacrifice of the Son of God, performed by the
priests" (72). Stroumsa argues that the Christian sacrifice was not a blood sacrifice as
was the sacrifices of Rome.

30. Leithart, *Defending Constantine*, 66–67.

31. Ibid., 325–27.

By recognizing the church's superiority to Rome Constantine acknowledged that the sacrifice of Christ, the blood of Jesus, is the end of bloodshed. "The church too was a sacrificial city, the true city of final sacrifice, which in the Eucharistic liturgy of sacrifice announced the end of animal sacrifice and the initiation of a new sacrificial order."[32] The rest, so to speak, is history. Constantine's refusal to sacrifice, his welcoming of the church as the true *polis*, created a non-sacrificial politics that became the norm even after the demise of Rome. Leithart celebrates this achievement, noting that "for millennia every empire, every city, every nation and tribe was organized around sacrifice. Every polity has been a sacrificial polity. We are not, and we have Constantine, to thank for that."[33]

It is not clear who Leithart thinks the "we" is in the last sentence. He has a brief account of Augustine's understanding of Christ's sacrifice now embodied in the Eucharist to suggest that any polity that acknowledges the church at least has the potential to be more just. So the church did not "fall" with the Constantinian settlement, but rather with that settlement a politics was begun that in all its variety can be thought to be Christian. The Middle Ages, in particular, are a model of the kind of political arrangement between church and state that Constantine made possible.

But, according to Leithart, Constantine's achievement has been lost in modernity. Modern states do not welcome the church as the true city because they are willing to recognize only a church that reduces itself to a religion or private piety. This is as true of totalitarian states as it is democratic, for both forms of the modern state are "secretly united in their anti-Constantinianism."[34] As a result, the modern state has reasserted its status as a sacrificial state so that it might be resacralized through the shedding of blood. Interestingly, this resacralization of the state is an expression of a nihilistic politics just to the extent that such states become ends in themselves, because there are no gods to receive the sacrifices the state asks of its members.[35]

Therefore the modern state in its refusal to welcome the church as teacher and judge has reasserted its status as a sacrificial state. It has done so, moreover, with a vengeance. The medieval world was bloody but the "Eucharistic blood of Jesus founded the true city," which meant there was a brake on bloodshed. Modern nations know no limits, attempting as they

32. Ibid., 329.
33. Ibid., 329.
34. Ibid., 340.
35. Ibid., 340–41.

must to be resacralized. That states now can "demand the 'ultimate sacrifice'" means, according to Leithart, in modernity "the 'Constantinianism' Yoder deplores becomes a horrific reality, as the church has too often wedded itself to power."[36]

This last remark, suggesting as it does how similar Leithart's position is to Yoder's ecclesiology, is why I find Leithart's criticism of Yoder so interesting. Like Yoder, Leithart thinks the church is the only true polity. Leithart, for example, seems to think Augustine is right to maintain that the church displays for the world what true justice is because true justice is first and foremost giving back to God what God has given us through the sacrifice of the Son. Leithart recognizes that Yoder is quite close to Augustine because like Augustine Yoder believes that the justice of a social order begins in the recognition that the church is a more determinative reality than the state. That the church is so, moreover, means the church betrays herself and the world when she identifies with the power structures of the world.

Leithart is a Calvinist. He therefore says that "if there is going to be a Christian politics, it is going to have to be an evangelical Christian politics, one that places Jesus, his cross and his resurrection at the center."[37] Yoder would not disagree as long as we remember that such a politics can only be found in the church. Leithart, I suspect, thinks that to be a mistake because he assumes that theocracy should always, at least in principle, be thought to be a possibility.

He also thinks Yoder is wrong about nonviolence. He acknowledges, however, that the most powerful argument for nonviolence is Yoder's contention that the cross makes nonviolence an unavoidable stance for Christians. For it was at the cross that Jesus' lordship was established, making clear that the one who is King refuses to save coercively. Leithart acknowledges the power of this reading of Jesus' death but suggests more "detailed exegesis" is required—although finally the matter cannot be determined by examination of specific texts but only by "attention to the full sweep of biblical history."[38] Yet "a full sweep of biblical history" is exactly what Yoder has given with his reading of the apocalyptic character of the gospel.

Leithart, like Yoder, wants to read history doxologically, but I am not convinced that he is right to suggest all politics after Constantine were non-sacrificial. That, however, is a topic for another time. More helpful for

36. Ibid., 340–41.

37. Ibid., 332.

38. Ibid., 333.

the argument I am trying to make is Leithart's contention that there has been an attempt to resacralize the state in modernity. By exploring that contention I hope to show that Yoder's understanding of what it means for Christ to be Lord is no less a challenge to the world in which we find ourselves than it was to Rome.

THE END OF SACRIFICE

These last remarks indicate that I think Yoder, though often criticized for tempting Christians to withdraw from politics, is the most political of theologians. For as Leithart suggests, Yoder challenges some of the deepest presuppositions of modern political reality, that is, that only the state has the right to ask that we make sacrifices that are life-changing. The problem with that presupposition is that the state that is legitimated by such sacrifices is not and cannot be acknowledged to be one that requires sacrifice. The sacrifices called for to legitimate the state are hidden even from those who sacrifice and are sacrificed because it is assumed that whatever anyone does they are acting as free individuals.

Paul Kahn, for example, argues in his book *Putting Liberalism in Its Place* that the liberal story of the birth of the modern state as an act of reason and free choice in which sacrifice is no longer necessary is a profound illusion.[39] It is an illusion of great power, however, because the presumption that a politics can be founded in reason between self-interested free individuals has become such a determinative story it creates its own reality. But Kahn argues that a politics so conceived cannot give an account of the body and, in particular, the experience of love that constitutes any politics. As a result, how liberal societies determine life and death remains out of sight in liberal theory.[40]

Kahn, however, observes that the political only properly begins at the point where people are organized sufficiently to imagine sacrificing their lives or killing others to maintain the state. Thus the general presumption that "the modern state has fully arrived not when it defends me against violence, but when it conscripts me into the armed force."[41] The legitimacy of claims to authority by the modern state depends, therefore, on the sacrifices we are asked to make on its behalf. Kahn argues such sacrifices are best understood as acts of love. Sacrifice is an act of love constituting

39. Kahn, *Putting Liberalism*, 93–94.
40. Ibid., 21.
41. Ibid., 240.

the very character of politics just to the extent sacrifice is "linked to the reciprocal possibility of infliction of injury."[42]

That is why war is so crucial for the legitimization of the modern state. The capacity of the nation-state to sacrifice its citizens in war was the great discovery, Kahn argues, of the nineteenth century. That discovery began with Napoleon's armies, shaped as they were by the popular enthusiasm of the Revolution. The fullest expression of that development is to be found in the American Civil War, in which democratic armies, based on mass conscription, confronted one another. As the result of these developments the conception of citizenship and political participation broadened, which meant so did the conception of the reach of military service. "The people's state is supported by people's armies."[43]

A liberal state is, therefore, no less dependent on sacrifice for legitimacy than the states of the past. In this respect, Western politics is but the expression of the faith of Western religious practices, that is, that only by being willing to die does one participate in the sacred. Liberal societies are, therefore, exemplifications of sacrificial politics just to the extent that the violent destruction of the self is "necessary for the realization of the transcendent character of the sovereign."[44]

Sacrifice and sovereignty are, therefore, linked in the politics of the state. For sacrifice transforms the finite self in order to express the infinite value of the sovereign. Sovereignty is brought into existence through the sacrificial destruction of the body. "The subject, or bearer, of sovereignty in the West has moved from God to monarch to the people. The point, however, is always the same. The sovereign is the source of meaning: it is not a means to any end apart from itself. It reveals itself in the act of sacrifice."[45]

Kahn's account of the relation of sovereignty and the state, a relation that depends on a memorialization of a chain of martyrs to the founding moment in which the state was born, obviously draws on the work of Carl Schmitt.[46] Schmitt's work is obviously disputed, but the way Kahn draws attention to the relation of sovereignty and sacrifice helps to illumine, and

---

42. Ibid., 234.

43. Ibid., 263.

44. Kahn, *Sacred Violence*, 184.

45. Ibid., 144.

46. Kahn discusses Schmitt's views in his recent book *Political Theology*. Kahn is quite critical of some aspects of Schmitt's work, but his fundamental understanding of modern political life owes much to Schmitt.

is illuminated by, Leithart's engagement of Yoder's apocalyptic politics. Kahn confirms Leithart's contention that the modern state has recovered the centrality of sacrifice for sustaining its legitimacy. What, however, is new about such states is the inability to make those sacrifices constitutive of the theory that informs their self-understanding.

WHERE DOES THIS LEAVE US?

Martyn's account of apocalyptic in Paul rightly suggested that the antinomies created by the new creation established by Christ are rightly understood to be in a cosmic conflict. Martyn, however, did not develop that insight politically. I suggested that Yoder's understanding of the church/world dualism, a dualism that expresses the tension between the two aeons, makes clear the political implications of the apocalyptic claim that Christ is Lord. That claim, that is, through Christ's sacrifice on the cross all worldly sacrifices have been brought to an end, creates a political alternative otherwise unimaginable.

The name of that political alternative is "church." The work of the church is to be an alternative to the world, that the world may know that all sacrifices that are not determined by the sacrifice of the cross are idolatrous. We do live, as Yoder argued, in two times. Apocalyptic is not some fantasy of the early church, but a claim about the cosmos. Martyn's and Yoder's work provide the tools to help us see what is before our eyes but too often we fail to see. Of course, that is the way the powers work. They cannot be seen because we think we can only see with them.

Christians continue to be a people of the new age at war with the old age. The old age is a time, a world, constituted by sacrifices to bloodthirsty gods. They are the gods of war. So understood, the question of Christian participation in war turns out to be a question not restricted to "the ethics of war," but instead it is a question of how Christians can at once say "Jesus is Lord," the end of all sacrifices, and yet continue to participate in the sacrifice of war.[47] Focus on that question and you will begin to understand how frightening and wonderful it is to be a people of a new age.

---

47. For the development of this way to put the matter see my *War and the American Difference*.

Bibliography

Adams, Edward. *Constructing the World: A Study in Paul's Cosmological Language.* Studies of the New Testament and Its World. Edinburgh: T. & T. Clark, 2000.

———. "Greco-Roman and Ancient Jewish Cosmology." In *Cosmology and New Testament Theology,* edited by Jonathan T. Pennington and Sean M. McDonough, 5–27. London: T. & T. Clark, 2008.

Adams, J., et al. *Dienst in Freiheit: Ernst Käsemann zum* 100. *Geburtstag.* Neukirchener-Vluyn: Neukirchener, 2008.

Adorno, Theodor. "The Essay as Form." In *The Adorno Reader,* edited by Brian O'Connor, 91–111. New York: Blackwell, 2000.

———. *Minima Moralia: Reflections from Damaged Life.* Translated by E. F. N. Jephcott. London: New Left, 1974.

Agamben, Giorgio. *The Time that Remains: A Commentary on the Letter to the Romans.* Translated by Patricia Dailey. Stanford, CA: Stanford University Press, 2005.

Agersnap, Søren. *Baptism and the Newness of Life: A Study of Romas 6:1–14.* Translated by Christine and Frederick Crowley. Aarhus, Netherlands: Aarhus University Press, 1999.

Altizer, Thomas J. J. *Genesis and Apocalypse: A Theological Voyage Toward Authentic Christianity.* Louisville: Westminster John Knox, 1991.

———. *The New Apocalypse: The Radical Christian Vision of William Blake.* East Lansing: Michigan State University Press, 1967.

Augustine of Hippo. "A Treatise on the Grace of Christ, and on Original Sin; Written against Pelagius and Coelestius." In *Nicene and Post-Nicene Fathers,* vol. 5, edited by Philip Schaff. Grand Rapids: Eerdmans, 1971.

Aulén, Gustaf. "Chaos and Cosmos: The Drama of the Atonement." *Interpretation* 4:2 (1950) 156–67.

———. *Christus Victor: An Historical Study of the Three Main Types of the Idea of the Atonement.* Translated by A. G. Herbert. London: SCM, 1970.

———. *The Faith of the Christian Church.* Translated by E. H. Wahlstrom. Philadelphia: Fortress, 1960.

Austin, J. L. *How to Do Things with Words.* Cambridge, MA: Harvard University Press, 1962.

Badiou, Alain. *Infinite Thought: Truth and the Return to Philosophy.* Edited by Justin Clemens and Oliver Feltham. London: Continuum, 2003.

———. *Saint Paul: The Foundation of Universalism.* Translated by Ray Brassier. Stanford: Stanford University Press, 2003.

Bibliography

Barclay, John M. G. "I Will Have Mercy on Whom I Have Mercy: The Golden Calf and Divine Mercy in Romans 9–11 and Second Temple Judaism." *Early Christianity* 1 (2010) 82–106.

———. "Manna and the Circulation of Grace: A Study of 2 Corinthians 8:1–15." In *The Word Leaps the Gap: Essays on Scripture and Theology in Honor of Richard B. Hays*, edited by J. Ross Wagner, C. Kavin Rowe, and A. Katherine Grieb, 409–26. Grand Rapids: Eerdmans, 2008.

———. "Why the Roman Empire Was Insignificant to Paul." In *Pauline Churches and Diaspora Jews*, 363–87. Tübingen: Mohr Siebeck, 2011.

The Barmen Theological Declaration. In *The Book of Confessions: Study Edition*, article 3. Louisville: Geneva, 1999.

Bar On, Bat-Ami. "Marginality and Epistemic Privilege." In *Feminist Epistemologies*, edited by Linda Alcoff and Elizabeth Potter, 83–100. New York: Routledge, 1993.

Barth, Karl. *Church Dogmatics*. Edited by T. F. Torrance and G. W. Bromiley, translated by A. T. MacKay et. al. 14 vols. Edinburgh: T. & T. Clark, 1936–70.

———. *The Epistle to the Romans*. Translated by Edwyn C. Hoskyns. Oxford: Oxford University Press, 1968.

———. *Karl Barth—Rudolf Bultmann Letters, 1922–1966*. Edited by B. Jaspert. Grand Rapids: Eerdmans, 1981.

———. *Protestant Theology in the Nineteenth Century: Its Background and History*. New ed. Grand Rapids: Eerdmans, 2002.

———. *Der Römerbrief*. Munich: Chr. Kaiser, 1922.

———. *Theology and Church: Shorter Writings, 1920–1928*. Translated by Louise Pettibone Smith. London: SCM, 1962.

———. *The Word of God and the Word of Man*. Translated by Douglas Horton. New York: Harper, 1957.

Baur, Ferdinand Christian. *Lehrbuch der christlichen Dogmengescheschichte*. Tübingen: Fues, 1858.

Behr, John. *The Mystery of Christ: Life in Death*. Crestwood, NY: St. Vladimir's Seminary Press, 2006.

Bell, Richard. *Deliver Us from Evil: Interpreting the Redemption from the Power of Satan in New Testament Theology*. Wissenschaftliche Untersuchungen Zum Neun Testament. Tübingen: Mohr Siebeck, 2007.

Benjamin, Walter. "On the Concept of History." In *Selected Writings*, vol. 4, 1938–1940, edited by Howard Eiland and Michael W. Jennings, 401–25. Cambridge, MA: Belknap, 2003.

———. "Theological-Political Fragment." In *Selected Writings*, vol. 3, 1935–1938, edited by Howard Eiland and Michael W. Jennings, 305–6. Cambridge, MA: Belknap, 2002.

Boer, Martinus C de. "Paul and Jewish Apocalyptic Eschatology." In *Apocalyptic and the New Testament: Essays in Honor of J. Louis Martyn*, edited by J. Marcus and M. L. Soards, 169–90. Sheffield: JSOT Press, 1989.

———. "Paul, Theologian of God's Apocalypse." *Interpretation* 56/1 (2002) 21–33.

Bonhoeffer, Dietrich. *Christ the Center*. New York: HarperOne, 1978.

———. *The Cost of Discipleship*. Edited by Geoffrey B. Kelly and John D. Godsey, translated by Barbara Green and Reinhard Kraus. Minneapolis: Fortress, 2003.

———. *Ethics*. Edited by Clifford J. Green, translated by Reinhard Krauss et al. Minneapolis: Fortress, 2005.

————. *No Rusty Swords: Letters, Lectures, and Notes, 1928–1936.* New York: Harper, 1965.

Bousset, Wilhelm. *Kyrios Christos: A History of the Belief in Christ from the Beginnings of Christianity to Irenaeus.* Translated by John E. Steely. Nashville: Abingdon, 1970.

————. *What Is Religion?* Translated by F. B. Low. New York: Putnam, 1907.

Bowie, Andrew. *Aesthetics and Subjectivity: From Kant to Nietzsche.* Manchester: Manchester University Press, 2003.

————. "Introduction." In *The Subject and the Text: Essays on Literary Theory and Philosophy,* edited by Andrew Bowie, translated by Helen Atkins, xxvi–xxxvi. Cambridge: Cambridge University Press, 1987.

Boyarin, Daniel. *A Radical Jew: Paul and the Politics of Identity.* Berkeley: University of California Press, 1994.

Braaten, Carl E. "The Recovery of Apocalyptic Imagination." In *The Last Things: Biblical and Theological Perspectives on Eschatology,* edited by C. E. Braaten and Robert W. Jenson, 14–32. Grand Rapids: Eerdmans, 2002.

————. "The Significance of Apocalypticism for Systematic Theology." *Interpretation* 25/4 (1971) 480–99.

Bradley, K. R. *Slaves and Masters in the Roman Empire: A Study in Social Control.* New York: Oxford University Press, 1989.

Breytenbach, Cilliers. *Versöhnung: Eine Studie zur paulinische Soteriologie.* Neukirchen-Vluyn: Neukirchener, 1989.

Brown, Alexandra R. *The Cross and Human Transformation: Paul's Apocalyptic Word in 1 Corinthians.* Minneapolis: Fortress, 1995.

Brueggemann, Walter. "The Epistemological Crisis of Israel's Two Histories (Jer 9:22–23)." In *Israelite Wisdom: Theological and Literary Essays in Honor of Samuel Terrien,* edited by J. G. Gammie, W. A. Brueggemann, W. L. Humphries, and James W. Ward, 85–105. Missoula, MO: Scholars Press, 1978.

Buber, Martin. *I and Thou.* Translated by Walter Kaufmann. New York: Scribner, 1970.

Bultmann, Rudolf. "Autobiographical Reflections." In *Existence and Faith,* 283–88. New York: Meridian Books, 1960.

————. "The Case for Demythologization: A Reply by Rudolf Bultmann." Translated by Norbert Guterman. In *Myth and Christianity: An Inquiry into the Possibility of Religion without Myth,* 57–71. New York: Noonday, 1958.

————. "Die christliche Hoffnung und das Problem der Entmythologisierung (1954)." In *Glauben und Verstehen: Gesammelte Aufsätze,* 3:81–90. Tübingen: Mohr, 1933–65.

————. "Ist die Apokalyptik die Mutter der christlichen Theologie?: Eine Auseinandersetzung mit Ernst Käsemann." In *Exegetica: Aufsätze zur Erforschung des Neuen Testaments,* edited by Erich Dinkler, 476–82. Tübingen. Mohr, 1967.

————. *Jesus Christ and Mythology.* New York: Scribner, 1958.

————. "Letter to Rev. Stanley D. Padgett." *Lutheran Quarterly* 2/4 (1988) 554.

————. "New Testament and Mythology: The Problem of Demythologizing the New Testament Proclamation (1941)." In *New Testament and Mythology and Other Basic Writings,* edited by Schubert M. Ogden, 1–43. Philadelphia: Fortress, 1984.

————. "On the Problem of Demythologizing (1952)." In *New Testament and Mythology and Other Basic Writings,* edited by Schubert M. Ogden, 95–130. Philadelphia: Fortress, 1984.

————. *Primitive Christianity in Its Contemporary Setting.* Translated by R. H. Fuller. Cleveland: World Publishing, 1956.

Bibliography

———. "Science and Existence (1955)." In *New Testament and Mythology and Other Basic Writings*, 131–44. German ed.: "Wissenschaft und Existenz." In *Glauben und Verstehen: Gesammelte Aufsätze*, 3:107–21. Tübingen: Mohr, 1933–65.

———. *Theology of the New Testament*. 2 vols. New York: Scribner, 1951; Waco: Baylor, 2007.

———. *Das verkündigte Wort: Predigten, Andachten, Ansprachen 1906–1941*. Edited by Erich Grässer and Martin Evang. Tübingen: Mohr, 1984.

———. "The Understanding of Man and the World in the New Testament and in the Greek World." In *Essays Philosophical and Theological*, 67–90. London: SCM, 1955.

Butler, Judith. *Bodies That Matter: On the Discursive Limits of "Sex"*. New York: Routledge, 1993.

Calvin, John. *Commentary on the Epistles of Paul the Apostle to the Corinthians*. Vol. 1. Grand Rapids: Eerdmans, 1948.

———. *The First Epistle of Paul the Apostle to the Corinthians*. Edinburg: Oliver and Boyd, 1960.

———. *Institutes of the Christian Religion*. Edited by John T. McNeill and translated by Ford Lewis Battles. Library of Christian Classics. Philadelphia: Westminster, 1960.

Campbell, Douglas. *The Deliverance of God: An Apocalyptic Reading of Justification in Paul*. Grand Rapids: Eerdmans, 2009.

Carr, Wesley. *Angels and Principalities: The Background, Meaning and Development of the Pauline Phrase* hai archai kai hai exousiai. Society for New Testament Studies Monograph Series. Cambridge: Cambridge University Press, 1981.

Casel, Odo. *The Mystery of Christian Worship*. Edited by Aidan Kavanagh. Milestones in Catholic Theology. New York: Crossroad, 1999.

Collins, Raymond F. *First Corinthians*. Sacred Pagina. Collegeville, MN: Liturgical, 1999.

Cone, James H. *Black Theology and Black Power*. 20th anniversary ed. San Francisco: Harper, 1989.

———. *The Cross and the Lynching Tree*. Maryknoll, NY: Orbis, 2011.

Cousar, Charles B. *Theology of the Cross: The Death of Jesus in the Pauline Letters*. Overtures to Biblical Theology. Minneapolis: Fortress, 1990.

Cranfield, C. E. B. *The Epistle to the Romans*. Vol. 1. International Critical Commentary Series. Edinburgh: T. & T. Clark, 1975.

Creegan, Nicola Hoggard. "The Salvation of Creatures." In *God of Salvation: Soteriology in Theological Perspective*, edited by Ivor J. Davidson and Murray A. Rae. Burlington, 77–87. VT: Ashgate, 2011.

Cullman, Oscar. *Christ and Time*. Translated by Floyd V. Filson. Philadelphia: John Knox, 1964.

———. *Salvation in History*. New York: Harper, 1967.

Danielson, Dennis Richard. *The Book of the Cosmos: Imagining the Universe from Heraclitus to Hawking*. New York: Basic Books, 2000.

Davis, Joshua. "Apocalyptic, Typology, and Metaphysics: Reflecting on Providence with Hans Frei." A paper presented at the Explorations in Theology and Apocalyptic group, American Academy of Religion, Atlanta, November 2010.

Dodson, Joseph R. *The 'Powers' of Personification: Rhetorical Purpose in the* Book of Wisdom *and the Letter to the Romans*. Berlin: de Gruyter, 2008.

Dorrien, Gary J. *The Barthian Revolt in Modern Theology: Theology without Weapons*. Louisville: WJK, 1999.

Durantaye, *Giorgio Agamben: A Critical Introduction.* Stanford, CA: Stanford University Press, 2009.

Eastman, Susan. "'Empire of Illusion': Sin, Evil, and the Good News in Romans." In *Comfortable Words: Essays in Honor of Paul F. M. Zahl.* Eugene, OR: Wipf and Stock, forthcoming.

———. "Israel and the Mercy of God: A Re-Reading of Galatians 6:16 and Romans 9–11." *New Testament Studies* 56/3 (2010) 356–95.

———. "Whose Apocalypse?: The Identity of the Sons of God in Romans 8:19." *Journal of Biblical Literature* 121 (2002) 263–77.

Eichhorn, Albert. *The Lord's Supper in the New Testament.* Translated by Jeffrey F. Cayzer. Atlanta: SBL, 2007.

Eller, Vernard. *Christian Anarchy: Jesus' Primacy over the Powers.* Eugene, OR: Wipf and Stock, 1999.

Elliott, Neil. *The Rhetoric of Romans: Argumentative Constraint and Strategy and Paul's Dialogue with Judaism.* Sheffield: Sheffield Academic, 1990.

Engberg-Pedersen, Troels. *Paul and the Stoics.* Louisville: Westminster John Knox, 2000.

———. "Response to Martyn." *Journal for the Study of the New Testament* 86 (2002) 103–14.

Erasmus, Desiderius. *Paraphrases on the Epistles to the Corinthians, Ephesians, Philippians, Colossians, and Thessalonians.* Edited by Robert D. Sider, translated by Mechtilde O'Mara and Edward Phillips. Collected Works of Erasmus 43. Toronto: University of Toronto Press, 2009.

Esler, Philip F. *Conflict and Identity in Romans: The Social Setting of Paul's Letter.* Minneapolis: Fortress, 2003.

Fahey, Michael A. "Sacraments." In *The Oxford Handbook of Systematic Theology.* Edited by Kathryn Tanner et al. Oxford: Oxford University Press, 2007.

Farley, Edward. *Divine Empathy: A Theology of God.* Philadelphia: Fortress, 1996.

Fee, Gordon D. *The First Epistle to the Corinthians.* Grand Rapids: Eerdmans, 1987.

Ferguson, Everett. *Baptism in the Early Church: History, Theology, and Liturgy in the First Five Centuries.* Grand Rapids: Eerdmans, 2009.

Fichte, J. G. "First Introduction." In *Science of Knowledge,* translated by A. E. Kroeger, 11–60. Philadelphia: Lippincott, 1808.

The First and Second Prayer Books of Edward VI. London: Dent and Sons, 1952.

Fischer, Simon. *Revelatory Positivism?: Barth's Earliest Theology and the Marburg School.* Oxford: Oxford University Press, 1988.

Fitzmyer, Joseph A. *Romans.* Anchor Bible 33A. New York: Doubleday, 1993.

Flannery, Austin. *Vatican Council.* Vol. 1. New rev. ed. Northport, NY: Costello, 1998.

Flett, John G. "The Spirit Went the Way of Mission: Robert Jenson on the Objectivity of the Gospel." Unpublished paper.

Forché, Carolyn. *Against Forgetting: Twentieth-Century Poetry of Witness.* New York: Norton, 1993.

Frank, Manfred. *Das individuelle Allgemeine: Textstrukturierung und –interpretation nach Schleiermacher. Frankfurt: Suhrkamp,* 1977.

———. "Metaphysical Foundations: A look at Schleiermacher's Dialectic." In *The Cambridge Companion to Friedrich Schleiermacher,* edited by Jacqueline Mariña, 15–34. Cambridge: Cambridge University Press, 2005.

———. *The Philosophical Foundations of Early German Romanticism.* Translated by Elizabeth Millán-Zaibert. New York: SUNY Press, 2004.

————. *Selbstgefühl: Eine historisch-systematische Erkundung.* Frankfurt: Suhrkamp, 2002.

Frei, Hans. "David Friedrich Strauss." In *Nineteenth-Century Religious Though in the West,* edited by Ninian Smart et al., 1:215–60. Cambridge: Cambridge University Press, 1985.

————. *The Identity of Jesus Christ.* Philadelphia: Fortress, 1975.

————. "Scripture as Realistic Narrative: Karl Barth as Critic of Historical Criticism." Online: http://www.library.yale.edu/div/Freitranscripts/Frei02-Narrative.htm.

Fulkerson, Mary McClintock. *Changing the Subject: Women's Discourses and Feminist Theology.* Eugene, OR: Wipf and Stock, 2001.

————. *Places of Redemption: Theology for a Worldly Church.* New York: Oxford University Press, 2007.

Fussell, Paul. *The Great War and Modern Memory.* London: Oxford University Press, 1975.

Gathercole, Simon. "What Did Paul Really Mean?" *Christianity Today,* August 2007. Online: http://www.christianitytoday.com/ct/2007/august/13.22.html.

Gaventa, Beverly Roberts. "'For the Glory of God': Theology and Experience in Paul's Letter to the Romans." In *Between Experience and Interpretation: Engaging the Writings of the New Testament,* edited by Mary F. Foskett and O. Wesley Allen Jr., 53–65. Nashville: Abingdon, 2008.

————. "From Toxic Speech to the Redemption of Doxology in Paul's Letter to the Romans." In *The Word Leaps the Gap: Essays on Scripture and Theology in Honor of Richard B. Hays,* edited by J. Ross Wagner, et al., 392–408. Grand Rapids: Eerdmans, 2008.

————. "God Handed Them Over." In *Our Mother Saint Paul,* 113–23. Louisville: Westminster John Knox, 2007.

————. "Interpreting the Death of Jesus Apocalyptically: Reconsidering Romans 8:32." In *Jesus and Paul Reconnected: Fresh Pathways into an Old Debate,* edited by Todd D. Still, 125–45. Grand Rapids: Eerdmans, 2007.

————. "On the Calling-into-Being of Israel: Romans 9:6–26." In *Between Gospel and Election.* Edited by Florian Wilk and J. Ross Wagner, 255–69. WUNT 1:257. Tübingen: Mohr Siebeck, 2010.

————. *Our Mother Saint Paul.* Louisville: Westminster John Knox, 2007.

Gilson, Etienne. *The Spirit of Medieval Philosophy.* Notre Dame: University of Notre Dame Press.

Grässer, E. "Schweitzer, Albert." In *Dictionary of Biblical Interpretation,* edited by John H. Hayes, 2:449–450. Nashville: Abingdon, 1999.

Griffiths, Paul J. "The Cross as the Fulcrum of Politics: Expropriating Agamben on Paul." In *Paul, Philosophy, and the Theopolitical Vision: Critical Engagements with Agamben, Badiou, Zizek and Others,* edited by Douglas Harink, 179–97. Eugene, OR: Cascade, 2010.

Grosz, Elizabeth. "Bodies and Knowledges: Feminism and the Crisis of Reason." In *Feminist Epistemologies,* edited by Linda Alcoff and Elizabeth Potter, 187–215. New York: Routledge, 1993.

Gunkel, Hermann. *Genesis.* Göttingen: Vandenhoeck & Ruprecht, 1901.

————. *The Legends of Genesis.* Translated by W. H. Carruth. Chicago: Open Court, 1901.

Gunton, Colin. *The Actuality of Atonement: A Study of Metaphor, Rationality and the Christian Tradition*. Edinburgh: T. & T. Clark, 1989.

Gutiérrez, Gustavo. *A Theology of Liberation: History, Politics, and Salvation*. Edited and translated by Sister Caridad Inda and John Eagleson. 15th anniversary ed. Maryknoll, NY: Orbis, 1988.

———. *We Drink from Our Own Wells: The Spiritual Journey of a People*. Translated by Matthew J. O'Connell. Maryknoll, NY: Orbis, 1983.

Hahne, Harry Alan. *The Corruption and Redemption of Creation: Nature in Romans 8.19–22 and Jewish Apocalyptic Literature*. London: T. & T. Clark, 2006.

Hammann, Konrad. *Rudolf Bultmann: Eine Biographie*. Tübingen: Mohr Siebeck, 2009.

Hannay, Alastair. *Kierkegaard*. Arguments of the Philosophers. London: Routledge, 1982.

Harding, Sandra. "Rethinking Standpoint Epistemology: What Is 'Strong Objectivity'?" In *Feminist Epistemologies*, edited by Linda Alcoff and Elizabeth Potter, 49–82. New York: Routledge, 1993.

Harink, Douglas. "Barth's Apocalyptic Exegesis and the Question of Israel in *Römerbrief*, Chapters 9–11." *Toronto Journal of Theology* 25/1 (2009) 5–18.

———. *1 & 2 Peter*. Brazos Theological Commentary on the Bible. Grand Rapids: Brazos, 2009.

———. "Jewish Priority, Election, and the Gospel." In *Introduction to Messianic Judaism*, edited by David Rudolf and Joel Willets. Grand Rapids: Zondervan, forthcoming.

———. "Paul and Israel: An Apocalyptic Reading." *Pro Ecclesia* 16/4 (2007) 359–80.

———. *Paul Among the Postliberals: Pauline Theology beyond Christendom and Modernity*. Grand Rapids: Brazos, 2003.

———. "Time and Politics in Four Commentaries on Romans." In *Paul, Philosophy, and the Theopolitical Vision: Critical Engagements with Agamben, Badiou, Zizek and Others*, edited by Douglas Harink, 282–312. Eugene, OR: Cascade, 2010.

Hatchett, Marion, J. *Commentary on the American Prayer Book*. New York: Harper-Collins, 1995.

Hays, Richard B. *The Faith of Jesus Christ: An Investigation of the Narrative Substructure of Galatians* 3:1—4:11. Biblical Resource Series. Chico, CA: Scholars Press, 1982.

———. *First Corinthians*. Interpretation. Louisville: John Knox, 1997.

———. "Review of J. Louis Martyn, *Galatians*." *Review of Biblical Literature* 3 (2001) 59–65.

Hauerwas, Stanley. *War and the American Difference: Theological Reflections on Violence and National Identity*. Grand Rapids: Brazos, 2011.

———. *With the Grain of the Universe: The Church's Witness and Natural Theology*. Grand Rapids: Brazos, 2001.

Hefner. "Introduction." In *Three Essays of Albrecht Ritschl*, edited by Philip J. Hefner, 1–50. Philadelphia: Fortress, 1972.

Hegel, G. W. F. *The Encyclopedia Logic*. Translated by T. F. Garaets, et al. Indianapolis: Hackett, 1992.

———. *Faith and Knowledge*. Translated by Walter Cerf and H. S. Harris. Albany, NY: SUNY Press, 1977.

———. *Lectures on the Philosophy of Religion*. 1 vol. ed. Edited by Peter C. Hodgson. Berkley: University of California Press, 1988.

Henrich, Dieter. *Between Kant and Hegel*. Edited by David S. Pacini. Cambridge, MA: Harvard University Press, 2003.

Bibliography

Henry, Michael. *Franz Overbeck: Theologian?: Religion and History in the Thought of Franz Overbeck*. Frankfurt: Peter Lang, 1995.

Hochschild, Adam. *To End All Wars: A Story of Loyalty and Rebellion, 1914–1918*. Boston: Houghton Mifflin Harcourt, 2011.

Hodgson, Peter C. *The Formation of Historical Theology: A Study of Ferdinand Christian Baur*. Philadelphia: Fortress, 2007.

————. *Hegel and Christian Theology: A Reading of the Lectures on the Philosophy of Religion*. Oxford: Oxford University Press, 2007.

Hofius, Otfried. "Der Mensch im Schatten Adams." In *Paulusstudien*, 2:104–54. Wissenschaftliche Untersuchungen Zum Neun Testament. Tübingen: Mohr Siebeck, 2002.

Holmes, Christopher R. J. *Ethics in the Presence of Christ*. London: T. & T. Clark, 2011.

Hooker, Morna D. "Interchange in Christ." In *From Adam to Christ: Essays on Paul*, 13–25. Cambridge: Cambridge University Press, 1990.

Horsley, Richard A. *1 Corinthians*. Abingdon New Testament Commentaries. Nashville: Abingdon, 1998.

Hultgren, Arland J. *Paul's Letter to the Romans: A Commentary*. Grand Rapids: Eerdmans, 2011.

Inwood, Michael James. *A Hegel Dictionary*. Malden, MA: Blackwell, 1992.

Irigaray, Luce. "Equal to Whom?" In *The Essential Difference*, edited by Naomi Schor and Elizabeth Weed, translated by Robert L. Mazzola, 63–81. Bloomington: Indiana University Press, 1994.

Ive, Jeremy. "Robert W. Jenson's Theology of History." In *Trinity, Time, and Church: A Response to the Theology of Robert W. Jenson*, edited by Colin E. Gunton, 146–57. Grand Rapids: Eerdmans, 2000.

Jacobi, Friedrich. *Über der Lehre des Spinoza in Briefen an den Herrn Moses Mendelssohn*. Breslau: Loewe, 1789.

————. *David Hume über den Glauben oder Idealismus und Realizmus*. Breslau: Loewe, 1787.

Jenson, Robert W. *Canon and Creed*. Interpretation. Louisville: Westminster John Knox, 2010.

————. "Catechesis for Our Time." In *Marks of the Body of Christ*, edited by Carl E. Braaten and Robert W. Jenson, 137–49. Grand Rapids: Eerdmans, 1999.

————. "Christ as Culture 1: Christ as Polity." *International Journal of Systematic Theology* 5/2 (2003) 323–29.

————. "Christ as Culture 3: Christ as Drama." *International Journal of Systematic Theology* 6/3 (2004) 194–200.

————. "Christian Civilization." *God, Truth, and Witness: Engaging Stanley Hauerwas*, edited by L. Gregory Jones et al., 153–63. Grand Rapids: Brazos, 2005.

————. "Election and Culture: From Babylon to Jerusalem." In *Public Theology in Cultural Engagement*, edited Stephen R. Holmes, 35–50. London: Paternoster, 2008.

————. "How the World Lost Its Story." *First Things* 36 (1993) 19–24.

————. "Review of *Christ, History and Apocalyptic: The Politics of Christian Mission*." *Pro Ecclesia* 20 (2011) 310–12.

————. "Scripture's Authority in the Church." In *The Art of Reading Scripture*, edited by Ellen F. Davis and Richard B. Hays, 27–37. Grand Rapids: Eerdmans, 2003.

————. "Toward a Christian Theology of Israel." *Pro Ecclesia* 9 (2000) 43–56.

———. *Visible Words: The Interpretation and Practice of Christian Sacraments.* Philadelphia: Fortress, 1978.

———. *Systematic Theology.* 2 vols. Oxford: Oxford University Press, 1997, 1999.

———. "You Wonder Where the Spirit Went." *Pro Ecclesia* 2 (1993) 296–304.

Jewett, Robert. *Romans: A Commentary.* Hermeneia. Minneapolis: Fortress, 2007.

Johnson, Roger A. *The Origins of Demythologizing: Philosophy and Historiography in the Theology of Rudolf Bultmann.* Leiden: Brill, 1974.

Jones, Jenny M. *The Annotated Godfather: The Complete Screenplay.* New York: Black Dog & Leventhal, 2007.

Joseph A. Fitzmyer. *First Corinthians.* Anchor Yale Bible Commentaries. New Haven, CT: Yale University Press, 2008.

Jüngel, Eberhard. *Justification: The Heart of the Christian Faith.* Translated by J. Webster. Edinburgh: T. & T. Clark, 2001.

Kahn, Paul. *Political Theology: Four New Chapters on the Concept of Sovereignty.* New York: Columbia University Press, 2011.

———. *Putting Liberalism in Its Place.* Princeton, NJ: Princeton University Press, 2005.

———. *Sacred Violence: Torture, Terror, and Sovereignty.* Ann Arbor: University of Michigan Press, 2011.

Kant, Immanuel. *Critique of Pure Reason.* Translated by Werner Pluhar. Indianapolis: Hackett, 1996.

———. *Kritik der reinen Vernunft.* Berlin: Georg Reimer, 1900.

———. *Religion within the Limits of Reason Alone.* New York: Harper, 1960.

Käsemann, Ernst. "Die Anfänge christlicher Theologie." *Zeitschrift für Theologie und Kirche* 57 (1960) 162–85.

———. "An Apologia for Primitive Christian Eschatology." In *Essays on New Testament Themes,* 169–95. Translated by W. J. Montague. Philadelphia: Fortress, 1982.

———. "The Beginnings of Christian Theology." In *New Testament Questions of Today,* 82–107. Translated by W. J. Montague. London: SCM Press, 1969. German ed.: "Die Anfänge christlicher Theologie," in *Exegetische Versuche und Besinnungen,* 2:82–104 (Göttingen: Vandenhoeck & Ruprecht, 1965).

———. "Blind Alleys in the 'Jesus of History' Controversy." In *New Testament Questions of Today,* translated by W. J. Montague, 23–65. London: SCM, 1969.

———. *Commentary on Romans.* Edited and translated by Geoffrey W. Bromiley. Grand Rapids: Eerdmans, 1980.

———. "Corporeality in Paul." In *On Being a Disciple of the Crucified Nazarene: Unpublished Lectures and Sermons,* edited by Wolfgang Kraus and Rudolf Landau, translated by Roy A. Harrisville, 38–51. Grand Rapids: Eerdmans, 2010.

———. "A Critical Analysis of Philippians 2:5–11." In *God and Christ: Existence and Providence,* edited by Robert W. Funk, translated by Alice F. Carse, 45–88. Journal for Theology and the Church. New York: Harper, 1968.

———. "The Divine *Agent Provocateur.*" *Religious Studies Review* 11/3 (1985) 217–63.

———. "The Doctrine of Reconciliation in the New Testament." In *The Future of our Religious Past: Essays in Honour of Rudolf Bultmann,* edited by J. M. Robinson, translated by C. E. Carlston and R. P. Scharlemann, 49–64. London: SCM, 1971.

———. "For and Against a Theology of the Resurrection." In *Jesus Means Freedom: A Polemical Survey of the New Testament,* 59–84. Translated by Frank Clarke. London: SCM, 1969.

———. "Für und wider eine Theologie der Auferstehung." In *Der Ruf der Freiheit*, 79–114. Tübingen: Mohr, 1972.

———. "God's Image and Sinners." In *On Being a Disciple of the Crucified Nazarene: Unpublished Lectures and Sermons*, edited by Wolfgang Kraus and Rudolf Landau, translated by Roy A. Harrisville, 108–19. Grand Rapids: Eerdmans, 2010.

———. "God's 'Yes' to All." In *On Being a Disciple of the Crucified Nazarene: Unpublished Lectures and Sermons,*edited by Wolfgang Kraus and Rudolf Landau, translated by Roy A. Harrisville, 216–25. Grand Rapids: Eerdmans, 2010.

———. "Justification and Salvation History in the Epistle to the Romans." In *Perspectives on Paul*, 60–78. Translated by Margaret Kohl. Philadelphia: Fortress, 1971.

———. *Kirchliche Konflikte*. Vol. 1. Göttingen: Vanderhoeck & Ruprecht, 1982.

———. *New Testament Questions of Today*. Translated by W. J. Montague. Philadelphia: Fortress, 1969.

———. *On Being a Disciple of the Crucified Nazarene: Unpublished Lectures and Sermons*. Edited by Wolfgang Kraus and Rudolf Landau, translated by Roy A. Harrisville. Grand Rapids: Eerdmans, 2010.

———. "On Paul's Anthropology." In *Perspectives on Paul*, translated by Margaret Kohl, 1–31. London: SCM, 1971.

———. "On the Subject of Primitive Christian Apocalyptic." In *New Testament Questions of Today*, translated by W. J. Montague, 108–37. London: SCM, 1969. German ed.: "Zum Thema der urchristlichen Apokalyptik." In *Exegetische Versuche und Besinnungen*, 2:105–31. Göttingen: Vandenhoeck & Ruprecht, 1965.

———. "The Pauline Doctrine of the Lord's Supper." In *Essays on New Testament Themes*, translated by W. J. Montague, 108–35. Philadelphia: Fortress, 1964.

———. *Perspectives on Paul*. Translated by Margaret Kohl. London: SCM, 1969.

———. "Rechtfertigung und Heilsgeschichte im Römerbrief." In *Paulinische Perspektiven*, 108–39. Tubingen: Mohr Siebeck, 1969.

———. "'The Righteousness of God' in Paul." In *New Testament Questions of Today*, translated by W. J. Monague, 168–83. London: SCM, 1969.

———. "The Saving Significance of the Death of Jesus in Paul." In *Perspectives on Paul*, translated by Margaret Kohl, 32–59. Philadelphia: Fortress, 1971.

———. "Theologians and the Laity." In *New Testament Questions of Today*, translated by W. J. Montague, 289–90. London: SCM, 1969.

———. *The Wandering People of God*. Translated by R. Harrisville and I. L. Sandberg. Philadelphia: Augsburg, 1984.

———. "What I Have Unlearned in 50 years as a German Theologian." *Currents in Theology and Mission* 15/4 (1988) 329–31.

Kaufman, Eleanor. "The Saturday of Messianic Time (Agamben and Badiou on the Apostle Paul)." *South Atlantic Quarterly* 107/1 (Winter 2008) 37–54.

Keck, Leander E. "Justification of the Ungodly and Ethics." In *Rechtfertigung: Festschrift für Ernst Käsemann zum 70. Geburtstag*, edited by Johannes Friedrich et al., 199–209. Tübingen: Mohr Siebeck, 1976.

———. *Paul and His Letters*. Rev. ed. Minneapolis: Fortress, 1988.

———. *Romans*. Abingdon New Testament Commentary. Nashville: Abingdon, 2005.

Kearney, Richard. *On Paul Ricoeur: The Owl of Minerva*. Burlington, VT: Ashgate, 2004.

Keen, Craig. *After Crucifixion: The Promise of Theology*. Eugene, OR: Cascade, forthcoming.

Keller, Catherine. *Apocalypse Now and Then: A Feminist Guide to the End of the World.* Boston: Beacon, 1996.

Kerr, Nathan R. "In Solidarity With the World: The Holiness of the Missionary Community." In *Nurturing the Prophetic Imagination*, edited by Jamie Gates and Mark Mann. Forthcoming.

Kierkegaard, Søren. *Concluding Unscientific Postscript to Philosophical Fragments.* Edited and translated by Howard V. and Edna H. Hong. Vol. 1. Kierkegaard's Writings 12. Princeton, NJ: Princeton University Press, 1992.

————. *For Self-Examination; Judge for Yourself.* Kierkegaard's Writings 21. Edited and translated by Howard V. and Edna H. Hong. Princeton, NJ: Princeton University Press, 1990.

Kline, Peter. "The Real Absence of Christ in the Liturgy of the Eucharist." Unpublished paper.

Kristof, Nicholas. "Three Cups of Tea, Spilled." *The New York Times*, April 20, 2011.

Künneth, Walter. *A Theology of the Resurrection.* Translated by James W. Leitch. St. Louis: Concordia, 1965.

Lehmann, Paul Louis. *The Transfiguration of Politics.* New York: Harper, 1975.

Leithart, Peter. *Defending Constantine: The Twilight of an Empire and the Dawn of Christendom.* Downers Grove: InterVarsity, 2010.

Liebing, Heinz, editor. *Die Marburger Theologen und der Arierparagraph in der Kirche: Eine Sammlung von Texten aus den Jahren 1933 und 1934.* Marburg: Elwert, 1977.

Lindemann, Andreas. "Anthropologie und Kosmologie in der Theologie des Paulus: Eine Auseinandersetzung mit Rudolf Bultmann und Ernst Käsemann." In *Theologie und Wirklichkeit: Diskussionen der Bultmann-Schule*, edited by Martin Bauspiess et al., 149–83. Neukirchen-Vluyn: Neukirchener, 2011.

Lohmann, Johann Friedrich. *Karl Barth und der Neukantianismus: Die Rezeption des Neukantianismus im "Römerbrief" und ihre Bedeutung für die weitere Ausarbeitung der Theologie Karl Barths.* Berlin: de Gruyter, 1995.

Lowe, Walter. "Christ and Salvation." In *The Cambridge Companion to Postmodern Theology*, edited by Kevin J. Vanhoozer, 235–51. Cambridge, MA: Cambridge University Press, 2003.

————. "Is There a Postmodern Gospel?" In *The Blackwell Companion to Postmodern Theology*, edited by Graham Ward, 490–504. Malden, MA: Blackwell, 2001.

————. "Postmodern Theology." In *The Oxford Handbook of Systematic Theology*, edited by John Webster et al., 617–33. Oxford: Oxford University Press, 2007.

————. "Prospects for a Postmodern Christian Theology: Apocalyptic without Reserve." *Modern Theology* 15/1 (1999) 17–24.

Luther, Martin. *Annotationes D. M. in Priorem epistolam ad Timotheum.* In *D. Martin Luthers Werke* (WA), 26:4–120. Weimar, Böhlau, 1902.

————. *A Commentary on Saint Paul's Epistle to the Galatians.* New York: R. Carter, 1856.

————. "Psalm 5." In *Operationes in Psalmos.* In *D. Martin Luthers Werke* (WA), 5:125–99. Weimar: Böhlau, 1892.

————. *Ein Sermon vom dem Heiligen Hochwirdigen Sacrament der Tauffe.* In *D. Martin Luthers Werke* (WA), 2:727–37. Weimar: Böhlau, 1884. English translation in *Luther's Works* vol. 35, edited by Jaroslav Pelikan et al., translated by Charles M. Jacobs and E. Theodore Bachmann. Philadelphia: Fortress, 1955–1986.

MacKinnon, Donald M. *The Stripping of the Altars.* Suffolk: Fontana, 1969.

Bibliography

Marcus, Joel. "The Evil Inclination in the Epistle of James." *Catholic Biblical Quarterly* 44 (1982) 606–21.

———. "The Evil Inclination in the Letters of Paul." *Irish Biblical Studies* 8 (1986) 8–21.

———. *Mark* 1–8. Anchor Yale Bible Commentaries. New Haven, CT: Yale University Press, 2002.

Martin, Dale. *The Corinthian Body.* New Haven, CT: Yale University Press, 1995.

Martyn, Dorothy. *Beyond Deserving: Children, Parents, and Responsibility Revisited.* Grand Rapids: Eerdmans, 2007.

Martyn, J. Louis. "The Abrahamic Covenant, Christ, and the Church." In *Theological Issues in the Letters of Paul,* 161–75. Nashville: Abingdon, 1997.

———. "Apocalyptic Antinomies." In *Theological Issues in the Letters of Paul,* 111–23. Edinburgh: T. & T. Clark; Nashville: Abingdon, 1997.

———. "The Apocalyptic Gospel in Galatians." *Interpretation* 54 (2000) 246–66.

———. "Christ and the Elements of the Cosmos." In *Theological Issues in the Letters of Paul,* 125–40. Nashville: Abingdon, 1997.

———. "The Daily Life of the Church in the War between the Spirit and the Flesh." In *Theological Issues in the Letters of Paul,* 251–66. Nashville: Abingdon, 1997.

———. "De-apocalypticizing Paul: An Essay Focused on *Paul and the Stoics* by Troels Engberg-Pedersen." *Journal for the Study of the New Testament* 86 (2002) 61–102.

———. "Epilogue: An Essay in Pauline Meta-Ethics." In *Divine and Human Agency in Paul and his Cultural Environment,* edited by John M. G. Barclay and Simon J. Gathercole, 173–83. London: T. & T. Clark, 2008.

———. "Epistemology at the Turn of the Ages." In *Theological Issues in the Letters of Paul,* 89–110. Nashville: Abingdon, 1997.

———. "Epistemology at the Turn of the Ages: 2 Corinthians 5:16." In *Christian History and Interpretation: Studies Presented to John Knox,* edited by W. R. Farmer, et al. 269–87. Cambridge: Cambridge University Press, 1967.

———. "Events in Galatia: Modified Covenantal Nomism versus God's Invasion of the Cosmos in the Singular Gospel: A Response to J. D. G. Dunn and B. F. Gaventa." In *Pauline Theology,* edited by Jouette M. Bassler, 1:160–79. Minneapolis: Fortress, 1991.

———. "A Formula for Communal Discord!" In *Theological Issues in the Letters of Paul,* 267–78. Nashville: Abingdon, 1997.

———. "From Paul to Flannery O'Connor with the Power of Grace." In *Theological Issues in the Letters of Paul,* 279–97. Nashville: Abingdon, 1997.

———. *Galatians.* Anchor Bible 33A. New York: Doubleday, 1997.

———. "Galatians 3:28, Faculty Appointments and the Overcoming of Christological Amnesia." *Katallegete* 8/1 (1982) 39–44.

———. "God's Way of Making Right What Is Wrong." In *Theological Issues in the Letters of Paul,* 141–56. Nashville: Abingdon, 1997.

———. "The Gospel Invades Philosophy." In *Paul, Philosophy, and the Theopolitical Vision,* edited by Douglas Harink, 13–33. Eugene, OR: Cascade, 2010.

———. *History & Theology in the Fourth Gospel.* Nashville: Abingdon, 1968.

———. *History & Theology in the Fourth Gospel.* Rev. ed. Nashville: Abingdon, 1979.

———. *History & Theology in the Fourth Gospel.* 3rd ed. Louisville: Westminster John Knox, 2003.

———. "John and Paul on the Subject of Gospel and Scripture." In *Theological Issues in the Letters of Paul,* 209–30. Nashville: Abingdon, 1997.

———. "Leo Baeck's Reading of Paul." In *Theological Issues in the Letters of Paul*, 47–69. Nashville: Abingdon, 1997.

———. "Nomos Plus Genitive Noun in Paul: The History of the Law." In *Early Christianity and Classical Culture: Comparative Studies in Honor of Abraham J. Malherbe*, edited by John T. Fitzgerald et al., 575–87. Leiden: Brill, 2003.

———. "Part II: Apolcalyptic Rectification." In *Theological Issues in the Letters of Paul*, 85–156. Nashville: Abingdon, 1997.

———. "Part IV: The Church's Everyday Life." In *Theological Issues in the Letters of Paul*, 231–97. Nashville: Abingdon, 1997.

———. "A Personal Word." In Meyer, Paul W. *The Word in This World: Essays in New Testament Exegesis and Theology*, edited by John T. Carroll, xvii–xxx. New Testament Library. Louisville: Westminster John Knox, 2004.

———. "Review of *New Testament Questions of Today* by Ernst Käsemann." *Union Seminary Quarterly Review* 25/4 (1970) 556–58.

———. *Theological Issues in the Letters of Paul*. Nashville: Abingdon, 1997.

———. "World without End or Twice-Invaded World?" In *Shaking Heaven and Earth: Essays in Honor of Walter Brueggemann and Charles B. Cousar*, edited by Christine Roy Yoder et al., 117–32. Louisville: Westminster John Knox, 2005.

Marx, Karl. *Critique of Hegel's Philosophy of Right*. Cambridge, MA: Cambridge University Press, 1970.

Matlock, R. Barry. *Unveiling the Apocalyptic Paul: Paul's Interpreters and the Rhetoric of Criticism*. Journal for the Study of the New Testament: Supplement Series. Sheffield: Sheffield Academic, 1996.

Maurice, F. D. *The Kingdom of Christ, or, Hints to a Quaker: Respecting the Principles, Constitution and Ordinances of the Catholic Church*. London: MacMillan, 1883.

McCarthy, Cormac. *The Crossing*. New York: Vintage, 1994.

McCormack, Bruce. *Karl Barth's Critically Realistic Dialectical Theology: Its Genesis and Development (1909–1936)*. Oxford: Clarendon, 1997.

———. "Review of Johann Friedrich Lohmann's *Karl Barth und der Neukantianismus*." In *Orthodox and Modern: Studies in the Theology of Karl Barth*, 305–7. Grand Rapids: Baker, 2008.

McDonald, Neil. *Karl Barth and the Strange New World within the Bible: Barth, Wittgenstein, and the Metadilemmas of the Enlightenment*. Carlisle, Cumbria: Paternoster, 2000.

McFarland, Ian A. *In Adam's Fall: A Meditation on the Christian Doctrine of Original Sin*. Malden, MA: Wiley-Blackwell, 2011.

McRae, Rachel M. "Eating with Honor: The Corinthian Lord's Supper in Light of Voluntary Association Meal Practices." *Journal of Biblical Literature* 130/1 (2011) 165–81.

Merton, Thomas. *New Seeds of Contemplation*. New York: New Directions, 1961.

Metz, Johan Baptiste. *Faith in History and Society*. Translated by J. Matthew Ashley. New York: Crossroad, 2007.

Meyer, Paul W. "Faith and History Revisited." In *The Word in This World: Essays in New Testament Exegesis and Theology*, edited by John T. Carroll, 19–26. New Testament Library. Louisville: Westminster John Knox, 2004.

———. "Romans: A Commentary." In *The Word in This World: Essays in New Testament Exegesis and Theology*, edited by John T. Carroll, 151–218. New Testament Library. Louisville: Westminster John Knox, 2004.

————. "The This-Worldliness of the New Testament." In *The Word in This World: Essays in New Testament Exegesis and Theology*, edited by John T. Carroll, 5–18. New Testament Library. Louisville: Westminster John Knox, 2004.

————. "The Worm at the Core of the Apple." In *The Conversation Continues: Studies in Paul and John*, edited by R. T. Fortna and B. R. Gaventa, 62–84. Nashville: Abingdon, 1990.

Minear, Paul S. "Gratitude and Mission in the Epistle to the Romans." In *Basileia: Tribute to Walter Freytag*, edited by Jan Hermelink and Hans Jochen Margull, 42–48. Stuttgart: Evang. Missionsverlag, 1959.

Mitchell, Richard. "Glassboro, NJ: A Voice Crying in the Wilderness." *Time*, January 29, 1979.

Moltmann, Jürgèn. *The Coming of God: Christian Eschatology*. Translated by Margaret Kohl. Minneapolis: Fortress, 1996.

————. *Theology of Hope: On the Ground and the Implications of a Christian Eschatology*. Translated by James W. Leitch. Minneapolis: Fortress, 1993.

Moo, Douglas. *The Epistle to the Romans*. New International Commentary on the New Testament. Grand Rapids: Eerdmans, 1996.

Morgan, Robert. "Ferdinand Christian Baur." In *Nineteenth Century Religious Thought in the West*, edited by Ninian Smart, et al., 1:261–89. Cambridge, MA: Cambridge University Press, 1985.

Morse, Christopher. *The Difference Heaven Makes: Rehearing the Gospel as News*. London: T. & T. Clark, 2010.

————. "Paul Lehmann as Nurturer of Theological Discernment." In *Explorations in Christian Theology and Ethics: Essays in Conversation with Paul L. Lehmann*, edited by Michelle J. Bartel and Philip G. Ziegler, 11–28. Farnam, Surrey: Ashgate, 2009.

————. "The Resurrection as Myth and as Fable." In *In Search of Humanity and Deity: A Celebration of John Macquarrie's Theology*, edited by Robert Morgan, 254–63. London: SCM, 2006.

————. "Tests of Doctrinal Faithfulness." In *Not Every Spirit: A Dogmatics of Christian Disbelief*, 45–70. 2nd ed. London: T. & T. Clark, 2009.

Mosès, Stéphane. *The Angel of History: Rosenzweig, Benjamin, Scholem*. Translated by Barbara Harshaw. Stanford, CA: Stanford University Press, 2009.

Myers, Ched. *Binding the Strong Man: A Political Reading of Mark's Story of Jesus*. Maryknoll, NY: Orbis, 1988.

Newbigen, Lesslie. *Sin and Salvation*. London: SCM, 1956.

Niebuhr, Reinhold. *The Nature and Destiny of Man*. Vol. 2. New York: Scribner, 1964.

O'Regan, Cyril. *Gnostic Apocalypse: Jacob Boehme's Haunted Narrative*. New York: SUNY Press, 2002.

————. *The Gnostic Turn in Modernity*. New York: SUNY Press, 2001.

————. *Theology and the Spaces of Apocalyptic: The Pere Marquette Lecture in Theology*. Milwaukee: Marquette University Press, 2009.

Origen. *On First Principles*. Translated by G. W. Butterworth. New York: Harper, 1966.

Orr, William F., and James Arthur Walter. *First Corinthians*. Anchor Yale Bible Commentaries. New York Doubleday, 1976.

Otto, Rudolph. *The Idea of the Holy*. Translated by John W. Harvey. Oxford: Oxford University Press, 1958.

Overbeck, Franz. *How Christian Is Our Present-Day Theology?* Translated by Martin Henry. New York: T. & T. Clark, 2005.

———. *On the Christianity of Theology.* Translated by John E. Wilson. San Jose, CA: Pickwick, 2002.

Ovey, Michael J. "Appropriating Aulén? Employing *Christus Victor* Models of the Atonement." *Churchman* 124/4 (2010) 297–330.

Passavant, Paul A. "The Contradictory State of Giorgio Agamben." *Political Theory* 35/2 (1997) 147–74.

Patterson, Orlando. *Slavery and Social Death: A Comparative Study.* Cambridge, MA: Harvard University Press, 1982.

Pecknold, Chad. "Beyond Our Intentions: An Augustinian Reading of *Hannah's Child.*" *Pro Ecclesia* 20/3 (2011) 297–309.

Placher, William C. *The Domestication of Transcendence: How Modern Theology about God Went Wrong.* Louisville: Westminster, 1996.

Portier-Young, Anathea. *Apocalypse Against Empire: Theologies of Resistance in Early Judaism.* Grand Rapids: Eerdmans, 2011.

Radner, Ephraim. *The End of the Church: A Pneumatology of Christian Division in the West.* Grand Rapids: Eerdmans, 1998.

Reno, R. R. *In the Ruins of the Church: Sustaining Faith in an Age of Diminished Christianity.* Grand Rapids: Brazos, 2002.

Reese, W. L. *Dictionary of Philosophy and Religion: Eastern and Western Thought.* Atlantic Heights, NJ: Humanities, 1980.

Riches, John. *Galatians Through the Centuries.* Blackwell Bible Commentaries. Oxford: Blackwell, 2008.

Rickert, Gailann. *Hekón and Akón in Early Greek Thought.* American Classical Studies. Atlanta: Scholars, 1989.

Rieske-Braun, Uwe. *Duellem mirabile: Studium zum Kampfmotif in Martin Luthers Theologie.* Göttingen: Vanderhoeck & Ruprecht, 1999.

Ritschl, Albrecht. *The Doctrine of Justification and Reconciliation.* Edited by H. R. MacKintosh and A. B. Macaulay. Vol. 3. Edinburgh: T. & T. Clark, 1900.

———. *Three Essays of Albrecht Ritschl.* Edited by Philip J. Hefner. Philadelphia: Fortress, 1972.

Robinson, James McConkey. *The Beginnings of Dialectical Theology.* Vol. 1. Louisville: John Knox, 1968.

Rose, Gillian. "The Final Notebooks of Gillian Rose." Edited by Howard Caygill. *Women: A Cultural Review* 9/1 (1998) 6–18.

———. *Hegel Contra Sociology.* Brooklyn: Verso, 2009.

———. *The Melancholy Science: An Introduction to the Thought of Theodor W. Adorno.* New York: Columbia University Press, 1978.

Rothstein, Edward. "400 Years Old and Ageless." *The New York Times,* September 30, 2011.

Rowe, C. Kavin. *World Upside Down: Reading Acts in the Graeco-Roman Age.* Oxford: Oxford University Press, 2009.

Rowland, Christopher. *The Open Heaven: A Study of Apocalyptic in Judaism and Early Christianity.* London: SPCK, 1982.

Rutledge, Fleming. *Not Ashamed of the Gospel: Sermons from Romans.* Grand Rapids: Eerdmans, 2008.

Saaranin, Risto. *Gottes Wirken auf uns: Die transzendentale Deutung des Gegenwart-Christi-Motivs in der Lutherforschung.* Stuttgart: Franz Steiner, 1989.

Sanders, E. P. *Paul and Palestinian Judaism.* Minneapolis: Fortress, 1977.

Bibliography

Sasse, Hermann. "κόσμος." In *Theological Dictionary of the New Testament*, edited by Gerhard Kittel. Grand Rapids: Eerdmans, 1964–74.

Schleiermacher, Friedrich. *The Christian Faith*. Edited by H. R. MacKintosh and J. S. Stewart. New York: T. & T. Clark, 1999.

———. *Der christliche glaube*. Berlin: Georg Reimer, 1861.

Schweitzer, Albert. *Christianity and the Religions of the World*. New York: George H. Doran, 1923.

———. *Civilization and Ethics*. London: A. & C. Black, 1923.

———. *Memoirs of Childhood and Youth*. New York: Macmillan, 1955.

———. *The Quest of the Historical Jesus: A Critical Study of Its Progress from Reimarus to Wrede*. New York: Macmillan, 1968.

Shannon, William H., et al. *The Thomas Merton Encyclopedia*. Maryknoll, NY: Orbis, 2002.

Sider, Alex. *To See History Doxologically: History and Holiness in John Howard Yoder's Ecclesiology*. Grand Rapids: Eerdmans, 2011.

Solberg, Mary M. *Compelling Knowledge: A Feminist Proposal for an Epistemology of the Cross*. Albany: SUNY Press, 1997.

Sölle, Dorothee. "Rudolf Bultmann und die politische Theologie." In *Rudolf Bultmann 100 Jahre: Oldenburger Vorträge*, edited by Stadt Oldenburg, Kulturdezernat, 62–80. Oldenburg: H. Holzberg, 1985.

Southall, David J. *Rediscovering Righteousness in Romans: Personified* dikaiosynē *within Metaphoric and Narratorial Settings*. Wissenschaftliche Untersuchungen Zum Neun Testament. Tübingen: Mohr Siebeck, 2008.

Spence, Alan. "A Unified Theory of the Atonement." *International Journal of Systematic Theology* 6/4 (2004) 404–20.

Spivak, Gayatri Chakravorty. "In a Word." Interview with Ellen Rooney. In *The Essential Difference*, edited by Naomi Schor and Elizabeth Weed, 151–184. Bloomington: Indiana University Press, 1994.

Stackhouse, John G., Jr., editor. *What Does It Mean to Be Saved?: Broadening Evangelical Horizons of Salvation*. Grand Rapids: Baker, 2002.

Stanton, Graham, et al. Review of *Galatians* by J. Louis Martyn. *Review of Biblical Literature* 3 (2001) 42–85.

Strauss, David Friedrich. *The Life of Jesus, Critically Examined*. Translated by George Eliot. Philadelphia: Fortress, 1972.

———. *The Christ of Faith and the Jesus of History: A Critique of Schleiermacher's* The Life of Jesus. Translated by Leander E. Keck. Philadelphia: Fortress, 1977.

———. *In Defense of My Life of Jesus Against the Hegelians*. Translated by Marilyn Chapin Massey. Hamden, CT: Archon, 1983.

Stroumsa, Guy. *The End of Sacrifice: Religious Transformations in Later Antiquity*. Translated by Susan Emanuel. Chicago: University of Chicago Press, 2009.

Sturm, Richard E. "Defining the Word 'Apocalyptic': A Problem in Biblical Criticism." In *Apocalyptic and the New Testament: Essays in Honor of J. Louis Martyn,* edited by Joel Marcus and Marion L. Soards, 17–47. Sheffield: JSOT Press, 1989.

Tannehill, Robert. *Dying and Rising with Christ: a Study in Pauline Theology*. Berlin: Töpelmann, 1967.

———. "Participation in Christ." In *The Shape of the Gospel*, 223–37. Eugene, OR: Cascade, 2007.

Tanner, Kathryn. *Christ the Key*. Cambridge: Cambridge University Press, 2010.

———. "Creation and Salvation in the Image of an Incomprehensible God." In *God of Salvation: Soteriology in Theological Perspective*, edited by Ivor J. Davidson and Murray A. Rae, 61–76. Surrey: Ashgate, 2011.

Taubes, Jacob. "Dialectic and Analogy." In *From Cult to Culture: Fragments Toward a Critique of Historical Reason*, edited by Charlotte Elisheva Fonrobert and Amir Engel, 165–76. Stanford, CA: Stanford University Press, 2010.

———. *Occidental Eschatology*. Translated by David Ratmoko. Stanford, CA: Stanford University Press, 2009.

———. "On the Nature of the Theological Method: Some Reflections on the Methodological Principles of Tillich's Theology." In *From Cult to Culture: Fragments Toward a Critique of Historical Reason*, edited by Charlotte Elisheva Fonrobert and Amir Engel, 195–213. Stanford, CA: Stanford University Press, 2010.

———, editor. *Religionstheorie und politische Theologie*. Vol. 1. Munich: Wilhelm Fink, 1983.

———. "Theology and the Philosophic Critique of Religion." *Zeitschrift für Religions- und Geistesgeschichte* 8/2 (1956) 129–38.

———. "Theodicy and Theology: A Philosophical Analysis of Karl Barth's Dialectical Theology." In *From Cult to Culture: Fragments Toward a Critique of Historical Reason*, edited by Charlotte Elisheva Fonrobert and Amir Engel, 177–94. Stanford, CA: Stanford University Press, 2010.

Thiselton, Anthony. *The First Epistle to the Corinthians*. New International Greek Testament Commentary. Grand Rapids: Eerdmans, 2000.

Torrance, Alan. *Persons in Communion: Trinitarian Description and Human Participation*. Edinburgh: T. & T. Clark, 1996.

Torrance, Thomas F. *The Trinitarian Faith: The Evangelical Theology of the Ancient Catholic Church*. Edinburgh: T. & T. Clark, 1988.

Trigg, Jonathan D. *Baptism in the Theology of Martin Luther*. Studies in the History of Christian Thought. Leiden: Brill, 1994.

Troeltsch, Ernst. "Historical and Dogmatic Method in Theology." In *Religion in History*, 11–32. Minneapolis: Fortress, 1991.

Vogel, Heinrich. "A Shortened Course of Instruction for a Soldier of Jesus Christ." In *The Iron Ration of a Christian*, translated by W. A. Whitehouse. London: SCM, 1941.

Vos, Gerhard. *Traditionsgeschichtliche Untersuchungen zur Paulinischen Pneumatologie*. Assen: Van Gorcom, 1973.

Wagner, J. Ross. *Heralds of the Good News: Isaiah and Paul in Concert in the Letter to the Romans*. Supplements to Novum Testamentum. Leiden: Brill, 2002.

Way, David V. *The Lordship of Christ: Ernst Käsemann's Interpretation of Paul's Theology*. Oxford: Oxford University Press, 1991.

Weaver, J. Denny. "Atonement for the Nonconstantinian Church." *Modern Theology* 6/4 (1990) 307–23.

———. *The Nonviolent Atonement*. Grand Rapids: Eerdmans, 2011.

Webster, John. "Reading Scripture Eschatologically (1)." In *Reading Texts, Seeking Wisdom: Scripture and Theology*, edited by David F. Ford and Graham Stanton, 245–56. Grand Rapids: Eerdmans, 2003.

———. "Soteriology and the Doctrine of God." In *God of Salvation: Soteriology in Theological Perspective,* edited by Ivor J. Davidson and Murray A. Rae, 15–34. Burlington, VT: Ashgate, 2011.

Weiss, Johannes. *Der erste Korintherbrief.* Göttingen: Dandenhoed & Ruprecht, 1910.

―――. *Earliest Christianity: A History of the Period A.D. 30–50.* Edited by Frederick C. Grant. New York: Harper, 1959.

―――. *Jesus' Proclamation of the Kingdom of God.* Edited by Richard H. Hiers and D. Larrimore Holland. Philadelphia: Fortress, 1971.

―――. *Die Predigt Jesu von Reich Gottes.* Göttingen: Vandenhoeck & Ruprecht, 1892.

Welborn, L. L. "'Extraction from the Mortal Site:' Badiou on the Resurrection in Paul." *New Testament Studies* 55/3 (2009) 295–314.

Westphal, Merold. *Becoming a Self: A Reading of Kierkegaard's Concluding Unscientific Postscript.* West Lafayette, IN: Purdue University Press, 1996.

Westhelle, Vítor. *The Church Event: Call and Challenge of a Church Protestant.* Minneapolis: Fortress, 2010.

White, Jr., Ronald C. *Lincoln's Greatest Speech.* New York: Simon & Schuster, 2002.

Wilkinson, David. *Christian Eschatology and the Physical Universe.* London: T. & T. Clark, 2010.

Williams, Rowan. "Incarnation and the Renewal of Community." In *On Christian Theology,* 225–37. Oxford: Blackwell, 2001.

Wink, Walter. *Naming the Powers: The Language of Power in the New Testament.* Philadelphia: Fortress, 1984.

Wladyslaw, Szpilman. *The Pianist: The Extraordinary True Story of One Man's Survival in Warsaw, 1939–1945.* New York: Picador, 1999.

Wrede, Wilhelm. *Paul.* Translated by Edward Lummis. London: Philip Green, 1907.

Wright, Archie T. *The Origin of Evil Spirits: The Reception of Genesis 6.1–4 in Recent Literature.* Wissenschaftliche Untersuchungen Zum Neun Testament. Tübingen: Mohr Siebeck, 2005.

Wright. N. T. *Justification: God's Plan and Paul's Vision.* London: SPCK, 2009.

―――. "The Letter to the Romans: Introduction, Commentary, and Reflections." In *The New Interpreter's Bible: A Commentary in Twelve Volumes,* edited by Leander E. Keck, 393–770. Nashville: Abingdon, 2002.

―――. *Paul: In Fresh Perspective.* Minneapolis: Fortress, 2005.

―――. *What Saint Paul Really Said.* Oxford: Lion Hudson, 1997.

Yoder, John Howard. *The Christian Witness to the State.* Scottdale, PA: Herald, 2002.

―――. *The Original Revolution: Essays on Christian Pacifism.* Scottdale, PA: Herald, 2003.

―――. *The Politics of Jesus: Vicit Agnus Noster.* 2nd ed. Grand Rapids: Eerdmans, 1994.

―――. *Preface to Theology: Christology and Theological Method.* Grand Rapids: Brazos, 2002.

―――. "To Serve Our God and to Rule the World." In *The Royal Priesthood: Essays Ecclesiological and Ecumenical,* edited by Michael Cartwright, 127–40. Grand Rapids: Eedmanns, 1994.

Zahl, Paul F. M. *Die Rechtfertigungslehre Ernst Käsemanns.* Stuttgart: Calwer, 1996.

―――. "A Tribute to Ernst Käsemann." *Anglican Theological Review* 80/3 (1998) 385.

Zwingli, Ulrich. *Sixty-Seven Articles of 1523.* In *Reformed Confessions of the 16th Century,* edited by Arthur C. Cochrane. Philadelphia: Westminster, 1966.

Name Index

Adams, Edward, 183n1, 185–86,
  186nn14–15
Adams, Robert Merrihew, 9n31
Adorno, Theodor, 4nn12–13,
  15n63, 26–27n116, 44
Agamben, Giorgio, 84n35,
  97–98, 100–101, 101n8,
  102, 102n12, 102n14, 103,
  103n17, 104–7, 109–11,
  114–17
Allison, Dale, 302n10
Altizer, Thomas J. J., 4
Anselm, Saint, 38, 319, 319n14
Aquinas, Thomas. *See* Thomas
  Aquinas
Augustine, Saint, 130n40, 291n87,
  300, 363–64
Aulén, Gustaf, 71, 200–201, 201n6,
  215–16
Austin, J. L., 97

Badiou, Alain, 97–98, 107, 107n27,
  108, 108n30, 109–10,
  110n40, 111–12, 114–17
Bar On, Bat-Ami, 239n6, 247–48,
  248n56, 249–50
Barrett, C. K., 194
Barth, Karl, 2, 3n4, 4, 25n105,
  27–30, 30nn123–24, 30n126,
  31–32, 35–36, 60, 60n24,
  69–70, 74n4, 75, 75n6,
  76, 82, 88, 93n53, 103,
  118, 125n27, 129, 129n35,
  130, 132, 134, 134–35n44,
  143–44, 152, 160, 178,

178n27, 221–22, 224–25,
  227, 229, 231–32, 234, 297,
  300, 302n11, 305n15, 310,
  325, 330, 338n20, 350
Bauer, Walter, 80, 80n22
Baur, Ferdinand Christian, 10,
  12–13, 13n50, 14–17, 17n71,
  18, 20, 25, 25n105, 30, 80
Beethoven, Ludwig van, 305,
  305n15, 345
Beker, J. Christiaan, 132
Belcher, J. David, 47,
Belcher, Jodi L. A., 47
Benjamin, Walter, 3, 36, 44, 84n35,
  86, 86n39, 87, 95, 101
Bloch, Ernst, 3, 36
Blumhardt, Christoph, 93n53, 143
Blumhardt, Johann Christoph,
  93n53, 143
Boer, Martinus C. de, 124n25,
  173n19
Bonhoeffer, Dietrich, 52, 93n53,
  132, 134, 315, 325, 332
Borg, Marcus, 22n100
Bousset, Wilhelm, 21–22
Bowie, Andrew, 10n33, 14n57
Boyarin, Daniel, 110n36
Braaten, Carl E., 202, 217, 276n46
Breytenbach, Cilliers, 191
Brown, Alexandra, 46, 243n28
Brown, Raymond E., 310n24
Brueggemann, Walter, 114
Buber, Martin, 53–55, 57, 59–63,
  65, 68, 271, 271n31, 277

Name Index

Subject Index

Abraham, 81n27, 85, 87–90, 169,
171, 177, 186–87, 227,
284n66, 317
Abrahamic blessing, 180, 220, 222,
225, 234, 284n66
absolute, the, 8–10, 13, 13n50, 15
abstract logic, 23–24, 29–30,
30n126, 31–32, 35–37,
44–45, 45n160, 123
Acts of the Apostles, 79n20, 302
actuality, 45, 51–52, 290, 339
Adam, 85, 88, 171, 174–76, 181–
82, 187, 189, 195, 205–6,
298–99, 304
Adam, the Second, 88, 171
agency, divine, 39–40, 90–91, 117,
125, 143, 146–47, 149, 213,
220, 301n9, 305–7, 310, 313,
319, 355–56, 358
agency, human, 39, 43, 46, 74,
90–91, 106, 146–47, 149,
220, 230, 234, 250, 253,
253n75, 254–55, 261, 306,
320, 324, 355–56
agency, political, 74, 91–92, 94
anthropology, 33, 170, 185, 202,
204–5, 209–10, 217, 262
anti-God powers, 90–91, 94,
146, 185, 189, 205, 236n2,
243–45, 251–55, 329, 356.
See also Death; Sin
antinomy, 23–24, 32, 36, 39, 41,
56–57, 61–62, 64, 102, 145,
147–48, 152, 184–85n6, 284,
284n66, 317, 325, 355, 367

apocalypse, apocalyptic, *apokalypsis, passim.*
apocalyptic, cosmological, 35,
38n143, 64, 69, 71–72, 123,
125–26, 204, 217, 236
apocalyptic, Jewish, 23, 86n39,
124n25, 128, 128n34, 130,
132, 135, 269n23
apocalyptic, Pauline, 37, 39–44,
47, 71–72, 77, 86, 88, 91–92,
96–97, 97n3, 98–99, 114–15,
117, 119, 124, 124n25,
127–28, 131–32, 138, 145,
147, 149, 159, 166–67, 174,
181, 202, 211, 215, 220,
228, 236–37, 247, 251, 256,
262–63, 265, 275, 278–79,
316, 318, 354–56, 361, 367
apocalyptic, primitive Christian,
1, 23–24, 26–27, 31, 120,
121n14, 124n25, 128n34,
144, 335, 335n6, 336, 346,
367
apocalyptic, theological appropriation of, 3–5, 6n16, 24, 28, 31,
36, 44–46, 60, 119–21
apocalyptic imagination, 2, 202,
218, 330, 361
apocalyptic imminence, 337,
343–44, 346
apocalyptic Jesus, 20, 22, 46, 55, 58,
138, 348, 350
apocalyptic theology, 3, 5, 28, 37,
42, 44–48, 118–21, 124,
124n25, 126n29, 127, 129,

393

kingdom of God (*cont.*)
344, 346–49, 351, 356–57,
360
knowledge, scientific, 6n16,
13, 20–21, 23, 26, 56,
250–51n69
knowledge and the body, 44, 237,
237n3, 255–57, 261
knowledge of God, 7–8, 8nn21–23,
9, 18n76, 19–20, 29, 32–33,
70, 193, 305, 313
kosmos. See cosmos
krisis, 31–32, 32n130, 34–37, 39.
See also theology of *krisis*
kurios, kyrios, 22, 33n131, 34–35,
38, 43–44, 83, 93, 301, 312,
336

Law, 39–40, 74, 85, 88–89, 92–93,
93n53, 94–95, 104, 158,
167, 170, 172, 175, 180, 184,
190n24, 215, 220, 223, 225–
27, 227n39, 228, 231–32,
234, 283–84nn65–66, 284,
320, 355
law, 41, 55, 84n35, 92, 92n51, 93,
93n53, 94–95, 97, 99–102,
102n11, 102n13, 103–6,
109–11, 116, 167–69, 173,
176, 180, 180n35, 188, 191,
194, 213, 221, 225–26, 231,
234, 284n66, 301, 311n29,
324, 353
law of Christ, 94–95, 227, 234, 356
liberal religion, 3, 26, 309, 309n23
liberalism, Protestant, 18, 24, 31
liberation, 36, 47, 72, 74, 85, 95,
97, 115, 117, 148, 165–68,
170, 172–74, 176, 178–79,
181–82, 184, 192, 199, 201,
208–9, 211, 214–15, 217–18,
223, 225, 228, 234, 239, 244,
246, 252–53, 255, 277n51,
286–88, 288–89n81, 292,

313, 316, 336, 339–40n23,
342, 344, 354
logos, Logos, 83, 94, 97, 112–13,
265
Lord's Supper. *See* Eucharist
Luke, 82, 188, 302

marginalization, marginalized,
the, 238n5, 239–41, 247–51,
250–51n69, 255, 347n54,
350, 352–53
Mark, 349–50
Mark, the Gospel of, 48, 113n45,
330n38, 337, 346–47,
347nn53–54, 349–50,
350n62, 351
Marxism, Marxist, 3, 3n6, 33n131,
36, 97, 107, 128–30, 133
Matthew, the Gospel of, xiii, 155,
302, 302n10, 303, 330n38
mediation, 12, 15, 24, 25n105, 70,
129n35, 134, 276n48
Messiah, the, 23, 74, 81n27, 84,
84n35, 85–89, 94–95, 101,
111, 156, 190, 244, 271–72,
301, 302n10
messianic community, 94–95, 104,
114
messianic time, 101–2, 104–6, 111,
116, 356
metaphysics, 7, 8n21, 11, 18, 131,
133, 136, 160, 336
modernity, 4, 4n11, 21, 26–27, 31,
60, 150, 324, 363–65
monism, 13, 18, 52, 54, 56
Moses, 81n27, 103, 301, 306
myth, 12, 16, 128n34, 132, 134,
151, 160, 211
mythical representation, 11, 16–17,
31, 120, 123, 132

negative determination, 10n33, 12,
14, 30

Subject Index

powers (*cont.*)
   337, 348–51, 355–57, 367.
   See also anti-God powers
practical reason, 7–8, 8n21, 19, 62
present evil age, 70, 72, 146, 167,
   170, 180, 184, 184n3, 185n7,
   189, 197, 221, 226, 276n49,
   316, 355

real and the ideal, the, 35–36, 45
Rebecca, 90
reconciliation, 9, 11–12, 15, 17,
   17n75, 18, 20, 30, 36, 43–44,
   129n35, 190–91, 200–01,
   209–11, 213, 216
rectification, 38–39, 39n145, 40,
   43, 47, 99, 146, 171–72, 176,
   190, 196n46, 208, 208n43,
   221, 221n7, 223, 225, 233,
   235, 278–79, 302, 311n29,
   312
redemption, 9, 35, 37–38, 40, 42,
   45, 47–48, 71–72, 86, 90,
   100–01, 107, 116–17, 128,
   128–29n34, 166, 169–70,
   174, 197, 197n49, 208, 267–
   68, 271, 280–81, 281n59,
   286, 291, 291n86
Reformation, the, 10, 33–34,
   37–38, 130, 267, 267n11,
   268n15, 287n77, 289, 320,
   320n16, 328–30
religion as sociocultural, 21–22,
   24–25, 25n107
remnant, the, 98n5, 99–101, 104–6,
   110–11, 116–17
resurrection, 31, 48, 85–86, 88,
   99, 107–8, 111–13, 116–17,
   121, 123, 135n45, 156,
   158, 171, 185, 197, 207n37,
   215n69, 216, 221–22, 234,
   234n71, 262, 266, 266n10,
   267, 267n13, 268, 268n15,
   268n19, 269, 269n25, 270,

271n30, 272, 272nn33–35,
   273, 273–74n37, 274–75,
   275–76nn45–46, 276,
   276–77nn50–51, 277,
   277–78nn53–54, 278–81,
   281–82nn59–60, 282,
   282–83n64, 283, 285–86,
   286n72, 287–88, 288n78,
   288n80, 289, 289n82, 290,
   302, 302n10, 311, 333,
   334–37, 339–40n23, 340n25,
   341, 343, 346, 349, 351–54,
   360, 364
revelation, 3n6, 29, 31–32, 39,
   51–52, 69–70, 98, 124–25,
   128–29n34, 156–57, 159–60,
   192, 209, 256n80, 262, 302,
   336, 338
Revelation, Book of, 120, 161, 357
righteousness, 33n131, 34, 39, 120,
   166, 169, 169n10, 171, 174,
   176, 202, 207, 207n39, 208,
   208n43, 209, 216, 221n7,
   227, 232, 274, 309, 314
Romans, Letter to the, 82, 85–86,
   88–90, 94, 99, 102–3, 115–
   17, 158, 171, 173n19, 176,
   185–86, 186n13, 187–89,
   189n21, 190, 190n24,
   192–93, 195–96, 196n46,
   197–98, 266n10, 280, 282,
   286, 286n74, 287, 309, 320,
   361

sacrament(s), 279, 281n59, 286,
   288n80, 290, 291n87,
   292n89, 318–20, 320n16,
   326, 331–32, 339. *See also*
   baptism; Eucharist
sacramental realism, 268, 268n16,
   318, 329
sacrifice, 48, 238, 257–58, 290, 307,
   356–57, 361–62, 362n29,
   363–67